Schriften zum Migrationsrecht

Volume 41

Janine Prantl

The legal framework for refugee resettlement to the European Union with lessons from the American model

Nomos

Published with the support of Austrian Science Fund (FWF): [PUB 993-G]

FWF Austrian Science Fund

The Deutsche Nationalbibliothek lists this publication in the Deutsche Nationalbibliografie; detailed bibliographic data are available on the Internet at http://dnb.d-nb.de

a.t.: Innsbruck, Univ., Diss., 2021

ISBN 978-3-8487-9007-4 (Print)
978-3-7489-3470-7 (ePDF)

British Library Cataloguing-in-Publication Data
A catalogue record for this book is available from the British Library.

ISBN 978-3-8487-9007-4 (Print)
978-3-7489-3470-7 (ePDF)

Library of Congress Cataloging-in-Publication Data
Prantl, Janine
The legal framework for refugee resettlement to the European Union with lessons from the American model
Janine Prantl
359 pp.
Includes bibliographic references.

ISBN 978-3-8487-9007-4 (Print)
978-3-7489-3470-7 (ePDF)

1st Edition 2023

Published by
Nomos Verlagsgesellschaft mbH & Co. KG
Waldseestraße 3–5 | 76530 Baden-Baden
www.nomos.de

Production of the printed version:
Nomos Verlagsgesellschaft mbH & Co. KG
Waldseestraße 3–5 | 76530 Baden-Baden

ISBN 978-3-8487-9007-4 (Print)
ISBN 978-3-7489-3470-7 (ePDF)
DOI https://doi.org/10.5771/9783748934707

Onlineversion
Nomos eLibrary

With thanks to
Univ.-Prof. Mag. Mag. Dr. Andreas Th. Müller, LL.M.
for encouraging, challenging, and supporting me in all stages of this doctoral project,
and to
Univ.-Prof. Dr. Werner Schroeder, LL.M.
for his thoughtful advice and feedback,
and to
my beloved sister
for believing in me in times when I did not believe in myself.

List of abbreviations

Formal abbreviations

Art(s)	Article(s)
ed(s)	editor(s)
e.g.	*exempli gratia*
f(f)	(forth)following
fn	footnote
ibid	*ibidem*
i.e.	*id est*, that is to say
lit	*litera*
no	number(s)
para(s)	paragraph(s)
Stat	Statutes

Substantive abbreviations

ACHR	American Convention on Human Rights
AG	Advocate General
ARIO	Articles on Responsibility of International Organizations
ARSIWA	Articles on Responsibility of States for Internationally Wrongful Acts
ASEAN	Association of South East Asian Nations
ATCR	Annual Tripartite Consultations on Resettlement
CAT	Convention against Torture and Other Cruel, Inhuman or Degrading Treatment or Punishment
CBP	US Customs and Border Protection
CEAS	Common European Asylum System
CEDAW	Convention on the Elimination of All Forms of Discrimination against Women
CFR	Code of Federal Regulations
CFSP	Common Foreign and Security Policy
the Charter	Charter of Fundamental Rights of the European Union

CJEU	Court of Justice of the European Union
CO	Cultural Orientation
Commission	European Commission
CPA	Comprehensive Plan of Action
CRC	United Nations Convention on the Rights of the Child
DHS	US Department of Homeland Security
EASO	European Asylum Support Office
EBCG	European Border and Cost Guard
ECHR	Convention for the Protection of Human Rights and Fundamental Freedoms
ECOSOC	Economic and Social Council
ECRE	European Council on Refugees and Exiles
ECtHR	European Court of Human Rights
EEA	European Economic Area
EMN	European Migration Network
ESMA	European Securities and Markets Authority
EU	European Union
EUAA	European Agency for Asylum
EUMS	Member States of the European Union
EXCOM	Conclusions of the Executive Committee of UN-HCR's Program
FBI	Federal Bureau of Investigation
FRA	European Union Agency for Fundamental Rights
GAMM	Global Approach to Migration and Mobility
GDP	Gross Domestic Product
HHS	US Department of Health and Human Services
IACtHR	Inter-American Court of Human Rights
ICESCR	International Covenant on Economic, Social and Cultural Rights
ICC	International Criminal Court
ICCPR	International Covenant on Civil and Political Rights
ICEM	Intergovernmental Committee on European Migration
ICJ	International Court of Justice
IDP	Internally Displaced Person
IGCR	Intergovernmental Committee on Refugees
IIRIRA	Illegal Immigration Reform and Immigrant Responsibility Act
ILC	International Law Commission

ILO	Immigration Liaison Officer
INA	Immigration and Nationality Act
IOM	International Organization for Migration
IRO	International Refugee Organization
LGBTQIA+	Lesbian, gay, bisexual, transgender, queer or questioning, intersex, asexual, and more
MAA	Mutual Assistance Association
MFF	Multiannual Financial Framework
MPI	Migration Policy Institute
NGO	Non-governmental organization
OHCHR	Office of the High Commissioner for Human Rights
ORR	Office of Refugee Resettlement
PCIJ	Permanent Court of International Justice
PRM	State's Bureau of Population, Refugees, and Migration
Refugee Convention	1951 Convention Relating to the Status of Refugees
RPP	Regional Protection Program
RRF	Resettlement Registration Form
RSC	Resettlement Support Center
RSD	Refugee Status Determination
TEU	Treaty on European Union
TFEU	Treaty on the Functioning of the European Union
TIQ	Tradable Immigration Quota
UDHR	Universal Declaration of Human Rights
UK	United Kingdom
UN	United Nations
UN Charter	Charter of the United Nations
UNCRPD	United Nations Convention on the Rights of Persons with Disabilities
UNGA	United Nations General Assembly
UNHCR	United Nations High Commissioner for Refugees
US	United States of America
USCIS	US Citizenship and Immigration Services
USRAP	US Refugee Admissions Program
WGR	Working Group on Resettlement

Table of Contents

1 Introduction[*]

1.1 Resettlement in the EU context

The United Nations High Commissioner for Refugees (UNHCR) recognizes refugee resettlement as one of three 'durable solutions'. The durable solutions aim at achieving self-reliance of refugees.[1] The three durable solutions consist of (i) voluntary repatriation to the home country, (ii) integration within a country of (first) refuge, or (iii) resettlement to a third country, i.e. the receiving country. Refugees who cannot return to their home country and who cannot integrate into the country of (first) refuge, constitute the target group for resettlements to a receiving country.[2] Therefore, "*resettlement remains an important protection tool which addresses the special needs of refugees whose fundamental human rights are at risk in the country of refuge*".[3]

Plenty of obstacles have hindered the efficient use of resettlement.[4] The so-called resettlement gap between the number of persons in need of resettlement and the number of actual resettlements to committing third countries remains significant to date. The UNHCR 2021 resettlement data

---

* The text was prepared with due attention to gender neutrality and ethical principles. Any and all deviations from this policy are exclusively for the sake of improving the readability of the text or for the authentic replication of legal texts. The generic masculine chosen in this work refers simultaneously to male, female, and other gender identities (and *vice versa*).

1 See UNHCR, 'The 10-Point Plan', Chapter 7 Solutions, 186 <https://www.unhcr.org/50a4c17f9.pdf> accessed 24 June 2022. See also UNHCR, 'Framework for durable solutions for refugees and persons of concern' (2003) para. 10 <https://www.unhcr.org/partners/partners/3f1408764/framework-durable-solutions-refugees-persons-concern.html> accessed 24 June 2022: "*The basic criterion for a good programme is self-reliance*".

2 See Kristin Bergtora Sandvik, 'On the Social Life of International Organizations: Framing Accountability' in Jan Wouters et al (eds), *Accountability for Human Rights Violations* (Intersentia 2010) 287 (296).

3 Garry G Troeller, 'UNHCR Resettlement: Evolution and Future Direction' in (2002) 14 International Journal of Refugee Law 1, 85 (95).

4 See Margret AM Piper, Paul Power and Graham Thom, 'Refugee Resettlement: 2012 and Beyond', UNHCR Research Paper n°253 (February 2013) 17 <https://www.unhcr.org/research/working/510bd3979/refugee-resettlement-2012-beyond-margaret-piper-paul-power-dr-graham-thom.html> accessed 13 February 2021.

show that only 39,266 actual departures out of 63,190 UNHCR referrals took place.[5] This is exacerbated by the fact that resettlement needs are expected to rise up to 2 million refugees in 2023, which represents a 36% increase compared to the needs in 2022 of 1.47 million.[6] In its attempts to close the gap, the UNHCR considered Member States of the European Union (EUMS) to be "*the major sticking point when it comes to achieving a significant increase in resettlement capacity*".[7]

In 2016, the European Union (EU) accounted for about 10% of resettlements globally.[8] The programs of the EUMS have remained small compared to the United States (US) or Canada. The past joint efforts[9] of EUMS were based on non-binding Commission communications, recommendations and European Council conclusions. Even though leaders have conveyed that migration and asylum issues need a European approach, "*actual policy and practice continue to be national in every way, including the migration decisions of those individuals arriving in the EU* [...] *as resettled refugees*".[10] Thus, EUMS' national resettlement policies have remained divergent.

Traditional resettlement countries, such as Sweden, Finland, the Netherlands and Ireland, had been resettling persons in need for protection on a regular basis even before resettlement was anchored in their asylum

5 See UNHCR, 'Resettlement Data' (as of 24 June 2022) <https://www.unhcr.org/resettlement-data.html> accessed 24 June 2022.

6 See UNHCR, 'Projected Global Resettlement Needs 2023' (June 2022) <https://www.unhcr.org/62b18e714> accessed 24 June 2022.

7 Margret AM Piper, Paul Power and Graham Thom, 'Refugee Resettlement: 2012 and Beyond', UNHCR Research Paper n°253 (February 2013) 20.

8 See Lyra Jakulevičienė and Mantas Bileišis, 'EU refugee resettlement: Key challenges of expanding the practice into new Member States' in (2016) 9 Baltic Journal of Law & Politics 1, 93.

9 See Elona Bokshi, 'Refugee Resettlement in the EU: The capacity to do it better and to do it more', KNOW RESET Research Report 2013/04 (European University Institute 2013) 1 <https://www.ecre.org/wp-content/uploads/2016/03/00013_20140108160733_knowresetrr-2013-04.pdf> accessed 13 February 2021; see also Commission, Communication 'Establishment of a joint EU resettlement programme', COM(2009) 447 final.

10 Joanne van Selm, 'Are asylum and immigration really a European Union issue?' in (2016) 51 Forced Migration Review, 60 (61).

legislation.[11] Other EUMS, for example, Italy, Luxembourg and Austria,[12] joined with *ad hoc* initiatives. In some EUMS there is no legal basis for resettlement in their respective national migration and/or asylum law. For instance, the Austrian Asylum Law does not expressly mention resettlement.[13]

Overall, heterogeneous policies make it difficult to objectively assess whether an EUMS has exhausted its full capacity to admit refugees ('inability' to contribute) or whether it deliberately holds back admissions ('unwillingness' to contribute).[14] This is reflected in the uneven resettlement contributions of EUMS. For example, between 2013 and 2015, EUMS had offered to resettle 38,000 refugees from third countries within their own territory, whereas Germany pledged 78% of the places, Sweden 7%, and the other EUMS just 14% in total.[15]

Against this backdrop, on 13 July 2016, the European Commission (Commission) proposed a Resettlement Framework Regulation "*to achieve*

11 See Delphine Perrin and Frank McNamara, 'Refugee Resettlement in the EU: Between Shared Standards and Diversity in Legal and Policy Frames', KNOW RESET Research Report 2013/03 (European University Institute 2013) 4 <https://cadmus.eui.eu/bitstream/handle/1814/29400/KnowReset_RR-2013_03.pdf> accessed 13 February 2021.

12 A regular resettlement program for Austria was proposed by a working group of Caritas Austria, Diakonie Austria, the International Organization for Migration (IOM), the Red Cross Austria and UNHCR in July 2017; see ARBEITSGRUPPE CARITAS, DIAKONIE, IOM, ÖRK, UNHCR, 'Resettlement in Österreich' (revised July 2017) <https://www.caritas.at/fileadmin/storage/global/pdf/Resettlement_Konzept_für_Ö_update_2017.pdf> accessed 13 February 2021.

13 The only provision in Austrian Asylum Law that may be considered as basis for resettlement procedures is § 3a Austrian Asylum Law [Bundesgesetz über die Gewährung von Asyl (Asylgesetz 2005 - AsylG 2005), BGBl 100/2005], allowing to recognize status *ex officio* (without further procedure) in cases where Austria has committed itself under international law to do so. See Delphine Perrin and Frank McNamara, 'Refugee Resettlement in the EU: Between Shared Standards and Diversity in Legal and Policy Frames', KNOW RESET Research Report 2013/03, 16.

14 See Philippe de Bruycker and Evangelia (Lilian) Tsourdi, 'In search of fairness in responsibility sharing' in (2016) 51 Forced Migration Review, 64.

15 See Commission, 'Relocation & Resettlement' (27 May 2015) <https://ec.europa.eu/home-affairs/sites/homeaffairs/files/what-we-do/policies/european-agenda-migration/background-information/docs/relocation_and_resettlement_factsheet_en.pdf> accessed 13 February 2021.

a degree of convergence for the resettlement practices and procedures".[16] At this point in time, the EU legislators have not adopted this Proposal. The Council of the EU and the European Parliament reached a partial and provisional agreement in June 2018, which, however, the Council did not endorse. The file was carried over to the Commission under *Ursula von der Leyen* in 2019,[17] who mentioned among the key actions in its New Pact on Migration and Asylum,[18] to "[c]*onclude swiftly negotiations on the Framework Regulation on Resettlement and Humanitarian Admission*".[19] According to the prevailing political view, the EU migration and asylum framework should not be reformed by a piecemeal adoption. While agreement on the whole package has been missing, progress in negotiations on parts of the reform package could be achieved.[20] In December 2022, the European Parliament and the Council reached an agreement on an updated text of the proposed EU Resettlement Framework Regulation.[21]

A common framework promises to open untapped resources of the EUMS. Receiving EUMS, in addition to resettlement beneficiaries, may benefit from increased quantity and quality of EU resettlement.[22]

In terms of quantity, recent commitments in response to the Afghan mass displacement following the take-over by the Taliban regime demonstrate that there is room for improvement. The pledges remained lopsided,

16 Commission, Proposal for a Regulation establishing a Union Resettlement Framework and amending Regulation (EU) No 516/2014 of the European Parliament and the Council, COM(2016) 468 final 2016/0225 (COD) 7.

17 See European Parliament, 'Legislative Train Schedule: EU Resettlement Framework' (as of 5 May 2022) <https://www.europarl.europa.eu/legislative-train/theme-towards-a-new-policy-on-migration/file-jd-eu-resettlement-framework> accessed 24 June 2022.

18 Commission, Communication on a New Pact on Migration and Asylum, COM(2020) 609 final.

19 Ibid 24.

20 For example, the establishment of the EU Asylum Agency. See Jacopo Bariagazzi, 'Mediterranean countries give green light to deal on EU asylum agency' (*Politico*, 8 June 2021) <https://www.politico.eu/article/mediterranean-countries-green-light-deal-eu-asylum-agency/> accessed 16 June 2021. Regulation 2021/2303 (EU) on the European Union Agency for Asylum and repealing Regulation (EU) No 439/2010 [2021] OJ L468/1-54.

21 European Parliament, 'Asylum and migration: deal reached on new EU resettlement framework' (*Press release*, 15 December 2022) <https://www.europarl.europa.eu/news/en/press-room/20221214IPR64717/asylum-and-migration-deal-reached-on-new-eu-resettlement-framework>.

22 See Volker Türk, 'Prospects for Responsibility Sharing in the Refugee Context' in (2016) 4 Journal on Migration and Human Security 3, 45 (48).

and the total number of pledges of EUMS was low compared to the US or Canada (see 2.3.16).

In terms of quality, an EU resettlement framework offers the opportunity to foster compliance with international law and counter recent criticism. In 2018, the African Union expressed dissatisfaction with "*EU's latest blueprint for stemming migration, claiming that it would breach international law by establishing 'de facto detention centres' on African soil, trampling over the rights of those being held*".[23] Moreover, EU and EUMS officials and agents have been accused of crimes against humanity,[24] "*committed as part of a premeditated policy to stem migration flows from Africa via the Central Mediterranean route, from 2014 to date*".[25] This shows the need for a policy intended to accommodate international law in order to regain trust of countries of (first) refuge, and persuade these countries to open their borders and keep their borders open for refugees.[26]

1.2 US resettlement policy as point of reference

This monography considers 'best practice' and 'bad precedent' derived from the US Refugee Admissions Program (USRAP) to draw conclusions for EU resettlement *de lege ferenda*.

The USRAP has a long history, dating back to the aftermath of World War II.[27] Scholars described the US refugee resettlement program as a

---

23 Daniel Boffey, 'African Union seeks to kill EU plan to process migrants in Africa' (*The Guardian*, 24 February 2019) <https://www.theguardian.com/world/2019/feb/24/african-union-seeks-to-kill-eu-plan-to-process-migrants-in-africa> accessed 13 February 2021.

24 See Owen Bowcott, 'ICC submission calls for prosecution of EU over migrant deaths' (*The Guardian*, 3 June 2019) <https://www.theguardian.com/law/2019/jun/03/icc-submission-calls-for-prosecution-of-eu-over-migrant-deaths> accessed 13 February 2021.

25 Omer Shatz and Juan Branco et al, 'EU Migration Policies in the Central Mediterranean and Libya (2014-2019)' (PSIA – Sciences Po 2017/2018, 2018/2019) <https://www.statewatch.org/news/2019/jun/eu-icc-case-EU-Migration-Policies.pdf> accessed 13 February 2021.

26 See Kathleen Newland, 'Legislative Developments and Refugee Resettlement in the Post-Cold War Era' in (1996) 19 In Defense of the Alien, 134 (138).

27 See Thomas Alexander Aleinikoff, David A Martin, Hiroshi Motomura, Maryellen Fullerton and Juliet P Stumpf, *Immigration and Citizenship: Process and Policy* (West Academic Publishing 8th ed 2016) 793.

long-term success.[28] In fact, the US has resettled more refugees than any other country in the world. This is confirmed, amongst others, by the UNHCR[29] and the Refugee Council of Australia.[30] Nevertheless, it is undeniable that US resettlement has faced serious difficulties. Following the events of 9/11, resettlements to the US stopped abruptly, but then slowly recovered. Terrorist attacks in France and Belgium compounded security concerns not only in Europe but also in the US, and several US states started to oppose admission.[31] Notably, figures from 2018 showed the lowest admission rate since the program's inception.[32] For the Fiscal Year 2021, President *Trump* determined a reduced ceiling of only 15,000.[33] President *Biden* raised this cap subsequently to 62,500.[34] He proclaimed

28 See Stephen H Legomsky, 'Refugees, Asylum and the Rule of Law in the USA' in Susan Kneebone (ed), *Refugees, asylum seekers and the rule of law: comparative perspectives* (Cambridge University Press 2009) 122-270; for current information on the US offshore permanent resettlement program see US Department of State, 'Refugee Admissions' <https://www.state.gov/status-of-the-u-s-refugee-admissions-program/> accessed 23 March 2021; see also United States Committee for Refugees and Immigrants, 'World Refugee Survey 2009 – United States' (17 June 2009) <http://www.refworld.org/docid/4a40d2b580.html> accessed 13 February 2021; see also Donald Kerwin, 'The US Refugee Resettlement Program – A Return to First Principles: How Refugees Help to Define, Strengthen, and Revitalize the United States' in (2018) 6 Journal on Migration and Human Security 3, 205-225 <https://journals.sagepub.com/doi/full/10.1177/2331502418787787> accessed 13 February 2021.

29 See UNHCR, 'Global Trends: Forced Displacement in 2018' (20 June 2019) <https://www.unhcr.org/5d08d7ee7.pdf> accessed 13 February 2021.

30 "*The United States has been by far the largest resettlement destination (828,128), followed by Canada (191,801), Australia (158,217), Sweden (24,649) and Norway (17,327). These five countries have been responsible for over 95% of all refugees resettled in that period. The United States alone has been responsible for nearly 65% of resettled refugees in this time*", Refugee Council of Australia, 'Global resettlement statistics' (as of 2 August 2019) <https://www.refugeecouncil.org.au/global-resettlement-statistics/> accessed 13 February 2021.

31 See Kevin J Fandl, 'States' Rights and Refugee Resettlement' in (2017) 52 Texas International Law Journal 1, 71 (100f).

32 See UNHCR, 'Global Trends: Forced Displacement in 2018' (20 June 2019).

33 See US Department of State, Department of Homeland and Security, Department of Health and Human Services, 'Report to Congress on Proposed Refugee Admissions for Fiscal Year 2021' <https://www.state.gov/wp-content/uploads/2020/10/FY21-USRAP-Report-to-Congress-FINAL-for-WEBSITE-102220-508.pdf> accessed 13 February 2021.

34 See Maanvi Singh, 'Biden raises US refugee admissions cap to 62,500 after delay sparks anger' (*The Guardian*, 3 May 2021) <https://www.theguardian.com/world/2021/may/03/biden-refugee-cap-us-immigration?utm_term=Autofeed&CMP=twt_

moral leadership, including the defense refugees and adherence to a rules based international order.[35] For the Fiscal Year of 2022, with the current displacements from Afghanistan and Ukraine, admission numbers are expected to further rise. President *Biden* set the 2022 admission ceiling at 125,000,[36] with further rises expected due to current mass displacements from Afghanistan and the Ukraine. The US' extensive resettlement experience is based on the exclusive competence of the federal government, which justifies a closer assessment. Such assessment is crucial in order to decide whether regulating resettlement at the EU level is necessary because resettlement targets cannot be sufficiently achieved at the national level, and the assessment could shed light on the issue of whether the EU can address currently untapped resources 'better' than national approaches.[37]

1.3 *Relevance of the topic*

A comprehensive research of the legal framework for EU resettlement – including US resettlement practice as a point of reference – fills a research gap. In general, there is scarce up to date literature on resettlement.[38]

---

gu&utm_medium&utm_source=Twitter#Echobox=1620096721> accessed 5 May 2021.

35 See Kemal Kirişci and Fulya Memisoglu, 'Biden's decision to pull troops from Afghanistan risks a major refugee crisis' (26 April 2021) <https://www.brookings.edu/articles/bidens-decision-to-pull-troops-from-afghanistan-risks-a-major-refugee-crisis/> accessed 15 May 2022.

36 See US Department of State, Department of Homeland and Security, Department of Health and Human Services, 'Report to Congress on Proposed Refugee Admissions for Fiscal Year 2022' (20 September 2021) <https://www.state.gov/report-to-congress-on-proposed-refugee-admissions-for-fiscal-year-2022/> accessed 15 May 2022.

37 "*The EU's principle of 'subsidiarity' says that there are three criteria for determining that EU-level intervention is desirable: Does the action have transnational aspects that cannot be resolved by Member States? Would national action or an absence of action be contrary to the requirements of the Treaty? Does action at European level have clear advantages?*", Joanne van Selm, 'Are asylum and immigration really a European Union issue?' in (2016) 51 Forced Migration Review, 61.

38 See Hanna Schneider, 'Implementing the Refugee Resettlement Process: Diverging Objectives, Interdependencies and Power Relations' in (2021) Frontiers in Political Science, 1 <https://www.frontiersin.org/articles/10.3389/fpos.2021.629675/full > accessed 21 June 2021.

Already in 2002 *Piper*, *Power* and *Thom* regretted that since *Troeller*[39], "*with the exception of some limited circulation documents produced by the UNHCR, writing about this area has been scant and in most cases, references to resettlement have either been specific to a particular situation or secondary to the main focus of the piece*".[40] By including the US perspective as well as EUMS practice in the analysis of the resettlement process, this monography responds to *Nakashiba*'s[41] call for dedicating future research to a comparative analysis on resettlement practices. So far, research on resettlement has for the most part been done independently in Europe[42] and in the US.[43] One of the rare cross-border studies dealt with resettlement programs in the US, Canada, Norway and Sweden as representative for an EUMS.[44] This study confirmed that "[t]*he size of the US resettlement program and the availability of data on refugee populations provide a unique opportunity to track outcomes for resettled refugees specifically*".[45] The US, with its Refugee Act

---

39 See Garry G Troeller, 'UNHCR Resettlement: Evolution and Future Direction' in (2002) 14 International Journal of Refugee Law 1, 85-95.

40 Margret AM Piper, Paul Power and Graham Thom, 'Refugee Resettlement: 2012 and Beyond', UNHCR Research Paper n°253 (February 2013) 1.

41 See Haruno Nakashiba, 'Clarifying UNHCR Resettlement: A few considerations from a legal perspective', UNHCR Research Paper n°264 (November 2013) 13 <https://www.unhcr.org/research/working/528e0a139/clarifying-unhcr-resettlement-few-considerations-legal-perspective-haruno.html> accessed 13 February 2021.

42 See Lyra Jakulevičienė and Mantas Bileišis, 'EU refugee resettlement: Key challenges of expanding the practice into new Member States' in (2016) 9 Baltic Journal of Law & Politics 1, 93-123; for relocation measures see Lars Carlsen, 'An Alternative View on Distribution Keys for the Possible Relocation of Refugees in the European Union' in (2017) 130 Social Indicators Research 3, 1147-1163; see also Commission Directorate-General Home Affairs, 'Study on the Feasibility of Establishing a Mechanism for a Relocation of Beneficiaries of International protection', JLX/2009/ERFX/PR/1005 (Final Report 2010) <https://ec.europa.eu/home-affairs/sites/homeaffairs/files/e-library/docs/pdf/final_report_relocation_of_refugees_en.pdf> accessed 13 February 2021.

43 For development and improvement of resettlement in the US see e.g., Donald Kerwin, 'The US Refugee Resettlement Program – A Return to First Principles: How Refugees Help to Define, Strengthen, and Revitalize the United States' in (2018) 6 Journal on Migration and Human Security 3, 205-225; see also Anastasia Brown and Todd Scribner, 'Unfulfilled Promises, Future Possibilities: The Refugee Resettlement System in the United States' (2014) 2 Journal on Migration and Human Security 2, 101-120.

44 See Randy Capps et al, 'Integrating refugees in the United States: The successes and challenges of resettlement in a Global context' in (2015) Statistical Journal of the IAOS, 341 (344).

45 Ibid 342f.

of 1980, is not only a pioneer in legislating refugee resettlement but also in collecting resettlement-related data, which justifies the choice to refer to the US program in this thesis. A comparative analysis with Canada is beyond the scope of this thesis but remains an area for further research. Regarding EUMS domestic resettlement frameworks and policies, this thesis complements the 2013 comparative report of *Perrin and McNamara*[46] as it adds more recent data, such as updated country chapters to the *Resettlement Handbook*[47] and reports[48]. Furthermore, as opposed to the 2013 recommendations of *Bokshi*[49] focusing on the resettlement capacity of individual EUMS, this monography sheds light on the EU perspective. One recent research project from *Schneider* adopts a broader approach by highlighting the multiplicity of stakeholders and bringing together the multiple steps in the resettlement process. However, as opposed to this thesis, *Schneider* focuses on policy rather than legal questions, and she focuses on the analysis of two different programs conducted by Germany.[50]

The underlying legal questions of this monography comprise (i) whether there is a (binding) international legal basis for resettlement, (ii) which international legal obligations must be respected in the course of resettlements to the EU, (iii) where is the location of resettlement in EU's legal framework and to what extent can it be regulated at EU level.[51]

---

46 See Delphine Perrin and Frank McNamara, 'Refugee Resettlement in the EU: Between Shared Standards and Diversity in Legal and Policy Frames', KNOW RESET Research Report 2013/03.

47 See Country Chapters to UNHCR *Resettlement Handbook* <https://www.unhcr.org/protection/resettlement/4a2ccf4c6/unhcr-resettlement-handbook-country-chapters.html> accessed 13 February 2021.

48 See Susan Fratzke and Lena Kainz, 'Preparing for the unknown: Designing effective predeparture orientation for resettling refugees' (May 2019) 1 <https://www.migrationpolicy.org/research/designing-effective-predeparture-orientation-resettling-refugees> accessed 13 February 2021.

49 See Elona Bokshi, 'Refugee Resettlement in the EU: The capacity to do it better and to do it more', KNOW RESET Research Report 2013/04.

50 See Hanna Schneider, 'Implementing the Refugee Resettlement Process: Diverging Objectives, Interdependencies and Power Relations' in (2021) Frontiers in Political Science, 2.

51 This monography provides a more extensive analysis than *Ziebritzki*'s contribution on resettlement within the EU's constitutional order as it complements EU law with a more holistic international law perspective. See Catharina Ziebritzki, 'The Objective of Resettlement in an EU Constitutional Perspective' in Marie-Claire Foblets and Luc Leboeuf (eds), *Humanitarian Admission to Europe: The Law between Promises and Constraints* (Hart/Nomos 2020) 285 (285ff).

1.4 Methodology and structure

Based on legal-dogmatic analysis, and the comparison with resettlement law and practice in the US, this monography comes up with recommendations for a future EU legal framework. This is accomplished through the following structure:

As a starting point, Chapter 2 clarifies the concept of resettlement. A better understanding of this concept is achieved by classifying resettlement as a responsibility-sharing mechanism, defining resettlement, putting it in the historical context, analyzing its functions, revealing the motives of states to engage in resettlement, as well as presenting the actors involved in the resettlement process. The main legal question of this Chapter is to reveal whether there is a (binding) international legal basis for resettlement.

Even though there might not be a binding obligation to resettle refugees, it is important to examine whether states must comply with obligations under international law when they carry out resettlement operations. Chapter 3 pursues this question by first examining the applicability of selected human rights and refugee law treaties in the resettlement process. Subsequently, substantive rights relevant throughout the resettlement process are discussed. Finally, it is shown whether the law of responsibility of states and international organizations for internationally wrongful conduct provides mechanisms to establish responsibility of the actors involved in the resettlement process for international law violations.

Chapter 4 is dedicated to the development and status of EU resettlement. This Chapter evaluates whether and to what extent resettlement has been regulated at the EU level. It elaborates on possibilities and barriers under EU's constitutional order for regulating resettlement and observes to what extent EU legal principles have been upheld in EU resettlement to date.

Eventually, Chapter 5 accounts for legal and practical issues throughout the resettlement process. It considers and compares European and US resettlement practice in the stages of selection, pre-departure and post-arrival orientation and placement, followed by long-term integration and naturalization. With a view to prospective EU legislation on resettlement, this Chapter identifies legal and practical issues demanding legal reform.

Against the backdrop of the findings, Chapter 6 concludes with a recap of the legal framework for resettlement to the EU with lessons from the US model.

2 The concept of refugee resettlement entrenched in international and EU law

2.1 *Responsibility sharing through resettlement*

Globally, low- and middle-income countries host 83 per cent of the world's refugees and other persons displaced abroad, and more than 70 per cent live in countries neighboring their countries of origin.[52] This 'responsibility by proximity'[53] misconstrues the definition of responsibility sharing, as Peter Sutherland, the former UN Special Representative of the Secretary-General for Migration and Development, warned.[54] All need to accept additional responsibilities to ensure protection for refugees and other forced migrants, and in particular to uphold the fundamental guarantee that refugees will not be expelled to territories in which they will be subject to persecution (see 3.3.1).

Against this backdrop, scholars identified resettlement as a 'burden sharing' or 'responsibility sharing' scheme.[55] Even though burden and responsibility sharing are sometimes used synonymously, they must be distinguished. According to *Hathaway* and *Neve*, responsibility sharing refers to the overall contributions by states towards ensuring refugee protection, while burden sharing refers to contributions by states to the protection

---

52 See UNHCR, 'Refugee Data Finder' (as of 16 June 2022) <https://www.unhcr.org/refugee-statistics/> accessed 27 June 2022.

53 See Janine Prantl, Mark J Wood and Michael W Doyle, 'Principles of Responsibility Sharing: Proximity, Culpability, Moral Accountability and Capability' in (June 2022) 110 California Law Review 3, 935 (937f) <https://www.californialawreview.org/print/principles-for-responsibility-sharing-proximity-culpability-moral-accountability-and-capability/> accessed 16 August 2022.

54 See UN, 'INTERVIEW: "Refugees are the responsibility of the world… Proximity doesn't define responsibility." – Peter Sutherland' (*UN News*, 2 October 2015) <https://news.un.org/en/story/2015/10/511282-interview-refugees-are-responsibility-world-proximity-doesnt-define> accessed 16 June 2021.

55 "*The system established by UNHCR to resettle a small number of especially vulnerable refugees in third countries reflects in a modest way the principle of sharing responsibility*", Astri Suhrke, 'Burden-sharing during Refugee Emergencies: The Logic of Collective versus National Action' in (1998) 11 Journal of Refugee Studies 4, 396 (397); see Eddie Bruce-Jones, 'Burden sharing in refugee law' in Satvinder Singh Juss (ed), *Research Handbook on International Refugee Law* (Edward Elgar 2019) 71.

of refugees in another state's territory.[56] Resettlement ensures refugee protection through physical transfer of protection seekers to the receiving country and is hence better described as a responsibility sharing scheme rather than that of burden sharing.

Sharing responsibility to protect refugees by means of physical transfer from countries of (first) refuge to a receiving country enables overburdened countries of (first) refuge to (better) cope with large numbers of refugees in their territories, and it enhances their ability to comply with international protection obligations. Therefore, resettlement constitutes a gesture of international solidarity to safeguard generous asylum policies of countries of (first) refuge.[57]

2.1.1 Responsibility sharing at the international level: left to the discretion of states

International authorities mention international cooperation, burden and responsibility sharing. In this regard, the Charter of the United Nations (UN Charter)[58] refers to 'international co-operation'. Its Art 1 para 3 envisages "*international co-operation in solving international problems of* [...] *humanitarian character, and in promoting and encouraging respect for human rights and for fundamental freedoms*". The Preamble to the 1951 Convention Relating to the Status of Refugees (Refugee Convention)[59] expressly mentions 'international co-operation' to counteract the problem that "*the grant of asylum may place unduly heavy burdens on certain countries*". Furthermore, the Final Act of the Conference of Plenipotentiaries which anchored the adoption of the Refugee Convention recommends that governments act "*in a true spirit of international co-operation in order that these refugees may*

56 See James C Hathaway and R Alexander Neve, 'Making international Refugee Law Relevant again: A proposal of Collectivized and Solution-Orientated Protection' in (1997) 10 Harvard Human Rights Journal, 115 (144f).

57 See Marjoleine Zieck, 'Doomed to Fail from the Outset? UNHCR's Convention Plus Initiative Revisited' in (2009) 21 International Journal of Refugee Law 3, 387 (398f).

58 See Charter of the United Nations (adopted 26 June 1945, entered into force 24 October 1945) 1 UNTS XVI.

59 See Convention Relating to the Status of Refugees (adopted 28 July 1951, entered into force 22 April 1954) 189 UNTS 137-220.

find asylum and the possibility of resettlement".[60] Additionally, UN General Assembly Resolutions[61] and several Conclusions of the Executive Committee of UNHCR's Program (EXCOM Conclusions)[62] refer to burden and responsibility sharing. The 2018 Global Compact for Refugees mentions resettlement as a key pillar for refugee solutions.[63] This Compact aims at "*more equitable and predictable burden- and responsibility-sharing*".[64] It anticipates Global Refugee Forums every four years where states announce, amongst others, concrete pledges for resettlement places.[65]

These references indicate a general awareness of an uneven refugee distribution.[66] Nonetheless, burden and responsibility sharing are, for instance, not included in the Refugee Convention's operative sections – thus cannot be considered as effectively binding obligations under international law.

---

60 UN General Assembly, 'Final Act of the United Nations Conference of Plenipotentiaries on the Status of Refugees and Stateless Persons', Recommendation D (25 July 1951) <https://www.unhcr.org/protection/travaux/40a8a7394/final-act-united-nations-conference-plenipotentiaries-status-refugees-stateless.html> accessed 13 February 2021.

61 See e.g., UNGA, A/RES/55/2 (18 September 2000); UNGA, A/RES/56/151 (11 October 2001); UNGA, A/RES/57/213 (18 December 2002); UNGA, A/RES/59/193 (20 December 2004).

62 See e.g., UNHCR EXCOM Conclusion No 74 (XLV) 'General' (1994) lit h; No 81 (XLVII) 'General' (1997) lit j; No 85 (XLIX) 'International Protection' (1998) lit o; No 89 (LI) 'General' (2000); No 90 (LII) 'General' (2001) lit f; No 95 (LIV) 'General' (2003) lit g; No 98 (LIV) 'Protection from Sexual Abuse and Exploitation' (2003) lit g; No 100 (LV) 'International Cooperation and Burden and Responsibility Sharing in Mass-Influx Situations' (2004) lit b; see also UNHCR, 'Conclusions on International Protection: Adopted by the Executive Committee of the UNHCR Programme 1975-2017 (Conclusion No 1 – 114)', UN Doc HCR/IP/3/Eng/REV 2017 (October 2017) <https://www.refworld.org/pdfid/5a2ead6b4.pdf> accessed 13 February 2021.

63 See UNHCR, Report 'Global compact on refugees', UN Doc A/73/12 (Part II) (13 September 2018) <https://www.unhcr.org/gcr/GCR_English.pdf> accessed 13 February 2021.

64 Ibid para 15; see Michael W Doyle, 'Responsibility Sharing: From Principle to Policy' in Wiebke Sievers, Rainer Bauböck, Christoph Reinprecht (eds), *Flucht und Asyl – Internationale und österreichische Perspektiven* (VÖAW 2021) 15.

65 See Michael W Doyle in Wiebke Sievers, Rainer Bauböck, Christoph Reinprecht (eds), *Flucht und Asyl – Internationale und österreichische Perspektiven*, 15.

66 See Marjoleine Zieck, 'Doomed to Fail from the Outset? UNHCR's Convention Plus Initiative Revisited' in (2009) 21 International Journal of Refugee Law 3, 400.

Since international legal norms "*almost always refrain from providing specifics, leaving it to States to determine the* [...] *responsibility-sharing mechanisms*",[67] it is the prevailing opinion that the engagement in resettlement is voluntary. For example, *van Selm* highlighted that "[t]*he establishment and operation of a resettlement programme is voluntary, however, and primarily an administrative and programmatic operation*".[68] Furthermore, according to *Hashimoto*, "[n]*o State has a legal obligation proactively to admit refugees via resettlement who are still outside their jurisdiction nor can a refugee claim a 'right' to be resettled*".[69]

2.1.2 Responsibility sharing at the EU level: mandatory relocation failed

The principle of solidarity and fair sharing of responsibility is incorporated in EU law through Art 80 of the Treaty on the Functioning of the European Union (TFEU)[70]. This principle contains an external component, i.e. between EUMS and third countries, and stipulates positive obligations for EUMS (see 4.1.2.1). Notwithstanding, mandatory resettlement cannot be derived from EU law.[71]

While neither EU nor international law stipulates an obligation to resettle, the Council Decision 2015/1601[72] introduced mandatory quota at the

67 Tally Kritzman-Amir, 'Not In My Backyard: On the Morality of Responsibility Sharing in Refugee Law' in (2009) 34 Brooklyn Journal of International Law 2, 355 (376); see Alexander Betts and Jean François Durieux, 'Convention Plus as a Norm-Setting Exercise' in (2007) 20 Journal of Refugee Studies 3, 509 (510).

68 Joanne van Selm et al, Study on 'The Feasibility of setting up resettlement schemes in EU Member States or at EU Level, against the background of the Common European Asylum system and the goal of a Common Asylum Procedure' (European Communities 2004) 17 (emphasis as in original removed).

69 Naoko Hashimoto, 'Refugee Resettlement as an Alternative to Asylum' in (2018) 37 Refugee Survey Quarterly, 162 (165).

70 See Consolidated version of the Treaty on the Functioning of the European Union [2012] OJ C326/47-390.

71 See Lyra Jakulevičienė and Mantas Bileišis, 'EU refugee resettlement: Key challenges of expanding the practice into new Member States' in (2016) 9 Baltic Journal of Law & Politics 1, 103; see also Catharina Ziebritzki in Marie-Claire Foblets and Luc Leboeuf (eds), *Humanitarian Admission to Europe: The Law between Promises and Constraints*, 298ff.

72 See Council Decision 2015/1601 (EU) establishing provisional measures in the area of international protection for the benefit of Italy and Greece [2015] OJ L248/80-94.

EU level to 'relocate' refugees among EUMS.[73] By definition, relocation involves "*the transfer of an applicant from the territory of the Member State* [...] *responsible for examining his or her application for international protection to the territory of the Member State of relocation*".[74] As a purely internal measure, relocation "*from one Member State to another is effectively transferring a refugee within an area which should have a uniform protection for refugees anyway*".[75] In other words, relocation applies to those who have already reached EU territory and are entitled to the respective protection under EU law, while resettlement offers a legal pathway to international protection in the EU and a durable solution for those who cannot remain in the country of (first) refuge.

Council Decision 2015/1601 faced stark opposition from Eastern European states.[76] Slovakia and Hungary filed actions of annulment against this Decision, which were dismissed by the Court of Justice of the European Union (CJEU).[77] In effect, Council Decision 2015/1601 and the previous Council Decision 2015/1523[78] only achieved about one fourth of the targeted relocations.[79] Particularly, the CJEU confirmed that the Czech Re-

---

73 See Delphine Perrin and Frank McNamara, 'Refugee Resettlement in the EU: Between Shared Standards and Diversity in Legal and Policy Frames', KNOW RESET Research Report 2013/03, 35.

74 Art 2 lit e Council Decision 2015/1601.

75 Delphine Perrin and Frank McNamara, 'Refugee Resettlement in the EU: Between Shared Standards and Diversity in Legal and Policy Frames', KNOW RESET Research Report 2013/03, 36.

76 The decision was adopted on the basis of Art 78(3) TFEU, which provides that "*in the event of one or more Member States being confronted by an emergency situation characterised by a sudden inflow of nationals of third countries, the Council, on a proposal from the Commission, may adopt provisional measures for the benefit of the Member State(s) concerned. It shall act after consulting the European Parliament*".

77 See Joined Cases C-643/15 and C-647/15 *Slovak Republic and Hungary v Council* [2017] EU:C:2017:631.

78 See Council Decision 2015/1523 (EU) establishing provisional measures in the area of international protection for the benefit of Italy and of Greece [2015] OJ L239/146-156 (not imposing a mandatory quota).

79 The temporary relocation scheme was officially ceased at the end of September 2017, whereas operations on pending cases were continued until the end of that year. In fact, only 31,503 of the 160,000 expected relocations took place by November 2017; see Commission, 'Relocation: EU Solidarity between Member States' (14 November 2017) <https://ec.europa.eu/home-affairs/sites/homeaffairs/files/what-we-do/policies/european-agenda-migration/20171114_relocation_eu_solidarity_between_member_states_en.pdf> accessed 13 February 2021; see also Darla Davitti, 'Biopolitical Borders and the State of Exception in the European Migration 'Crisis'' in (2018) 29 European Journal of International Law

public, Hungary and Poland[80] did not fulfill their relocation obligations.[81] Overall, the implementation of the 2015 *intra*-EU relocation scheme failed and raised doubts regarding the normative force of the principle of solidarity and fair sharing of responsibilities stated in Art 80 TFEU (see 4.1.2.1).[82]

2.1.3 Preliminary conclusion

Resettlement constitutes a means of responsibility sharing (as opposed to burden sharing). Even though international law recognizes the uneven refugee "*burden*" amongst states, calling for co-operation, there is no resettlement mechanism under binding international law. It is left to the discretion of states to bear responsibility by taking a share. At the EU

4, 1173 (1190); Sertan Sanderson, 'EU relocation scheme ends to mixed reviews' (*InfoMigrants*, 26 September 2017) <https://www.infomigrants.net/en/post/5270/eu-relocation-scheme-ends-to-mixed-reviews> accessed 27 June 2022. Further statistics are provided by Asylum Information Database <https://www.asylumineurope.org> accessed 20 March 2021.

80 Poland distinguishes from the Czech Republic and Hungary in terms of legal migration, inasmuch as there was an increase in the number of permits issued by Poland (since 2008), mostly for short-term period/seasonal work. "*If one excludes the large number of permits issued by Poland, the number of permits issued for the purpose of work in the rest of the EU-25 countries decreased from 326,000 in 2011 to 198,400 in 2015 before increasing in 2016 (226,000) and in 2017 (289,000)*", speech of Fabian Lutz, 'Legal migration (focus on economic migration)' (*ULB Odysseus Summer University*, 11 July 2019).

81 In July 2017, the Commission initiated infringement proceedings that were brought before the CJEU; see Commission, 'Relocation: Commission launches infringement procedures against Czech Republic, Hungary and Poland' (*Press release*, 14 June 2017) <http://europa.eu/rapid/press-release_IP-17-1607_en.htm> accessed 13 February 2021; see also Commission, 'Relocation: Commission refers the Czech Republic, Hungary and Poland to the Court of Justice' (*Press release*, 7 December 2017) <http://europa.eu/rapid/press-release_IP-17-5002_en.htm> accessed 13 February 2021; see also Sergio Carrera, *An Appraisal of the European Commission of Crisis: Has the Juncker Commission delivered a new start for EU Justice and Home Affairs?* (Centre of European Policy Studies 2018) 21 <https://www.ceps.eu/wp-content/uploads/2019/01/Commission%20of%20Crisis.pdf> accessed 13 February 2021; in 2020, the Court found that the defendant EUMS infringed their relocation obligations, see Joined Cases C-715/17, C-718/17 and C-719/17 *Commission v Republic of Poland, Hungary and Czech Republic* [2020] EU:C:2020:257.

82 See Arne Niemann and Natascha Zaun, 'EU Refugee Policies and Politics in Times of Crisis: Theoretical and Empirical Perspectives' in (2018) 56 Journal of Common Market Studies 1, 3 (6).

level, mandatory refugee distribution between EUMS, i.e. relocation, was attempted but failed. In terms of responsibility sharing between EUMS and third countries through resettlement, a binding obligation does not exist and is also not provided for in the Proposal for a Union Resettlement Framework Regulation (see 4.2.11.1).

2.2 Defining resettlement

The Refugee Convention, the most relevant legal instrument with regard to international refugee law, does not define refugee resettlement. It neither addresses the circumstances of a refugee's arrival in the country of refuge or the receiving country, nor does it legally define resettlement. Instead, it applies to all refugees, regardless of whether they arrive in an uncontrolled or controlled manner.[83]

The UNHCR put effort into the conceptualization of resettlement. The legal nature of UNHCR's resettlement definition and standards will be analyzed in the following section. Moreover, light will be shed on the EU and the US legislators' attempts to define resettlement.

2.2.1 The United Nations High Commissioner for Refugees

From UNHCR's perspective, refugee resettlement constitutes one of three durable solutions (see 1.1). Among the durable solutions, resettlement is considered to be the solution which is the least entrenched and implemented in national and/or international law.[84] Against this backdrop, the UNHCR has used its mandate to promote durable solutions (see 2.5.2.1) and has elaborated on a standardized concept of resettlement.[85]

83 See Marjoleine Zieck, 'The Limitations of Voluntary Repatriation and Resettlement of Refugees' in Vincent Chetail and Céline Bauloz (eds), *Research Handbook on International Law and Migration* (Edward Elgar Publishing 2014) 562 (578).

84 See Naoko Hashimoto, 'Refugee Resettlement as an Alternative to Asylum' in (2018) 37 Refugee Survey Quarterly, 162.

85 See Marjoleine Zieck in Vincent Chetail and Céline Bauloz (eds), *Research Handbook on International Law and Migration*, 562.

In its most recent *Resettlement Handbook*,[86] the UNHCR defined resettlement as follows:[87]

> *Resettlement involves the selection and transfer of refugees from a State in which they have sought protection to a third State which has agreed to admit them – as refugees – with permanent residence status. The status provided ensures protection against refoulement and provides a resettled refugee and his/her family or dependents with access to rights similar to those enjoyed by nationals. Resettlement also carries with it the opportunity to eventually become a naturalized citizen of the resettlement country.*

Besides this definition, the *Resettlement Handbook* sets out guidelines for the resettlement process, which aim at ensuring adequate protection of resettlement refugees in line with international law. Whether UNHCR's standards actually spur legal entrenchment of resettlement depends on the acceptance and practice of states. To that effect, international custom determines the standards' legal relevance.[88] To put it differently, it needs to be tackled whether the UNHCR's concept of resettlement, mainly based on the UNHCR *Resettlement Handbook*, has surpassed the status of non-

---

86 In 1997, the first UNHCR *Resettlement Handbook* was published. A revised version followed in 2004 and the most recent revised edition was published in 2011. It has been recognized as a useful information tool; see Joanne van Selm et al, Study on 'The Feasibility of setting up resettlement schemes in EU Member States or at EU Level, against the background of the Common European Asylum system and the goal of a Common Asylum Procedure', 11; see also UNHCR, *Resettlement Handbook* (revised ed July 2011) <http://www.unhcr.org/protection/resettlement/46f7c0ee2/unhcr-resettlement-handbook-complete-publication.html?query=resettlementhttp://www.unhcr.org/protection/resettlement/46f7c0ee2/unhcr-resettlement-handbook-complete-publication.html ?query=resettlement> accessed 13 February 2021.

87 UNHCR, *Resettlement Handbook* (revised ed July 2011) 3 (emphasis added); the definition of resettlement included in the IOM Glossary is derived from the definition in the *Resettlement Handbook*: "*The transfer of refugees from the country in which they have sought protection to another State that has agreed to admit them – as refugees – with permanent residence status*", IOM, 'Glossary on Migration No 34' (2019) 184 <https://publications.iom.int/system/files/pdf/iml_34_glossary.pdf> accessed 13 February 2021.

88 See Michael Bothe, 'Legal and Non-Legal Norms – a meaningful distinction in international relations?' in (1980) 11 Netherlands Yearbook of International Law, 65 (67).

binding soft law. Soft law standards would not be enforceable in a legal sense.[89]

As a preliminary point, it must be noted that the *Resettlement Handbook* differs from a binding treaty signed by state parties. It constitutes an internal UNHCR document, namely a guide to UNHCR staff, and a "*key reference tool* [...] *for resettlement countries, NGOs and other partners*".[90]

Still, (parts of) the *Resettlement Handbook* could become binding as customary international law if (i) a general practice exists and (ii) it is accepted as international law, i.e. *opinio juris*.[91] The first requirement demands "*extensive and virtual uniform*"[92] practice. General practice can be given in case of relevant practice of those states whose interests are especially affected.[93] In the resettlement context, accessible information about state practice mostly comes from a (relatively small) group of receiving countries that accept resettled refugees on a constant basis and in cooperation with the UNHCR. Arguing extensive practice on that basis likely undermines the relevant threshold to be met.[94] As regards uniformity, there is a certain degree of leeway. Uniformity does not mean absolute rigorous conformity, rather consistency is sufficient.[95]

Beyond state practice, the second major requirement of *opinio juris* demands a feeling of states that they are committing to what amounts to a legal obligation.[96] Whether this means acceptance or mere belief that the legal obligation exists is contested among scholars, and some of them argue that *opinio juris* is superfluous.[97] Yet, even under the less restrictive belief-theory, general practice among states remains the main

89 See Chris Inglese, 'Soft law' in (1993) 20 Polish Yearbook of International Law, 75 (77).
90 UNHCR, *Resettlement Handbook* (revised ed July 2011) cover page.
91 See James Crawford, *Brownlie's Principles of Public International Law* (Oxford University Press 9th ed 2019) 21; see also Chris Inglese, 'Soft law' in (1993) 20 Polish Yearbook of International Law, 81; see also *North Sea Continental Shelf* [1969] ICJ Rep 3.
92 *North Sea Continental Shelf* [1969] ICJ Rep 43, para 74.
93 See ibid 43, para 74; see also Tullio Treves, 'Customary International Law' (MPIL, November 2006) para 36 <https://opil.ouplaw.com/view/10.1093/law:epil/9780199231690/law-9780199231690-e1393 > accessed 13 February 2021.
94 See Tullio Treves, 'Customary International Law' (November 2006) para 78.
95 See *Military and Paramilitary Activities in und against Nicaragua (Nicaragua v United States of America)* (Merits) [1986] ICJ Rep 14, para 186.
96 See ibid para 207.
97 For an overview of the different positions in the literature, see Christian Dahlman, 'The function of Opinio Juris in Customary International Law' in (2012) Nordic Journal of International Law, 328 (330ff).

indicator that states believe that the norm is valid international law, which demonstrates the interdependence of the two requirements. That being said, *opinio juris* regularly presupposes general practice.

In order to determine whether the above requirements are met, domestic legislation counts among the material sources of custom[98] because it reflects "*what States believe to be the law*".[99] If states implement the definition and guidelines of UNHCR's *Resettlement Handbook* in domestic legislation, those standards determine their national resettlement practice and become relevant practice, provided that the executive branch complies with the domestic legislation.

A comparative study by *Perrin* and *McNamara* (2013)[100] as well as the current versions of EUMS' Country Chapters to the *Resettlement Handbook* revealed that not all EUMS legally implemented resettlement. Those who incorporated resettlement into their asylum and/or immigration laws rarely introduced a legal definition of resettlement. For instance, Section 8 Danish Aliens Act[101] stipulates that resettlement to Denmark takes place based on an arrangement with the UNHCR or a similar international organization; at the same time, Denmark has not implemented UNHCR's resettlement definition, nor has it established any other legal definition of resettlement. Similarly, Finland has not defined resettlement in its Alien Act,[102] and the French Code of the Entry and Stay of Foreigners and Asylum Law does not set out a resettlement definition.[103] Germany currently conducts resettlement on the basis of Section 23 para 4 German Residence Act. It has followed UNHCR's recommendations and has generally recognized the UNHCR standards, but the UNHCR resettlement defi-

---

98 See James Crawford, *Brownlie's Principles of Public International Law*, 21f.

99 Tullio Treves, 'Customary International Law' (November 2006) para 26.

100 See Delphine Perrin and Frank McNamara, 'Refugee Resettlement in the EU: Between Shared Standards and Diversity in Legal and Policy Frames', KNOW RESET Research Report 2013/03, Annex 1, 43ff.

101 See Danish Aliens Act <https://www.legislationline.org/download/id/1222/file/4f98cdeb46c52d328c99626728c6.pdf> accessed 13 February 2021; see also Danish Country Chapter to the UNHCR *Resettlement Handbook* <https://www.unhcr.org/3c5e57b07.html> accessed 13 February 2021.

102 See Finish Alien Act <https://finlex.fi/fi/laki/kaannokset/2004/en20040301.pdf> accessed 13 February 2021.

103 See French Code of the Entry and Stay of Foreigners and Asylum Law <https://www.legifrance.gouv.fr/affichTexte.do?cidTexte=JORFTEXT000000624655&dateTexte=&categorieLien=id> accessed 13 February 2021.

nition has not been incorporated into German law.[104] And Ireland legally defines a so-called 'program refugee' as a person "*to whom permission to enter and remain in the State for resettlement, or for temporary protection* [...] *has been given by the Government or the Minister and whose name is entered in a register established and maintained by the Minister,* [...]" in Section 59 Irish International Protection Act 2015.[105] Since program refugees can be admitted either for resettlement or temporary protection, Ireland does not necessarily offer a durable solution to program refugees – but it has transposed essential elements of the UNHCR resettlement definition into its national law. Amongst other rights, Irish law grants program refugees a right to seek employment; engage in any business, trade or profession; and access education and training *to the like extent in all respects as an Irish citizen*. This reflects the UNHCR definition's reference to "*access to rights similar to those enjoyed by nationals*". Another rare example of a legal resettlement definition can be found in Romanian law.[106] The Romanian definition incorporates the main ideas of the UNHCR definition and recognizes the character of resettlement as a durable solution. Furthermore, it expressly mentions UNHCR's pre-determination of refugee status (see 5.2.1). As opposed to Denmark, Finland and Sweden, Romania restricts access to resettlement to Convention refugees.

From this short and rudimentary examination it is discovered that only two receiving countries, namely two of the few countries that regularly resettle and report to the UNHCR, have adopted a resettlement definition at all. Their definitions diverge from each other and from the UNHCR definition.

---

104 See German Country Chapter to the UNHCR *Resettlement Handbook* <https://www.unhcr.org/5162b3bc9.html> accessed 13 February 2021.

105 See Irish International Protection Act <http://www.irishstatutebook.ie/eli/2015/act/66/section/59/enacted/en/html#sec59> accessed 18 June 2020; see also Irish Country Chapter to the UNHCR *Resettlement Handbook* <https://www.unhcr.org/3cac29da4.html> accessed 13 February 2021.

106 Accordingly, a refugee in need of resettlement is "*an alien found on the territory of another state who has been recognized as a refugee in accordance with the 1951 Geneva Refugee Convention, or an alien recognized as a refugee by the UNHCR in accordance with Article 1 A of the 1951 Geneva Refugee Convention and Art. 1(2) of its Protocol, who is not benefiting from effective protection, and does not have the possibility of integration in the country of asylum or the possibility of voluntary repatriation to his or her country of origin in conditions of safety and dignity*", Romanian Country Chapter to the UNHCR *Resettlement Handbook* <https://www.unhcr.org/4e2d64679.html> accessed 13 February 2021.

So far, the numerous states from which resettlement should take place have not been mentioned. There are, however, hardly any significant references to resettlement in their national laws. One of the few examples is Turkish law, where resettlement is used in the context of 'conditional refugee status'. In the Turkish case, protection standards for potential resettlement refugees are restricted rather than strengthened. As explicitly stated in Art 62 Turkish Law on Foreigners and International Protection (LFIP)[107], 'conditional refugees' "*shall be allowed to reside in Turkey temporarily until they are resettled to a third country*";[108] but they are, amongst others, excluded from family reunification rights and they have no prospect of long-term legal integration in Turkey.[109]

It seems obvious from all these inconsistencies that a uniform and consistent practice has not emerged. The lack of general practice, in particular the fact that many receiving countries have not implemented the main characteristics of the UNHCR definition into their domestic laws, indicates that states do not consider the *Resettlement Handbook* to be binding international law. Indeed, states initially did not accept the *Resettlement Handbook* as a binding instrument, but rather as a guiding document, which speaks against the existence of *opinio juris*. As a result, the UNHCR resettlement definition and guidelines under the *Resettlement Handbook* cannot be considered as binding customary international law.

The requirements of customary international law are not met, but has the formation process even started? In this regard, the will of states, namely a true belief, voluntarily made with the purpose of starting or influencing

107 Law No 6458 of 2013 on Foreigners and International Protection (as amended 29 October 2016) [unofficial translation] <https://www.refworld.org/docid/5a1d828f4.html> accessed 3 July 2021.

108 This is also indicated on the webpage of the Turkish Directorate General of Migration Management; see <https://en.goc.gov.tr/conditional-refugee> accessed 16 June 2021.

109 For further details on Turkey's reservation and the LFIP, see AIDA & ECRE, 'Country Report: Introduction to the asylum context in Turkey' (last updated 30 November 2020) <https://asylumineurope.org/reports/country/turkey/introduction-asylum-context-turkey/> accessed 16 June 2021; see also N Ela Gökalp Aras and Zeynep Sahin Mencütek, '*Refugee Protection: Turkey Report*', Paper 2020/30 (January 2020) 26 <https://www.researchgate.net/profile/Zeynep-Mencutek/publication/340236818_Refugee_Protection_Turkey_Report_Working_Papers_Global_Migration_Consequences_and_Responses/links/5e7e4ee192851caef4a56b41/Refugee-Protection-Turkey-Report-Working-Papers-Global-Migration-Consequences-and-Responses.pdf> accessed 16 June 2021.

the formation of customary law constitutes a relevant indicator.[110] It is difficult, but decisive to distinguish the aim of creating customary law from the aim of establishing new rules of soft law.[111] Since the nature of the definition and standards set out in the *Resettlement Handbook* are rather defined as guidelines than rules that should become binding on states (at a later stage), it is hard to establish any indication that the formation process of customary international law has started. States have continuously insisted on the voluntary nature of resettlement, and a significant change towards creating binding international obligations in this regard cannot be expected at this point in time.

Another attempt would be to vest normative force into the UNHCR *Resettlement Handbook* by considering it as a binding decision of an international organization. However, the UNHCR as a subsidiary organ of the UN has no legislative competences in the sense of passing normative acts with direct effect and/or primacy over national norms in the legal systems of receiving countries.

It can be invoked that the current version of UNHCR's *Resettlement Handbook* along with its two predecessors "*are the result of extensive round table consultations with governments, NGOs and UNHCR personnel from all over the globe*".[112] This shows that resettlement standards have been subjected to repeated international negotiations. They have been reciprocally endorsed. Thus, the argument that the conduct of resettlement operations by receiving countries constitutes an exclusive domestic affair does not hold true.[113]

The fact remains that the UNHCR resettlement standards are not perceived as 'legal norms', rather they constitute non-binding soft law. This classification is supported by scholars, e.g. *Garnier*, *Sandvik* and *Jubilut* expressly referred to "*UNHCR's soft law*".[114] Specifically, *Garnier* described

110 See Tullio Treves, 'Customary International Law' (November 2006) para 9.

111 See ibid para 29.

112 Kristin Bergtora Sandvik, 'A Legal History: The Emergence of the African Resettlement Candidate in International Refugee Management' in Adèle Garnier, Liliana Lyra Jubilut and Kristin Bergtora Sandvik (eds), *Refugee Resettlement: Power, Politics, and Humanitarian Governance* (Berghahn 2018) 46 (61).

113 See Chris Inglese, 'Soft law' in (1993) 20 Polish Yearbook of International Law, 83.

114 Adèle Garnier, Kristin Bergtora Sandvik and Liliana Lyra Jubilut, 'Introduction: Refugee Resettlement as Humanitarian Governance' in Adèle Garnier, Liliana Lyra Jubilut and Kristin Bergtora Sandvik (eds), *Refugee Resettlement: Power, Politics, and Humanitarian Governance* (Berghahn 2018) 1 (7).

the UNHCR *Resettlement Handbook* as a "*main source of 'soft law' aiming to guide resettlement globally*".[115] The analysis has confirmed that currently, this remains more a matter of guidance than of binding international law. However, not to undermine the value of soft law and its standard-setting nature, UNHCR's *Resettlement Handbook* could still serve as a model in international and EU law making.[116]

2.2.2 The European Union

The Commission defined resettlement in Art 2 Union Resettlement Framework Regulation Proposal. As part of a regulation, once adopted, this definition would have a legally binding effect upon all EUMS. The proposed Article states that

> [...] *'resettlement' means the admission of third-country nationals and stateless persons in need of international protection from a third country, to which or within which they have been displaced to the territory of the Member States with a view to granting them international protection*.[117]

The Commission followed the main ideas of UNHCR's resettlement definition. One particularity is the Commission's inclusion of persons from a third country "*within which they have been displaced*", thereby extending the scope of beneficiaries to Internally Displaced Persons (IDPs), i.e. persons who have not left their home countries. By comparison, the UNHCR definition refers to 'refugees' only. IDPs may be in need for international protection for the same reasons as Convention refugees, who are, by definition, outside their home country (see 2.5.4.1). It follows that cases of internal displacement[118] demand for resettlement operations as well.

---

115 Adèle Garnier, 'The COVID-19 Resettlement Suspension: Impact, Exemptions and the Road Ahead' (*FluchtforschungsBlog*, 16 June 2020) <https://blog.fluchtforschung.net/the-covid-19-resettlement-suspension/> accessed 13 February 2021.

116 See Daniel Thürer, 'Soft law' (MPIL, March 2019) para 32 <https://opil.ouplaw.com/view/10.1093/law:epil/9780199231690/law-9780199231690-e1469> accessed 13 February 2021.

117 Art 2 Proposal for a Union Resettlement Framework Regulation (emphasis added) <https://eur-lex.europa.eu/legal-content/EN/TXT/?uri=CELEX%3A52016PC0468&qid=1605104443607> accessed 3 August 2021.

118 The Guiding Principles on Internal Displacement provide the normative framework for protecting and assisting internally displaced persons. Therein such persons are defined as those "*who have been forced or obliged to flee or to leave their homes or places of habitual residence, in particular as a result of or in order to avoid*

However, implementing the extended scope of the Commission Proposal would entail a significant rise in resettlement needs. The gap between needs and actual resettlements would grow if receiving states were not willing to increase the pledged quotas.

Furthermore, adopted in 2014, Art 2 lit a Regulation 2014/516 (EU) establishing the Asylum, Migration and Integration Fund (AMIF)[119] set out a binding resettlement definition. It stated that resettlement means "*the process whereby, on a request from the* [...] [UNHCR] *based on a person's need for international protection, third-country nationals are transferred from a third country and established in a Member State where they are permitted to reside* [...]". The residence should be based either on refugee status, subsidiary protection status or "*any other status which offers similar rights and benefits under national and Union law*".

In contrast to the definition in the 2016 Proposal for a Resettlement Framework Regulation (see 4.2.11.2), the 2014 AMIF Regulation did not literally refer to IDPs. Nonetheless, the definition in the 2014 AMIF Regulation included "*any other status which offers similar rights and benefits under national and Union law*". Depending on the national legal situation, IDPs could fall under this category. It should also be noted that subsidiary protection status, a more temporary status than refugee status, was explicitly mentioned (for further elaboration on subsidiary protection status see 2.5.4.1). Yet not all EUMS envisage the resettlement of persons eligible for subsidiary protection (see 5.2.1). The explicit reference and the associated funding could provide an incentive for EUMS to expand the scope of resettlement beneficiaries to persons eligible for subsidiary protection. In the absence of an explicit reference, however, this is less clear for IDPs.

As opposed to the UNHCR resettlement definition, neither the Commission's definition under Art 2 Union Resettlement Framework Regulation Proposal, nor the definition under Art 2 lit a of the 2014 AMIF Regulation mention permanent residence status or (potential) naturalization. This means that the Commission did not necessarily characterize resettlement as a durable solution, but left the door open for resettlement

the effects of armed conflict, situations of generalized violence, violations of human rights or natural or human-made disasters, and who have not crossed an internationally recognized State border", ECOSOC, 'Guiding Principles on International Displacement', UN Doc E/CN4/1998/53/Add2 (11 February 1998) Annex, para 2 <https://undocs.org/E/CN.4/1998/53/Add.2> accessed 20 March 2021.

119 See Regulation 2014/516 (EU) establishing the Asylum, Migration and Integration Fund [2014] OJ L150/168-195.

as a temporary substitution of the country of (first) refuge.[120] In a more recent resettlement definition from December 2019, the Commission still refrained from any express reference to resettlement's role as a durable solution:[121]

> *Resettlement means the admission of non-EU nationals in need of international protection from a non-EU country to a Member State where they are granted protection. It is a safe and legal alternative to irregular journeys and a demonstration of European solidarity with non-EU countries hosting large numbers of persons fleeing war or persecution.*

In this definition the Commission described resettlement as a demonstration of European solidarity towards countries of (first) refuge. Unburdening countries of (first) refuge by taking a share can, in turn, help to (re)establish stable situations and durable settlement opportunities in those countries. The 2019 resettlement definition also exemplifies a terminological problem, namely the usage of the terms 'irregular' *versus* 'illegal'. The Commission's choice confirms the trend of the prevailing usage of the term 'irregular' instead of 'illegal',[122] which is also reflected in the terminology used in this monography.

Eventually, a reference to resettlement as durable solution can be found in the current 2021 AMIF Regulation.[123] It defines resettlement in Art 2 para 8 as "*admission following a referral from the UNHCR of third-country nationals or stateless persons from a third country to which they have been displaced, to the territory of the Member States, and who are granted international protection and have access to a <u>durable solution</u> in accordance with Union and national law*"[124].

---

120 See Marjoleine Zieck, 'Refugees and the Right to Freedom of Movement: From Flight to Return' in (2018) 39 Michigan Journal of International Law 1, 19 (105).

121 Commission, 'Resettlement: EU Member States' pledges exceed 30,000 places for 2020' (*Press release*, 18 December 2019) <https://ec.europa.eu/commission/presscorner/detail/de/ip_19_6794> accessed 13 February 2021.

122 See for an elaboration Tobias Klarmann, *Illegalisierte Migration: Die (De-)Konstruktion migrationsspezifischer Illegalitäten im Unionsrecht* (Nomos 2021) 38-50.

123 See Regulation 2021/1147 (EU) establishing the Asylum, Migration and Integration Fund [2021] OJ L251/1-47 (consolidated version of 12 April 2022).

124 Emphasis added.

2.2.3 The United States of America

In the US, eligibility for resettlement depends on the situation in the country of (first) refuge. To that effect, US law describes the situation where an alien is firmly resettled. Only persons who are not firmly resettled in a country of (first) refuge qualify for resettlement to the US. Firm resettlement can be assumed if:[125]

> *prior to arrival in the United States, he or she entered into another country with, or while in that country received, an offer of permanent resident status, citizenship, or some other type of permanent resettlement unless he or she establishes:*
> *(a) That his or her entry into that country was a necessary consequence of his or her flight from persecution, that he or she remained in that country only as long as was necessary to arrange onward travel, and that he or she did not establish significant ties in that country; or*
> *(b) That the conditions of his or her residence in that country were so substantially and consciously restricted by the authority of the country of refuge that he or she was not in fact resettled. In making his or her determination, the asylum officer or immigration judge shall consider the conditions under which other residents of the country live; the type of housing, whether permanent or temporary, made available to the refugee; the types and extent of employment available to the refugee; and the extent to which the refugee received permission to hold property and to enjoy other rights and privileges, such as travel documentation that includes a right of entry or reentry, education, public relief, or naturalization, ordinarily available to others resident in the country.*

By emphasizing the conditions of residence in the country of (first) refuge, the US firm resettlement bar takes account of situations where fundamental rights of refugees are at risk in overburdened countries of (first) refuge. It reflects the interest of the country of (first) refuge to be relieved in overburdened situations, and the interest of refugees to be protected from serious human rights violations in that country. By the same token, it bars those individuals from international protection in the US who can effectively receive such protection elsewhere – this in turn is a relief for the US.

---

125 Section 208.15 Title 8 Code of Federal Regulations 2012 <https://www.govinfo.gov/content/pkg/CFR-2012-title8-vol1/pdf/CFR-2012-title8-vol1-part208.pdf> accessed 13 February 2021.

2.2.4 Preliminary conclusion

As of today, there is no binding definition of resettlement in international (refugee) law. The UNHCR made conceptualization efforts, which however do not go beyond the status of non-binding soft law. Remarkably, as opposed to the UNHCR definition, the Commission attempted to extend the scope of resettlement beneficiaries by generally including IDPs in its Proposal for a Union Resettlement Framework Regulation. US law is unique because it focuses on the conditions in the country of (first) refuge as bar for resettlement eligibility. Thereby, the US implicitly recognizes resettlement as a durable solution for those refugees who cannot find such solution in the country of (first) refuge. In EU legislation, explicit reference to resettlement as a durable solution was only introduced recently through the 2021 AMIF Regulation.

While all three outlined definitions consider resettlement as a tool to protect persons in need who cannot find protection in a respective third country, there is no clear common denominator on the durability and eligibility for resettlement.

For the sake of clarity on the concept of resettlement, the traditional UNHCR definition of resettlement as a durable solution is used as a reference point. In this regard, traditional resettlement is distinct from humanitarian admission, which includes more temporal measures. In terms of the scope of resettlement beneficiaries, all three elaborated definitions include refugees. The potential extension of the scope to other forcibly displaced persons will be discussed in 2.5.4 and 5.2.3.2.

2.3 *Historical background and development of resettlement (with focus on the US)*

The historical background and development of resettlement helps to clarify the concept of resettlement. The following section shows in which contexts resettlement has been used as a response to forced displacements and reveals which factors have determined international resettlement efforts.

2.3.1 The beginning of systematic and organized resettlement

Globally, organized resettlements to protect vulnerable persons, such as Belarussians fleeing to China after the Russian Revolution as well as Jews facing persecution by the Nazis, emerged in the period between the two World Wars.[126]

During that time, the US did not pursue what could be described as an immigration-friendly policy. For example, the US did not approve the so-called Emigrants Charter[127] in May 1924. This Charter's focus on equal treatment between nationals and foreigners[128] contradicted the then existing US law on quotas discriminating against populations that were deemed to potentially harm US society and economy.[129]

In the aftermath of World War II, resettlement was soon considered the only viable option to deal with "*21 million displaced people throughout Europe*".[130] Many of the displaced people had valid reasons not to return home, which created a situation that required solutions apart from voluntary repatriation.[131] Against this backdrop, movements of refugees from their country of (first) refuge to other countries started in 1945, under the auspices of the Intergovernmental Committee on Refugees (IGCR).[132]

In the following years, the US – together with Canada, Australia and the free countries of Western Europe – supported the UN in establishing the International Refugee Organization (IRO).[133] From 20 April 1946, the IRO "*provided the vehicle for resettlement, but it could only be successful if each of the member nations agreed to accept a portion of the group for the*

126 See Margret AM Piper, Paul Power and Graham Thom, 'Refugee Resettlement: 2012 and Beyond', UNHCR Research Paper n°253 (February 2013) 4.

127 See 'Final Act of the International Conference on Emigration and Immigration' in Giuseppe de Michelis, *Conference international de l'émigration et de l'immigration, Rome 15-31 mai 1924* (Imprimerie de la Chambre des Députés – Raison C Colombo 1925).

128 See Vincent Chetail, *International Migration Law* (Oxford University Press 2019) 54f.

129 See International Crisis Group, 'How to Save the US Refugee Admissions Program', Crisis Group United States Report N°2 (12 September 2018) 4 <https://www.crisisgroup.org/united-states/002-how-save-us-refugee-admissions-program> accessed 13 February 2021.

130 Ibid 4.

131 See ibid 4.

132 See Atle Grahl-Madsen, *The Status of Refugees in International Law: Volume II* (AW Sijthoff 1972) 230.

133 See Vincent Chetail, *International Migration Law*, 58; see also Aristide R Zolberg, 'From Invitation to Interdiction: US Foreign Policy and Immigration since 1945' in Michael S Teitelbaum and Miron Weiner (eds), *Threatened Peoples, Threatened Borders* (WW Norton Company 1995) 117 (123).

permanent residence".[134] Between 1947 and 1951, the IRO presided over the resettlement of more than one million refugees, 80% of which were resettled to destinations outside of Europe.[135]

The scale of IGCR and subsequent IRO resettlements demanded a legal foundation in the form of resettlement agreements concluded with the governments of receiving countries.[136] IRO's responsibility for determining which individuals were in need of resettlement was a characteristic feature of these agreements. At the same time, governments reserved the exclusive right to carry out the final selection of the resettlement beneficiaries under the respective agreements.[137]

The US recognized that "*pre-war efforts, especially on behalf of Jewish refugees, had been shamefully inadequate*"[138] and altered its restrictive policy. In the following era, "*Congress passed several pieces of legislation to admit large-scale refugee populations*".[139] Strategic considerations and foreign policy played a significant factor in the US decision to resettle refugees.[140] The Cold War, i.e. the geopolitical tension between the Soviet Union and the US with its allies, also impacted US immigration policy. In June 1948, America's first refugee act, the Displaced Persons Act,[141] was signed. The

---

134 Stephen H Legomsky, *Immigration Law and Policy* (The Foundation Press 1992) 827.

135 See Margret AM Piper, Paul Power and Graham Thom, 'Refugee Resettlement: 2012 and Beyond', UNHCR Research Paper n°253 (February 2013) 4.

136 The earliest agreement concerning resettlement to a Western European Country was the Agreement between His Britannic Majesty's Government (Control Commission for Germany), the Belgian Government and the IGCR for the Resettlement in Belgium of Displaced Persons and Refugees in the British Zone of Germany of 13 February 1947, IRO Doc IRO/LEG/GOV/10/Add I, 25 March 1949; for further examples see Atle Grahl-Madsen, *The Status of Refugees in International Law: Volume II*, 231ff (233): e.g. the Luxembourg Resettlement Agreement of 9 March 1947, the Norwegian Agreement following the Hungarian exodus in 1956.

137 See Atle Grahl-Madsen, *The Status of Refugees in International Law: Volume II*, 233.

138 Thomas Alexander Aleinikoff et al, *Immigration and Citizenship: Process and Policy*, 793.

139 Donald Kerwin, 'The US Refugee Resettlement Program – A Return to First Principles: How Refugees Help to Define, Strengthen, and Revitalize the United States' in (2018) 6 Journal on Migration and Human Security 3, 208.

140 See International Crisis Group, 'How to Save the US Refugee Admissions Program', Crisis Group United States Report N°2 (12 September 2018) 4.

141 See Displaced Persons Act 1948, Public Law 80-774, 62 Stat 1009, Chapter 647.

law provided for the admission of 202,000 persons.[142] In fact, those fleeing from communist or communist-dominated nations were prioritized for refugee status.[143] The amendments of 1950 expanded admission to 400,000 refugees.[144] The Displaced Persons Act "*was followed by additional ad hoc enactments responsive to the imperatives of the cold war*".[145]

2.3.2 Resettlement under the UNHCR

In 1950, the UNHCR followed the IRO.[146] Together with the Intergovernmental Committee on European Migration (ICEM),[147] the UNHCR continued IRO's resettlement tradition[148] and spurred the development of an international refugee regime, culminating in the enactment of the 1951 Refugee Convention. Notwithstanding its leading role in this development, the US was not among the signatories of the Refugee Convention.[149]

The *post*-IRO period with the adoption of the Refugee Convention was marked by a shift away from the past practice of concluding resettlement agreements. The UNHCR and the ICEM operated on a much smaller scale than the IRO because selection practices had already been firmly

142 See Aristide R Zolberg in Michael S Teitelbaum and Miron Weiner (eds), *Threatened Peoples, Threatened Borders*, 123.
143 See Kathryn M Bockley, 'A Historical Overview of Refugee Legislation: The Deception of Foreign Policy in the Land of Promise' in (1995) 21 North Carolina Journal of International Law and Commercial Regulation 1, 253 (262).
144 See Stephen H Legomsky, *Immigration Law and Policy*, 828; see also Donald Kerwin, 'The US Refugee Resettlement Program – A Return to First Principles: How Refugees Help to Define, Strengthen, and Revitalize the United States' in (2018) 6 Journal on Migration and Human Security 3, 208.
145 Aristide R Zolberg in Michael S Teitelbaum and Miron Weiner (eds), *Threatened Peoples, Threatened Borders*, 123.
146 This did not imply succeeding to the rights and obligations of the IRO as predecessor; see Marjoleine Zieck, *UNHCR's worldwide presence in the field* (Wolf Legal Publishers 2006) 19.
147 The Intergovernmental Committee for European Migration was established in 1951, originally under the name Provisional Intergovernmental Committee for the Movement of Migrants from Europe; see Atle Grahl-Madsen, *The Status of Refugees in International Law: Volume II*, 230.
148 See Stephen H Legomsky, *Immigration Law and Policy*, 829.
149 See Joanne van Selm, 'European Refugee Policy: is there such a thing?', UNHCR Research Paper n°115 (May 2005) 4 <https://www.refworld.org/pdfid/4ff166f31e.pdf> accessed 13 February 2021.

established and the Refugee Convention made the conclusion of detailed agreements superfluous.[150] The ordinary practice then was that receiving countries demanded the individual refugee to be in possession of a Convention travel document (see Art 28 Refugee Convention) including the usual return clause,[151] which entitled the refugee to return to the issuing state, namely the country of (first) refuge.[152]

2.3.3 Adjustments in US immigration law

The realization of UNHCR's resettlement initiatives in the 1950s and 1960s to reconstruct Europe[153] strongly depended on US admissions.[154] In turn, this required adjustments of the US refugee regime. At that time, US immigration law had not yet contained "*a standing mechanism for bringing refugees into the country, or even recognize the concept of 'refugee'*".[155] US resettlement was largely conducted on an *ad hoc* basis. Three means allowed entry to refugees: (i) visas issued by the President through borrowing against existing quotas, (ii) (time-limited) visas created by Congress without quota, or (iii) parole authority invoked by the President, i.e. the President directed discretionary power to the Attorney General "*to 'parole' any alien into the United States for reasons of emergency or if it were 'deemed*

150 See Atle Grahl-Madsen, *The Status of Refugees in International Law: Volume II*, 233.

151 See Annex to the Refugee Convention, 'Specimen Travel Document', para 2 <https://cms.emergency.unhcr.org/documents/11982/55726/Convention+relating+to+the+Status+of+Refugees+%28signed+28+July+1951%2C+entered+into+force+22+April+1954%29+189+UNTS+150+and+Protocol+relating+to+the+Status+of+Refugees+%28signed+31+January+1967%2C+entered+into+force+4+October+167%29+606+UNTS+267/0bf3248a-cfa8-4a60-864d-65cdfece1d47> accessed 13 February 2021.

152 See Atle Grahl-Madsen, *The Status of Refugees in International Law: Volume II*, 234.

153 "[A]*fter the onset of the cold war, under the leadership of Secretary of State George Marshall, the Truman administration began to treat the reconstruction of Europe as a major priority.* [...] *Given local conditions, the solution required some sort of resettlement*", Aristide R Zolberg in Michael S Teitelbaum and Miron Weiner (eds), *Threatened Peoples, Threatened Borders*, 123.

154 See ibid 123.

155 International Crisis Group, 'How to Save the US Refugee Admissions Program', Crisis Group United States Report N°2 (12 September 2018) 5.

strictly in the public interest.'".[156] Parole power became the favored tool.[157] It should be mentioned that the usage of parole power was not regulated by standardized procedures. Furthermore, due to its discretionary nature, parole power was outside the scope of judicial review.[158]

The Refugee Relief Act of 1953,[159] another temporary US measure, allowed non-quota admission of special immigrants in times of international crisis.[160] Over the following three years, it provided for 209,000 non-quota slots.[161] In fact, the Act constituted a "[...] *device to 'encourage' defection of all* [Soviet] *nations and 'key' personnel from the satellite countries*".[162]

2.3.4 The Hungarian exodus

In 1956, the first large-scale resettlement operation, namely UNHCR's "*first major emergency*"[163] took place. It was triggered by the Soviet invasion of Hungary. When the Hungarian revolution was ended on 4 November 1956, Austria had welcomed some 200,000 Hungarian refugees on the condition of rapid resettlement to other countries.[164] The resettlements

156 Aristide R Zolberg in Michael S Teitelbaum and Miron Weiner (eds), *Threatened Peoples, Threatened Borders*, 124.

157 See International Crisis Group, 'How to Save the US Refugee Admissions Program', Crisis Group United States Report N°2 (12 September 2018) 5.

158 See Kathryn M Bockley, 'A Historical Overview of Refugee Legislation: The Deception of Foreign Policy in the Land of Promise' in (1995) 21 North Carolina Journal of International Law and Commercial Regulation 1, 268.

159 See Refugee Relief Act 1953, Public Law 203, 67 Stat 400, Chapter 336.

160 See Kathryn M Bockley, 'A Historical Overview of Refugee Legislation: The Deception of Foreign Policy in the Land of Promise' in (1995) 21 North Carolina Journal of International Law and Commercial Regulation 1, 265.

161 See Donald Kerwin, 'The US Refugee Resettlement Program – A Return to First Principles: How Refugees Help to Define, Strengthen, and Revitalize the United States' in (2018) 6 Journal on Migration and Human Security 3, 208.

162 Aristide R Zolberg in Michael S Teitelbaum and Miron Weiner (eds), *Threatened Peoples, Threatened Borders*, 123f.

163 Erika Feller and Anja Klug, 'Refugees, United Nations High Commissioner for (UNHCR)' (MPIL, January 2013) para 4 <https://opil.ouplaw.com/view/10.1093/law:epil/9780199231690/law-9780199231690-e530> accessed 20 March 2021.

164 See Aristide R Zolberg in Michael S Teitelbaum and Miron Weiner (eds), *Threatened Peoples, Threatened Borders*, 124; see also Gil Loescher, 'The UNHCR and World Politics: State Interest vs Institutional Autonomy' in (2001) 35 The International Migration Review 1, Special Issue, 'UNHCR at 50: Past, Present and Future of Refugee Assistance', 33 (36).

started only one week after the first refugee had arrived in Austria.[165] Within three years, about 180,000 Hungarians were resettled to 37 countries.[166] For instance, the Norwegian government dispensed with formal selection and waived the right to return undesirables to Austria. The Norwegian government declared to "*admit for resettlement any Hungarian refugee who – upon having received adequate information on the conditions in the country – freely expressed his desire to go to Norway*".[167] Other European countries, however, only admitted limited numbers of refugees. Thus, relief for Austria could only be achieved through resettlements to overseas countries.[168] The role of the US was particularly important because refugees were reluctant to accept offers from Canada "*as long as there remained hope of gaining asylum in the US*".[169] Despite initial opposition,[170] more than 30,000 Hungarians were paroled in the US.[171] Given the limited number of visas available under the 1953 Refugee Relief Act, the US administration used parole authority.[172] To facilitate integration, the US government initiated a propaganda campaign to counter the hostility of the American public towards Hungarian refugees.[173]

The Hungarian exodus exemplifies that resettlement was "*used both as a politically motivated protection tool and as a measure for sharing the burden*

165 See Amanda Cellini, 'The resettlement of Hungarian refugees in 1956' in (2017) 54 Forced Migration Review, 7 <https://www.refworld.org/docid/58cbcb314.html> accessed 13 February 2021.

166 Among the European states, Sweden was one of the first respondents to Austria's call for solidarity, whereas Norway first held a domestic debate; see ibid 6ff.

167 Atle Grahl-Madsen, *The Status of Refugees in International Law: Volume II*, 233.

168 See James P Niessen, 'The Culture of Welcome and the January, 1957 Austrian Refugee Quota Proposal' (2016) 11 <https://rucore.libraries.rutgers.edu/rutgers-lib/50546/PDF/1/play/> accessed 13 February 2021.

169 Ibid 10.

170 See Gil Loescher, 'The UNHCR and World Politics: State Interest vs Institutional Autonomy' in (2001) 35 The International Migration Review 1, Special Issue, 'UNHCR at 50: Past, Present and Future of Refugee Assistance', 36.

171 See Donald Kerwin, 'The US Refugee Resettlement Program – A Return to First Principles: How Refugees Help to Define, Strengthen, and Revitalize the United States' in (2018) 6 Journal on Migration and Human Security 3, 208.

172 See Aristide R Zolberg in Michael S Teitelbaum and Miron Weiner (eds), *Threatened Peoples, Threatened Borders*, 124.

173 See Kathryn M Bockley, 'A Historical Overview of Refugee Legislation: The Deception of Foreign Policy in the Land of Promise' in (1995) 21 North Carolina Journal of International Law and Commercial Regulation 1, 266f.

with Austria".[174] The efforts to resettle Hungarians from Austria are considered one of the most successful demonstrations of international solidarity in response to forced migration.[175] Nevertheless, the claim of Austria's Minister of Internal Affairs at that time, Oskar Helmer, to introduce mandatory resettlement quotas for all 'freedom-loving countries' with a ratio of 1:1000 to their population was not considered in the resolutions passed by the fourth session of the United Nations Refugee Emergency Fund (UNREF) in early 1957.[176]

2.3.5 Towards a more diverse US immigration policy

Upon expiration of the 1953 Refugee Relief Act, the Refugee Escape Act of 1957 followed. In support of US foreign policy interests,[177] it redefined the legal term refugee by including persons who departed from a "*Communist, Communist-dominated, or Communist-occupied area*".[178] Subsequently, Congress passed the Fair Share Refugee Law in 1960,[179] enabling the parole of large refugee groups in the US.[180] The US thereby admitted refugees from European camps in the proportion of one for every refugee resettled by other nations.[181]

---

174 Joanne van Selm et al, Study on 'The Feasibility of setting up resettlement schemes in EU Member States or at EU Level, against the background of the Common European Asylum system and the goal of a Common Asylum Procedure', 7.

175 See Amanda Cellini, 'The resettlement of Hungarian refugees in 1956' in (2017) 54 Forced Migration Review, 6.

176 See UNHCR, 'Report of the United Nations High Commissioner for Refugees', UN Doc A/3585/Rev.1 (1 January 1958) <https://www.refworld.org/docid/3ae68c710.html> accessed 17 June 2021; see also James P Niessen, 'The Culture of Welcome and the January, 1957 Austrian Refugee Quota Proposal' (2016) 12f.

177 See Kathryn M Bockley, 'A Historical Overview of Refugee Legislation: The Deception of Foreign Policy in the Land of Promise' in (1995) 21 North Carolina Journal of International Law and Commercial Regulation 1, 266.

178 See Section 15 lit c point a Refugee Escape Act 1957, Public Law 85-316, 71 Stat 639; see also Aristide R Zolberg in Michael S Teitelbaum and Miron Weiner (eds), *Threatened Peoples, Threatened Borders*, 124.

179 See Fair Share Refugee Act 1960, Public Law 86-648, 74 Stat 504.

180 See Kathryn M Bockley, 'A Historical Overview of Refugee Legislation: The Deception of Foreign Policy in the Land of Promise' in (1995) 21 North Carolina Journal of International Law and Commercial Regulation 1, 268.

181 See Aristide R Zolberg in Michael S Teitelbaum and Miron Weiner (eds), *Threatened Peoples, Threatened Borders*, 124f.

The 1965 Amendments to the Immigration and Nationality Act[182] introduced a shift in US immigration policy towards ethnic and cultural diversification[183], as they ended the national-origin quota prioritizing migration from northern and western European countries. Finally, the US agreed to the definitions and protections set forth in the Refugee Convention as it became party to the 1967 Protocol to that Convention.[184]

2.3.6 The mechanized resettlement of Vietnamese

With the consolidation of power in the Socialist Republic of Vietnam in 1975, an era of mechanized resettlement began. The US perceived it as a moral obligation to admit a large portion of the several thousand people who reached the Thai border in April 1975.[185] This happened under the so-called Orderly Departure Program.[186] The Senate unanimously approved President *Ford*'s request to parole 150,000 Indochinese in the US.[187] When Saigon fell a week later,[188] Congress responded within less than a month by approving the Indochina Migration and Refugee Assistance Act.[189] This Act authorized funds for a massive two-year resettlement program.[190] After the emergency program had expired, the admission rate of Indochinese refugees dropped to a mere 100 per month. Due to calls for additional

182 See The Immigration and Nationality Act Amendments 1965, Public Law 89-236, 79 Stat 911.

183 See International Crisis Group, 'How to Save the US Refugee Admissions Program', Crisis Group United States Report N°2 (12 September 2018) 5.

184 See Protocol to the Convention Relating to the Status of Refugees (adopted 31 January 1967, entered into force 4 October 1967) 606 UNTS 267; see also Aristide R Zolberg in Michael S Teitelbaum and Miron Weiner (eds), *Threatened Peoples, Threatened Borders*, 125f; see also Thomas Alexander Aleinikoff et al, *Immigration and Citizenship: Process and Policy*, 793.

185 See Aristide R Zolberg in Michael S Teitelbaum and Miron Weiner (eds), *Threatened Peoples, Threatened Borders*, 130.

186 See International Crisis Group, 'How to Save the US Refugee Admissions Program', Crisis Group United States Report N°2 (12 September 2018) 6.

187 See Aristide R Zolberg in Michael S Teitelbaum and Miron Weiner (eds), *Threatened Peoples, Threatened Borders*, 130ff.

188 See ibid 131f.

189 See Indochina Migration and Refugee Assistance Act 1975, Public Law 94-23, 89 Stat 87.

190 See Aristide R Zolberg in Michael S Teitelbaum and Miron Weiner (eds), *Threatened Peoples, Threatened Borders*, 131f.

resettlements within the State Department, US admissions were extended more generally throughout the 1980s.[191]

In 1978 (global) resettlement declined.[192] At the same time, Vietnamese refugees crossed the high seas to find safety, whereas countries of the Association of South East Asian Nations (ASEAN) started to oppose to admitting boat people from Vietnam.[193] The idea that the Vietnamese could obtain long-term asylum in neighboring countries failed to convince Thailand and Malaysia, who "*made it very clear that they would accept refugees only for temporary asylum, and on condition that they be quickly resettled elsewhere*".[194] Eventually, agreements for temporary asylum in neighboring ASEAN countries and resettlement to third countries were achieved under the initiative of the UNHCR.[195]

Under the initiative of the *Carter* administration, the International Conference on Indochinese Refugees took place in July 1979 in Geneva.[196] Over the course of this Conference, Western states and South East Asian governments re-established consensus on offering entry to Indochinese refugees in exchange for resettlement commitments.[197] The US, together with Canada, Australia, France and some thirty other nations, "*embarked on a huge and costly resettlement programme that was to continue into the 1990s*".[198]

---

191 See ibid 132.

192 See Garry G Troeller, 'UNHCR Resettlement as an Instrument of International Protection: Constraints and Obstacles in the Arena of Competition for Scarce Humanitarian Resources' in (1991) 3 International Journal of Refugee Law 3, 564 (575).

193 See International Crisis Group, 'How to Save the US Refugee Admissions Program', Crisis Group United States Report N°2 (12 September 2018) 6, fn 19.

194 Aristide R Zolberg in Michael S Teitelbaum and Miron Weiner (eds), *Threatened Peoples, Threatened Borders*, 130f.

195 See Erika Feller and Anja Klug, 'Refugees, United Nations High Commissioner for (UNHCR)' (MPIL, January 2013) para 7.

196 See Aristide R Zolberg in Michael S Teitelbaum and Miron Weiner (eds), *Threatened Peoples, Threatened Borders*, 134.

197 See Margret AM Piper, Paul Power and Graham Thom, 'Refugee Resettlement: 2012 and Beyond', UNHCR Research Paper n°253 (February 2013) 5.

198 Gil Loescher, *The UNHCR and World Politics: A perilious path* (Oxford University Press 2001) 207.

2.3.7 The 1980 Refugee Act

Later, the 1980 Refugee Act[199], a significant legislative milestone in the US, was enacted and has remained in force until today. This new legislation shifted the emphasis away from geopolitics.[200] The Refugee Act (formally) eliminated the presumption that all those fleeing from Communist countries were *de facto* refugees, and it finally implemented the Refugee Convention's refugee definition.[201] It established a permanent resettlement program with annual resettlement quotas (the normal flow) and emergency procedures (refugees of special humanitarian concern). The annual ceiling under this Act has since then been subject to executive (presidential) determination, after consultation with Congress.[202] Initially, the Refugee Act was intended to narrow the President's parole power.[203] Actually, "*Congress' intent to establish a geographically and ideologically neutral system of refugee admissions has been undermined*"[204] because the usage of parole power in favor of those fleeing from Communist countries continued.

2.3.8 The disintegration of Yugoslavia

In the 1990s, forced displacement increased in Europe. Due to the disintegration of Yugoslavia, Eastern Europe faced a sudden wave of mass migration. According to the UNHCR, from 1989 to 1992, 2.3 million people

---

199 See Section 201 para 42 Title II Refugee Act 1980, Public Law 96-212, 94 Stat 102 <https://www.govinfo.gov/content/pkg/STATUTE-94/pdf/STATUTE-94-Pg102.pdf> accessed 13 February 2021.

200 See Aristide R Zolberg in Michael S Teitelbaum and Miron Weiner (eds), *Threatened Peoples, Threatened Borders*, 95.

201 See ibid 138f.

202 See Kathryn M Bockley, 'A Historical Overview of Refugee Legislation: The Deception of Foreign Policy in the Land of Promise' in (1995) 21 North Carolina Journal of International Law and Commercial Regulation 1, 281f.

203 See Aristide R Zolberg in Michael S Teitelbaum and Miron Weiner (eds), *Threatened Peoples, Threatened Borders*, 138f; see also Initiative of the Harvard Immigration and Refugee Clinical Program, 'Fulfilling US Commitment to Refugee Resettlement: Protecting Refugees, Preserving National Security, & Building the US Economy through Refugee Admissions' in (2017) 5 Texas A&M Law Review, 155 (170f).

204 Kathryn M Bockley, 'A Historical Overview of Refugee Legislation: The Deception of Foreign Policy in the Land of Promise' in (1995) 21 North Carolina Journal of International Law and Commercial Regulation 1, 282.

fled their homes, leading to a significant rise in asylum applications in Western Europe.[205] Remarkably, this so-called Balkan crisis triggered first attempts to encourage solidarity and responsibility sharing among EUMS, including a (failed) German proposal on mandatory refugee distribution (see 4.2.2).[206] In December 1995, when the Bosnian War ended with the signing of the Dayton Peace Agreement, there were still an estimated 1.3 million Bosnian IDPs and 500,000 other refugees displaced in the sub-region, with an additional 700,000 refugees in Western Europe.[207] Instead of urging receiving countries to increasee resettlement contributions, the UNHCR coordinated and facilitated large-scale returns.[208]

2.3.9 The decade of voluntary repatriation and reconceptualization of resettlement

The early 1990s became known as the decade of voluntary repatriation, with decreasing resettlement numbers. In 1979, the resettlement rate, i.e. the percentage of the global refugee population that had access to resettlement, was 5%; it dropped to 1% in 1990 and to 0.25% in 1996.[209] The decreased political interest in resettlement induced a shift of UNHCR's priorities,[210] resulting in the retreat and reconceptualization of resettlement.[211] A 1991 UNHCR paper introduced definitions of concrete categories of

---

205 See Garry G Troeller, 'UNHCR Resettlement as an Instrument of International Protection: Constraints and Obstacles in the Arena of Competition for Scarce Humanitarian Resources' in (1991) 3 International Journal of Refugee Law 3, 575.

206 See ibid 575.

207 See Guido Ambroso, 'The Balkans at a crossroads: Progress and challenges in finding durable solutions for refugees and displaced persons from the wars in the former Yugoslavia', UNHCR Research Paper n°133 (November 2006) 2 <https://www.unhcr.org/4552f2182.pdf> accessed 13 February 2021.

208 See ibid 3.

209 See Margret AM Piper, Paul Power and Graham Thom, 'Refugee Resettlement: 2012 and Beyond', UNHCR Research Paper n°253 (February 2013) 6.

210 See ibid 7.

211 See Haruno Nakashiba, 'Postmillennial UNHCR refugee resettlement: New developments and challenges', UNHCR Research Paper n°265 (November 2013) 2 <https://www.unhcr.org/research/working/528e15259/postmillenial-unhcr-refugee-resettlement-new-developments-old-challenges.html> accessed 13 February 2021.

refugees qualifying for resettlement.[212] Developments at the administrative level involved the establishment of the Working Group on Resettlement (WGR) composed of UNHCR representatives and government officials from resettlement partner countries. Furthermore, Annual Tripartite Consultations on Resettlement (ATCR) took place, where selected Non-Governmental Organization (NGO) partners were also invited.[213] The WGR and the ATCR became "*the principal multilateral institutions in which states, UNHCR and non-governmental organisations (NGOs) engage on issues specific to the resettlement of refugees*".[214]

In July 1997, the UNHCR published its first *Resettlement Handbook*. It further developed the categories of refugees qualifying for resettlement introduced in the 1991 paper[215] and "*comprehensively outlined the process, criteria, goals and objectives of the UNHCR programme*".[216] UNHCR's efforts also comprised the establishment of a trust fund through financial contributions from Sweden, Norway, Denmark, Finland and the US.[217] The primary aim to engage new resettlement countries via funding incentives,[218] however, was not achieved.[219]

---

212 See UNHCR, 'Resettlement as an Instrument of Protection: Traditional Problems Achieving This Durable Solution and New Directions in the 1990s', EC/SCP/65 (9 July 1991) <https://www.unhcr.org/excom/scip/3ae68ccc10/resettlement-instrument-protection-traditional-problems-achieving-durable.html> accessed 13 February 2021.

213 See Joanne van Selm et al, Study on 'The Feasibility of setting up resettlement schemes in EU Member States or at EU Level, against the background of the Common European Asylum system and the goal of a Common Asylum Procedure', 8.

214 Carol Batchelor and Edwina O'Shea, 'The internationalization of resettlement: lessons from Syria and Bhutan' in (2017) 54 Forced Migration Review, 9 <https://www.refworld.org/docid/58cbcb314.html> accessed 13 February 2021.

215 See Haruno Nakashiba, 'Postmillennial UNHCR refugee resettlement: New developments and challenges', UNHCR Research Paper n°265 (November 2013) 4.

216 Ibid 3.

217 See Joanne van Selm et al, Study on 'The Feasibility of setting up resettlement schemes in EU Member States or at EU Level, against the background of the Common European Asylum system and the goal of a Common Asylum Procedure', 13.

218 See ibid 13.

219 See ibid 14 (with further references).

2.3.10 Convention Plus

In September 2002, UN High Commissioner for Refugees *Lubbers* pushed the Convention Plus initiative with the "*ambitious goal of adding substantial obligations to the acquis of the* [Refugee Convention] *and the 1967 Protocol* [...] *regarding burden-sharing*".[220] This initiative was dedicated to the 'strategic use of resettlement',[221] shedding new light on the benefits of responsibility sharing as an additional function of resettlement.[222] It culminated in a Multilateral Framework of Understanding on Resettlement.[223] This is a non-binding understanding among state parties to use resettlement for the benefit of a greater number of refugees and to conclude special, situation-specific, multilateral agreements.[224] However, Convention Plus failed to provide an answer as to why state parties should engage in responsibility sharing at all. The initiative also failed for systematic reasons.[225] The controversy was that states were not bound to provide durable solutions while the UNHCR was entrusted to do so.[226] Moreover, Convention Plus referred to specific situations rather than providing a normative framework

220 Marjoleine Zieck, 'Doomed to Fail from the Outset? UNHCR's Convention Plus Initiative Revisited' in (2009) 21 International Journal of Refugee Law 3, 387.

221 See UNHCR, 'The Strategic Use of Resettlement', EC/53/SC/CRP.10/Add.1 (3 June 2003) <https://www.unhcr.org/excom/standcom/3edf57cd4/strategic-use-resettlement.html> accessed 13 February 2021.

222 See Haruno Nakashiba, 'Postmillennial UNHCR refugee resettlement: New developments and challenges', UNHCR Research Paper n°265 (November 2013) 11.

223 See UNHCR, 'Multilateral Framework of Understandings on Resettlement', FORUM/2004/6 (16 September 2004) <https://www.unhcr.org/protection/convention/414aa7e54/multilateral-framework-understandings-resettlement-emforum20046em.html?query=Multilateral%20Framework%20of% 20Understandings%20on%20Resettlement> accessed 13 February 2021; see also Marjoleine Zieck, 'Doomed to Fail from the Outset? UNHCR's Convention Plus Initiative Revisited' in (2009) 21 International Journal of Refugee Law 3, 405.

224 The designation 'special agreement' derives from Art 8 lit b UNHCR Statute: "*Promoting through special agreements with Governments the execution of any measures calculated to improve the situation of refugees and to reduce the number requiring protection*"; see Marjoleine Zieck, 'Doomed to Fail from the Outset? UNHCR's Convention Plus Initiative Revisited' in (2009) 21 International Journal of Refugee Law 3, 390.

225 See ibid 387.

226 *Zieck* refers to the statement of the Assistant High Commissioner at the High Commissioner's Forum on 20 May 2005 who emphasized durable solutions as being at the very heart of UNHCR's mandate; see ibid 396.

for responsibility sharing.[227] When the initiative was closed in November 2005 "*'generic agreements' had not been created and there were no documents with even the 'soft law' status intended by the High Commissioner*".[228]

2.3.11 The terrorist attacks of 9/11

The USRAP experienced a "*sharp decline following the terrorist attacks of 11 September 2001*".[229] It was completely shut down in the months following the attacks. Nevertheless, on condition to new security requirements and with the involvement of the Federal Bureau of Investigation (FBI), the USRAP continued to operate. The *Bush jr* administration kept admission numbers at a normal level, i.e. not below 70,000 per year.[230]

2.3.12 Harmonization efforts

In parallel, the UNHCR refined and harmonized the common selection criteria in 2004, resulting in the publication of the second edition of the *Resettlement Handbook*.[231] Nonetheless, some traditional resettlement countries, i.e. states with long-standing resettlement programs, such as the US, Australia and Canada,[232] adopted different criteria and alternative entry streams in addition to resettlements based on UNHCR's referrals.[233]

---

227 See ibid 395ff.

228 Ibid 394.

229 Donald Kerwin, 'The Faltering US Refugee Protection System: Legal and Policy Responses to Refugees, Asylum-Seekers, and Others in Need of Protection' in (2012) 31 Refugee Survey Quarterly 1, 1.

230 See International Crisis Group, 'How to Save the US Refugee Admissions Program', Crisis Group United States Report N°2 (12 September 2018) 8.

231 See Haruno Nakashiba, 'Postmillennial UNHCR refugee resettlement: New developments and challenges', UNHCR Research Paper n°265 (November 2013) 4.

232 "*Certain States are considered 'traditional' resettlement States because of their long-standing programmes, namely: Australia, Canada, New Zealand, the Netherlands, the Nordic countries (Denmark, Finland, Norway and Sweden) and the United States of America*", UNHCR, 'Frequently Asked Questions about Resettlement' (September 2013) 6 <https://www.refworld.org/pdfid/4ac0d7e52.pdf> accessed 13 February 2021.

233 See Margret AM Piper, Paul Power and Graham Thom, 'Refugee Resettlement: 2012 and Beyond', UNHCR Research Paper n°253 (February 2013) 11.

These traditional resettlement countries have continued to resettle refugees outside the realm of UNHCR referrals.[234]

2.3.13 Regained recognition of resettlement

Subsequently, refugee resettlement programs regained recognition.[235] There were various reasons behind this development, such as the appearance of new 'safe' refugees, namely refugees that were considered to less likely pose a security threat to the receiving country; for instance, the Burmese were seen as less 'risky' refugees than those coming from Iraq, Afghanistan and Somalia.[236] A further new development consisted of addressing protracted refugee situations. Protracted refugee situations involved "*refugees who did not benefit from repatriation efforts of the 1990s because the situation in their home countries had not changed sufficiently to enable safe return*".[237] Enthusiasm about repatriation vanished because several major repatriation operations (to Afghanistan, Iraq, and South Sudan) posed difficulties. In 2010, the numbers of returnees reached a 20-year low.[238] Still, resettlement did not gain momentum. While UNHCR resettlement referrals increased, departures were progressively decreasing. In 2013, this resulted in a resettlement gap of 100,000 places.[239]

Further efforts on conceptualizing resettlement and redefining common resettlement criteria resulted in the third (and currently latest) version of the *Resettlement Handbook* in 2011.[240] New resettlement states were slow in adjusting to UNHCR's standards and failed to keep pace with the number of UNHCR referrals. Resettlement was criticized, even within the

---

234 See Adèle Garnier, 'The COVID-19 Resettlement Suspension: Impact, Exemptions and the Road Ahead' (*FluchtforschungsBlog*, 16 June 2020).

235 See Margret AM Piper, Paul Power and Graham Thom, 'Refugee Resettlement: 2012 and Beyond', UNHCR Research Paper n°253 (February 2013) 12; see also Haruno Nakashiba, 'Postmillennial UNHCR refugee resettlement: New developments and challenges', UNHCR Research Paper n°265 (November 2013) 6.

236 See Margret AM Piper, Paul Power and Graham Thom, 'Refugee Resettlement: 2012 and Beyond', UNHCR Research Paper n°253 (February 2013) 12.

237 Ibid 12.

238 See ibid 12f.

239 See ibid 13f.

240 See Haruno Nakashiba, 'Postmillennial UNHCR refugee resettlement: New developments and challenges', UNHCR Research Paper n°265 (November 2013) 4.

UNHCR, for being expensive, time consuming, blocking other solutions and encouraging fraud.[241]

2.3.14 The 2015-2016 refugee crisis

In the course of the refugee crisis 2015-2016, UNHCR referrals increased again. Responses were necessary to unburden the countries in the immediate region surrounding conflicts, given that they hosted 90% of the world's refugees.[242] The UNHCR initiated 'High Meetings on Global Responsibility Sharing', which brought offers to resettle more than 201,000 Syrian refugees.[243] The number of countries offering resettlement or humanitarian admission as part of UNHCR's resettlement program also increased.[244] According to UNHCR statistics, the year 2016 brought a 22% rise in persons referred to as in need for resettlement (compared to 2015). Still, a resettlement gap remained because only 126,291 out of 163,206 refugees actually departed to a receiving country for resettlement.[245]

From the nearly 130,000 UNHCR departures in 2016, 78,340 departed to the US.[246] Nonetheless, security concerns remained after ISIS-inspired terrorist attacks in November 2015 in Paris.[247] In the aftermath of these attacks, tensions between the federal US government and states arose when thirty-one governors expressed the wish to block resettlement for security reasons. For example, "*Texas and Indiana sued to keep refugees away*".[248]

241 See Margret AM Piper, Paul Power and Graham Thom, 'Refugee Resettlement: 2012 and Beyond', UNHCR Research Paper n°253 (February 2013) 14ff; see also UNHCR, 'UNHCR receives report on Nairobi' (*Press release*, 25 January 2002) <https://www.unhcr.org/news/press/2002/1/3c513a284/unhcr-receives-report-nairobi-investigation.html> accessed 13 February 2021.

242 See Volker Türk, 'Prospects for Responsibility Sharing in the Refugee Context' in (2016) 4 Journal on Migration and Human Security 3, 46.

243 See ibid 55.

244 See European Parliament, 'Resettlement of refugees: EU framework' (*Briefing*, April 2017) 2 <http://www.europarl.europa.eu/RegData/etudes/BRIE/2016/589859/EPRS_BRI%282016%29589859_EN.pdf> accessed 13 February 2021.

245 See UNHCR, 'Resettlement Data' (as of 25 February 2019).

246 See ibid.

247 See International Crisis Group, 'How to Save the US Refugee Admissions Program', Crisis Group United States Report N°2 (12 September 2018) 11f.

248 Ibid 12.

They argued that suspects involved in the Paris terrorist attacks entered Europe with the wave of Syrian refugees.[249]

2.3.15 The Trump administration

President *Obama*, in consultation with Congress, set an exceptionally high admission ceiling of 110,000 for 2017,[250] but President *Trump* obstructed admissions through his Executive Order of 27 January 2017[251] ('Muslim ban'). This order barred nationals from seven Muslim countries and suspended all pending refugee admissions for a 120-day period of security review.[252] As a result, the initial 2017 admission ceiling was reduced to 50,000.[253] The following 45,000 refugee admission ceiling for 2018 meant a drastic cut compared to the 2017 *Obama* ceiling and *ex post*, the 2018 ceiling was never exhausted.[254] For the fiscal year 2019,[255] President

---

249 See James Y Xi, 'Refugee Resettlement Federalism' in (2017) Stanford Law Review 69, 1197 (1199); see also Ashley Fantz and Ben Brumfield, 'More than half the nation's governors say Syrian refugees not welcome' (19 November 2014) <https://edition.cnn.com/2015/11/16/world/paris-attacks-syrian-refugees-backlash/index.html> accessed 13 February 2021.

250 See Initiative of the Harvard Immigration and Refugee Clinical Program, 'Fulfilling US Commitment to Refugee Resettlement: Protecting Refugees, Preserving National Security, & Building the US Economy through Refugee Admissions' in (2017) 5 Texas A&M Law Review, 170.

251 See Executive Order 13769 'Protecting The Nation from Foreign Terrorist Entry Into The United States' (27 January 2017) <https://trumpwhitehouse.archives.gov/presidential-actions/executive-order-protecting-nation-foreign-terrorist-entry-united-states/> accessed 20 March 2021; see also Executive Order 13780 'Protecting The Nation from Foreign Terrorist Entry Into The United States' (6 March 2017) <https://trumpwhitehouse.archives.gov/presidential-actions/executive-order-protecting-nation-foreign-terrorist-entry-united-states-2/> accessed 20 March 2021.

252 See International Crisis Group, 'How to Save the US Refugee Admissions Program', Crisis Group United States Report N°2 (12 September 2018) 15.

253 See Refugee Council USA, 'Where are the Refugees?: Drastic Cuts to Refugee Resettlement Harming Refugees, Communities, and American Leadership' (12 June 2019) 17 <http://www.rcusa.org/report> accessed 13 February 2021.

254 See Donald Kerwin, 'The US Refugee Resettlement Program – A Return to First Principles: How Refugees Help to Define, Strengthen, and Revitalize the United States' in (2018) 6 Journal on Migration and Human Security 3, 208f.

255 See US Department of State, Department of Homeland and Security, Department of Health and Human Services, 'Report to Congress on Proposed Refugee Admissions for Fiscal Year 2019' <https://www.state.gov/wp-content/uploads/

Trump proposed an even lower admission cap of 30,000 in his report to Congress.[256]

As a response to the former opposition of governors to admit resettlement refugees, the Presidential Executive Order of 26 September 2019 established that "*the State and the locality's consent to the resettlement of refugees under the Program is taken into account to the maximum extent consistent with law.* [...] [I]*f either a State or locality has not provided consent to receive refugees under the Program, then refugees should not be resettled within that State or locality* [...]".[257] With this Executive Order, the *Trump* administration was the first to grant individual American states a veto to oppose admission of resettlement refugees. In fact, most US governors affirmed their support to continued refugee resettlement.[258]

Eventually, President *Trump* approved a cap of 18,000 for 2020.[259] In that respect, Congress, through its Judiciary Committee, expressed frustration about lacking adherence to the consultation requirement.[260] In

---

2018/12/Proposed-Refugee-Admissions-for-Fiscal-Year-2019.pdf> accessed 13 February 2021.

256 The *Trump* administration considered further cuts, even down to zero. See Ted Hesson, 'Trump officials pressing to slash refugee admissions to zero next year' (*Politico*, 18 July 2019) <https://www.politico.com/story/2019/07/18/trump-officials-refugee-zero-1603503> accessed 13 February 2021; see also Amanda Taub and Max Fisher, 'Trump's Refugee Cuts Threaten Deep Consequences at Home and Abroad' (*The New York Times*, 11 September 2019) <https://www.nytimes.com/2019/09/11/world/middleeast/bahamas-refugees.html> accessed 13 February 2021.

257 Section 2 Executive Order 13888 'Enhancing State and Local Involvement in Refugee Resettlement' (26 September 2019) <https://www.hsdl.org/?view&did=829794> accessed 13 February 2021.

258 See Muzaffar Chishti and Sarah Pierce, 'Despite Trump Invitation to Stop Taking Refugees, Red and Blue States Alike Endorse Resettlement' (29 January 2020) <https://www.migrationpolicy.org/article/despite-trump-invitation-stop-taking-refugees-red-and-blue-states-alike-endorse-resettlement> accessed 13 February 2021.

259 See UNHCR, 'UNHCR troubled by latest US refugee resettlement cut' (*Press release*, 4 November 2019) <https://www.unhcr.org/news/press/2019/11/5dbd87337/unhcr-troubled-latest-refugee-resettlement-cut.html> accessed 13 February 2021; see also US Department of State, Department of Homeland and Security, Department of Health and Human Services, 'Report to Congress on Proposed Refugee Admissions for Fiscal Year 2020' <https://www.politico.com/f/?id=0000016d-bb51-d0d8-af6d-ff79261f0002> accessed 13 February 2021.

260 "*The statute requires the Administration to initiate such consultation prior to the start of each fiscal year by reporting to the Committees, the 'foreseeable number of refugees who will be in need of resettlement', and the 'anticipated allocation of refugee admissions during the fiscal year'. The Administration must also meet 'in person' with*

terms of implementation of this cap, by March 2020, only 7,163 refugees were actually resettled to the US. From 19 March to 29 July 2020, the COVID-19 pandemic led to a suspension of resettlement to the US, except for emergency cases. In the end, 11,814 refugees were admitted in 2020.[261] For 2021, President *Trump* further reduced the ceiling to only 15,000.[262] A substantial shift was expected with the current *Biden* administration. As President-elect, *Biden* committed to "*raising the refugee admissions target to at least 125,000 refugees a year*".[263] The Immigration and Nationality Act (INA)[264], specifically Section 207 lit b INA,[265] provides a legal basis

---

the Committees prior to the President making a final determination on the allocation of refugee admissions", Section 1157 lit d para 1 Title 8 US Code; see Committee on the Judiciary, Letter of 13 September 2019 <https://judiciary.house.gov/sites/democrats.judiciary.house.gov/files/documents/2019-09-13%20Letter%20to%20Admin%20re%20Refugee%20Admissions.pdf> accessed 13 February 2021; see also Committee on the Judiciary, 'Grassley, Feinstein: Congress Requires More Thorough Engagement with State Dept. on Refugee Numbers' (27 September 2017) <https://www.judiciary.senate.gov/press/rep/releases/grassley-feinstein-congress-requires-more-thorough-engagement-with-state-dept-on-refugee-numbers> accessed 13 February 2021; see also Kristie de Peña, 'Congress is letting the administration violate consultation requirements for refugee admissions' (*The Hill*, 26 August 2019) <https://thehill.com/opinion/immigration/458860-congress-is-letting-the-trump-administration-violate-consultation> accessed 13 February 2021.

261 By November 2020, almost 7,000 of the 18,000 places available remained unused. See Adèle Garnier, 'The COVID-19 Resettlement Suspension: Impact, Exemptions and the Road Ahead' (*FluchtforschungsBlog*, 16 June 2020).

262 See US Department of State, Department of Homeland and Security, Department of Health and Human Services, 'Report to Congress on Proposed Refugee Admissions for Fiscal Year 2021'.

263 International Rescue Committee, 'What does a Joe Biden presidency mean for refugees and asylum seekers?' (8 November 2020) <https://www.rescue.org/article/what-does-joe-biden-presidency-mean-refugees-and-asylum-seekers> accessed 13 February 2021.

264 See Immigration and Nationality Act 1952 <https://www.uscis.gov/laws-and-policy/legislation/immigration-and-nationality-act> accessed 13 February 2021.

265 Section 207 lit b INA: "*If the President determines, after appropriate consultation, that (1) an unforeseen emergency refugee situation exists, (2) the admission of certain refugees in response to the emergency refugee situation is justified by grave humanitarian concerns or is otherwise in the national interest, and (3) the admission to the United States of these refugees cannot be accomplished under subsection (a), the President may fix a number of refugees to be admitted to the United States during the succeeding period (not to exceed twelve months) in response to the emergency refugee situation and such admissions shall be allocated among refugees of special humanitarian concern to the United States in accordance with a determination made by the President after the appropriate consultation provided under this subsection.*"

for a presidential mid-year increase[266] of the annual refugee ceiling.[267] On 16 April 2021, however, President *Biden* announced to keep former President *Trump*'s refugee cap. The argument was that the system had been overwhelmed due to the high numbers of crossings at the Mexican border by unaccompanied minors. This neglects the fact that the US system is historically based on complementary protection, i.e. the admission of asylum seekers at the border does not supplant overseas admission through the USRAP. President *Biden*'s announcement came with backlash from Democrats and human rights activists.[268] In the end, President *Biden* raised the US cap on refugee admissions to 62,500 for the Fiscal Year 2021.[269] For the Fiscal Year 2022, the admission ceiling was increased to 125,000,[270] but around 100,000 places remained unused by the end of that Fiscal Year. On 8 September 2022, the State Department published the report for Fiscal Year 2023. The total resettlement ceiling of 125,000, as well as most regional quotas stayed the same.[271]

2.3.16 Afghan mass displacement and the revival of parole power

Against the backdrop of the withdrawal of US troops and the Taliban regime's take-over of Afghanistan in August 2021, the US administration admitted a large number of individuals from Afghanistan under the Special Immigrant Visas for Afghans (SIV) program; Congress enacted this

266 See International Refugee Assistance Project, 'Refugee Reset: Mid-Year Increase to the US Refugee Admission Target' (28 January 2021) <https://refugeerights.org/wp-content/uploads/2021/01/Refugee-Reset-Mid-Year-Increases-to-the-U.S.-Refugee-Admissions-Target.pdf> accessed 13 February 2021.

267 See International Refugee Assistance Project, 'Refugee Reset: Mid-Year Increase to the US Refugee Admission Target' (28 January 2021).

268 See Zolan Kanno-Youngs, 'After backlash, Biden will increase the limit on refugee admissions' (*The New York Times*, 16 April 2021) <https://www.nytimes.com/2021/04/16/us/biden-refugees-cap.html> accessed 16 April 2021.

269 See Maanvi Singh, 'Biden raises US refugee admissions cap to 62,500 after delay sparks anger' (*The Guardian*, 3 May 2021).

270 See US Department of State, Department of Homeland and Security, Department of Health and Human Services, 'Report to Congress on Proposed Refugee Admissions for Fiscal Year 2022' (20 September 2021).

271 See US Department of State, Department of Homeland and Security, Department of Health and Human Services, 'Report to Congress on Proposed Refugee Admissions for Fiscal Year 2023' (8 September 2022) <https://www.state.gov/report-to-congress-on-proposed-refugee-admissions-for-fiscal-year-2023/>.

program already in 2009, and due to the 2021 developments, it expanded the program's scope through the adoption of the Emergency Appropriations Act 2021[272]. Overall, SIV holders are eligible for the same benefits accorded to refugees admitted under the USRAP, and they receive access to lawful permanent residence in the US. Some of the evacuees who do not qualify for SIV are eligible for the USRAP, on the basis of a newly created group in the Priority 2 (P-2) category,[273] i.e. an admission category particularly designed for groups of special concern to the US.[274] Those who do not meet the criteria of the P-2 category can still be admitted under the (pre-existing) Priority 1 (P-1) category, for example on the basis of a referral of the UNHCR.[275]

In practice, few Afghan refugees have been admitted under the USRAP. Most of them have been paroled to the US instead.[276] Functioning as fast track for legal entry, admission under parole power initially left parolees from Afghanistan without the same benefits as SIV holders and refugees admitted under the USRAP. Congress took action to counteract the described differential treatment. On 30 September 2021, it passed the Extending Government Funding and Delivering Emergency Assistance Act, which allowed Afghans granted humanitarian parole between 31 July 2021 and 30 September 2022 to receive federal benefits to the same extent as parolees with pending SIV applications, SIVs, and refugees admitted under the USRAP.[277] However, due to the limited time period covered, the rights of those who are subsequently admitted through humanitarian parole remains open. Furthermore, the Emergency Appropriations Act

---

272 Emergency Security Supplemental Appropriations Act 2021 <https://www.congress.gov/bill/117th-congress/house-bill/3237> accessed 27 June 2022.

273 See US Department of State, 'US Refugee Admissions Program Priority 2 Designation for Afghan Nationals' (2 August 2021) <https://www.state.gov/u-s-refugee-admissions-program-priority-2-designation-for-afghan-nationals/> accessed 20 July 2022.

274 See Michael Posner, 'How To Address The Legal Status of Afghan Refugees' (*Forbes*, 8 September 2021) <https://www.forbes.com/sites/michaelposner/2021/09/08/how-to-address-the-legal-status-of-afghan-refugees/?sh=7d25a18d572f> accessed 27 June 2022.

275 See Daniel J Steinbock, 'The Qualities of Mercy: Maximizing the Impact of US Refugee Resettlement' in (2003) 36 U. Mich. J.L. Reform, 951 (959).

276 The legal authority for parole can be found in section 212(d)(5) of the Immigration and Nationality Act and the regulations at 8 C.F.R. 212.5.

277 Public Law 117-43 (30 Sept. 2021) <https://www.congress.gov/117/plaws/publ43/PLAW-117publ43.pdf> accessed 2 May 2023.

2021 does not ensure status adjustment, respectively access to long-term residence for parolees.[278]

2.3.17 Attempts towards private sponsorship

Drawing on the Canadian example, the Biden administration has explored private sponsorship for refugees.

To that effect, the Report to Congress on Proposed Refugee Admissions for the Fiscal Year 2022 first mentioned a new Priority 4 (P-4) category to admit privately sponsored refugees, which was finally endorsed in the Report to Congress for Fiscal Year 2023. This category covers "*refugees supported by private sponsors who accept primary responsibility for funding and providing core resettlement services*".[279] A private sponsorship pilot program linked to this category was announced to be launched in early 2022. However, the launch was delayed until January 2023. The pilot program will include a matching component (for refugees who already have access to the USRAP) and an identification component (for refugees referred by sponsors). Groups of individual US citizens or permanent residents, as well as established organizations or formal entities, will be able to apply to serve as sponsors. Sponsorship opportunities include families sponsoring relatives, institutions of higher education sponsoring refugee students, and affinity organizations sponsoring members of their community, such as LGBTQIA+, religious, and veteran organizations.[280]

---

278 See Janine Prantl, 'Afghan Mass Displacement: The American Response in Light of International Human Rights and Refugee Law, and the Need for International Cooperation to achieve a Satisfactory Solution' in (2022) ALJ, 17 (21f).

279 US Department of State, Department of Homeland and Security, Department of Health and Human Services, 'Report to Congress on Proposed Refugee Admissions for Fiscal Year 2022' (20 September 2021) 18.

280 See US Department of State, Department of Homeland and Security, Department of Health and Human Services, 'Report to Congress on Proposed Refugee Admissions for Fiscal Year 2023' (8 September 2022).

2.3.18 Preliminary conclusion

When US resettlement numbers hit their all-time low, the EU did not sufficiently counteract.[281] Even though the numbers of receiving countries in Europe increased from 16 countries in 2005 to 29 countries in 2019,[282] the numbers of actual resettlement remained low. The implementation of resettlement commitments under the EU-Turkey Statement "*to end irregular migration flows from Turkey to the EU*"[283] went slow. By 2018, after two years, only about 12,476 Syrians were resettled in the EU under this Statement,[284] and even after five years of implementation in 2021, the critics[285] remained harsh (for a detailed analysis on the EU-Turkey Statement see 4.2.10). Moreover, of the 29,500 pledges made by EUMS for 2020, only 11,200 actual resettlements occurred as of late February 2021, i.e. only 38% (for recent EU developments see 4.2.12). In the course of the COVID-19 pandemic, resettlement was suspended,[286] but EUMS have adopted new

---

281 See Janine Prantl, 'A strong EU resettlement program is more important than ever' (*FluchtforschungsBlog*, 13 May 2020) <https://blog.fluchtforschung.net/a-strong-eu-resettlement-program-is-more-important-than-ever/> accessed 21 February 2021. In August 2022, the Senate introduced the Afghan Adjustment Act, which would establish access to permanent residence for parolees from Afghanistan. At the time of writing, this law has not been adopted. See Danilo Zak, 'Bill Summary: The Afghan Afjustment Act' (*National Immigration Forum*, 11 August 2022) <https://immigrationforum.org/article/bill-summary-the-afghan-adjustment-act/> accessed 3 September 2022.

282 See Hanna Schneider, 'Implementing the Refugee Resettlement Process: Diverging Objectives, Interdependencies and Power Relations' in (2021) Frontiers in Political Science, 4.

283 Commission, 'The EU-Turkey Statement: Two years on' (April 2018) <https://ec.europa.eu/home-affairs/sites/default/files/what-we-do/policies/european-agenda-migration/20180314_eu-turkey-two-years-on_en.pdf> accessed 17 June 2021.

284 See ibid.

285 See e.g., ECRE, 'EU-Turkey Deal 5 Years on: Fundamentals Remain Unchanged' (19 March 2021) <https://mailchi.mp/ecre/ecre-weekly-bulletin-19032021#edito> accessed 17 June 2021; see also Daphne Panayotatos, 'Undermining Protection in the EU: What Nine Trends Tell Us About The Proposed Pact on Migration and Asylum' (June 2021) 16 <https://www.refugeesinternational.org/reports/2021/6/1/undermining-protection-in-the-eu-what-nine-trends-tells-us-about-the-proposed-pact-on-migration-and-asylum> accessed 17 June 2021.

286 As a response to the temporary hold, seven civil society organizations launched a joint statement in September 2020 urging the EU to revive resettlement efforts. See International Rescue Committee, Caritas Europe, European Council on Refugees and Exiles, International Catholic Migration Commission, Curches' Commission for Migrants in Europe, SHARE Network and Red Cross

procedures to allow for the resumption of the resettlement process, including remote dossier selection, interviewing and orientation.[287] In response to the Afghan mass displacement, the commitments of EUMS remained diverse and comparably small. On 9 December 2021, 15 EUMS agreed to take in 40,000 Afghans through resettlement, humanitarian admission or evacuation programs, with Germany pledging 25,000 places.[288] By comparison, the US committed to 100,000 global places, Canada to 40,000, and the United Kingdom to 20,000.[289]

Overall, resettlement has been used in various contexts and has experienced several ebbs and flows, generally depending on the willingness of the prospective receiving countries to resettle as well as on international events with global impact, such as the Cold War, 9/11, the Covid-19 pandemic, the Taliban take-over in Afghanistan, or the war in Ukraine.[290] In the recent history of resettlement, there has been no serious political aspiration or even discussion to make resettlement a binding obligation under international law. The present lack of permanent and ongoing commitment of receiving countries to engage in resettlement is reflected in the unsolved problem of the resettlement gap, which is evident from the 2021 UNHCR statistics,[291] showing only 39,266 departures out of

EU Office, 'Joint Resettlement: Resettlement Can't Wait' (21 September 2020) <https://www.ecre.org/joint-statement-resettlement-cant-wait/> accessed 17 June 2021.

287 See Daphne Panayotatos, 'Undermining Protection in the EU: What Nine Trends Tell Us About The Proposed Pact on Migration and Asylum' (June 2021) 12.

288 See Zaini Majeed, 'European Nations To Resettle 40,000 Afghan Refugees To Prevent 'irregular Arrivals'' (11 December 2021) <https://www.republicworld.com/world-news/europe/european-nations-to-resettle-40000-afghan-refugees-to-prevent-irregular-arrivals.html> accessed 24 June 2022.

289 See Priyanka Shankar, 'EU, fearful of refugee crisis, delays response on Afghan asylum' (*Al Jazeera*, 15 October 2021) <https://www.aljazeera.com/news/2021/10/15/eu-fearful-of-refugee-crisis-delays-response-on-afghan-asylum-2> accessed 24 June 2022.

290 See Adèle Garnier, 'The COVID-19 Resettlement Suspension: Impact, Exemptions and the Road Ahead' (*FluchtforschungsBlog*, 16 June 2020).

291 Resettlement submission and departure figures reported by the UNHCR may not match resettlement statistics published by States as Government figures may include submissions received outside of UNHCR processes. UNHCR figures may also include cases in which the UNHCR assisted, i.e. obtained exit permits for humanitarian admissions or family reunion but did not initially submit.

63,190 referrals.[292] The US reluctance in the fiscal years 2018, 2019 and 2020 shows that solely relying on traditional resettlement countries is not enough to catch up and close the gap. The COVID-19 outbreak and the related global health crisis worsened the situation.[293] In the midst of the war in Ukraine, EUMS have been confronted with unprecedented mass displacement and must cope with challenges in their role as neighboring countries of (first) refuge. In the end, durable solutions for those fleeing Ukraine may also depend on resettlement commitments of the US.[294] The "*history of resettlement from Europe provides for legitimate reciprocity demands: the continent could be expected to invest into a system from which it has already benefited in the past*"[295] – and from which it would continue to benefit in current and future crises.

2.4 *Functions of and motives behind resettlement*

History reveals that resettlement initiatives have served multiple functions and receiving countries have pursued various motives when engaging in resettlement. The most prominent conclusion from the history of resettlement is that resettlement constitutes a crucial means to persuade countries of (first) refuge to open their borders and to keep their borders open. This is exemplified by the outlined major large-scale resettlement operations, specifically the Hungarian refugees in Austria and the Vietnamese refugees in the ASEAN countries, and more recently the mass displacement from Afghanistan. These examples demonstrate that resettlement serves (i) to share international responsibility and (ii) to provide international protection. Conversely, resettlement also serves to manage migration and to shift responsibility to countries of (first) refuge. The insufficient imple-

292 See UNHCR, 'Resettlement Data' (as of 28 June 2022) <https://www.unhcr.org/resettlement-data.html>.

293 "*UNHCR had planned the departure of 70,000 refugees for resettlement in 2020. According to its Resettlement Data Finder, as of June 9,758 refugees had been resettled worldwide*", Adèle Garnier, 'The COVID-19 Resettlement Suspension: Impact, Exemptions and the Road Ahead' (*FluchtforschungsBlog*, 16 June 2020).

294 See Ted Hesson and Kristina Cooke, 'Explainer: Why did the United States resettle only 12 Ukrainian refugees in March?' (*Reuters*, 11 April 2022) <https://www.reuters.com/world/why-isnt-us-accepting-more-ukrainian-refugees-2022-03-16/> accessed 28 June 2022.

295 Gregor Noll and Joanne van Selm, 'Rediscovering Resettlement' in (2003) 3 Migration Policy Institute Insight, 10 <https://www.migrationpolicy.org/research/rediscovering-resettlement> accessed 13 February 2021.

mentation of the 2016 EU-Turkey Statement by EUMS demonstrates that receiving countries did not keep their resettlement promises (see 4.2.10). Functions and motives behind resettlement are interrelated because the functions attached to a resettlement scheme shift according to specific motives of a state to engage in resettlement.[296] Against this backdrop, the following section elaborates on the functions of resettlement as defined by the UNHCR as well as motives pursued by the US and the EU. This is to show the risk that UNHCR's core functions of resettlement are undermined by controversial state motives.

2.4.1 Functions

The UNHCR has followed the concept that resettlement benefits the country of (first) refuge, the receiving country, the home country, and the resettlement beneficiaries. It specified three equally important core functions of resettlement in its *Resettlement Handbook*,[297] namely (i) providing international protection, (ii) offering a durable solution alongside voluntary repatriation to the home country and local integration in the country of (first) refuge, and (iii) expressing international solidarity.

> *First, it is a tool to provide international protection and meet the specific needs of individual refugees whose life, liberty, safety, health or other fundamental rights are at risk in the country where they have sought refuge.*
> *Second, it is a durable solution for larger numbers or groups of refugees alongside the other durable solutions of voluntary repatriation and local integration.*
> *Third, it can be a tangible expression of international solidarity and a responsibility sharing mechanism, allowing States to help share responsibility for refugee protection, and reduce problems impacting the country of asylum.*[298]

Feller and *Klug* endorsed achievements of the UNHCR "*in strengthening the functions of resettlement* [...]. *Resettlement provided solutions for more than*

296 See Catharina Ziebritzki in Marie-Claire Foblets and Luc Leboeuf (eds), *Humanitarian Admission to Europe*, 288, 305f.

297 See UNHCR, *Resettlement Handbook* (revised ed July 2011) 3; see also Haruno Nakashiba, 'Clarifying UNHCR Resettlement: A few considerations from a legal perspective', UNHCR Research Paper n°264 (November 2013) 2.

298 UNHCR, *Resettlement Handbook* (revised ed July 2011) 3 (emphasis in original removed).

330,000 refugees between 2007 and 2011, and, as a result of its strategic use, it is serving to expand asylum space in a number of host countries and leverage wider protection and solution dividends benefitting the refugee population as a whole".[299] The Social Science principle of path-dependency elucidates the fundamental role of resettlement for the relationship between countries of (first) refuge and receiving countries.[300] *Sewell* explained path-dependency as "*what happened at an earlier point in time will affect the possible outcomes of a sequence of events occurring at a later point*".[301] *Levi* took a narrower view of this concept by pointing out that "*once a country or region has started down a track, the costs of reversal are very high*".[302]

In this light, several countries of (first) refuge generously and continuously stayed on track to keep their borders open and to offer refugees short-term shelter until they could repatriate or resettle. Nevertheless, camps grew over time. Humanitarian involvement was gradually prolonged beyond immediate assistance as a result of expanded triangular relationships between countries of (first) refuge, donor states and humanitarian actors, such as the UNHCR.[303] That triangle triggered so-called protracted refugee situations, i.e. situations "*which have moved beyond the initial emergency phase but for which solutions do not exist in the foreseeable future*".[304] Generally, such protracted situations entail the risk of becoming unbearable for countries of (first) refuge. Consequently, in view of the prevailing public interests in closing the borders, countries of (first) refuge may close their borders. In other words, if prospective receiving countries neglect their resettlement commitments by blindly relying on countries of

---

299 Erika Feller and Anja Klug, 'Refugees, United Nations High Commissioner for (UNHCR)' (MPIL, January 2013) para 99.

300 See e.g., Brendon J Cannon and Hirotaka Fujibayashi, 'Security, structural factors and sovereignty: Analyzing reactions to Kenya's decision to close the Dadaab refugee camp complex' in (2018) 27 African Security Review 1, 20-41.

301 William Sewell, 'Three Temporalities: Toward a Sociology of the Event', CSST Working Paper No 58, CRSO Working Paper No 448 (October 1990) 16 <https://deepblue.lib.umich.edu/bitstream/handle/2027.42/51215/448.pdf?sequence=1&isAllowed=y> accessed 13 February 2021.

302 Margaret Levi, 'A Model, a Method, and a Map: Rational Choice in Comparative and Historical Analysis' in Mark Lichtback and Ellen Zuckerman (eds), *Comparative Politics: Rationality, Culture, and Structure* (Cambridge University Press 1997) 19 (28).

303 See Dana Schmalz, *Refugees, Democracy and the Law: Political Rights at the Margins of the State* (Routledge 2020) 125.

304 Gil Loescher and James Milner, 'Understanding the challenge' in (2009) 33 Forced Migration Review, 9 <https://www.fmreview.org/sites/fmr/files/FMRdownloads/en/FMRpdfs/FMR33/FMR33.pdf> accessed 13 February 2021.

(first) refuge, they risk that those countries – unexpectedly – close their borders. This in turn aggravates the migratory pressure and encourages uncontrolled border-crossings.

For example, the developments of the Dadaab camp complex in Kenya hosting hundreds and thousands of refugees from Somalia for decades culminated in an unbearable, protracted situation.[305] Nevertheless, Kenya's security concerns were vehemently dismissed. When Kenya eventually made its warnings real, unilaterally closing the Dadaab camp for national security reasons, the international community reacted with shock.[306] The result was that refugees from Somalia were forced to repatriate without adequate information about the conditions in their home country.[307] The example of Kenya demonstrates the consequence of the lack of adequate response from receiving countries to actual humanitarian needs in countries of (first) refuge.[308] In doing so, they have dismissed the stated core functions of resettlement as an international protection tool, a durable solution, and an instrument of international solidarity. In many cases, receiving countries have instead based their decisions to engage in resettlement (or not to do so) on national security interests, "*good economic sense*"[309] and/or international reputation.

2.4.2 US motives

The US has conducted resettlement not only for purely humanitarian purposes, but primarily for foreign policy reasons.[310] This is evident from

305 See Brendon J Cannon and Hirotaka Fujibayashi, 'Security, structural factors and sovereignty: Analyzing reactions to Kenya's decision to close the Dadaab refugee camp complex' in (2018) 27 African Security Review 1, 25.

306 See ibid 32.

307 See Leomoi Ochan, Abikar Abdikadir and Kim HaEun, 'Educating for return: Somali refugees in Dadaab' in (2019) Forced Migration Review, 36-37 <https://www.fmreview.org/sites/fmr/files/FMRdownloads/en/return/leomoi-abikar-kim.pdf> accessed 13 February 2021.

308 See International Crisis Group, 'How to Save the US Refugee Admissions Program', Crisis Group United States Report N°2 (12 September 2018) 1.

309 Volker Türk, 'Prospects for Responsibility Sharing in the Refugee Context' in (2016) 4 Journal on Migration and Human Security 3, 54.

310 See Donald Kerwin, 'The US Refugee Resettlement Program – A Return to First Principles: How Refugees Help to Define, Strengthen, and Revitalize the United States' in (2018) 6 Journal on Migration and Human Security 3, 205-225;

the historical outline, specifically from US resettlement during the Cold War period (see 2.3.1).

As an example, the 2017 Report of the Syrian Refugee Resettlement Project highlighted the following political objectives pursued by the US: (i) international leverage, (ii) international credibility, (iii) regional stability, (iv) counter measures against terrorist recruitment, (v) security screening and (vi) economic policy.[311]

According to this Report, US cooperation with countries of (first) refuge, namely with Turkey, Jordan and Iraq, was a vital incentive for offering to resettle Syrian refugees to the US. It seems, however, that the US resettlement offer was not purely motivated by humanitarian concerns but instead by the fact that Turkey, Jordan and Iraq hosted US military bases. Still, US resettlement commitments encouraged these countries of (first) refuge to keep their borders open through international leverage.[312]

Furthermore, the 2017 Report highlighted the US' acknowledgement that resettlement strengthened its international credibility, while withdrawal from resettlement would have induced other countries to abandon their own resettlement pledges.[313] The Report also showed that resettlement contributed to regional stability[314] and accelerated regional conflict resolution.

Moreover, under the Syrian Refugee Resettlement Project, resettlement constituted a means to counter terrorism. The US helped "*to undermine the recruitment efforts of ISIS, al Qaida, and other armed terrorist groups*"[315] by rebutting their propaganda strategy, namely refuting the message that the US and Europe were unwilling to offer protection to persons harmed by the war. From a security policy perspective, the US resettlement program

see also International Crisis Group, 'How to Save the US Refugee Admissions Program', Crisis Group United States Report N°2 (12 September 2018) 20.

311 See Initiative of the Harvard Immigration and Refugee Clinical Program, 'Fulfilling US Commitment to Refugee Resettlement: Protecting Refugees, Preserving National Security, & Building the US Economy through Refugee Admissions' in (2017) 5 Texas A&M Law Review, 155-236.

312 See Refugee Council USA, 'Where are the Refugees?: Drastic Cuts to Refugee Resettlement Harming Refugees, Communities, and American Leadership' (12 June 2019) 9.

313 See Initiative of the Harvard Immigration and Refugee Clinical Program, 'Fulfilling US Commitment to Refugee Resettlement: Protecting Refugees, Preserving National Security, & Building the US Economy through Refugee Admissions' in (2017) 5 Texas A&M Law Review, 174ff.

314 See ibid 176.

315 Ibid 177.

has required refugees to undergo "*the highest degree of security screening and background checks for any category of traveler*".[316] Syrian refugees, compared to refugees from other nations, were subject to a more enhanced review process.[317] This was confirmed by US government officials, who described the security-focused refugee resettlement screening process[318] as extensive and careful. They emphasized that the resettlement program promoted, instead of undermining, national security interests.[319] What is more, the US benefited economically from resettlement [320] since refugees have "*impressively*"[321] integrated in the US. One study pointed to a tenfold return on investment.[322]

2.4.3 EU motives

The negotiations on a Union Resettlement Framework Regulation revealed various motives behind EUMS' commitment to resettlement (see 4.2.11), "*from value-based to strategic protection considerations in first countries of asylum to foreign policy interests and border management goals*".[323]

Similar to the US, the Commission proposed to add a security angle by linking resettlement to Eurodac. The Commission viewed the access to Eurodac data as incentive for EUMS to engage in resettlement. It would

316 Ibid 178ff.
317 See ibid 180.
318 See ibid 178ff.
319 See ibid 181.
320 See ibid 182.
321 Donald Kerwin, 'The US Refugee Resettlement Program – A Return to First Principles: How Refugees Help to Define, Strengthen, and Revitalize the United States' in (2018) 6 Journal on Migration and Human Security 3, 212.
322 See Initiative of the Harvard Immigration and Refugee Clinical Program, 'Fulfilling US Commitment to Refugee Resettlement: Protecting Refugees, Preserving National Security, & Building the US Economy through Refugee Admissions' in (2017) 5 Texas A&M Law Review, 182; "[T]*he Department of Health and Human Service prepared a draft report that weighed the costs of its resettlement support programs against the benefits that refugees produced for the economy, and found a net benefit to the economy of $63 billion over the period 2005-2014*", International Crisis Group, 'How to Save the US Refugee Admissions Program', Crisis Group United States Report N°2 (12 September 2018) 20.
323 Katharina Bamberg, 'The EU Resettlement Framework: From a humanitarian pathway to a migration management tool?', Discussion Paper European Migration and Diversity Programme (26 June 2018) 6 <http://aei.pitt.edu/94238/1/pub_8632_euresettlement.pdf> accessed 13 February 2021.

enable them to share data more easily and to obtain better control over EU resettlement entries.[324]

As a result, two conflicting approaches evolved among the EU institutions: While the European Parliament opposed a control-orientated approach towards resettlement, the Council of the EU emphasized the potential to control the numbers and profiles of individuals being granted protection under the new resettlement framework. The Council of the EU further highlighted that resettlement served "*as leverage in political dialogues with third countries*"[325] which in turn enabled the building of sustainable relationships with third countries.[326]

In addition, EU funding under the AMIF was considered an incentive (see 4.3.1). According to stakeholders, EU funding has not only induced the expansion of existing resettlement capacities but also the increase of the numbers of refugees actually resettled.[327] Nevertheless, EU funding has been disproportionately small. *Thielemann* critically reflected upon EU funding by stating that[328]

> *EU resources remain, and are likely to remain, small in comparison to domestic spending in the Member States and unlikely to provide credible incentives for those less affected to make significantly greater protection contributions* [...].

2.4.4 Preliminary conclusion

Overall, the motives behind the decisions of US and European policy makers to pursue resettlement are similar.[329] Besides humanitarian interests, their rationale is based on foreign policy, security and economic interests.

---

324 See ibid 9.
325 Ibid 10.
326 See ibid 3.
327 See Elona Bokshi, 'Refugee Resettlement in the EU: The capacity to do it better and to do it more', KNOW RESET Research Report 2013/04, 31.
328 Eiko R Thielemann, 'Why Refugee Burden-Sharing Initiatives Fail: Public Goods, Free-Riding and Symbolic Solidarity in the EU' in (2018) 56 Journal of Common Market Studies 1, 63 (76).
329 See Initiative of the Harvard Immigration and Refugee Clinical Program, 'Fulfilling US Commitment to Refugee Resettlement: Protecting Refugees, Preserving National Security, & Building the US Economy through Refugee Admissions' in (2017) 5 Texas A&M Law Review, 155-236.

Excessive focus on national security can implicate a shift of resettlement's function from humanitarian protection to migration control. Hereto, *Davitti* pointed out that "*through the administration of humanitarian assistance, the lives of refugees are stabilized, managed and controlled by sovereign power*".[330] To reiterate: The term 'humanitarian' comprises *humanity*, defined as encompassing all mankind, and *humaneness*, defined as a non-cruel attitude towards human beings.[331] When states use resettlement to prevent forced migrants from reaching their border, to control (the entry of) people and to discriminate against particular groups, they apparently undermine the humanitarian function of resettlement.

Indeed, it is important to consider and maintain the difference between resettlement as a protective form of third country processing and other forms of external migration control, where states have started externalizing key elements of their own asylum system to third countries.[332] From a legal point of view, such externalization policies must not result in serious human rights violations. Beyond hard law, scholars suggested that a good faith duty of cooperation and responsibility sharing is implicit in international refugee law and expressed by instruments such as the Global Compact on Refugees (see 2.1.1).[333]

For the US, as a long-term major resettlement contributor who has tailored its resettlement operations around foreign policy and national security interests, it is counterintuitive to proclaim its position as a role model but at the same time neglecting human rights and outsourcing responsibilities.

---

330 Darla Davitti, 'Biopolitical Borders and the State of Exception in the European Migration 'Crisis'' in (2018) 29 European Journal of International Law 4, 1185f.

331 See Dana Schmalz, *Refugees, Democracy and the Law: Political Rights at the Margins of the State*, 121.

332 See David Cantor, Nikolas Feith Tan, Marianna Gkiliati, Elisabeth Mavropoulou et al, 'Externalisation, Access to Territorial Asylum, and International Law' in (2022) International Journal of Refugee Law, 1 (22).

333 See ibid 5f; for wider discussion of responsibility sharing duties, see Rebecca Dowd and Jane Mc Adam, 'International Cooperation and Responsibility-Sharing to Protect Refugees: What, Why, and How?' in (2017) 66 International and Comparative Law Quaterly, 863-892.

2.5 Actors in the resettlement process

States are considered the predominant actors[334] in international (migration) law. Although they determine international efforts to resettle refugees, they are not the only actors involved in the resettlement process. When voluntarily committing to resettlement, prospective receiving countries engage in so-called tripartite agreements with countries of (first) refuge and with the UNHCR.[335] Besides the states and the UNHCR, NGOs have also participated in the ATCRs since the 1990s.[336] Additionally, private actors, the receiving communities, and the resettlement beneficiaries themselves have equally shaped the resettlement process.

2.5.1 States

There are three types of states involved in resettlement, namely the home country of the resettlement beneficiaries, the country of (first) refuge, and the receiving country.

Home countries determine the very beginning of a resettlement beneficiary's journey because, in essence, several home countries interfere with the right to leave one's own country by preventing its citizens from fleeing abroad (see 3.3.2). Moreover, IDPs are individuals who have not left their home country, but they may equally be in need for resettlement (see 2.2.2). The resettlement of IDPs implies that receiving countries also conduct selection missions in home countries. Furthermore, the conditions in home countries are decisive for considering voluntary repatriation from a country of (first) refuge as an alternative to resettlement; also, after resettlement to the receiving country, a resettlement beneficiary may seek voluntary repatriation to his or her home country.

Apart from home countries, countries of (first) refuge are crucial actors in the resettlement process. Protection seekers flee from their home countries to a country of (first) refuge. Their presence on the territory of the country of (first) refuge entails the responsibility of this country to

334 See Gil Loescher, 'The UNHCR and World Politics: State Interest vs Institutional Autonomy' in (2001) 35 The International Migration Review 1, Special Issue, 'UNHCR at 50: Past, Present and Future of Refugee Assistance', 33.

335 See Kristin Bergtora Sandvik in Jan Wouters et al (eds), *Accountability for Human Rights Violations*, 298.

336 See Margret AM Piper, Paul Power and Graham Thom, 'Refugee Resettlement: 2012 and Beyond', UNHCR Research Paper n°253 (February 2013) 7.

comply with protection obligations under international law. Since countries of (first) refuge are often overwhelmed by massive refugee influx, resettlement constitutes a means to ease the burden. The essential role of countries of (first) refuge must not be underestimated since receiving countries need to conduct selection missions on their territories and – just like the home countries – the countries of (first) refuge may impede the resettlement process by refusing to grant resettlement beneficiaries the right to leave (see 3.3.2).[337]

Eventually, resettlement depends on the willingness of receiving countries to accept a refugee for legal stay within its territory, "*in accordance with its laws and regulations*".[338] Each resettlement country has its own regulations and procedures with respect to the resettlement of refugees. Receiving countries decide whether they accept resettlement cases referred by the UNHCR. When deciding upon UNHCR's referrals, state authorities use two general bases, i.e. (i) dossier only and (ii) selection missions.[339] When a receiving country selects on a dossier only basis, it refrains from conducting a direct interview with the refugee. The receiving country thereby either specifies from which refugee population it wishes to receive dossier submissions or leaves this to the discretion of the UNHCR. Receiving countries consistently conduct personal interviews with potential resettlement beneficiaries. These interviews typically take place during resettlement selection missions in the countries of (first) refuge or home countries.[340] In addition to UNHCR referrals, some receiving countries also admit individuals for resettlement on other bases.[341]

As shown, receiving countries have the power to decide if and how to resettle persons in need for protection. Beyond the national level, receiving countries influence how resettlement-related issues are tackled at the international level. As a general rule, receiving countries who regularly engage

---

337 See UNHCR, *Resettlement Handbook* (revised ed July 2011) 385: "*Collaboration between resettlement partners extends across the resettlement continuum, from identification and referral in the field, to processing, acceptance and travel, and to reception and integration in a third country.*"

338 Ibid 361.

339 See Joanne van Selm et al, Study on 'The Feasibility of setting up resettlement schemes in EU Member States or at EU Level, against the background of the Common European Asylum system and the goal of a Common Asylum Procedure', 176.

340 See UNHCR, *Resettlement Handbook* (revised ed July 2011) 354.

341 See Margret AM Piper, Paul Power and Graham Thom, 'Refugee Resettlement: 2012 and Beyond', UNHCR Research Paper n°253 (February 2013) 11.

in resettlement on the basis of UNHCR referrals are full members of the WGR/ATCR process (see 2.3.9).[342]

2.5.2 United Nations High Commissioner for Refugees

After the IRO, the UNHCR has marked the evolution of resettlement from the aftermath of World War II until today (see 2.3.2). Resettlement constitutes an essential part of UNHCR's mandate because the UNHCR is determined to work with states on durable solutions to the global refugee problem.[343]

2.5.2.1 Legal basis, mandate and funding

The UNGA Resolution 319 (IV) of 3 December 1949, based on Art 22 UN Charter[344], established the UNHCR as a subsidiary organ of the UN General Assembly. The Statute of the Office (UNHCR Statute)[345] laid down UNHCR's original mandate, adopted through UNGA Resolution 428 (V) of 14 December 1950. In 1958, the UN's Economic and Social Council (ECOSOC) followed the request of the General Assembly under the UNGA Resolution 1166 (XII) and established an Executive Committee to advise the work of the UNHCR.[346] It still exists and consists of representatives from UN Member States or members of any UN specialized agency; meetings take place in annual plenary sessions.[347] In 2003, another Resolution (UNGA Res 58/153) removed the initial temporal limitation of UNHCR's mandate, authorizing the UNHCR to continue its work "*until the refugee problem is solved*". Subsequently, through the adoption

---

342 See UNHCR, *Resettlement Handbook* (revised ed July 2011) 386.

343 See Erika Feller and Anja Klug, 'Refugees, United Nations High Commissioner for (UNHCR)' (MPIL, January 2013) paras 97ff.

344 "*The General Assembly may establish such subsidiary organs as it deems necessary for the performance of its functions*".

345 See Statute of the Office of the United Nations High Commissioner for Refugees (14 December 1950) <https://www.unhcr.org/4d944e589.pdf> accessed 13 February 2021.

346 See ECOSOC Resolution 672 (XXV).

347 See Dana Schmalz, *Refugees, Democracy and the Law: Political Rights at the Margins of the State*, 122; see also UNHCR, 'The Executive Committee's origins and mandate' <https://www.unhcr.org/executive-committee.html> accessed 13 February 2021.

of numerous UN General Assembly and ECOSOC resolutions, the scope of UNHCR's mandate was broadened without formal amendment of its Statute, with the outcome that the UNHCR has a "*somewhat fragmented legal basis*".[348]

Art 8 lit c UNHCR Statute makes the UNHCR competent to assist in "*assimilation within new national communities*". Principally, the UNHCR is tasked with "*providing international protection to refugees and working with States to seek permanent solutions to their plight on a non-political and humanitarian basis*".[349] The requirement of cooperation[350] between governments and the UNHCR explicitly and implicitly derives from Art 8 UNHCR Statute. UNHCR's authority to directly conclude treaties with states (Art 8 lit b UNHCR Statute[351]) constitutes a remarkable tool to foster its cooperation with states as well as among states, particularly in the resettlement context. For example, the UNHCR played a crucial role in achieving agreements between ASEAN countries and receiving countries to stimulate the resettlement of Vietnamese refugees (see 2.3.6).

UNHCR's actual scope of action to foster cooperation strongly depends on the commitment and political will of states. In fact, Art 8 UNHCR Statute limits its functions to tasks of promotion, assistance, and facilitation.[352] To put it in other words, the success or failure of the UNHCR hinges on the states' endeavors. This means that UNHCR faces the challenge to reconcile dependency on state partners with its non-partisan nature.[353] According to Art 2 UNHCR Statute UNHCR's work shall be of an "*entirely non-political character*". The subsequent phrase clarifies the object of its work, namely that it "*shall be humanitarian and social and shall relate, as a rule, to groups and categories of refugees*". Accordingly, UNHCR's "*entirely non-political character*" means that the UNHCR is determined

348 Erika Feller and Anja Klug, 'Refugees, United Nations High Commissioner for (UNHCR)' (MPIL, January 2013) para 39.

349 Ibid para 3 (emphasis added).

350 The cooperation requirement is legally anchored in the UNHCR Statute, and UNHCR's practice has broadly met the *acquiescence* of states. See Volker Türk, 'The UNHCR's role in the supervising international protection standards in the context of its mandate' in James C Simeon (ed), *The UNHCR and the Supervision of International Refugee Law* (Cambridge University Press 2013) 39 (58).

351 "*Promoting through special agreements with Governments the execution of any measures calculated to improve the situation of refugees and to reduce the number requiring protection*".

352 See Marjoleine Zieck, *UNHCR's worldwide presence in the field*, 26.

353 See Dana Schmalz, *Refugees, Democracy and the Law: Political Rights at the Margins of the State*, 121f.

to serve humanitarian and social purposes rather than (other) political objectives of receiving countries. As opposed to other UN organizations, the UNHCR financially depends on donor states.[354] It is crucial that the UNHCR remains independent even if funded by receiving or other countries. In this light, UNHCR's discretion constitutes a vital tool to uphold its non-political character, meaning that the UNHCR, rather than the donor states, decides the distribution of resources. Art 10 UNHCR Statute allows the UNHCR to distribute resources among private and public agencies "*which he* [the High Commissioner] *deems best qualified to administer such assistance*". While UNHCR's dependency on donors entails power imbalance, voices in the literature nonetheless highlight the role of the UNHCR as 'agenda setter' and 'counterweight', defending the larger interests instead of the interests of individual states.[355]

2.5.2.2 The UNHCR and the US

The US has traditionally opposed to autonomous international institutions. It has been concerned about the delegation of power to international organizations, including the UN.[356] Accordingly, the US considered the UNHCR a progressive but powerless agent of the state, namely "*a mechanism through which states act*".[357] Initially, the US did not intend to assign an operational role to the UNHCR. Instead, the US limited the functional

354 See Kristin Bergtora Sandvik in Jan Wouters et al (eds), *Accountability for Human Rights Violations*, 295.

355 See Hanna Schneider, 'Implementing the Refugee Resettlement Process: Diverging Objectives, Interdependencies and Power Relations' in (2021) Frontiers in Political Science, 16; see also Adèle Garnier, 'Migration Management and Humanitarian Protection: The UNHCR's 'Resettlement Expansionism' and its Impact on Policy-Making in the EU and Australia' in (2014) 40 Journal of Ethnic and Migration Studies 6, 942 (954): refers to the "*significant autonomy*" of the UNHCR; see also Bhupinder S Chimni, 'The Geopolitics of Refugee Studies: A View from the South' in (1998) 11 Journal of Refugee Studies 4, 350 (368): describes the UNHCR as "*guardian of the larger interests of the coalition which establishes and sustains it, not the individual interests of its members. This often brings the organization in confrontation with even its more powerful members*".

356 See Kenneth W Abbott and Duncan Snidal, 'Hard and Soft Law in International Governance', in (2000) 54 Legalization and World Politics 3, Special Issue, 'International Organization', 421 (438).

357 Gil Loescher, 'The UNHCR and World Politics: State Interest vs Institutional Autonomy' in (2001) 35 The International Migration Review 1, Special Issue, 'UNHCR at 50: Past, Present and Future of Refugee Assistance', 34.

scope and independence of the UNHCR by establishing and funding own American-led refugee organizations whose mandates directly overlapped with UNHCR's mandate.[358] Notwithstanding, over the years, the US has continuously cooperated with the UNHCR to support UNHCR's operations. The US is a major UNHCR donor state. The 2022 statistics on contributions to UNHCR programs revealed that the US contributed the most, followed by Germany, the EU, Japan and Sweden.[359]

2.5.2.3 The UNHCR and the EU

The EU and its EUMS have gradually opened their attitude towards UNHCR's involvement. While France and Belgium took quite a narrow view on UNHCR's functions when submitting the first concrete proposal on its creation in 1949,[360] its influence on the policies of EUMS today is significant. The UNHCR participated in the EU harmonization process, namely the development of the CEAS, through legal opinions on draft texts as well as substantial background information.[361] It took part in the drafting of the 2016 Commission Proposal for a Union Resettlement Framework Regulation and is explicitly mentioned therein. In its explanatory memorandum, the Proposal highlights that the "*UNHCR has over the past years urged the Union and its Member States to increase commitments to receive refugees through sustainable resettlement programmes*".[362]

Furthermore, the Proposal's Recital 27 states that "[g]*iven the expertise of UNHCR in facilitating the different forms of admission of persons in need of international protection from third countries, to which they have been displaced, to Member States willing to admit them, UNHCR should continue to play a <u>key role</u> in resettlement efforts conducted under the Union Resettlement Framework*".[363] To that end, Art 8 para 2 Proposal specifies that the admission of protection seekers shall be recorded in "*practical cooperation arrangements*

358 See ibid 35.

359 See UNHCR, 'Contributions' (as of 29 June 2022) <https://reporting.unhcr.org/contributions> accessed 29 June 2022.

360 See Marjoleine Zieck, *UNHCR's worldwide presence in the field*, 19f.

361 See Volker Türk in James C Simeon (ed), *The UNHCR and the Supervision of International Refugee Law*, 45.

362 Commission, Proposal for a Regulation establishing a Union Resettlement Framework, 2.

363 Emphasis added; see Luc Leboeuf and Marie-Claire Foblets, 'Introduction: Humanitarian Admission to Europe' in Marie-Claire Foblets and Luc Leboeuf

among Member States, [...] and with third countries, and UNHCR or other partners".

2.5.2.4 Criticism and shortfalls

The extent of UNHCR's involvement has been critically reflected among scholars,[364] asserting shortfalls in UNHCR's resettlement practice. *Loescher* stated the following major issues: (i) poor UNHCR case identification causing a resettlement backlash; (ii) the need to clarify procedures; (iii) the related responsibilities; (iv) incidences of fraud and misuse as well as (v) the absence of an autonomous resource base.[365] Furthermore, *Smrkolj*[366] highlighted due process concerns, namely a lack of judicial review mechanism, whereby states accepted that cooperation with the UNHCR implied procedural inconsistencies. She also pointed to the lack of binding force of UNHCR's Mandate Refugee Certificates,[367] which left states with a leeway to disregard them.[368] This implies that individuals seeking international protection usually have no means to legally enforce the recognition of their refugee status by the UNHCR before national authorities or courts.

(eds), *Humanitarian Admission to Europe: The Law between Promises and Constraints* (Hart/Nomos 2020) 11 (26).

364 See Janine Prantl, 'The UNHCR in 2021: Refugee Resettlement as a Challenge of Underfunding, Power Imbalance and Impartiality' (*Völkerrechtsblog*, 20 July 2021) <https://voelkerrechtsblog.org/the-unhcr-in-2021-refugee-resettlement-as-a-challenge-of-underfunding-power-imbalance-and-impartiality/> accessed 7 August 2021.

365 See Gil Loescher, 'The UNHCR and World Politics: State Interest vs Institutional Autonomy' in (2001) 35 The International Migration Review 1, Special Issue, 'UNHCR at 50: Past, Present and Future of Refugee Assistance', 43.

366 See Maja Smrkolj, 'International Institutions and Individualized Decision-Making: An Example of UNHCR's Refugee Status Determination' in (2008) 9 German Law Journal 11, 1779-1803.

367 "*UNHCR Offices should issue a UNHCR Refugee Certificate to every individual who is determined in UNHCR mandate RSD procedures to meet the criteria for refugee status, including family members/dependents who are determined to be eligible for derivative refugee status*", UNHCR, 'Procedural Standards for Refugee Status Determination under UNHCR's Mandate', Unit 8, 8-1 <https://www.refworld.org/pdfid/42d66dd84.pdf> accessed 13 February 2021.

368 See Maja Smrkolj, 'International Institutions and Individualized Decision-Making: An Example of UNHCR's Refugee Status Determination' in (2008) 9 German Law Journal 11, 1786f, 1802.

Ultimately, critiques claimed that the UNHCR has expanded and developed in a sense that it "*has compromised its capacity and willingness to provide protection and has put the agency at the mercy of a much broader set of political and strategic calculations*".[369] Such development is problematic in light of the aforementioned Art 2 UNHCR Statute, requiring UNHCR's work to be of an "*entirely non-political character*". Even though UNHCR's mandate comprises cooperation with states, thus being inevitably confronted with political interests, its work must focus on the humanitarian and social needs.

2.5.3 Other non-state actors

Besides the UNHCR, other non-state actors[370], namely NGOs[371], have been increasingly active in the resettlement process at the global, regional and sub-regional levels.

Overall, there are five stages in the resettlement process where NGOs can "*have a stake*":[372] (i) the referral stage, (ii) the placement decision, (iii) the greeting on arrival, (iv) the provision of integration and social services and (v) the involvement in policymaking. The involvement of NGOs has benefitted resettlement in various aspects. As opposed to the UNHCR, these non-state actors do not have to deal with the full enormity of a refugee crisis. They generally have more resources available to verify

369 Gil Loescher, 'The UNHCR and World Politics: State Interest vs Institutional Autonomy' in (2001) 35 The International Migration Review 1, Special Issue, 'UNHCR at 50: Past, Present and Future of Refugee Assistance', 49.

370 *Wagner* described non-state actors as "*a superordinate concept that encompasses all those actors that are not State*[s]", Markus Wagner, 'Non-State Actors' (MPIL, July 2013) para 1 <https://opil.ouplaw.com/view/10.1093/law:epil/9780199231690/law-9780199231690-e1445?rskey=0oAy0H&result=1&prd=MPIL> accessed 13 February 2021.

371 According to the Organization for Economic Co-Operation and Development (OECD) the term 'NGO' "*may include profit-making organisations, foundations, educational institutions, churches and other religious groups and missions, medical organisations and hospitals, unions and professional organisations, co-operatives and cultural groups, as well as voluntary agencies*", cited in Stephan Hobe, 'Non-Governmental Organizations' (MPIL, June 2019) para 2 <https://opil.ouplaw.com/view/10.1093/law:epil/9780199231690/law-9780199231690-e968?rskey=LXvy3A&result=1&prd=MPIL> accessed 13 February 2021.

372 Joanne van Selm, 'Public-Private Partnerships in Refugee Resettlement: Europe and the US' in (2003) 4 Journal of International Migration and Integration 2, 157 (162ff).

case merits on site in countries of (first) refuge or home countries in order to find the most vulnerable cases of refugees in need for resettlement. It has even become a well-established practice that NGOs support the UNHCR by loaning resettlement staff.[373] In addition, NGOs can rely on private funding earmarked for resettlement.[374] This means that unlike the UNHCR, they are not dependent on donor states. One major drawback, however, is that the question of "whom to hold responsible for misconduct" becomes more complex with the involvement of NGOs in the process. In particular, it needs to be tackled whether the acts of NGO staff can be attributed to states and/or the UNHCR (see 3.4.3).

2.5.3.1 Voluntary resettlement agencies in the US

From a US perspective, voluntary agencies have traditionally played a crucial role in the various stages of the resettlement process.[375] The US resettlement model is based on public-private partnerships between the government and voluntary non-profit resettlement agencies. The 1980 Refugee Act (Sections 301 lit b para 7 and 412 lit b) provides the legal basis for this relationship.[376] The Office of Refugee Resettlement (ORR), located in the Department of Health and Human Services (HHS), is authorized to fund cooperative agreements with nine voluntary agencies,[377] known as 'Volags'.

---

373 See Melonee Douglas, Rachel Levitan and Lucy W Kiama, 'Expanding the role of NGOs in resettlement' in (2017) 54 Forced Migration Review, 34 (35); see also Amy Slaughter, 'How NGOs have helped shape resettlement' in (2017) 54 Forced Migration Review, 32 (32f).

374 See ibid 35.

375 See Joanne van Selm, 'Public-Private Partnerships in Refugee Resettlement: Europe and the US' in (2003) 4 Journal of International Migration and Integration 2, 169.

376 See Anastasia Brown and Todd Scribner, 'Unfulfilled Promises, Future Possibilities: The Refugee Resettlement System in the United States' in (2014) 2 Journal on Migration and Human Security 2, 101.

377 Church World Service, Ethiopian Community Development Council, Episcopal Migration Ministries, Hebrew Immigrant Aid Society, International Rescue Committee, US Committee for Refugees and Immigrants, Lutheran Immigration and Refugee Services, United States Conference of Catholic Bishops, World Relief Corporation; see <https://www.acf.hhs.gov/orr/grant-funding/resettlement-agencies> accessed 13 February 2021.

Mutual Assistance Associations (MAAs) constitute another important pillar of the USRAP. MAAs are community-based groups frequently established by people who arrived in the US as resettled refugees and who wish to help others integrate in the local community in the long run.[378] Beyond the provision of services, Volags and MAAs engage in advocacy and lobbying tasks.[379]

Even though as opposed to Canada, private refugee sponsorships are not formally anchored in US Immigration Law, the concept of community-based sponsorships to support refugees without federally appropriated funds was already explored by the Reagan administration.[380] This so-called Public Sector Initiative nonetheless discontinued in 1996. Inspired by practices in Canada and other countries, new initiatives to engage in private sponsorships for forcibly displaced individuals came up in the US as well. For example, as a response to Afghan mass displacement after the Taliban take-over, the Sponsor Circle Program was launched in the fall of 2021.[381] A similar program called 'Uniting for Ukraine' followed in spring 2022, enabling the admission of privately sponsored Ukrainians and family members fleeing the Russian invasion through parole.[382]

---

378 See Gregor Noll and Joanne van Selm, 'Rediscovering Resettlement' in (2003) 3 Migration Policy Institute Insight, 23.

379 See ibid 23.

380 See Vasudha Talla (with the assistance of IRAP and Human Rights First), 'Private Sponsorship of Refugee Resettlement in the United States: Guiding Principles and Recommendations' (October 2016) <https://www.humanrightsfirst.org/sites/default/files/Private_Sponsorship_of_Refugees_in_the_United_States_White_Paper.pdf#page=3> accessed 29 June 2021; see also National Immigration Forum, 'Explainer: Private Sponsorship Programs for Refugees' (25 April 2022) <https://immigrationforum.org/article/a-guide-to-private-sponsorship-for-refugees/> accessed 29 June 2022.

381 See US Department of State, 'Launch of the Sponsor Circle Program for Afghans' (25 October 2021) <https://www.state.gov/launch-of-the-sponsor-circle-program-for-afghans/> accessed 29 June 2021.

382 See USCIS, 'Uniting for Ukraine' (April 2022) <https://www.uscis.gov/ukraine> accessed 12 August 2022.

2.5.3.2 From state-orientation to greater NGO-involvement in Europe

Europe's resettlement traditions are more state-orientated compared to those of the US. *Van Selm* portrayed the differences in refugee assistance in (four) European states and the US:[383]

> *The Netherlands, Finland and Sweden and the UK all see the provision of most services (as for accepted asylum seekers) as part of the welfare state system. The systems are all of the from-the cradle-to-grave type. And where the cradle to grave happens to be does not matter in determining that while legally resident in the states in question there will be a lifejacket of welfare support to some degree. [...] The US, meanwhile, takes a sink-or-swim approach. The voluntary agencies are made formal partners in a process that offers (limited) support using government money (as well as charitable donations), in part because the system is such that no other structures are in place to assist citizens with what they need to survive.*

The situation described by *van Selm* dates back to 2003. Recent developments indicate that the involvement of non-governmental actors has gained momentum in Europe. As observed by *Arakaki*, "*participation in the legislative, judicial and administrative processes relating to the application of treaties*", namely the Refugee Convention, "*is no longer confined to states*"[384] and the UNHCR. The Commission has formally recognized the contributions of NGOs in EU policy-making through different instruments, such as consultations through Green and White Papers, Communications, advisory committees, business test panels and ad hoc consultations.[385] For example, in its Proposal for a Union Resettlement Framework Regulation, the Commission expressly mentioned a campaign "*led by the International Organization for Migration (IOM) and five non-governmental organisations active in the field of refugee protection*".[386] The Commission reinforced its en-

383 Joanne van Selm, 'Public-Private Partnerships in Refugee Resettlement: Europe and the US' in (2003) 4 Journal of International Migration and Integration 2, 171.

384 Osamu Arakaki, 'Non-state actors and UNHCR's supervisory role' in James C Simeon (ed), *The UNHCR and the Supervision of International Refugee Law* (Cambridge University Press 2013) 286 (291).

385 See Matthias Freise, 'NGOs in the European Union' in Thomas Davies (ed), *Routledge Handbook of NGOs and International Relations* (2019) 433-447.

386 Commission, Proposal for a Regulation establishing a Union Resettlement Framework, 2 (emphasis added); the organizations to which reference is made are Amnesty International (AI) <https://www.amnesty.org/> accessed 13 Febru-

deavors towards collaboration with NGOs in 2020, recommending NGO involvement in the different stages of the resettlement process "*from identification of those in need of international protection in the non-EU country to integration following their arrival*".[387]

Since the peak of asylum-seekers in 2015, community sponsorship models have been established and piloted in several EUMS.[388] Under the New Pact on Migration and Asylum, the Commission highlighted its commitment to support civil society cooperation and private refugee sponsorships.[389] In its 2020 Recommendation on legal pathways to protection in the EU, it literally invited EUMS "*to put in place or expand community sponsorship schemes that aim to ensure better and faster integration and social inclusion of those granted international protection in the host societies and improved public support by creating more welcoming and inclusive societies*".[390] Furthermore, the Commission mentioned the benefits of community sponsorship schemes in the Action plan on Integration and Inclusion.[391] Such schemes "*not only help Member States increase the number of places for people in need of protection (through resettlement, humanitarian admission and*

---

ary 2021, Churches Commission for Migrants in Europe (CCME) <http://www.ccme.be> accessed 13 February 2021, European Council on Refugees and Exiles (ECRE) <https://www.ecre.org> accessed 13 February 2021, International Catholic Migration Commission (ICMC) <https://www.icmc.net/icmc-unhcr-resettlement-deployment-scheme> accessed 13 February 2021, Save me <https://www.saveme.org.in/ngo/> accessed 13 February 2021.

387 Commission, Recommendation on legal pathways to protection in the EU: promoting resettlement, humanitarian admission and other complementary pathways, C(2020) 6467 final, 9, para 14.

388 For example, Germany, Ireland, France, Italy, Belgium and (former EUMS) UK. See European Parliament, 'Community sponsorship schemes under the new pact on migration and asylum' (*Briefing*, June 2021) <https://www.europarl.europa.eu/RegData/etudes/BRIE/2021/690675/EPRS_BRI(2021)690675_EN.pdf> accessed 29 June 2022.

389 Commission, Communication on a New Pact on Migration and Asylum, 22f: "*The EU will also support Member States wishing to establish community or private sponsorship schemes through funding, capacity building and knowledge-sharing, in cooperation with civil society, with the aim of developing a European model of community sponsorship, which can lead to better integration outcomes in the longer term.*"

390 Commission, Recommendation on legal pathways to protection in the EU: promoting resettlement, humanitarian admission and other complementary pathways, 9, para 14.

391 See Commission, Communication 'Action plan on Integration and Inclusion 2021-2027', COM(2020) 758 final <https://eur-lex.europa.eu/legal-content/EN/TXT/PDF/?uri=CELEX:52020DC0758&from=EN> accessed 19 July 2022.

other complementary pathways) but also to successfully integrate them into welcoming host communities, that are aware of and prepared for their arrival".[392]

2.5.4 Resettlement beneficiaries

The discretionary nature of resettlement entails that the scopes of resettlement beneficiaries vary among receiving countries (see 5.2). In order to determine the (minimum) rights of resettlement beneficiaries under international and EU law, it is necessary to define and differentiate legal core categories of potential resettlement beneficiaries.[393]

UNHCR's resettlement definition makes *refugees* the target group for resettlement. It expressly refers to the admission "*as refugees*", but it lacks specifications on the meaning and legal status of (resettlement) refugees.

The Refugee Convention contains the most internationally recognized legal definition of 'refugee'. It differs from the usage of 'refugee' in everyday language.[394] The term 'refugee' under the Refugee Convention[395] is defined "*on only five distinct categories*",[396] namely persecution or a well-founded fear of persecution on account of (i) race, (ii) religion, (iii) nationality, (iv) membership in a particular social group, and (v) political opinion.

The refugee definition under the Refugee Convention is restrictive because it limits protection to these five grounds of persecution. It does not cover individuals who are forced to flee for other reasons than those mentioned in the Convention. Especially individuals trying to escape war regularly fail to meet the Convention's definitional criteria, even though

---

392 Ibid 20.

393 See Fulvio Attina, 'Tackling the Migrant Wave: EU as a Source and a Manager of Crisis' in 70 Revista Espanola de Derecho Internacional, 49 (53).

394 See *Goodwin-Gill* gives an overview of the evolution of the definition 'refugee'; see also Guy S Goodwin-Gill and Jane McAdam, *The Refugee in International Law* (Oxford University Press 3rd ed 2007) Chapter 2, 15-49.

395 According to Art 1 A para 2 Refugee Convention, the term refugee refers to "*any person who owing to well-founded fear of persecution for reasons of race, religion, nationality, membership of a particular social group or political opinion, is outside the country of his nationality or and is unable or, owing to such fear, is unwilling to avail himself of the protection of that country*".

396 Michael J Parrish, 'Redefining the Refugee: The Universal Declaration of Human Rights as a Basis for Refugee Protection' in (2000) 22 Cardozo Law Review, 223 (224).

they may be in need of international protection and a durable solution, including resettlement.

As an additional requirement, the person persecuted or fearing persecution on account of at least one of these categories must be outside his or her home country and unable or unwilling to avail him- or herself of the protection of the home country. As mentioned before, IDPs who have not left their home country are not covered by the Refugee Convention – even if they fear persecution on account of one of the stated categories.

2.5.4.1 Refugee and subsidiary protection status in the EU

In terms of the definition and substantive rights of refugees, EU legislation follows the Refugee Convention. Art 2 lit d Qualification Directive[397] implements the definition of the Refugee Convention:

> '[R]*efugee' means a third-country national who, owing to a well-founded fear of being persecuted for reasons of race, religion, nationality, political opinion or membership of a particular social group, is outside the country of nationality and is unable or, owing to such fear, is unwilling to avail himself or herself of the protection of that country, or a stateless person, who, being outside of the country of former habitual residence for the same reasons as mentioned above, is unable or, owing to such fear, unwilling to return to it* [...].

Serving as a complement to the restrictive refugee definition in the Refugee Convention, the specific EU law development of *subsidiary protection status* embodied in the Qualification Directive is remarkable. It provides special protection for individuals not qualifying as refugees under the Refugee Convention.[398] Recital 33 Qualification Directive stipulates that "[s]*ubsidiary protection should be complementary and additional to the refugee protection enshrined in the Geneva Convention* [Refugee Convention]". The need to offer protection beyond refugee status primarily arises from EUMS' human rights obligations, namely the principle of *non-refoule-*

397 See Directive 2011/95 (EU) on standards for the qualification of third-country nationals or stateless persons as beneficiaries of international protection, for a uniform status for refugees or for persons eligible for subsidiary protection, and for the content of the protection granted [2011] OJ L337/9-26.

398 See Hemme Battjes, *European Asylum Law and International Law* (Martinus Nijhoff 2006) 490.

ment (see 3.3.1). Subsidiary protection status is based on the idea that an individual must not be returned to a country where it would face serious harm.[399] Against this backdrop, Art 2 lit f Qualification Directive defines the term 'person eligible for subsidiary protection' as[400]

> *a third-country national or a stateless person who does not qualify as a refugee but in respect of whom substantial grounds have been shown for believing that the person concerned, if returned to his or her country of origin, or in the case of a stateless person, to his or her country of former habitual residence, would face a real risk of suffering serious harm* [...] *and is unable, or, owing to such risk, unwilling to avail himself or herself of the protection of that country.*

Generally, the rights and entitlements of individuals eligible for subsidiary protection are more limited than those of refugees.[401] Moreover, the nature of subsidiary protection status is more temporary than refugee status: Eligibility for subsidiary protection has to be re-examined and the status renewed.[402]

Despite the introduction of the subsidiary protection status, "*a comprehensive and systemic consolidation of all protection possibilities within interna-*

399 See Dieter Kugelmann, 'Refugees' (MPIL, March 2010) para 36 <https://opil.ouplaw.com/view/10.1093/law:epil/9780199231690/law-9780199231690-e866> accessed 4 July 2021.

400 Serious harm in the sense of Art 15 Qualification Directive consists of: (i) the death penalty or execution; or (ii) torture or inhuman or degrading treatment or punishment of an applicant in the country of origin; or (iii) serious and individual threat to a civilian's life or person by reason of indiscriminate violence in situations of international or internal armed conflict.

401 Even if the right on *non-refoulement*, on information, on access to education, on unaccompanied minors, on access to accommodation, on freedom to movement within the EUMS and on repatriation apply without distinction, remaining provisions define a lower level of benefits for subsidiary protection status beneficiaries; see Hemme Battjes, *European Asylum Law and International Law*, 490f.

402 Art 16 Qualification Directive stipulates that "[a] *third-country national or a stateless person shall cease to be eligible for subsidiary protection when the circumstances which led to the granting of subsidiary protection status have ceased to exist or have changed to such a degree that protection is no longer required*".

tional law"[403] has not been achieved. EUMS continue to apply various types of non-harmonized complementary protection statuses.[404]

Resettlement is also characterized by diverse approaches. Only a number of EUMS have considered persons eligible for subsidiary protection as resettlement beneficiaries (see 5.2.1). Under the proposed Resettlement Framework Regulation, all EUMS would have to include them as well as IDPs who, similarly to persons eligible for subsidiary protection, do not meet the refugee definition but might equally be in need for resettlement (see 4.2.11).

2.5.4.2 US refugee definition

The 1980 Refugee Act incorporated the Refugee Convention's refugee definition in US law, even today providing the legal basis for the USRAP. As a general rule, persons eligible for resettlement to the US must meet the refugee definition under the Refugee Act (see 5.2.2).[405]

> *The term 'refugee' means (A) any person who is outside any country of such person's nationality or, in the case of a person having no nationality, is outside any country in which such person last habitually resided, and who is unable or unwilling to return to, and is unable or unwilling to avail himself or herself of the protection of, that country because of persecution or a well-founded fear of persecution on account of race, religion, nationality, membership in a particular social group, or political opinion, or (B) in such special circumstances as the President after appropriate consultation* [...] *may specify, any person who is within the country of such person's nationality or, in the case of a person having no nationality, within the country in which such person is habitually residing, and who is persecuted or who has a well-founded fear of persecution on account of race, religion, nationality, membership in a particular social group, or political opinion.*

With the Refugee Act of 1980, the US legislator intended to eliminate any discrepancies with the Refugee Convention. Yet, *Fitzpatrick* claimed that

403 Evangelia (Lilian) Tsourdi, 'The Emerging Architecture of EU Asylum Policy: Insights into the Administrative Governance of the Common European Asylum System' in Francesca Bignami (ed), *EU Law in Populist Times: Crises and Prospects* (Cambridge University Press 2020) 191 (198).

404 See ibid 198.

405 Section 201 para 42 Title II Refugee Act 1980, Public Law 96-212, 94 Stat 102.

the US practice remained discriminatory and inconsistent with the object and purpose of the Refugee Convention and the Protocol. The Refugee Act then still provided for discretionary admission to the US through parole power. Persons fleeing from communist countries were prioritized for admission through parole.[406] The discretionary parole power conferred to Attorneys General led to arbitrary decisions. Even after the restriction of parole authority in 1996 (see 5.2.2), the criteria for exercising parole power have remained blurred. A revival of parole power usage can be witnessed in the context of the 2021/22 mass displacements from Afghanistan and Ukraine (see 2.3.16).

By comparison to the EU approach, subsidiary protection status is alien to US law. Under US law, withholding of removal accounts for *non-refoulement* situations and protects individuals who do not meet the refugee definition from forced return. However, unlike subsidiary protection status, withholding of removal is not linked to an automatic right to remain; there is no possibility to directly access permanent residence status and there is no entitlement to most federally funded benefits.[407]

2.5.4.3 Climate migrants

The ongoing climate change also creates the need for resettlement of so-called 'climate migrants'.[408] According to the World Bank, by 2050, climate change will drive 143 million people in Latin America, Africa and South Asia – especially from poor regions, which actually have contributed little to global warming – to leave their homes. Yet, only in rare cases individuals experiencing climate-induced forced displacement meet the requirements to qualify as refugee under the Refugee Convention, because

406 See Robert Kogod Goldman and Scott M Martin, 'International Legal Standards Relating to the Rights of Aliens and Refugees and United States Immigration Law' in (1983) 5 Human Rights Quarterly 3, 302 (323).

407 See Dree K Collopy, *AILA's Asylum Primer* (7th ed American Immigration Lawyers Association 2015) Chapter 2.

408 "*Environmental migrants are not covered by the 1951 Geneva Convention Relating to the Status of Refugees* [Refugee Convention], *which is designed to protect those fleeing persecution, war or violence. The UN agencies most involved in refugee rights, the UN Refugee Agency (UNHCR) and the UN Development Programme, agree that the term 'climate refugee' should not be used to describe those displaced for environmental reasons*", WH, 'Why climate migrants do not have refugee status' (*The Economist*, 6 March 2018) <https://www.economist.com/the-economist-explains/2018/03/06/why-climate-migrants-do-not-have-refugee-status> accessed 13 February 2021.

this definition does not acknowledge climate change. Even if the Refugee Convention does not apply, governments might still risk violations of the principle of *non-refoulement* under international human rights law by sending people back to situations where climate change has created life-threatening conditions (see 3.3.1.1.2).

2.5.5 Preliminary conclusion

The resettlement process depends on the willingness of receiving countries to admit refugees from a country of (first) refuge or, in the case of IDPs, from their home country to their territory. The UNHCR cooperates with receiving countries, countries of (first) refuge and home countries in order to facilitate resettlement. Amongst others, the UNHCR is competent to formalize the cooperation with and between these countries by concluding treaties. While the UNHCR financially depends on state donors, its humanitarian and social work shall be of an "*entirely non-political character*". In addition, the resettlement process regularly involves cooperation with (other) non-state actors. The US has traditionally relied on public-private partnerships with Volags, primarily tasked to spur self-sufficiency in resettled refugees. In addition, to expand capacities, the US government has currently been exploring the potential of private refugee sponsorships. In resettlement to the EU, NGO involvement and community and private sponsorship models are growing as well. Eventually, resettlement beneficiaries constitute the focal point in the resettlement process. Besides refugees, who are explicitly mentioned in UNHCR's resettlement definition as beneficiaries, there are other (groups of) individuals who may be in need for resettlement.

3 The international law framework for resettlement

3.1 *The relevant human rights and refugee law framework*

As a first step to assess the interrelation between refugee resettlement and international law, it is necessary to identify the respective normative framework. States enjoy discretion when deciding whether to engage in resettlement.[409] However, when actually conducting resettlement, states must operate within the framework of their international obligations.[410]

Human rights create entitlements for individuals *vis à vis* states. Those entitlements are internationally guaranteed and acknowledged by states as fundamental. They are deemed to be necessary to safeguard human dignity and the development of the person. The acknowledgement of these fundamental entitlements has materialized in a broad framework of universal and regional human rights instruments.[411]

The following considerations are limited to legal issues that are relevant to the resettlement process (see Chapter 5). The analysis comprises major universal human rights instruments, namely the Universal Declaration of Human Rights (UDHR)[412], the International Covenant on Economic, Social and Cultural Rights (ICESCR)[413], the International Covenant on Civil and Political Rights (ICCPR)[414], and the International Convention Against Torture (CAT)[415]. Other pertinent treaties include the United Nations

---

409 See Catharina Ziebritzki in Marie-Claire Foblets and Luc Leboeuf (eds), *Humanitarian Admission to Europe*, 290.

410 See Marjoleine Zieck in Vincent Chetail and Céline Bauloz (eds), *Research Handbook on International Law and Migration*, 577.

411 See Walter Kälin and Jörg Künzli, *The Law of International Human Rights Protection* (Oxford University Press 2nd ed 2019) 28f.

412 See Universal Declaration of Human Rights (adopted 10 December 1948) UNGA Res 217 A(III).

413 See International Covenant on Economic, Social and Cultural Rights (adopted 16 December 1966, entered into force 3 January 1976) 993 UNTS 3.

414 See International Covenant on Civil and Political Rights (adopted 16 December 1966, entered into force 23 March 1976) 999 UNTS 171.

415 See International Convention against Torture and Other Cruel, Inhuman or Degrading Treatment or Punishment (adopted 10 December 1984) 1465 UNTS 85.

Convention on the Rights of the Child (CRC)[416], the Convention on the Elimination of All Forms of Discrimination against Women (CEDAW)[417], as well as the United Nations Convention on the Rights of Persons with Disabilities (UNCRPD)[418]. Discrimination on the basis of race is specifically addressed by the International Convention on the Elimination of All Forms of Racial Discrimination (CERD)[419]. The analysis also deals with the Convention for the Protection of Human Rights and Fundamental Freedoms (European Convention on Human Rights, ECHR)[420].

Refugees as human beings enjoy protection under the aforementioned human rights instruments. The evolution of general human rights treaties, however, has not rendered refugee-specific rights redundant. The most important international law source for refugee-specific rights is the Refugee Convention and its Protocol. In a nutshell, there is no right to resettlement, but there are rights within resettlement that deserve consideration.

3.2 *Extraterritorial application*

The obligations of states under international and European human rights and international refugee law when engaging in resettlement depend on the applicability of the respective international instruments. Given that resettlement entails the extraterritorial action of receiving countries in the countries of (first) refuge or in the case of IDPs, the respective home countries, the subsequent analysis of the receiving countries' obligations focuses on the extraterritorial application of human rights, namely the pre-

416 See United Nations Convention on the Rights of the Child (adopted 20 November 1989, entered into force 2 September 1990) 1577 UNTS 3.

417 See Convention on the Elimination of All Forms of Discrimination Against Women (adopted 18 December 1981, entered in to force 3 September 1981) 1249 UNTS 13.

418 See United Nations Convention on the Rights of Persons with Disabilities (adopted 13 December 2006, entered into force 3 May 2008) 2515 UNTS 3.

419 See International Convention on the Elimination of All Forms of Racial Discrimination (adopted 21 December 1965, entered into force 4 January 1969) 660 UNTS 195; for instance in Austria, this Convention has the status of Constitutional law [Bundesverfassungsgesetz vom 3. Juli 1973 zur Durchführung des Internationalen Übereinkommens über die Beseitigung aller Formen rassischer Diskriminierung, BGBl 390/1973].

420 See Convention for the Protection of Human Rights and Fundamental Freedoms (adopted 4 November 1950, entered into force 3 September 1953) ETS No 5.

requisite of extraterritorial jurisdiction, before turning to the substantive scope of the respective rights (see 3.3). Other dimensions and principles of jurisdiction in international law, such as jurisdiction of states based on the nationality or protective principle,[421] are not immediately relevant in determining the obligations of receiving countries towards potential resettlement beneficiaries, and will not be the subject of this analysis.

Moreover, for this analysis of human rights obligations, the personal scope of application of human right treaties is neglectable because the majority of human rights guarantees are universal in terms of their personal scope; notably with the exception of, amongst others, the CRC, CEDAW and the UNCRPD, targeting a specific group of vulnerable individuals, and obviously the Refugee Convention, whose personal scope of application is limited to refugees (see 3.2.2.)

3.2.1 Extraterritorial application of human rights

It is undisputed that once an individual finds itself within the territory of a receiving country, this country exercises territorial jurisdiction and is bound to uphold the guarantees under the respective human rights treaties towards this individual.[422] However, whether receiving countries establish jurisdiction through extraterritorial action, for example when selecting resettlement beneficiaries in a country of (first) refuge, constitutes a pertinent legal issue.[423]

---

421 For further elaborations on different forms of jurisdiction, see Bruno Simma and Andreas Th Müller, 'Exercise and limits of jurisdiction' in James Crawford and Martti Koskenniemi (eds), *The Cambridge Companion to International Law* (Cambridge University Press 2012) 135 (137ff).

422 The jurisdiction of a state as a prerequisite for the application of domestic norms exists within its territory. See Walter Kälin and Jörg Künzli, *The Law of International Human Rights Protection*, 121; see also Olivier de Schutter, *International Human Rights Law: Cases, Materials, Commentary* (Cambridge University Press 3rd ed 2019) 146.

423 See Dirk Hanschel, 'Humanitarian Admission Under Universal Human Rights Law: Some Observations Regarding the International Covenants' in Marie-Claire Foblets and Luc Leboeuf (eds), *Humanitarian Admission to Europe: The Law between Promises and Constraints* (Hart/Nomos 2020) 49 (56f).

3.2.1.1 Legal standard

While formulations and requirements of the respective human rights treaties differ,[424] generally-speaking, they bind states with persons *subject to or within* their jurisdiction.

As a prominent example, Art 2 para 1 ICCPR provides that "[e]*ach State Party to the present Covenant undertakes to respect and ensure to all individuals within its territory and subject to its jurisdiction the rights recognised in the present Covenant*".[425] The Human Rights Committee interpreted this Article expansively in its General Comment No 31. Accordingly, Art 2 para 1 ICCPR requires State Parties to respect and ensure the Covenant rights "*to all persons who may be within their territory and to all persons subject to their jurisdiction*".[426] Moreover, the Human Rights Committee found in *Delia Saldias de Lopez v Uruguay* that "*it would be unconscionable to so interpret the responsibility under Article 2 of the Covenant as to permit a state party to perpetrate violations of the Covenant on the territory of another State, which violations it could not perpetrate on its own territory*".[427] Indeed, the General Comments and views adopted by the Human Rights Committee

424 See Olivier de Schutter, *International Human Rights Law: Cases, Materials, Commentary*, 145; see also Fabiane Baxewanos, 'Relinking power and responsibility in extraterritorial immigration control' in Thomas Gammeltoft-Hansen and Jens Vedsted-Hansen (eds), *Human rights and the dark side of globalisation: Transnational law enforcement and migration control* (Routledge 2016) 193 (198); see also Ibrahim Kanalan, 'Extraterritorial State Obligations Beyond the Concept of Jurisdiction' in (2018) 19 German Law Journal 1, 43 (45).

425 Art 2 para 1 ICCPR (emphasis added).

426 OHCHR, 'General comment No 31: The nature of the general legal obligation imposed on States Parties to the Covenant', UN Doc CCPR/C/21/Rev1/Add.13 (26 May 2004) para 10 (emphasis added) <https://www.refworld.org/docid/478b26ae2.html> accessed 13 February 2021; see Marko Milanovic, 'Extraterritoriality and Human Rights: Prospects and challenges' in Thomas Gammeltoft-Hansen and Jens Vedsted-Hansen (eds), *Human rights and the dark side of globalisation: Transnational law enforcement and migration control* (Routledge 2016) 53; "*The HRC* [Human Rights Committee], *relying on the ICCPR, which uses more restrictive language than the ECHR, has in fact adopted a more expansive view of jurisdiction than the ECtHR*", Yuval Shany, 'Taking Universality Seriously: A Functional Approach to Extraterritoriality in International Human Rights Law' in (2013) 7 Law and Ethics of Human Rights, 47 (51).

427 OHCHR, 'Communication No 52/1979: Delia Saldias de Lopez v Uruguay', UN Doc CCPR/C/OP/1 (1984) para 12.3 <https://juris.ohchr.org/Search/Details/298> accessed 13 February 2021; see Annick Pijnenburg, 'Containment Instead of *Refoulement*: Shifting State Responsibility in the Age of Cooperative Migration Control' in (2020) Human Rights Law Review, 306 (322f).

remain legally non-binding, but states are still required "*to at least consider and weigh the reasons*"[428] of non-compliance. The ICJ has supported and fostered the authority of the Committee's decisions.[429] Additionally, the ICJ itself observed in its Advisory Opinion in *Legal Consequences of the Construction of a Wall in the Occupied Palestinian Territory* that certain human rights instruments, including the ICCPR, the ICESCR, and the CRC, were applicable in the occupied Palestinian territory.[430]

Similarly, in the regional European context, Art 1 ECHR stipulates that the "*High Contracting Parties shall secure to everyone within their jurisdiction the rights and freedoms defined in Section I of this Convention*".[431] The *travaux préparatoires* of the ECHR suggest a broader understanding of jurisdiction that goes beyond jurisdiction in the territorial sense. The initial reference in Art 1 ECHR to "*all persons residing within their territories*" was replaced by persons "*within their jurisdiction*".[432]

Consistently, the European Commission on Human Rights[433] and the European Court of Human Rights (ECtHR) set out criteria for exceptions to the territorial notion of jurisdiction.[434]

428 Walter Kälin and Jörg Künzli, *The Law of International Human Rights Protection*, 218f.

429 See *Ahmado Sadio Diallo (Republic of Guinea v Democratic Republic of the Kongo)* [2010] ICJ Rep 639 (669, para 66).

430 *Legal Consequences of the Construction of a Wall in the Occupied Palestinian Territory* (Advisory Opinion) [2004] ICJ Rep 136 (178ff); furthermore, the ICJ acknowledged that *de facto* effective control over areas triggers extraterritorial jurisdiction in *Armed Activities on the Territory of Congo Case (Democratic Republic of the Congo v Uganda)* [2005] ICJ Rep 168.

431 Art 1 ECHR (emphasis added).

432 *MN and Others v Belgium* App No 3599/18 (ECtHR 5 May 2020), para 100.

433 "*High Contracting Parties are bound to secure the* [...] *rights and freedoms* [in the ECHR] *to all persons under their actual authority and responsibility, not only when the authority is exercised within their own territory but also when it is exercised abroad*", *W v Ireland* App No 9360/81 (Commission Decision 28 February 1983) para 14 (emphasis added).

434 See e.g., *MN and Others v Belgium*, paras 101ff.

3.2.1.2 Relevant ECtHR case law, decisions of other regional courts and UN Treaty bodies

The starting point for the assessment of jurisdiction is territory. The ECtHR highlighted the strong tie between jurisdiction and the own territory of a Contracting State, for instance, in *Ilaşcu*.[435]

Beyond the own territory of a Contracting State, the ECtHR confirmed jurisdiction in *Hirsi Jamaa*,[436] where Italy sent its vessels in international waters. It would, however, be too far-fetched to draw an analogy from the jurisdiction of a vessel's flag state in international waters to extraterritorial selection for resettlement, which usually takes place on foreign territory.

In *M v Denmark*,[437] *Öcalan v Turkey*,[438] and *Al Skeini v UK*,[439] the establishment of extraterritorial jurisdiction on foreign territory was based on physical control over a person. In general, the agents of receiving countries do not exercise physical control over potential resettlement beneficiaries in the course of extraterritorial selection missions. Usually, a resettlement candidate is not physically forced by an officer to take part in a resettlement eligibility interview, and the candidate is free to end the interview and leave. In other words, listening to prospective resettlement beneficiaries on the territory of a third country does not necessarily involve effective control over a person.

In other cases, such as *Cyprus v Turkey*[440], the ECtHR relied on *de facto* control over the territory of another state. These cases also do not apply in the resettlement context. It cannot be claimed that agents of receiving countries exercise *de facto* control over the territory of the country where they select resettlement beneficiaries.

---

435 See *Ilaşcu and Others v Moldowa and Russia* App No 48787/99 (ECtHR 8 July 2004) para 33: In this case, the ECtHR confirmed that even the lack of *de facto* control of a state over (parts of) its own territory did not rule out jurisdiction of that state; see also Olivier de Schutter, *International Human Rights Law: Cases, Materials, Commentary*, 155f.

436 See *Hirsi Jamaa and Others v Italy* App No 27765/09 (ECtHR 23 February 2012).

437 See *M v Denmark* App No 17392/90 (Commission Decision 14 October 1992).

438 See *Öcalan v Turkey* App No 46221/99 (ECtHR 12 May 2005).

439 See *Al-Skeini and Others v United Kingdom* App No 55721/07 (ECtHR 7 July 2011).

440 See *Cyprus v Turkey* App No 25781/94 (ECtHR 10 May 2001) para 77.

Yet, the 'public powers doctrine' as established, e.g., in *Banković*[441] and *Al Skeini*[442], deserves further consideration. In this context, the question raised is whether the implementation of national resettlement policy qualifies as exercise of public powers normally to be exercised by the country of (first) refuge (or home country in the case of IDPs).[443] *Moreno-Lax* proposed to extend the exercise of public powers to situational control, whereby she based her arguments, amongst others, on policy delivery. Her proposition is that extraterritorial policy implementation qualifies as an exercise of state authority. *Dippel* confirmed that granting extraterritorially applicable rights for non-resident foreigners under the domestic law of the granting state amounts to an exercise of authority to the extent that this state applies its national law regulating the specific situation.[444] Applying these considerations to the resettlement selection process leads to the following conclusion: Officials of prospective receiving countries implement the resettlement policy of their sending state on the territory of the country of (first) refuge. By implementing the domestic policy and laws of the sending state, they deliberately exercise public power. The key point is that the officials of the receiving country exercise public power only with regards to the actions and rights related to the implementation of the refugee's sending country's resettlement policy. This is consistent with the approach that the ECtHR took in *al Skeini* that only those specific rights "*relevant to the situation of that individual*" apply.[445]

In addition to the exercise of public powers, the ECtHR required in *Banković* that the exercise of those powers was "*a consequence of military occupation or through the consent, invitation or acquiescence*".[446] In the normal case, the receiving country does not militarily occupy the country of (first) refuge when conducting resettlement selection, but public powers can be exercised through consent or at least *acquiescence*, i.e. acceptance in the

441 See *Banković and Others v Belgium and 16 Other Contracting States* App No 52207/99 (ECtHR 19 December 2001) para 71.

442 See *Al-Skeini and Others v United Kingdom*, para 135.

443 See James C Hathaway, *The Rights of Refugees Under International Law*², 189ff.

444 See Annika Dippel, *Extraterritorialer Grundrechtsschutz gemäß Art 16a GG* (Duncker & Humboldt 2020) 38.

445 *Al-Skeini and Others v United Kingdom*, para 137 (the treaty rights can be "*divided and tailored*" by situation). This is in contrat to UN treaty body practice suggesting the application of the full range of treaty rights. See David Cantor, Nikolas Feith Tan, Marianna Gkiliati, Elisabeth Mavropoulou et al, 'Externalisation, Access to Territorial Asylum, and International Law' in (2022) International Journal of Refugee Law, 8.

446 *Banković and Others v Belgium and 16 Other Contracting States*, para 71.

form of silence or absence of protest.[447] One can imagine a receiving country using its military bases in a third country to conduct interviews and vetting procedures; for instance, this is current practice between the US and Kosovo with regards to evacuees from Afghanistan.[448] Such military bases are commonly subject to Status of Forces Agreements "*that exclude the territorial state from exercising legal jurisdiction*"[449] over the activities of the sending country. Under such Status of Forces Agreements, the territorial state consents to the exercise of jurisdiction of the sending state.

Even without express agreement between a receiving country and a country of (first) refuge, *acquiescence* can be assumed. *Dippel* pointed out that granting an extraterritorially applicable right does not interfere with the territorial sovereignty of another state, as long as the granting of that right does not entail additional obligations for the foreign country.[450] Resettlement, in principle, meets this requirement since the receiving country takes on protection obligations of the country of (first) refuge rather than imposing additional obligations on that country. On this basis, it can be argued that countries of (first) refuge generally *acquiesce* to the conduct of resettlement selection missions on their territory.[451]

---

447 See Ian MacGibbon, 'The Scope of Acquiescence in International Law' in (1954) 31 British Yearbook of International Law, 143.

448 Agreement between the United States and Kosovo (25 August 2021) paras 1-3 <https://www.state.gov/wp-content/uploads/2021/11/21-825-Kosovo-Transit-Afghanistan.pdf> accessed 2 May 2023: "*The United States and the Republic of Kosovo [...] agree to cooperate regarding efforts to relocate from the territory of Afghanistan into the territory of another State identified individuals. [...] In furtherance of this cooperation, the Republic of Kosovo agrees to host, on a temporary basis, for up to 365 days identified individuals to facilitate efforts to resettle such individuals on a permanent basis in another location. [...] The United States agrees to relocate identified individuals to another location within 365 days after the day such individuals arrived in the Republic of Kosovo. Unless otherwise agreed, the Parties expect that the identified individuals will ultimately be resettled by the United States either in the United States or in another location outside of the United States and the Republic of Kosovo.*"

449 Sarah Cleveland, 'The United States and the Torture Convention, Part I: Extraterritoriality' (*Just Security*, 14 November 2014) <https://www.justsecurity.org/17435/united-states-torture-convention-part-i-extraterritoriality/> accessed 7 July 2022.

450 See Annika Dippel, *Extraterritorialer Grundrechtsschutz gemäß Art 16a GG*, 38f.

451 See Elspeth Guild and Vladislava Stoyanova, 'The Human Right to Leave Any Country: A Right to be Delivered' in Wolfgang Benedek et al (eds) *European Yearbook on Human Rights 2018* (Intersentia 2018) 373 (380).

Finally, in *Banković*, the ECtHR required attribution, i.e. the act in question must be attributable to the state acting extraterritorially rather than to the territorial state.[452] Such attribution is given in the course of selection missions conducted by a receiving country's field officers on the territory of a country of (first) refuge or a home country. However, attribution remains questionable when it comes to the mere provision of equipment, training, money, or intelligence by receiving countries to officials of countries of (first) refuge.[453] Furthermore, attribution cannot generally be assumed beyond the actual actions related to the policy implementation of the receiving country.

One contentious point remains. Even if most essential requirements of the 'public powers' doctrine are met in the resettlement context, it is difficult to argue that this doctrine applies directly to resettlement. The ECtHR used the exercise of public powers complementary, either in relation with *de facto* control over foreign territory (*Bankovic*),[454] or physical control over a person (*Al Skeini*)[455].[456] In *MN and Others v Belgium*, where a Syrian refugee family invoked urgent humanitarian reasons to obtain short-term visas via the Belgian embassy in Beirut, the ECtHR upheld the approach that the 'exercise of public powers' cannot be an independent model

---

452 See *Banković and Others v Belgium and 16 Other Contracting States*, para 71; see also Elspeth Guild and Vladislava Stoyanova in Wolfgang Benedek et al (eds) *European Yearbook on Human Rights 2018*, 380.

453 See ibid 380.

454 See *Banković and Others v Belgium and 16 Other Contracting States*, para 71: "[...] *when the respondent State, through the effective control of the relevant territory and its inhabitants abroad* [...] *exercises all or some of the public powers* [...]".

455 See *Al-Skeini and Others v United Kingdom*, para 149: "[...] the United Kingdom (together with the United States of America) assumed in Iraq the exercise of some of the public powers normally to be exercised by a sovereign government. [...] In these exceptional circumstances, the Court considers that the United Kingdom, through its soldiers [...] exercised authority and control over individuals killed in the course of [...] security operations, so as to establish a jurisdictional link [...]".

456 For example, *Besson* considers the exercise of public powers as one of the constitutive arguments in the spatial as well as in the personal jurisdiction model. See Samantha Besson, 'The Extraterritoriality of the European Convention on Human Rights: Why Human Rights Depend on Jurisdiction and What Jurisdiction Amounts to' in (2012) Leiden Journal of International Law, 857-884. See also Vladislava Stoyanova, 'M.N. and Others v Belgium: no ECHR protection from refoulement by issuing visas' (*EJIL: Talk!*, 12 May 2020) <https://www.ejiltalk.org/m-n-and-others-v-belgium-no-echr-protection-from-refoulement-by-issuing-visas/> accessed 6 July 2022.

without additional elements of personal or territorial physical control. Indeed, the ECtHR confirmed that Belgian authorities exercised public powers when taking decisions concerning the conditions for entry to the territory of Belgium,[457] but it found that this was not enough to establish a jurisdictional link (even though the consent requirement is likely fulfilled in the case of an embassy).

Apart from the 'public powers doctrine', courts (other than the ECtHR) and UN human rights bodies have found common ground in a test that focuses on direct and foreseeable effects on the rights of the person concerned by a specific extraterritorial action.[458] Amongst others, such functional approach was applied by the German Constitutional Court, the Inter-American Court of Human Rights (IACtHR), as well as the Human Rights Committee.

In 1999, the German Constitutional Court made it clear that protection of telecommunications privacy was not restricted to the domestic territory of Germany.[459] Subsequently, in its judgement of 19 May 2020 dealing with the German Act on the Federal Intelligence Service,[460] the Court went beyond its previous decision of 1999, finding that there were no restrictive requirements making the binding effect of fundamental rights dependent on a territorial connection or on the exercise of specific sovereign powers.[461] The Court concluded that "*German state authority is bound by fundamental rights even in relation to actions taken vis-à-vis foreigners in other countries*".[462]

In the same vein, the IACtHR did not limit extraterritorial jurisdiction to instances of physical control over a person or effective control over a territory. In its Advisory Opinion of 15 November 2017, it pointed out

---

457 *MN and Others v Belgium*, para 112.

458 David Cantor, Nikolas Feith Tan, Marianna Gkiliati, Elisabeth Mavropoulou et al, 'Externalisation, Access to Territorial Asylum, and International Law' in (2022) International Journal of Refugee Law, 8.

459 BVerfG, Order of the First Senate of 14 July 1999 – 1 BvR 2226/94, para 176 [BverfGE 100, 313 (363f) – Telekommunikationsüberwachung I] <https://www.bundesverfassungsgericht.de/SharedDocs/Entscheidungen/DE/1999/07/rs19990714_1bvr222694.html> accessed 28 March 2021; see Annika Dippel, *Extraterritorialer Grundrechtsschutz gemäß Art 16a GG*, 60f.

460 See BverfG, Judgment of the First Senate of 19 May 2020 – 1 BvR 2835/17 <https://www.bundesverfassungsgericht.de/SharedDocs/Entscheidungen/EN/2020/05/rs20200519_1bvr283517en.html;jsessionid=616AA65B0D67A6BAEA9FCF97F6FFA0AB.1_cid377> accessed 28 March 2021.

461 Ibid para 88.

462 Ibid para 93.

that extraterritorial jurisdiction was also given when a Contracting State exercised "*effective control over the activities that caused the damage and the consequent human rights violation*".[463]

Finally, the Human Rights Committee highlighted the effective control over the rights of a person in its General Comment No. 36.[464] It pointed out that persons under the jurisdiction of a Contracting State means "*all persons over whose enjoyment of the right to life it exercises power or effective control*".[465] The Committee reconfirmed its approach, among others, in *AS, DI, OI and GD v Italy*.[466]

---

463 IACtHR, Advisory Opinion OC-23/17 *The Environment and Human Rights* (15 November 2017) para 104 lit h.

464 See OHCHR, 'General Comment No 36: Article 6 (Right to Life)', UN Doc CCPR/C/GC/36 (3 September 2019) <https://tbinternet.ohchr.org/_layouts/15/treatybodyexternal/Download.aspx?symbolno=CCPR/C/GC/36&Lang=en> accessed 13 February 2021.

465 Ibid para 63.

466 OHCHR, 'Communication No 3042/2017: AS, DI, OI and GD v Italy', UN Doc CCPR/C/130/D/3042/2017 (27 January 2021) para 7.8: "*As a result, the Committee considers that the individuals on the vessel in distress were directly affected by the decisions taken by the Italian authorities in a manner that was reasonably foreseeable in light of the relevant legal obligations of Italy, and that they were thus subject to Italy's jurisdiction*". See also Committee on Economic Social and Cultural Rights, 'General Comment No 24 on State obligations under the International Covenant on Economic, Social and Cultural Rights in the context of business activities', UN Doc E/C.12/GC/24 (10 August 2017) para 32: "*The responsibility of the State can be engaged in such circumstances even if other causes have also contributed to the occurrence of the violation, and even if the State had not foreseen that a violation would occur, provided such a violation was reasonably foreseeable*"; see also Committee on the Rights of a Child, 'Decision adopted by the Committee on the Rights of the Child under the Optional Protocol to the Convention on the Rights of the Child on a communications procedure in respect of Communication No 104/2019: Sacchi et al v Argentina', UN Doc CRC/C/88/D/104/2019 (8 October 2021) para 10.7: "*Having considered the above, the Committee finds that the appropriate test for jurisdiction in the present case is that adopted by the Inter-American Court of Human Rights in its Advisory Opinion on the Environment and Human Rights. This implies that when transboundary harm occurs, children are under the jurisdiction of the State on whose territory the emissions originated for the purposes of article 5 (1) of the Optional Protocol if there is a causal link between the acts or omissions of the State in question and the negative impact on the rights of children located outside its territory, when the State of origin exercises effective control over the sources of the emissions in question.*" See also Committee on the Rights of a Child, 'Decision adopted by the Committee under the Optional Protocol to the Convention on the Rights of the Child on a communications procedure, concerning communications No 79/2019 and No 109/2019', UN Doc CRC/C/85/D/79/2019 – CRC/C/85/D/109/2019 (2 November 2020) para 9:

Scholars have argued likewise. *Çali* purported in her effective control over the rights of a person doctrine that "*control over someone else's territory or control over person are sub-themes of a more basic, but a more coherent idea: effective control over the rights of a person*".[467] The major idea is that the State Party exercises jurisdiction if the violation of a right is the foreseeable consequence of its extraterritorial action.[468] This is in line with the previously expressed view of *Shaw*. He claimed that jurisdiction related to a state's ability "*to regulate or otherwise impact upon people, property and circumstances*".[469] Similarly, *Pijnenburg* purported that receiving countries exercised jurisdiction "*on account of the effects that their policies have on the rights of intercepted migrants*".[470]

The concept of jurisdiction based on the control over the rights of a person affected by targeted extraterritorial action that implements domestic laws and/or policy is mirrored in a strand of ECtHR cases. In these cases, the Court confirmed the application of the Convention where state authorities directed executive or judicial measures at persons abroad.[471] Specifically, in *Güzelyurtlu and Others v Cyprus and Turkey*, the ECtHR held that jurisdiction was given "*if the investigative or judicial authorities of a Contracting State institute their own criminal investigation or proceedings concerning a death which has occurred outside the jurisdiction of that State, by virtue of their domestic law*".[472] On the surface, this case may look like a detention case, involving physical control over the person being investigat-

---

"[A]*s the State of the children's nationality,* [France] *has the capability and the power to protect the rights of the children in question by taking action to repatriate them or provide other consular responses.*"

467 Başak Çali, 'Has 'Control over rights doctrine' for extra-territorial jurisdiction come of age? Karlsruhe, too, has spoken, now it's Strasbourg's turn' (*EJIL: Talk!*, 21 July 2020) <https://www.ejiltalk.org/has-control-over-rights-doctrine-for-extra-territorial-jurisdiction-come-of-age-karlsruhe-too-has-spoken-now-its-strasbourgs-turn/> accessed 27 March 2021.

468 See David Cantor, Nikolas Feith Tan, Marianna Gkiliati, Elisabeth Mavropoulou et al, 'Externalisation, Access to Territorial Asylum, and International Law' in (2022) International Journal of Refugee Law, 9.

469 Malcolm Shaw, *International Law* (Cambridge University Press 6th ed 2008) 645.

470 See Annick Pijnenburg, 'Containment Instead of *Refoulement*: Shifting State Responsibility in the Age of Cooperative Migration Control' in (2020) Human Rights Law Review, 325.

471 For instance, *Romeo Castaño v Belgium* App No 8351/17 (ECtHR 9 July 2018); *Big Brother Watch and Others v UK* Apps Nos 58170/13 (ECtHR 13 September 2018).

472 See *Güzelyurtlu and Others v Cyprus and Turkey* App No 36925/07 (ECtHR 29 January 2019) para 188.

ed, but it contained fact patterns that deviate from physical control over a person, namely vast information gathering. Specifically, the Cypriot Government submitted that throughout the investigations "[m]*ore than 180 statements had been taken from various persons, including the relatives of the victims, persons who knew or had connections with the victims*".[473] It follows that the ECtHR assumed jurisdiction in a case involving extraterritorial investigations that went beyond physical control over a person.

The ECtHR based its distinction between cases like *Güzelyurtlu and Others v Cyprus and Turkey* and *MN and Others* on the unilateral choice of the individual. In *MN and Others*, the ECtHR rejected the administrative – also referred to as procedural[474] – control exercised by the Belgian embassy agents as "*not sufficient to bring every person* [...] *within Belgium's jurisdiction*".[475] The Court made it clear that individuals cannot create a jurisdictional link by submitting an application, thus provoking obligations under the ECHR which would not otherwise exist.[476]

Targeted action of the receiving country, rather than the individual choice, is also the distinguishing factor between resettlement selection missions and (humanitarian) visa applications. In the course of selection missions, the prospective receiving country's action is not initiated by an application of the protection seeker. For instance, German officials came to Addis Ababa for the specific purpose of conducting personal interviews and security checks with prospective resettlement beneficiaries residing in the Jijiga and Dolo Ado camps. Thereby, only a few were invited to meet the German authorities, while several of the resettlement candidates referred to Germany by the UNHCR had already been rejected after initial review.[477] This example shows that the potential receiving country,

473 Ibid para 47.

474 See Samantha Besson, 'Due Diligence and Extraterritorial Human Rights Obligations – Mind the Gap!' in (2020) 9 ESIL Reflections <https://esil-sedi.eu/wp-content/uploads/2020/04/ESIL-Reflection-Besson-S.-3.pdf> accessed 6 July 2022.

475 *MN and Others v Belgium*, para 119.

476 See ibid para 123.

477 See IOM, 'First IOM International Charter Flight from Ethiopia Brings 154 Refugees to New Homes in Germany' (18 October 2019) <https://www.iom.int/news/first-iom-international-charter-flight-ethiopia-brings-154-refugees-new-homes-germany> accessed 14 February 2021; see also Bundesamt für Migration und Flüchtlinge 'Äthiopien: Resettlement Mission 2019' in Tagungsdokumentation, *Resettlement und komplementäre Zugangswege: Neue Wege – neue Länder* (Frankfurt am Main 13-14 May 2019) <https://resettlement.de/wp-content/uploads/Dokumentation-Fachtagung-Resettlement-Mai-2019.pdf> accessed 14 February 2021.

Germany in this case, took targeted action on its own initiative. The application for a humanitarian visa at the Belgian Embassy in Beirut in *MN and others* is not a targeted action by Belgium. Moreover, it would be too far-reaching to assume that Belgium had exclusive and/or effective control over any violation of the *refoulement* principle (which was under dispute in *MN and others*) because the applicants could leave the embassy at any time, and in Beirut, they remained subject to the law of Beirut and the executive authority of Beirut officials. On the other hand, if the Belgian Embassy officials had taken concrete actions in application of Belgian law and policy that directly and foreseeably resulted in a violation of the applicants' rights, for example, violating their right to privacy in the course of data collection during a visa interview to which they had been invited, Belgium would arguably have exercised jurisdiction through the targeted actions of its officials.

On account of all these considerations, extraterritorial jurisdiction can be triggered by the exercise of public power on foreign territory through targeted actions of policy implementation, namely the effective control over those rights of a person that are affected by the specific action taken towards an individual in furtherance of the respective policy and/or application of the domestic law of the receiving country.

However, when detaching the question of jurisdiction from territorial and physical control, other ways need to be found, apart from borders, to demarcate when a state is responsible and when it is not. Here, the temporal aspect comes into play, involving the following questions: At what point in time does a state start to exercise control over the rights affected by its policy? And when does it end? It seems obvious that a state does not exercise control over the rights of an individual merely by adopting a certain policy and/or law, because the individual will never be affected if the policy or law is not actually implemented. Since it is the actual targeted action of implementation that makes the relevant difference, jurisdiction arguably starts with the targeted action. Coming back to the example of the German selection missions, the targeted action most probably starts when the state officials identify and consider (or reject) a certain potential resettlement candidate referred to them by the UNHCR for an interview. Conversely, the receiving country, Germany, should no longer be held responsible for human rights violations experienced by those individuals after the German officials have made their decision.

From the perspective of the receiving country, the application of the control over the rights doctrine must not result in responsibility for violations of human rights in cases where its officials are unable to effectively control the respective right at issue. As a matter of fact, in most cases, resettlement candidates remain subject to the law of the state on whose territory they are located,[478] and the actions of that state cannot be effectively controlled by the receiving state.

3.2.2 Extraterritorial application of refugee law

The territorial scope of the Refugee Convention differs from general human rights treaties because the Refugee Convention is not limited by a jurisdiction clause. When Contracting States engage in extraterritorial action, they must observe the Convention.[479]

However, for the rights under the Refugee Convention, the level of attachment to the receiving country is decisive. Most of these rights inhere only once a refugee is either lawfully staying or durably residing in a receiving country.[480] There is a small number of rights that apply without such qualification. Among those rights, there are "*two core refugee rights*"[481] of general practical relevance, namely Art 3 Refugee Convention, which sets out a rule of non-discriminatory application of the Convention rights (see 3.3.4.2); and Art 33 Refugee Convention, stipulating *non-refoulement* obligations (see 3.3.1.2). These Articles remain completely silent on their territorial scope. From the absence of a defined territorial scope, it cannot be inferred that the application of these Articles is limited to the own territory of the receiving country. The Preamble of the Refugee Convention suggests interpretation in conformity with fundamental rights. It reiterates that the UN envisages to assure refugees "*the widest possible exercise*" of fun-

---

478 As mentioned above, there may be rare exceptions, for example, when the application of the law of the territorial state is excluded on the basis of an agreement (for example, under a Status of Forces Agreement).

479 See David Cantor, Nikolas Feith Tan, Marianna Gkiliati, Elisabeth Mavropoulou et al, 'Externalisation, Access to Territorial Asylum, and International Law' in (2022) International Journal of Refugee Law, 5; see also see also Guy Goodwin-Gill, Jane Mc Adam and Emma Dunlop, *The Refugee in International Law* (Oxford University Press 4th ed 2021) 308-313.

480 See James C Hathaway, *The Rights of Refugees Under International Law*[2], 176ff, 219; see also idem in Brian Opeskin, Richard Perruchoud and Jillyann Redpath-Cross (eds), *Foundations of International Migration Law*, 191; see also Vincent Chetail, *International Migration Law*, 178; see also Guy S Goodwin-Gill and Jane McAdam, *The Refugee in International Law*, 524ff.

481 James C Hathaway, *The Rights of Refugees Under International Law*[2], 182.

damental rights and freedoms.[482] It follows that the standard of protection under the general human rights treaties should not be compromised in the context of refugee rights. The consistent approach is therefore to consider jurisdiction as the decisive criterion for the application of Arts 3 and 33 Refugee Convention – just like for the above-mentioned human rights treaties. Scholars confirmed that Art 33 Refugee Convention applies when a person is subject to or within the jurisdiction of a state.[483] Furthermore, the Michigan Guidelines on Freedom of Movement highlight that the duty of *non-refoulement* not only binds states at or inside their borders but also extraterritorially where they exercise jurisdiction.[484] The same has been acknowledged for other Convention rights not subject to a territorial or other level of attachment, including Art 3 Refugee Convention.[485] Consequently, in line with the jurisdictional threshold under general human rights treaties, Arts 3 and 33 Refugee Convention apply extraterritorially in cases where (consular) agents exercise physical control over persons abroad, and in cases where a state exercises significant public power on the territory which it has occupied or in which it is present by consent, invitation or *acquiescence*.[486]

Eventually, the lack of elaboration on the extraterritorial application in the text of the stated Articles of the Refugee Convention can arguably be interpreted as less constraining than the requirement of jurisdiction under other human rights treaties. In this context, *Hathaway* purported that "[t]*he decision generally to constrain the application of rights on a territorial or other basis creates a presumption that no such limitation was intended to govern the applicability of the rights not subject to such textual limitations*".[487] Against

482 See Nula Frei in Constantin Hruschka (ed), *Genfer Flüchtlingskonvention: Handkommentar* (Nomos 2022) Art 3, para 22.

483 See James C Hathaway, *The Rights of Refugees Under International Law*², 185f; see also Walter Kälin, Martina Caroni and Lukas Heim in Andreas Zimmermann (ed), *The 1951 Convention Relating to the Status of Refugees and its 1967 Protocol* (Oxford University Press 2011) Art 33 para 1 Refugee Convention, para 90; see also David Cantor, Nikolas Feith Tan, Marianna Gkiliati, Elisabeth Mavropoulou et al, 'Externalisation, Access to Territorial Asylum, and International Law' in (2022) International Journal of Refugee Law, 5.

484 See University of Michigan Law School, 'The Michigan Guidelines on Refugee Freedom of Movement' (May 2017) para 9 <https://www.refworld.org/docid/592ee6614.html> accessed 14 February 2021.

485 See James C Hathaway, *The Rights of Refugees Under International Law*², 193.

486 See ibid 188ff.

487 Ibid 182.

this backdrop, it appears to be even more valid to assume a broad(er) scope of application for Convention rights without express territorial limitation.

3.2.3 Preliminary conclusion

In the resettlement selection process, the question of extraterritorial jurisdiction arises when a receiving country acts through its field officers implementing its resettlement policy during selection missions on foreign territory. The analysis showed that extraterritorial jurisdiction in the course of resettlement selection procedures cannot be clearly deduced from ECtHR case law. Still, a common denominator for extraterritorial jurisdiction can be found in the exercise of public powers on foreign territory through actions of policy implementation, namely the effective control over those rights of a person that are affected by targeted extraterritorial actions implementing the respective resettlement policy of the receiving country.

With regards to refugee rights, only a few rights under the Refugee Convention remain without express territorial limitation. Two of those rights bear relevance in the resettlement context, namely Art 3 (non-discrimination) and Art 33 (*non-refoulement*) Refugee Convention. Since the wording of these Articles remains silent on their territorial scope, interpretative efforts are necessary. Accordingly, these Articles may apply extraterritorially (at least) when the threshold to establish extraterritorial jurisdiction under general human rights treaties is met.

3.3 Substantive rights

Once a human rights treaty or the Refugee Convention applies, attention needs to be drawn to the substantive rights relevant to the course of the resettlement process.

3.3.1 Non-refoulement

Referred to as a fundamental principle governing the admission of non-nationals, human rights law, humanitarian law, refugee law and criminal law endorse the prohibition of *refoulement*. This principle "*includes at a minimum the absolute and underogable prohibition of refoulement toward a state where there is a real risk of torture, inhuman, or degrading treatment or punish-*

ment".[488] In terms of refugee law, *non-refoulement* is explicitly stipulated in Art 33 Refugee Convention.[489] Universal human rights treaties include explicit *non-refoulement* provisions, such as Art 3 para 1 CAT, and implicit *non-refoulement* provisions, namely Art 7 ICCPR, and Art 37 CRC;[490] examples of *non-refoulement* provisions in regional human rights treaties are Art 22 para 8 American Convention on Human Rights (ACHR)[491] (explicit), as well as Art 3 ECHR[492] and Art 5 Banjul Charter[493] (both implicit). In the EU law context, Art 19 para 2 Charter of Fundamental Rights of the European Union (the Charter)[494] sets out an explicit prohibition of *refoulement* and Art 4 Charter provides for an implicit prohibition of *refoulement* (for the applicability of Charter rights see 4.1.2.2).

The difference between explicit and implicit *refoulement* provisions is significant because the wording of explicit *refoulement* provisions may limit the application of the principle. For instance, a *refoulement* prohibition that is literally directed to those who have actually crossed the border of the receiving country is difficult to apply in the resettlement context – apart from its application in the (not less important) scenarios where beneficiaries already find themselves on the territory of the receiving country. For this reason, it is crucial to assess the content beyond the wording by applying the rules of interpretation under Art 31 para 3 lit c Vienna

488 Vincent Chetail, *International Migration Law*, 124; see Walter Kälin and Jörg Künzli, *The Law of International Human Rights Protection*, 324; see also *Chahal v United Kingdom* App No 22414/93 (ECtHR 15 November 1996) paras 78ff, 96.

489 See Vincent Chetail, *International Migration Law* 119.

490 See Annick Pijnenburg, 'Containment Instead of *Refoulement*: Shifting State Responsibility in the Age of Cooperative Migration Control' in (2020) Human Rights Law Review, 315f.

491 American Convention on Human Rights, OAS Treaty Series No 36 (adopted 22 November 1969, entered into force 18 July 1978) <https://www.oas.org/dil/treaties_b-32_american_convention_on_human_rights.pdf> accessed 13 May 2021.

492 The principle of *non-refoulement* is not explicitly contained in the ECHR; significantly, the ECtHR considers Art 3 ECHR as providing an effective means against all forms of return to places where there is a risk that an individual would be subjected to torture, or to inhuman or degrading treatment or punishment; see e.g., *Soering v United Kingdom* App No 14038/88 (ECtHR 7 July 1989).

493 African Charter on Human and Peoples' Rights (adopted 27 June 1981, entered into force 21 October 1986) 1520 UNTS 217 (Banjul Charter).

494 Art 19 para 2 Charter of Fundamental Rights of the European Union [2000] OJ C364/1-22 states: "*No one may be removed, expelled or extradited to a State where there is a serious risk that he or she would be subjected to the death penalty, torture or other inhuman or degrading treatment or punishment*".

Convention on the Law of Treaties (VCLT)[495] (an analysis of specific *non-refoulement* provisions is provided in the following sections 3.3.1.1 and 3.3.1.2). Beyond treaty law, commentators affirmed the customary law nature of the principle of *non-refoulement*.[496] Some commentators qualified the prohibition of *refoulement* as *jus cogens*.[497]

In practice, a state may violate the *non-refoulement* principle when it does not (fully) assess an individual's risk of being exposed to conditions where his or her right to life, or the prohibition of ill-treatment or torture, are at stake. A *non-refoulement* violation can already be triggered if a state *ought* to have known that it would expose an individual to such conditions,[498] including subsequent *refoulement*.[499] The required standard of the *non-refoulement* principle under customary international law is, for example, reflected in Guideline 3 of the guidance on how to reduce the risk of *refoulement* in external border management when working in or together with third countries, published by the EU Agency for Fundamental Rights (FRA). It states that third countries "*should not be requested to intercept*

495 See Vienna Convention on the Law of Treaties (adopted 23 May 1969, entered into force 27 January 1980) 1155 UNTS 331.

496 Evelien Wauters and Samuel Cogolati, 'Crossing the Mediterranean Sea: EU Migration Policies and Human Rights' in Valsamis Mitsilegas, Violeta Moreno-Lax and Niovi Vavoula (eds), *Securitising Asylum Flows: Deflection, Criminalisation and Challenges for Human Rights* (Brill 2020) 102 (105). The customary law nature of *non-refoulement* was acknowledged by non-treaty parties like Myanmar and Bangladesh. See Vincent Chetail, *International Migration Law*, 120ff; see also James C Hathaway, *The Rights of Refugees Under International Law*, 363-370; see also Guy S Goodwin-Gill and Jane McAdam, *The Refugee in International Law*, 345ff.

497 See Annick Pijnenburg, 'Containment Instead of *Refoulement*: Shifting State Responsibility in the Age of Cooperative Migration Control' in (2020) Human Rights Law Review, 316; see also Jean Allain, 'The Jus Cogens Nature of Non-Refoulement' in (2002) 13 International Journal of Refugee Law, 533-558.

498 See *MSS v Belgium and Greece* App No 30696/09 (ECtHR 21 January 2011) para 358: "*In the light of the foregoing, the Court considers that at the time of the applicant's expulsion the Belgian authorities knew or ought to have known that he had no guarantee that his asylum application would be seriously examined by the Greek authorities. They also had the means of refusing to transfer him*"; see also Christoph Grabenwarter, *European Convention on Human Rights: Commentary* (CH Beck/Hart/Nomos 2014) Art 3 ECHR, para 14; see also William A Schabas, *The European Convention on Human Rights: A Commentary* (Oxford University Press 2015) 96; see James C Hathaway, *The Rights of Refugees Under International Law*[2], 327: "*This risk may also follow from failure of even a carefully designed procedure to take notice of the most accurate human rights data*".

499 See James C Hathaway, *The Rights of Refugees Under International Law*[2], 367.

people on the move before they reach the EU external border, when it is known or ought to be known that the intercepted people would as a result face persecution or a real risk of other serious harm".[500]

Consequently, it arises from the principle of *non-refoulement* that – regardless of whether the refugee status determination procedure takes place at the border or within the territory of the State , certain basic procedural requirements (such as access to an appeal with automatic suspensive effect, where applicable) must be ensured.[501]

Must receiving countries conducting procedures concerning resettlement eligibility and status determination outside their territory uphold these procedural standards? The preliminary analysis about extraterritorial jurisdiction (see 3.2.1.2) suggests that the application of *non-refoulement* obligations under human rights treaties remains exceptional for receiving countries engaging in resettlement selection missions.

---

500 FRA, 'Guidance on how to reduce the risk of refoulement in external border management when working in or together with third countries' (5 December 2016) (emphasis added) 3 <https://fra.europa.eu/sites/default/files/fra_uploads/fra-2016-guidance-reducing-refoulement-risk-0_en.pdf> accessed 14 February 2021; see Nula Frei and Constantin Hruschka, 'Circumventing Non-Refoulement or Fighting "Illegal Migration"?' (*Eumigrationlawblog.eu*, 23 March 2018) <https://eumigrationlawblog.eu/circumventing-non-refoulement-or-fighting-illegal-migration/> accessed 14 February 2021.

501 See UNHCR EXCOM Conclusion No 8 (XXVIII) 'Determination of Refugee Status' (1977) <https://www.unhcr.org/excom/exconc/3ae68c6e4/determination-refugee-status.html> accessed 6 July 2022; UNHCR EXCOM Conclusion No 30 (XXXIV) 'The Problem of Manifestly Unfounded or Abusive Applications for Refugee Status or Asylum' (1983) <https://www.unhcr.org/excom/exconc/3ae68c6118/problem-manifestly-unfounded-abusive-applications-refugee-status-asylum.html> accessed 6 July 2022. See also Sibel Uranues, '"Pushback" – Rechtliches über das "Unwort des Jahres" 2021 (Teil I)' (*Blogasyl*, June 30, 2022) <https://www.blogasyl.at/2022/06/pushback-teil-1/> accessed 6 July 2022. Procedural requirements also arise from the prohibition of expulsion. "*In essence, the prohibition translates to a due process right for each individual to have the act of removal administratively and judicially assessed.*" David Cantor, Nikolas Feith Tan, Marianna Gkiliati, Elisabeth Mavropoulou et al, 'Externalisation, Access to Territorial Asylum, and International Law' in (2022) International Journal of Refugee Law, 17.

3.3.1.1 Human rights

The following analysis sheds light on whether specific *non-refoulement* obligations in human rights treaties, namely the CAT, ICCPR, the CRC or/and the ECHR, are applicable during resettlement operations.

3.3.1.1.1 Art 3 para 1 CAT

Art 3 para 1 CAT states that "[n]*o State Party shall expel, return ('refouler') or extradite a person* <u>*to another State*</u> *where there are substantial grounds for believing that he would be in danger of being subject to torture*".[502] This Article constitutes an example of an explicit *non-refoulement* provision.

The first element of the general rule on treaty interpretation (Art 31 para 1 VCLT) requires consideration of the ordinary meaning of the terms of a treaty. A literal reading of Art 3 para 1 CAT, namely not to "*expel, return ('refouler') or extradite a person to another State*", holds that this provision covers situations where a resettlement beneficiary has already been transferred to the territory of a receiving country and is then returned to another state, i.e. the country of (first) refuge or the home country. On the surface, returning a person to another state implies that this person has already reached the territory of the returning country. However, the Special Rapporteur on torture and other cruel, inhuman or degrading treatment or punishment pointed to situations where "*States operate and hold individuals abroad, as in the context of* [...] *offshore detention or refugee processing facilities*". He took the position that "[w]*henever States are operating extraterritorially and are in the position to transfer persons, the prohibition against non-refoulement applies in full.* [...] *A person under the authority of State agents anywhere cannot be returned when facing risk of torture*".[503]

The purpose of the CAT speaks in favor of extraterritorial applicability. The prohibitions of torture are universal and "[...] *the purpose of the CAT was to 'make more effective' those prohibitions, which were already universal, by creating express obligations on States to prevent, prosecute, and remedy viola-*

502 Art 3 para 1 CAT (emphasis added).

503 OHCHR, 'Interim report of the Special Rapporteur on torture and other cruel, inhuman or degrading treatment or punishment', UN Doc A/70/303 (7 August 2015) para 38 <https://www.ohchr.org/en/documents/thematic-reports/a77502-interim-report-special-rapporteur-torture-and-other-cruel-inhuman> accessed 5 May 2023.

tions, as the Preamble makes clear. [...] *This universal prohibition is illustrated by the number of provisions of the CAT that include no express territorial limit. These include the obligation* [...] *not to return individuals to torture (Art 3)* [...]".[504] That being said, Art 3 CAT – in contrast to other CAT provisions – does not set an express limit on its territorial scope, which can be interpreted as a manifestation of the universal nature of the prohibitions underlying the CAT.

Besides, "*any subsequent agreement between the parties regarding the interpretation of the treaty or the application of its provisions*" shall be taken into account (Art 31 para 3 lit a VCLT), including decisions of a treaty organ.[505] In this regard, the General Comments of the Committee against Torture provide interpretative guidance – even though they are not legally binding.[506] With regard to Art 3 CAT, General Comment No 4 (2007)[507] is pertinent. This General Comment supports to extend the wording of Art 3 para 1 CAT to cases of extraterritorial action when a Contracting State exercises jurisdiction. The Committee clarified in its General Comment No 4 para 10 that a Contracting State was bound to the principle of *non-refoulement* "*in any territory under its jurisdiction or any area under its control or authority, or on board a ship or aircraft registered in the State party, to any person, including persons requesting or in need of international protection*".

In line with the above analysis, *Koh*, the (then) Legal Advisor for the US Department of State concluded in his Memorandum of 21 January 2013 that "*exhaustive analysis of all available sources of treaty interpretation requires rejection of an interpretation that would impose a categorical bar against the Convention's extraterritorial scope* [...]. *The object and purpose, text and context of the CAT, the negotiating history of the Convention* [...] *all support these conclusions*".[508]

---

504 Sarah Cleveland, 'The United States and the Torture Convention, Part I: Extraterritoriality' (*Just Security*, 14 November 2014).

505 See Oliver Dörr in Oliver Dörr and Kirsten Schmalenbach (eds), *Vienna Convention on the Law of Treaties: A Commentary* (Springer 2nd ed 2018) para 76.

506 See Walter Kälin and Jörg Künzli, *The Law of International Human Rights Protection*, 214.

507 See Committee against Torture, 'General Comment No 4 (2017) on the implementation of Article 3 of the Convention in the context of Article 22', CAT/C/GC/4 (4 September 2018) <https://tbinternet.ohchr.org/_layouts/15/treatybodyexternal/Download.aspx?symbolno=CAT%2fC%2fGC%2f4&Lang=en> accessed 14 February 2021.

508 Harold Hongju Koh, 'Memorandum Opinion on the Geographic Scope of the Convention Against Torture and Its Application in Situations of Armed

It can be deduced from interpretation according to the VCLT that Art 3 para 1 CAT applies extraterritorially whenever a jurisdictional link exists (see 3.2.1),[509] provided that "*there are 'substantial grounds' for believing that the person concerned would be in danger of being subjected to torture in a State to which the person is facing deportation*".[510]

3.3.1.1.2 Arts 6 and 7 ICCPR

The ICCPR contains two provisions from which an implicit prohibition of *refoulement* has been derived. First, Art 6 para 1 ICCPR sets out that "[e]*very human being has the inherent right to life. This right shall be protected by law. No one shall be arbitrarily deprived of his life*". Next, Art 7 ICCPR (first sentence) stipulates that "[n]*o one shall be subjected to torture or to cruel, inhuman or degrading treatment or punishment*".

The Human Rights Committee interpreted Art 6 ICCPR as a *non-refoulement* obligation in its General Comment No 36.[511] In addition, the Committee dealt with Art 7 ICCPR in its General Comment No 20 as a *non-refoulement* prohibition requiring Contracting States not to expose individuals "*to the danger of torture or cruel, inhuman or degrading treatment or punishment upon return to another country by way of their extradition, expulsion or refoulement*".[512] With this statement, the Committee abided by the wording of Art 3 para 1 CAT. Eventually, in *Mohammad Munaf v Rumania*, the Committee acknowledged that the prohibition of *refoulement* under Arts 6 and 7 ICCPR did not depend on a physical border crossing. Instead, the Commission considered the exercise of jurisdiction as the main issue.[513]

Conflict' (21 January 2013) 6 <https://www.documentcloud.org/documents/20986585-20130121-dos-torture-convention> accessed 5 May 2023.

509 Committee against Torture, 'General Comment No 4 (2017) on the implementation of article 3 of the Convention in the context of article 22', CAT/C/GC/4 (4 September 2018) para 11.

510 Ibid para 12.

511 OHCHR, 'General Comment No 36: Article 6 (Right to Life)', UN Doc CCPR/C/GC/36 (3 September 2019) para 31.

512 OHCHR, 'General Comment No 20: Article 7 (Prohibition of torture, or other cruel, inhuman or degrading treatment or punishment)', UN Doc HRI/GEN/1/Rev9 (Vol I) (10 March 1992) para 9 <https://www.refworld.org/docid/453883fb0.html> accessed 14 February 2021.

513 See OHCHR, 'Communication No 1539/2006: Mohammad Munaf v Romania', UN Doc CCPR/C/96/D/1539/2006 (21 August 2009) para 14.2 <https://www.re

As regards the answer whether a state exercises extraterritorial jurisdiction during resettlement selection missions, it has already been pointed out that the Human Rights Committee itself referred to the exercise of power or effective control over the right to life of a person as jurisdictional threshold (see 3.2.1). If targeted actions of the receiving country concerning its resettlement policy implementation have direct and foreseeable effects on the *non-refoulement* rights derived from Arts 6 and 7 ICCPR, the receiving country is arguably bound by these provisions, irrespective of whether the individual has already reached their territory.

For climate migrants (see 2.5.4.3), the Human Rights Committee has generally accepted the application of the *non-refoulement* principle in relation to life-threatening conditions caused by climate change. While the Committee rejected the appeal of Ioane Teitiota,[514] it "*accepted, in principle that it is unlawful for states to send people to places where the impacts of climate change expose them to life-threatening risks or a risk of cruel, inhuman, or degrading treatment*".[515] Specifically, the Committee observed that "*it and regional human rights tribunals have established that environmental degradation can compromise effective enjoyment of the right to life, and that severe environmental degradation can adversely affect an individual's well-being and lead to a violation of the right to life*".[516] In the specific case of Ioane Teitiota, the Committee found, however, that Kiribati could still take measures to remedy and prevent harm, though the Committee did not

---

fworld.org/cases,HRC,4acf500d2.html> accessed 14 February 2021: "*The main issue to be considered by the Committee is whether, by allowing the author to leave the premises of the Romanian Embassy in Baghdad, it exercised jurisdiction over him in a way that exposed him to a real risk of becoming a victim of violations of his rights under articles 6, 7, 9, 10, paragraph 1 and 14 of the Covenant, which it could reasonably have anticipated.*"

514 See OHCHR, 'Communication No 2728/2016: Ione Teitiota v New Zealand', UN Doc CCPR/C/127/D/2728/2016 (23 September 2020) para 9.11 <https://demaribus.files.wordpress.com/2020/02/2728-2016.pdf> accessed 19 June 2021.

515 Jane McAdam, 'Protecting People Displaced by the Impacts of Climate Change: The UN Human Rights Committee and the Principle of Non-refoulement' (2020) 114 American Journal of International Law 4, 708 (708); see also Katharine M Donato, Amanda Carrico and Jonathan M Gilligan, 'As more climate migrants cross borders seeking refuge, laws will need to adapt' (*The Conversation*, 8 June 2021) <https://theconversation.com/as-more-climate-migrants-cross-borders-seeking-refuge-laws-will-need-to-adapt-159673> accessed 16 June 2021.

516 OHCHR, 'Communication No 2728/2016: Ione Teitiota v New Zealand', UN Doc CCPR/C/127/D/2728/2016 (23 September 2020) para 9.5. See also ibid paras 8.6, 9.4.

clearly specify them. This means that future cases need to clarify when the threshold is met so that no measures can still be taken to prevent a life-threatening situation and, thus *non-refoulement* would apply. In such situations, provided that the conditions for extraterritorial jurisdiction are met, *non-refoulement* obligations could also arise for receiving countries towards climate migrants.

3.3.1.1.3 Art 37 lit a CRC

Art 37 lit a CRC states that "[n]*o child shall be subjected to torture or other cruel, inhuman or degrading treatment or punishment.* [...]". The Committee on the Rights of the Child clarified that Contracting Parties to the CRC face an implicit obligation not to return a child to a country when there are substantial grounds for assuming a real risk of irreparable harm. This obligation mainly concerns Arts 6 (right to life) and 37 CRC (stated above) but is not limited to those provisions.[517]

It shall be noted upfront that in the specific context of the rights of the child, the assessment of the risk of irreparable harm must be conducted more thoroughly than with regard to adults.[518]

The Committee on the Rights of the Child did not address extraterritorial *refoulement* obligations in its General Comment No 6.[519] However, it affirmed the extraterritorial application of *non-refoulement* with regard to Art 38 CRC, a provision concerning recruitment and participation in hostilities.[520] While the Committee made reference to "*the borders*" of a state which militates against the application in the resettlement selection process, it also used the expression "*in any manner whatsoever*", which is the wording of Art 33 para 1 Refugee Convention and indicates that the prohibition includes multiple types of state actions (see 3.3.1.2).

Furthermore, interpretation in consideration of other applicable treaties pursuant to Art 31 para 3 lit c VCLT suggests that the extraterritorial application of Art 37 lit a CRC in the resettlement (selection) process is ex-

---

517 See Committee on the Rights of the Child, 'General Comment No 6: Treatment of Unaccompanied and Separated Children Outside Their Country of Origin' (1 September 2006) 10, para 13 <https://digitallibrary.un.org/record/566055?ln=en> accessed 14 February 2021.

518 See ibid 10, para 27.

519 See ibid 10, para 27.

520 See ibid 10, para 28.

ceptionally possible, subject to the condition that the prospective receiving country exercises jurisdiction.

3.3.1.1.4 Arts 2 and 3 ECHR

In the regional European context, Art 2 para 1 ECHR sets forth that "[e]*veryone's right to life shall be protected by law. No one shall be deprived of his life intentionally save in the execution of a sentence of a court following his conviction of a crime for which this penalty is provided by law*". Furthermore, Art 3 ECHR states that "[n]*o one shall be subjected to torture or to inhuman or degrading treatment or punishment*". Both Articles inhere an implicit *refoulement* prohibition.[521] However, this does not answer the question whether a country is obligated to extraterritorially *admit* an individual if the individual would otherwise be subject to treatment contrary to Arts 2 and/or 3 ECHR.

Famously, in the *Hirsi Jamaa* judgement, the ECtHR found that Italy violated Art 3 ECHR and Art 4 Protocol No 4 to the ECHR.[522] Italy should have known that the return of Somali and Eritrean migrants intercepted by Italian ships (on these ships Italy exercised jurisdiction based on the flag principle) in the Mediterranean Sea, i.e. outside Italy's territorial waters, exposed them to the risk of serious human rights violations in Libya and arbitrary repatriation to Eritrea and Somalia.[523]

Furthermore, the ECtHR affirmed that obligations under Art 3 ECHR existed irrespective of any physical border crossing. For instance, in *Al-Sadoon and Mufdhi v United Kingdom*, the Court held that the transfer of detainees from British to Iraqi custody, i.e. a situation of physical *de facto* control, involved a breach of Art 3 ECHR because this transfer exposed

521 See Christoph Grabenwarter, *European Convention on Human Rights: Commentary* (CH Beck/Hart/Nomos 2014) Art 2 ECHR, para 5; see also ibid Art 3 ECHR, paras 13f; see also *Bader and Others v Sweden* App No 13284/04 (ECtHR 8 November 2005) paras 42, 48; see also *Saadi v Italy* App No 37201/06 (ECtHR 28 February 2008) para 125; see also *Tarakhel v Switzerland* App No 29217/12 (ECtHR 4 November 2014) para 122.

522 See Protocol No 4 to the Convention for the Protection of Human Rights and Fundamental Freedoms, securing certain rights and freedoms other than those already included in the Convention and in the first Protocol thereto (entered into force 2 May 1968) ETS No 46.

523 See *Hirsi Jamaa & Others v Italy* App No 27765/09 (ECtHR 23 February 2012), paras 137, 158, 186.

the affected individuals to a real risk of being sentenced to death and executed.[524]

Nonetheless, the ECtHR has yet to refrain from extending the scope of *non-refoulement* under the ECHR to a positive obligation (under the condition that the state exercises jurisdiction) to offer legal pathways such as resettlement. Specifically, it avoided to do so in *ND and NT v Spain*.[525] In this case, the ECtHR dealt with the Spanish policy of 'hot expulsions' of irregular migrants and thereby addressed the prohibition of collective expulsion pursuant to Art 4 Protocol No 4 to the ECHR.[526] The Court denied a violation of this Article because the applicants brought themselves in the situation of collective expulsion and did not make use of the possibility of entering Spain by legal means. At the same time, the ECtHR expressly set out the requirement for Contracting States to "*make available genuine and effective access to means of legal entry*", which allowed "*all persons who face persecution to submit an application for protection*".[527] However, it cannot be implied that this (vague) reference to legal pathways triggers an autonomous positive obligation for prospective receiving countries under Art 3 ECHR. When relying on the applicant's self-caused forfeit by not taking recourse to legal pathways, the ECtHR solely commented on Art 4 Protocol No 4 to the ECHR but refrained from considering Art 3 ECHR.[528] Essentially, Art 4 Protocol No 4 to the ECHR differs from Art 3 ECHR because it does not deal with torture, inhuman or degrading treatment in the country of (first) refuge or in the home country.[529]

Also, in the subsequent case of *Shahzad v Hungary*, where the ECtHR specified the standards set out in *ND and NT*, the Court did not compre-

524 See *Al-Sadoon and Mufdhi v United Kingdom* App No 61498/08, Merits and Just Satisfaction (ECtHR 2 March 2010) para 143.

525 See *ND and NT v Spain* App No 8675/15 and 8697/15 (ECtHR 13 February 2020).

526 See Daniel Thym, 'A Restrictionist Revolution?: A Counter-Intuitive Reading of the ECtHR's ND & NT-Judgment on 'Hot Expulsions' at the Spanish-Moroccan Border' (*Verfassungsblog*, 17 February 2020) <https://verfassungsblog.de/a-restrictionist-revolution/> accessed 15 February 2021.

527 *ND and NT v Spain*, paras 209, 229.

528 See Sarah Progin-Theuerkauf, 'Grenzen des Verbots von Kollektivausweisungen: Das Urteil des EGMR im Fall ND und NT gegen Spanien' in (2020) sui generis, 309 (314, para 26).

529 See ibid 311, para 10. See also Constantin Hruschka, 'Hot Returns Remain Contrary to the ECHR: ND & NT before the ECHR' (*Eumigrationlawblog.eu*, 28 February 2020) <https://eumigrationlawblog.eu/hot-returns-remain-contrary-to-the-echr-nd-nt-before-the-echr/> accessed 6 July 2022.

hensively comment on Art 3 ECHR. It is notable though, that the ECtHR expressly highlighted the importance that entry points "*secure the right to request protection under the Convention, and in particular Article 3, in a genuine and effective manner*"[530]. Sure, this does not answer the question of extraterritorial *non-refoulement* obligations to admit persons in need for protection. Instead, as regards (extra)territoriality, *Shahzad v Hungary* confronted the ECtHR with a new situation, namely the mirror question of whether expulsion can take place before having crossed the border.[531]

The ECtHR's strong insistence on the access to legal pathways in *Shahzad v Hungary* (and also *MH v Croatia*[532]) could have been interpreted as signaling to Contracting States an obligation to provide legal pathways.[533] However, in *AA and others v North Macedonia*[534], the ECtHR took a more restrictive stance than in *ND and NT* and found the applicants culpable of circumventing legal pathways, even though such pathways were arguably not available in practice.

Overall, the ECtHR has not provided clarity about the existence of an obligation to provide legal pathways. It avoided to deal with Art 3 ECHR in *ND and NT v Spain* and subsequent case law, and it denied jurisdiction in respect of this Article in *MN and others v Belgium* (see 3.2.1). Given these considerations, a definitive answer from the ECtHR regarding the question whether a receiving country is obligated to extraterritorially *admit* a potential resettlement beneficiary if he or she would otherwise be subject to treatment contrary to Arts 2 and/or 3 ECHR is still missing.

---

530 *Shahzad v Hungary* App No 12625/17 (ECtHR 8 July 2021) para 62.

531 Outside the border fence in Hungary remains a strip of land that is still Hungarian territory, and the Court held that this did not preclude expulsion. See ibid para 49; see also Dana Schmalz, 'Rights that are not Illusory' (*Verfassungsblog*, 9 July 2021) <https://verfassungsblog.de/rights-that-are-not-illusory/> accessed 9 July 2021.

532 *MH and others v Croatia* App Nos 15670/18 and 43115/18 (ECtHR 4 April 2022).

533 See Vera Wriedt, 'Expanding Exceptions? AA and Others v North Macedonia, Systematic Pushbacks and the Fiction of Legal Pathways' (*Eumigrationlawblog.eu*, 7 June 2022) <https://eumigrationlawblog.eu/expanding-exceptions-aa-and-others-v-north-macedonia-systematic-pushbacks-and-the-fiction-of-legal-pathways/> accessed 7 July 2022.

534 *AA and others v North Macedonia* App Nos 55798/16 and 4 others (ECtHR 2nd Section 5 April 2022).

3.3.1.2 Refugee law

Art 33 para 1 Refugee Convention states:[535]

> *No Contracting State shall expel or return ("refouler") a refugee in any manner whatsoever* <u>*to the frontiers of territories*</u> *where his life or freedom would be threatened on account of his race, religion, nationality, membership of a particular social group or political opinion.*

The wording of Art 33 para 1 Refugee Convention addresses cases where a receiving country expels or returns refugees to the country of (first) refuge or to their home country.

According to the observations of the English Court of Appeal in the *Prague Airport* case, Art 33 Refugee Convention "*cannot comprehend action which causes someone to remain on the same side of the frontier as they began; nor indeed could such a person be said to have been returned to any frontier*".[536]

In the earlier *Sale* case[537], the US Circuit Courts and the US Supreme Court dealt with Haitians who were interdicted on the high seas and returned home. The UNHCR submitted an *amicus curiae* brief, claiming that the *non-refoulement* obligation was binding regardless of whether the return decision concerned a person inside or outside the state's territory taking the return decision.[538] The US Supreme Court rejected such broad scope of the principle of *non-refoulement* and concluded as follows:[539]

> [...] *a treaty cannot impose uncontemplated extraterritorial obligations on those who ratify it through no more than its general humanitarian intent. Because the text of Article 33 cannot reasonably be read to say anything at all about a nation's actions toward aliens outside its own territory, it does not prohibit such actions.*

Subsequently, Judge *Albuquerque* criticized in his Concurring Opinion to the *Hirsi Jamaa* ruling of the ECtHR that the Supreme Court's interpreta-

---

535 Art 33 para 1 Refugee Convention (emphasis added).

536 *R (European Roma Rights Centre and Others) v Immigration Officer at Prague Airport* [2003] EWCA Civ 666 (Eng CA, 20 May 2003) para 31.

537 See *Acting Commissioner, Immigration and Naturalization Service, et al v Haitian Centers Council, Inc* 509 US 155, 113 S Ct 2549 (1993) <https://cdn.loc.gov/service/ll/usrep/usrep509/usrep509155/usrep509155.pdf> accessed 15 February 2021.

538 See UNHCR, *The Haitian Interdiction Case* 1993, Brief *Amicus Curiae* in (1994) 6 International Journal of Refugee Law 85, 94-97.

539 *Acting Commissioner, Immigration and Naturalization Service, et al v Haitian Centers Council, Inc* 509 US 155 (158) (1993).

tion of Art 33 Refugee Convention was contrary to the common rules on treaty interpretation.[540]

> *With all due respect, the United States Supreme Court's interpretation contradicts the literal and ordinary meaning of the language of Article 33 of the United Nations Convention relating to the Status of Refugees and departs from the common rules of treaty interpretation.*

Judge *Albuquerque* raised, amongst others, two essential points demonstrating that already the ordinary meaning of the terms of Art 33 para 1 Refugee Convention speaks in favor of extraterritorial *refoulement* obligations. First, he pointed out that unlike most other provisions in the Refugee Convention, the application of Art 33 para 1 Refugee Convention did not depend on the presence of a refugee in the territory of a receiving Contracting State (see 3.2.2). Second, he asserted that the expression "*in any manner whatsoever*" included "*all types of State actions to expel, extradite or remove an alien in need of international protection*"[541] – subject to a state's exercise of jurisdiction.

Even if one is not convinced that the literal text of Art 33 Refugee Convention already includes extraterritorial *non-refoulement* obligations, the purpose of the Refugee Convention supports the argument that extraterritorial *refoulement* obligations can be derived from Art 33 Refugee Convention and directed at refugees who have not left the territory of the country of (first) refuge or their home country yet. According to its Preamble, the Refugee Convention endeavors to ensure refugees "*the widest possible exercise*" of fundamental rights and freedoms. *Kälin et al* contend that an interpretation "*that allowed measures whereby a State, acting outside its territory, returns or otherwise transfers refugees to a country where they risk persecution would be fundamentally inconsistent with the purpose of the 1951 Convention and 1967 Protocol*".[542] In this vein, *Hathaway* highlighted that

---

540 See Walter Kälin, Martina Caroni and Lukas Heim in Andreas Zimmermann (ed), *The 1951 Convention Relating to the Status of Refugees and its 1967 Protocol*, Art 33 para 1 Refugee Convention, para 91; see also James C Hathaway, *The Rights of Refugees Under International Law*, 339; see also *Hirsi Jamaa & Others v Italy*, Concurring Opinion of Judge Pinto Albuquerque, 67.

541 *Hirsi Jamaa & Others v Italy*, Concurring Opinion of Judge Pinto Albuquerque, 68.

542 Walter Kälin, Martina Caroni and Lukas Heim in Andreas Zimmermann (ed), *The 1951 Convention Relating to the Status of Refugees and its 1967 Protocol*, Art 33 para 1 Refugee Convention, para 89.

"*the essential purpose of the Refugee Convention is to provide rights to seriously at-risk persons able to escape from their own countries*".[543]

Consequently, the essential purpose of the Refugee Convention would be undermined if Art 33 Refugee Convention was not extraterritorially applicable. As outlined, the prevailing opinion supports that this Article applies extraterritorially where Contracting States exercise jurisdiction (see 3.2.2).

3.3.1.3 Concluding remarks

The overall disputed extraterritorial application of the *non-refoulement* principle[544] suggests that the respective provisions in general human rights treaties and the Refugee Convention show differences, which in turn made it necessary to analyze the provisions separately. The findings revealed interpretative arguments in favor of extraterritorial *refoulement* obligations, provided that states exercise jurisdiction.

Starting with Art 3 para 1 CAT, the mere interpretation of the wording of this explicit *refoulement* provision makes a claim for extraterritorial *non-refoulement* obligations in the resettlement context difficult because at first glance, return "*to another State*" presupposes a prior border crossing. However, the Special Rapporteur as well as the Committee against Torture acknowledged that returns are not contingent on the territory of the returning Contracting State and that this Article applies extraterritorially where that State exercises jurisdiction.

In a similar vein, the Human Rights Committee interpreted the implicit *refoulement* obligations derived from Arts 6 and 7 ICCPR to apply extraterritorially in cases where a Contracting State exercises jurisdiction.

With regard to Art 37 lit a CRC, an implicit *non-refoulement* provision, interpretative guidance from the Committee on the Rights of the Child, together with an interpretation pursuant to Art 31 para 3 lit c VCLT in light of the CAT, the ICCPR and the Refugee Convention indicate that

---

543 James C Hathaway, *The Rights of Refugees Under International Law*, 338 (emphasis added).

544 See e.g., Thomas Gammeltoft-Hansen, *Access to asylum: international refugee law and the globalisation of migration control* (Cambridge University Press 2011); see also Marko Milanovic in Thomas Gammeltoft-Hansen and Jens Vedsted-Hansen (eds), *Human rights and the dark side of globalisation: Transnational law enforcement and migration control*, 53-78.

this Article inheres extraterritorial *non-refoulement* obligations once a state exercises jurisdiction.

In terms of the implicit *non-refoulement* obligations under Arts 2 and 3 ECHR, ECtHR case law does not provide definite answers whether a Contracting State is obligated to extraterritorially *admit* (e.g. via resettlement) an individual if the individual would otherwise be subject to treatment contrary to Arts 2 and/or 3 ECHR.

Finally, it is claimed that extraterritorial *non-refoulement* obligations can be deduced from the wording of Art 33 para 1 Refugee Convention. Interpreting this Article in the light of the object and purpose of the Refugee Convention strengthens this argument.

All of the analyzed provisions allow for interpretation in favor of extraterritorial *non-refoulement* obligations. This, however, does not mean that any extraterritorial rejection of admission, namely any non-selection of potential resettlement beneficiaries, constitutes a violation of the *non-refoulement* principle. The core question is whether the receiving country exercises jurisdiction. In most cases, such jurisdictional link cannot be established and the *non-refoulement* obligations are left to the state on whose territory resettlement beneficiaries are located.[545] Still, it cannot be ruled out that in particular situations, the receiving country exercises jurisdiction due to effective control over the resettlement candidate's *non-refoulement* right through targeted actions of its officials that directly and foreseeably affect this right and/or physical control over an individual (e.g. when the individual is deprived of its liberty and held in a certain location, such as a military basis, where the receiving country has exclusive legal authority) during vetting procedures. In such situations, the receiving country might violate applicable *non-refoulement* provisions when deporting individuals who do not pass the vetting process.[546]

545 As mentioned above, there may be rare exceptions, for example, when the application of the law of the host country is excluded on the basis of a written agreement, such as a Status of Forces Agreement.

546 For example, the US conduct of vetting procedures in Kosovo at Camp Bondsteel. See Janine Prantl, 'Afghan Mass Displacement: The American Response in Light of International Human Rights and Refugee Law, and the Need for International Cooperation to achieve a Satisfactory Solution' in (2022) ALJ, 17-46.

3.3.2 Right to leave and to seek asylum

Forced migrants not only face *refoulement* by (prospective) receiving countries. Even before taking on their journey, home countries as well as countries of (first) refuge might interfere with the right to leave by preventing them from leaving their territory. Moreover, "[t]*he non-refoulement principle* [...] *falls short of granting asylum in the sense of permission to enter and remain on the state's territory*."[547] Thus, the question arises whether prospective receiving countries, when implementing resettlement policies on foreign territory, breach the right to seek asylum and the right not to be punished for irregularly entering a country.[548]

3.3.2.1 Human rights

The right to leave the country of one's presence constitutes the prerequisite to seek international protection in a foreign country. In contemporary international law, such right is proclaimed in the non-binding Art 13 para 2 UDHR.[549] In line with the UDHR, the ICCPR, as a binding treaty, reiterates that "*everyone shall be free to leave any country, including its own*".[550] Furthermore, in the European regional setting, Art 2 para 2 Protocol 4 ECHR states that "*everyone shall be free to leave any country, including his own*". Eventually, the right to leave has been established as a rule of customary international law.[551]

In essence, the right to leave is an independent right[552] that exists irrespective of whether there exists a right to enter a specific country of destination.[553] The substantive scope of the right to leave primarily

---

547 Nikolas Feith Tan, 'International models of deterrence and the future of access to asylum' in Satvinder Singh Juss (ed), *Research Handbook on International Refugee Law* (Edward Elgar 2019) 170.

548 See Sabrina Ardalan, 'EU and US Border Policy: Externalisation of Migration Control and Violation of the Right to Asylum' in Valsamis Mitsilegas, Violeta Moreno-Lax and Niovi Vavoula (eds), *Securitising Asylum Flows: Deflection, Criminalisation and Challenges for Human Rights* (Brill 2020) 282 (308ff).

549 "*Everyone has the right to leave any country, including his own, and the right to return to his country*".

550 Art 12 para 2 ICCPR; see Vincent Chetail, *International Migration Law*, 80.

551 See Vincent Chetail, *International Migration Law*, 85ff.

552 See Elspeth Guild and Vladislava Stoyanova in Wolfgang Benedek et al (eds) *European Yearbook on Human Rights 2018*, 382.

553 See ibid 382, 385.

contains a negative duty not to restrict exit and a positive duty to issue travel documents.[554]

With regard to the implementation of resettlement policies, the right to leave has gained relevance. Receiving countries have developed control policies to prevent irregular migration flows, whereas countries of (first) refuge have acted as gate keepers. This entails that countries of (first) refuge engage in practices that can negatively affect the right to leave, e.g. Libyan coast guards (as a result of EU support to Libya[555], agreements between Libya and Italy[556], and between Malta and Libya); Morocco stopping people crossing into Spanish enclaves of Melilla and Ceuta;[557] or Mali deploying personnel at the border to Niger and Burkina Faso[558].[559] This raises the question whether the right to leave can be addressed to the countries of first refuge and/or to receiving countries.

The right to leave is not absolute. Restrictions of Art 12 para 2 ICCPR must be (i) provided by law and (ii) necessary to protect national security, public order, public health or morals, or the right and freedoms of others.

---

554 See for passport refusal *Stamose v Bulgaria* App No 29713/05 (ECtHR 27 November 2012); see also Elspeth Guild and Vladislava Stoyanova in Wolfgang Benedek et al (eds) *European Yearbook on Human Rights 2018*, 384.

555 See Commission, 'EU Trust Fund for Africa: new actions adopted to support vulnerable migrants, foster socio-economic development and improve border management in North of Africa' (14 December 2018) <Commission, 'EU Trust Fund for Africa: new actions adopted to support vulnerable migrants, foster socio-economic development and improve border management in North of Africa' (14 December 2018) <https://ec.europa.eu/commission/presscorner/detail/ro/IP_18_6793> accessed 8 July 2022.

556 Memorandum d'intesa sulla cooperazione nel campo dello sviluppo, del contrasto all'immigrazione illegale, al traffico di esseri umani, al contrabbando e sul rafforzamento della sicurezza delle frontiere tra lo Stato della Libia e la Repubblica Italiana (February 2017, renewed in 2020) <https://www.governo.it/sites/governo.it/files/Libia.pdf> accessed 8 July 2022; Memorandum of Understanding Between the Government of National Accord of the State of Libya and The Government of The Republic of Malta in the Field of Combatting Illegal Immigration (28 May 2020) <https://www.statewatch.org/media/documents/news/2020/jun/malta-libya-mou-immigration.pdf> accessed 8 July 2022.

557 See 'Morocco: 18 migrants die in attempt to enter Spain's Melilla' (*Al Jazeera*, updated 25 June 2022) <https://www.aljazeera.com/news/2022/6/24/hundreds-of-migrants-storm-border-fence-in-spains-melilla> accessed 8 July 2022.

558 See 'After Mali exit, Niger accepts foreign forces to secure border' (*Al Jazeera*, 18 February 2022) <https://www.aljazeera.com/news/2022/2/18/after-mali-exit-niger-accepts-foreign-forces-to-secure-border> accessed 8 July 2022.

559 See Elspeth Guild and Vladislava Stoyanova in Wolfgang Benedek et al (eds) *European Yearbook on Human Rights 2018*, 377.

Furthermore, restrictive measures must conform with the principle of proportionality.[560] Scholars have agreed that general measures limiting the right to leave on a massive scale are incompatible with the right to leave if no proportionality assessment has been made in relation to the specific individuals affected.[561]

The most obvious addressee for responsibility in case of a respective human rights violation is the state where the individual concerned is physically present and which he or she seeks to leave, i.e. the country of (first) refuge. Besides, receiving countries could become responsible for violations of the right to leave by countries of (first) refuge due to aid or assistance (see 3.4.1).

As counterpart to the right to leave, the UDHR accounts for the right to seek asylum. It was first addressed in Art 14 UDHR, stating that "[e]*veryone has the right to seek and to enjoy in other countries asylum from persecution*". However, this provision is neither legally binding nor has it reached the (secured) status of international customary law.[562] It does not guarantee that asylum is actually granted if the required conditions are fulfilled. Beyond the UDHR, there is no right to seek and be granted asylum in general human rights law.[563] It follows that under international human rights law, individuals in need for resettlement cannot invoke a right to seek for and to be granted asylum in a receiving country.

Being particularly vulnerable, children enjoy protection under Art 22 CRC. According to the Committee on the Rights of the Child, this Article sets out a right for children to access asylum procedures and other

560 See OHCHR, 'General Comment No 27: Article 12 (Freedom of Movement)', UN Doc CCPR/C/21/Rev1/Add 9 (2 November 1999) para 14 <https://www.refworld.org/docid/45139c394.html> accessed 16 February 2021; see also Vincent Chetail, *International Migration Law*, 82.

561 See Annick Pijnenburg, 'Containment Instead of *Refoulement*: Shifting State Responsibility in the Age of Cooperative Migration Control' in (2020) Human Rights Law Review, 321; see also Elspeth Guild and Vladislava Stoyanova in Wolfgang Benedek et al (eds) *European Yearbook on Human Rights 2018*, 393.

562 See Andreas Th Müller, 'Solidarität in der gemeinsamen europäischen Asylpolitik' in (2015) Zeitschrift für öffentliches Recht, 463 (471).

563 See Vincent Chetail, *International Migration Law*, 191. See also Michael Lysander Fremuth, 'Access Denied? – Human Rights Approaches to Compensate forthe Absence of a Right to Be Granted Asylum' in (2020) 4 University of Vienna Law Review 1 Special Issue: Slovenian-Austrian Law Conference, 79 (85ff).

complementary mechanisms providing international protection.[564] Resettlement constitutes such – possible but not mandatory – complementary mechanism. The Committee on the Rights of the Child encourages states to "*provide resettlement opportunities in order to meet all the resettlement needs related to unaccompanied and separated children*".[565]

3.3.2.2 Refugee law

As opposed to human rights law, the Refugee Convention does not expressly state a right to leave but a right to be issued identity papers as well as travel documents. Art 27 Refugee Convention obliges Contracting States to issue identity papers "*to any refugee in the territory who does not possess a valid travel document*". This means that any refugee in the territory of a Contracting State can invoke Art 27 Refugee Convention when he or she is not in the possession of travel documents. Art 27 Refugee Convention also applies to asylum seekers not yet lawfully registered in the territory of a Contracting State who are in need of such document to prove refugee status.[566] Furthermore, a refugee can claim travel documents from a Contracting State under Art 28 para 1 Refugee Convention for the purpose of travel outside their territory. As opposed to Art 27 Refugee Convention, its Art 28 demands lawful stay. Moreover, the latter Article allows a Contracting State to refrain from issuing travel documents if there are compelling reasons of national security or public order.

For the resettlement process, this means that any country of (first) refuge that is party to the Refugee Convention has the obligation under Art 27 of this Convention to issue identity papers to those refugees who do not possess travel documents. Notably, however, Art 27 Refugee Convention does not state the specific nature of identity papers which must be issued.[567] Still, some receiving countries may require travel documents,

564 See Committee on the Rights of the Child, 'General Comment No 6: Treatment of Unaccompanied and Separated Children Outside Their Country of Origin' (1 September 2006) 19, para 66.

565 Ibid 26, para 94.

566 See James C Hathaway, *The Rights of Refugees Under International Law*, 626.

567 Circumvention of documentation obligations is even more problematic considering that a large number of Contracting States reaffirmed their commitment to registration and documentation and individualized status determination in the non-binding Global compact on refugees (GCR) and Global Compact for Migration (GCM). [see GCR para 58 (committing to support States in expand-

which potential resettlement beneficiaries cannot claim from countries of (first) refuge if they are not lawfully present there.

What is more, the Refugee Convention lacks a comprehensive right to seek and to be granted asylum.[568] As a minimum, Art 31 Refugee Convention prohibits Contracting States to "*impose penalties, on account of their illegal entry or presence, on refugees* [...] *provided they present themselves without delay to the authorities and show good cause for their illegal entry or presence*". Effective implementation of Art 31 Refugee Convention requires clear legislative or administrative action ensuring that penalties are not imposed. While the term 'penalty' is not defined under this Article, consideration of general human rights law suggests a notion going beyond criminal law, focusing on whether the respective measure is reasonable and necessary, as opposed to arbitrary and discriminatory.[569]

In this vein, the UNHCR Executive Committee emphasized that states are required to grant protection seekers access to their territory and to fair and efficient asylum procedures.[570] Also, the Michigan Guidelines on Freedom of Movement point out that states must provide reasonable access and opportunity for a protection claim to be made. Thus, they may not lawfully construct or maintain a physical barrier that fails to provide protection seekers access to their territory.[571]

---

ing capacity for registration and documentation); GCM Objective 7, para 23 lit h (undertaking to enable individual status assessments of all migrants).]

568 Some scholars have argued in favor of an implicit right to seek asylum derived from the Refugee Convention; see French delegate cited in Alice Edwards, 'Human Rights, Refugees and the Right 'to Enjoy' Asylum' in (2005) 17 International Journal of Refugee Law, 293 (301); see Sabrina Ardalan in Valsamis Mitsilegas, Violeta Moreno-Lax and Niovi Vavoula (eds), *Securitising Asylum Flows: Deflection, Criminalisation and Challenges for Human Rights*, 308; see also Guy S Goodwin-Gill and Jane McAdam, *The Refugee in International Law*, Chapters 5 to 7.

569 See Guy S Goodwin-Gill, 'Article 31 of the 1951 Convention Relating to the Status of Refugees: non-penalization, detention, and protection' (2001) 193ff <https://www.unhcr.org/en-us/publications/legal/419c778d4/refugee-protection-international-law-article-31-1951-convention-relating.html> accessed 8 July 2022.

570 See UNHCR, 'Advisory Opinion on the Extraterritorial Application of Non-Refoulement Obligations under the 1951 Convention relating to the Status of Refugees and its 1967 Protocol' (26 January 2007) 3 <https://www.refworld.org/docid/45f17a1a4.html> accessed 16 February 2021.

571 See University of Michigan Law School, 'The Michigan Guidelines on Refugee Freedom of Movement' (May 2017) para 10.

3.3.2.3 Concluding remarks on the right to leave and to seek asylum

International and European human rights law acknowledges an independent right to leave. This right can be at stake when receiving countries implement resettlement policies in cooperation with countries of (first) refuge. In contrast, refugee law does not include a right to leave. The Refugee Convention recognizes the difficulties faced by refugees in leaving the territory of a country and has for this reason imposed obligations on Contracting States to provide identity papers and travel documents.

A right to seek and be granted asylum in the receiving country is established neither under international human rights nor refugee law. In the context of resettlement, this means that a potential resettlement beneficiary cannot invoke an international right to seek and be granted asylum towards a potential receiving country during selection missions.

3.3.3 Procedural rights

Receiving countries are obliged to grant due process guarantees under international and European human rights and international refugee law in the resettlement process, although this process itself is not regulated through binding international law. Such guarantees are particularly important in the resettlement selection, namely in case of a negative selection decision (see 5.2.3.9).

3.3.3.1 Human rights

A potential resettlement beneficiary who obtains a negative selection decision may want to appeal against it. This raises the question of whether human rights law stipulates a right to an effective review.

As a starting point, it must be noted that the Human Rights Committee and the ECtHR considered that the right to a fair trial does not apply to decisions of entry, stay or expulsion of aliens because they do not include a determination of civil rights or criminal obligations as required under the respective provisions in the ICCPR and the ECHR.[572]

572 See Vincent Chetail, *International Migration Law*, 141.

In this light, Art 14 para 1 ICCPR expressly links due process rights to the determination of "*any criminal charge*" and of "*rights and obligations in a suit at law*":

> *All persons shall be equal before the courts and tribunals. In the determination of any criminal charge against him, or of his rights and obligations in a suit at law, everyone shall be entitled to a fair and public hearing by a competent, independent and impartial tribunal established by law.*

The Human Rights Committee specified in its General Comment No 32 that the right to access a court or a tribunal pursuant to Art 14 ICCPR "*does not apply to extradition, expulsion and deportation procedures*".[573]

Similarly, Art 6 ECHR restricts the entitlement to a "*fair and public hearing within a reasonable time by an independent and impartial tribunal established by law*" to the determination of civil rights and obligations as well as to criminal charges. The non-application of Art 6 ECHR to asylum and other immigration proceedings is supported by case law.[574] For instance, in *MN and Others*, the ECtHR reiterated its previous case law and found that the decision on the entry to Belgian territory in the context of the issuance of humanitarian visas fell outside the scope of Art 6 ECHR.[575]

This means for the resettlement process that Art 14 ICCPR and Art 6 ECHR as such do not provide a sufficient legal basis to challenge a negative selection decision before the court.

Nevertheless, a right to an effective review under the ICCPR and the ECHR exists in situations where there is an arguable claim of violation of rights under the respective treaty.[576] This could be relevant, e.g. in the course of interviews during a resettlement selection mission. For example,

573 OHCHR, 'General Comment No 32: Article 14: Right to equality before courts and tribunals and to a fair trial', UN Doc CCPR/C/GC/32 (23 August 2007) para 17 <https://www.refworld.org/docid/478b2b2f2.html> accessed 18 February 2021.

574 See *Maaouia v France* App No 39652/98 (ECtHR 5 October 2000) para 40; see also *MN and Others v Belgium*.

575 See *MN and Others v Belgium*, para 137.

576 See Vincent Chetail, *International Migration Law*, 141f; see also, e.g. OHCHR, 'Communication No 1477/2006: Maksudov and Others v Kyrgyzstan', UN Doc CCPR/C/93/D/1461,1462,1476 and 1477/2006 (31 July 2008) para 12.7 <https://www.refworld.org/cases,HRC,4a93a0cd2.html> accessed 18 February 2021; see also *GHH and Others v Turkey* App No 43258/98 (ECtHR 11 October 2000) paras 34, 36.

one could imagine assaults by field officers amounting to a violation of Art 3 ECHR.[577]

Under EU law, the Charter provides additional due process guarantees (see 5.2.1).

3.3.3.2 Refugee law

According to Art 16 para 1 Refugee Convention, "[a] *refugee shall have free access to the courts of law on the territory of all Contracting States*". *Elberling* purported that the wording of this Article does not require physical presence of the refugee concerned in any Contracting State.[578] Furthermore, *Hathaway* confirmed that this right is not limited "*to the courts of the country in which the refugee is located*".[579] In fact, refugees can only benefit from whatever judicial remedies exist in a Contracting State. This entails for resettlement that despite the guarantee under Art 16 para 1 Refugee Convention, judicial review of a decision (not) to select a refugee for resettlement remains contingent on the remedies available under domestic law (arguably of the receiving country, i.e. the decision-making country).[580]

3.3.3.3 Concluding remarks

Resettlement refugees cannot invoke Art 14 ICCPR and Art 6 ECHR to challenge a negative selection decision. Still, the ICCPR and the ECHR

---

577 When it comes to misconduct by field officers (and also other actors involved), women as potential victims are particularly vulnerable. It therefore deserves mention that in its General Comment No 32, the Committee on the Elimination of Discrimination against Women affirmed the extraterritorial application of the CEDAW, including with regard to violations of private persons and other non-state actors, subject to the condition of jurisdiction. See Committee on the Elimination of Discrimination against Women, 'General recommendation No 32 on the gender-related dimensions of refugee status, asylum, nationality and statelessness of women', UN Doc CEDAW/C/GC/32 (14 November 2014) para 7 <https://www.refworld.org/docid/54620fb54.html> accessed 21 June 2021.

578 See Björn Elberling in Andreas Zimmermann (ed), *The 1951 Convention Relating to the Status of Refugees and its 1967 Protocol* (Oxford University Press 2011) Art 16 Refugee Convention, para 27.

579 James C Hathaway, *The Rights of Refugees Under International Law* (2005) 645.

580 See James C Hathaway, *The Rights of Refugees Under International Law*², 915ff.

acknowledge the right to an effective review when there is an arguable claim of violation of rights under the respective treaty. If, for example, such a right is violated during an interview when the receiving country exercises jurisdiction over a potential resettlement beneficiary through its field officers, then this right to review must be granted. Thus, at least for misconduct during selection interviews, there is protection for potential resettlement beneficiaries in the form of a right to review. Furthermore, Art 16 para 1 Refugee Convention grants any refugee access to courts in all Contracting States, but refugees are limited to the judicial remedies available under the respective domestic law.

3.3.4 Non-discrimination

Discrimination in the resettlement process may occur in multiple forms. In the resettlement selection process, discrimination can happen between (groups of) refugees, e.g. on the basis of their nationality or religion. Specifically, differences in legal status may result in discrimination between resettlement refugees and other refugees. Another source of discrimination derives from the fact that generally the rights of non-nationals, including resettlement beneficiaries, are less comprehensive than the rights of nationals. In this context, discrimination may be an issue during the process of naturalization for resettlement beneficiaries as opposed to other forced migrants (see 5.4.3.4).

The principle of non-discrimination is recognized under Art 1 para 3 UN Charter.[581] It is a well-established principle in international and European human rights law, enshrined in Art 2 UDHR, Arts 2 and 26 ICCPR, Art 2 ICESCR, Art 14 ECHR, Art 1 Protocol No 12 to the ECHR[582] and Art 21 Charter, as well as in international refugee law, namely in Art 3 Refugee Convention.

---

581 See Art 1 para 3 UN Charter stipulates that one of the purposes of the United Nations is "[t]*o achieve international co-operation in solving international problems of an economic, social, cultural, or humanitarian character, and in promoting and encouraging respect for human rights and for fundamental freedoms for all without distinction as to race, sex, language, or religion*".

582 See Protocol No 12 to the Convention for the Protection of Human Rights and Fundamental Freedoms (entered into force 1 April 2005) ETS No 177.

3.3.4.1 Human rights

Prominently, Art 2 UDHR stipulates a general prohibition of non-discrimination:

> *Everyone is entitled to all the rights and freedoms set forth in this Declaration, without distinction of any kind, such as race, colour, sex, language, religion, political or other opinion, national or social origin, property, birth or other status. Furthermore, no distinction shall be made on the basis of the political, jurisdictional or international status of the country or territory to which a person belongs, whether it be independent, trust, non-self-governing or under any other limitation of sovereignty.*

While the UDHR remains a non-binding instrument, Art 2 UDHR was incorporated in legally binding universal human rights treaties, namely Arts 2 para 1 and 26 ICCPR, and Art 2 para 2 ICESCR.

Art 2 para 1 ICCPR sets forth that each Contracting State shall "*ensure to all individuals within its territory and subject to its jurisdiction the rights recognized in the present Covenant, without distinction of any kind, such as race, colour, sex, language, religion, political or other opinion, national or social origin, property, birth or other status*". More precisely, Art 26 ICCPR stipulates:

> *All persons are equal before the law and are entitled without any discrimination to the equal protection of the law. In this respect, the law shall prohibit any discrimination and guarantee to all persons equal and effective protection against discrimination on any ground such as race, colour, sex, language, religion, political or other opinion, national or social origin, property, birth or other status.*

Similarly, Art 2 para 2 ICESCR states that the Contracting States "*undertake to guarantee that the rights enunciated in the present Covenant will be exercised without discrimination of any kind as to race, colour, sex, language, religion, political or other opinion, national or social origin, property, birth or other status*".

Moreover, Art 2 CRC rules out "*any discrimination on the basis of the status of a child as being [...] a refugee, asylum seeker or migrant*".[583]

583 Committee on the Rights of the Child, 'General Comment No 6: Treatment of Unaccompanied and Separated Children Outside Their Country of Origin' (1 September 2006) 8, para 18.

Based on these provisions, it is recognized that international human rights law prohibits discrimination among and between refugees.[584]

Under European human rights law, the ECHR does not establish a general principle of equality comparable to the UDHR. Art 14 ECHR prohibits discrimination, but its scope of application is limited to the rights and freedoms laid down in the ECHR.[585] This, however, does not presuppose that a respective Convention right applies; it is rather sufficient that the situation at issue falls within the ambit of a Convention right.[586] Furthermore, Art 1 Protocol No 12 to the ECHR contains a general principle of equality. Though to date, this Protocol has only been ratified by twenty Contracting States,[587] and its prohibition of discrimination is restricted to any rights set forth by law. It would therefore only apply if resettlement gained the status of a right under EU or domestic law.[588]

For the assessment whether a respective practice constitutes a discriminatory act violating one of the stated rules, it must be noted that "[d]*ifferential treatment of migrants does not always equal discrimination*".[589] According to the prevailing opinion, a difference in treatment is not discriminatory when three cumulative conditions are fulfilled, i.e. reasonableness, objectivity and proportionality to achieve a legitimate aim.[590]

This is reflected in the Human Rights Committee's General Comment No 15[591] with regard to the ICCPR, and also in the ECtHR's ruling in *Belgian Linguistics* with respect to the ECHR. According to the latter,

---

584 See James C Hathaway, *The Rights of Refugees Under International Law*[2], 265ff.

585 See Christoph Grabenwarter and Katharina Pabel, *Europäische Menschenrechtskonvention: Ein Studienbuch* (CH Beck/Helbig Lichtenhahn Verlag/Manz 6th ed 2016) 627, para 1.

586 See *The Church of Jesus Christ of Latter-Day Saints v Great Britain* App No 7552/09 (ECtHR 28 March 2014) para 30.

587 See Council of Europe, 'Chart of signatures and ratifications of Treaty 177' (as of 10 July 2022) <https://www.coe.int/en/web/conventions/full-list/-/conventions/treaty/177/signatures?p_auth=Zn0fdiIA> accessed 10 July 2022.

588 See Tom de Boer and Marjoleine Zieck, 'The Legal Abyss of Discretion in the Resettlement of Refugees: Cherry-Picking and the Lack of Due Process in the EU' in (2020) 32 International Journal of Refugee Law 1, 54 (79, 81).

589 Nikolaos Sitaopoulos, 'Why International Migration Law Does not Give a License to Discriminate' (*EJIL: Talk!*, 20 May 2015) <https://www.ejiltalk.org/why-international-migration-law-does-not-give-a-license-to-discriminate/> accessed 20 February 2021.

590 See Vincent Chetail, *International Migration Law*, 148.

591 See OHCHR, 'CCPR General Comment No 15: The position of aliens under the Covenant', UN Doc HRI/GEN/1/Rev1 (11 April 1986) <https://www.refworld.org/docid/45139acfc.html> accessed 20 February 2021.

a violation of the principle of equality could be assumed if a "*distinction has no objective or reasonable justification*".[592] Even earlier, the issue reached the ICJ. Judge *Tanaka* highlighted in his Dissenting Opinion in *South West Africa (Second Phase)* that equality does not exclude differentiation.[593]

When it comes to differential treatment on the basis of race, such distinction has special significance under international law authorities and has crystallized as discrimination *per se* under customary international law.[594] In this vein, the ECtHR found no objective justification for differential treatment based exclusively (or to a decisive extent) on race or ethnicity in a contemporary democratic society.[595] The Human Rights Committee applied a similar standard.[596]

Nationality constitutes another frequent source of discrimination among and between (groups of) refugees. This is particularly relevant where resettlement or humanitarian admission programs only apply to forced migrants with a certain nationality or are geographically restricted (such tendencies have been evident, for example, in the course of the Russian invasion of Ukraine).[597] As opposed to national origin, nationality is not an enumerated ground in Art 2 ICCPR, but Contracting States must nonetheless base justification of differential treatment on grounds

---

592 "*Relating to certain aspects of the laws on the use of languages in education in Belgium" v Belgium* App No 1474/62; 1677/62; 1691/62; 1769/63; 1994/63; 2126/64 (ECtHR 23 July 1968) 30f, para 10.

593 See *South West Africa, Second Phase* (Dissenting Opinion of Judge Tanaka) [1966] ICJ Rep 250.

594 See William A Schabas, *The Customary International Law of Human Rights* (Oxford University Press 2021) Chapter 5, 161ff.

595 See *Timishev v Russia* App No 55762/00 and 55974/00 (ECtHR 13 December 2005) para 58; *DH and Others v Czech Republic* App No 57325/00 (ECtHR 13 November 2007) para 176.

596 The Committee found identity checks for the purposes of immigration control to be discriminatory because "*racial characteristics*" were the "*decisive factor*". See OHCHR, 'Communication No 1493/2006: Lecraft v Spain', UN Doc CCPR/C/96/D/1493/2006 (17 August 2009) para 7.4 <https://documents-dds-ny.un.org/doc/UNDOC/GEN/G09/442/84/PDF/G0944284.pdf?OpenElement> accessed 10 July 2022.

597 See Janine Prantl and Ian Kysel, 'Generous, but Equal Treatment? Anti-Discrimination Duties of States Hosting Refugees Fleeing Ukraine' (*EJIL: Talk!*, 2 May 2022) <https://www.ejiltalk.org/generous-but-equal-treatment-anti-discrimination-duties-of-states-hosting-refugees-fleeing-ukraine/> accessed 10 July 2022.

of nationality or citizenship on reasonable and objective criteria.[598] The ECtHR has underscored repeatedly that only "*very weighty reasons*" could justify such differential treatment.[599]

In point of fact, states have invoked distinctions to justify unequal treatment between foreigners and their own nationals.[600] Specifically, with regard to Art 26 ICCPR, the Human Rights Committee has accepted categorical distinctions such as citizenship as an inherently reasonable basis upon which individuals may be treated differently.[601] In this context, *Hathaway* pointed out that "*non-discrimination law has not yet evolved to the point that refugees and other non-citizens can safely assume that it will provide a sufficient answer to the failure to grant them rights on par with citizens*".[602] Prominent examples of rights restricted to citizens are access to public services and the right to take part in elections and referendums (Art 25 ICCPR).[603] Inequalities, e.g., in the form of limited political participation, evidently impede integration.[604]

There are a few indications in EU law accounting for the link between the integration of foreigners and equal treatment with nationals. The Directive concerning the status of non-EU nationals who are long-term residents (Long-term Residents Directive)[605] provides for equal treatment with nationals in certain areas, such as access to employment and self-employed activity; education and vocational training; core benefits of social assistance; and access to goods and services (see Art 11 Long-term Residents Directive).

---

598 OHCHR, 'Communication No 196/1985: Gueye v France' (1989) para 9.4 <http://hrlibrary.umn.edu/undocs/session35/196-1985.html> accessed 10 July 2022.

599 See *Gayusuz v Austria* App No 17371/90 (ECtHR 16 September 1996) para 42; *Koua Poirrez v France* App No 40892/98 (ECtHR 30 December 2003) para 46; *Andrejeva v Latvia* App No 55707/00 (ECtHR 18 February 2009) para 87.

600 See OHCHR, 'General Comment No 18: Non-discrimination', UN Doc HRI/GEN/1/Rev9 (Vol I) (10 November 1989) para 8 <https://www.refworld.org/docid/453883fa8.html> accessed 20 February 2021.

601 See ibid para 8.

602 James C Hathaway, *The Rights of Refugees Under International Law*[2], 265.

603 See Walter Kälin and Jörg Künzli, *The Law of International Human Rights Protection*, 524.

604 See Kiran Banerjee, 'Rethinking the Global Governance of International Protection' in (2018) 56 Columbia Journal of Transnational Law, 313 (321).

605 See Directive 2003/109 (EC) concerning the status of third-country nationals who are long-term residents [2004] OJ L16/44 amended by Directive 2011/51/EU [2011] OJ L132/1.

3.3.4.2 Refugee law

Under international refugee law, Art 3 of the Refugee Convention constitutes the pivotal provision on non-discrimination. It states that "[t]*he Contracting States shall apply the provisions of this Convention to refugees without discrimination as to race, religion or country of origin*".

With respect to discrimination among refugees, Art 3 Refugee Convention does not contain a general prohibition of discrimination between refugees, meaning that refugee law offers limited protection in this regard. It is therefore described as overridden by international human rights, particularly by Art 26 ICCPR.[606]

Still, Art 3 of the Refugee Convention deserves consideration as it sets a specific threshold in terms of reasonableness. This threshold makes it more difficult for Contracting States to objectively justify differential treatment whenever the subject matter of a differentiation between or among (groups of) refugees is a right expressly guaranteed under the Refugee Convention, since "*these are rights that are explicitly intended to inhere in persons who are refugees <u>simply because</u> they are refugees*".[607] It follows that Contracting States have scarce reasons to justify differential protection of some part of the refugee population.

In terms of equal treatment between refugees and nationals, the UNHCR resettlement definition emphasizes that resettled refugees should have access to rights *similar* to those enjoyed by nationals. The term 'similar' must be distinguished from 'same'. In fact, there is only a limited number of Convention rights demanding the *same* treatment as nationals; for instance, Art 22 para 1 Refugee Convention states that "[t]*he Contracting States shall accord to refugees the same treatment as is accorded to nationals with respect to elementary education*". At a minimum, Convention States must treat refugees equally in areas where they are obliged to do so.[608]

3.3.4.3 Concluding remarks

Human rights law offers refugees protection in cases where they are discriminated against by other refugees, which is relevant, among others, in

606 See James C Hathaway, *The Rights of Refugees Under International Law*², 276.

607 Ibid 289 (emphasis as in original).

608 See Elena Andreevska, 'The Legal Protection of Refugee: Western Balkanas' in (2016) 23 Lex ET Scientia International Journal 2, 85 (88).

the resettlement selection process and with regard to the legal status of resettlement beneficiaries in the receiving country. Concerning discrimination between refugees and nationals of the receiving country, there is, however, no comprehensive protection provided by human rights law. Also, the Refugee Convention does not account for equal treatment between refugees and nationals in a comprehensive manner since only a few rights in this Convention require such treatment. Overall, the lack of equal treatment between resettled refugees and nationals impacts the integration process since the resettled refugees may face substantial hurdles due to the prioritization of nationals – even if the refugees have already obtained long-term residence status.

3.3.5 Reception conditions

The rights analyzed in the following concern the legal status of resettlement beneficiaries after the resettlement selection process. The listed human rights treaties as well as the Refugee Convention oblige receiving countries to grant resettlement beneficiaries specific rights and liberties upon arrival on their territory, which must be reflected in corresponding reception conditions. For the purpose of this analysis, the term 'reception conditions' refers to the full set of measures that a receiving country must grant to a resettlement beneficiary to establish a situation that complies with international human rights and refugee law.[609]

---

609 Under EU law 'reception conditions' are defined as follows: "*The full set of measures that EU Member States grant to* <u>*applicants for international protection*</u>" (emphasis as in original), see Art 2 lit f Directive 2013/33 (EU) laying down standards for the reception of applicants for international protection [2013] OJ L180/96-116 (Recast Reception Conditions Directive); see also European Migration Network, 'Asylum and Migration Glossary 7.0' (July 2020) <https://ec.europa.eu/home-affairs/what-we-do/networks/european_migration_network/glossary_search/reception-conditions_en> accessed 3 July 2021; definition of 'material reception conditions': "*The reception conditions that include housing, food and clothing provided in kind, or as financial allowances or in vouchers, or a combination of the three, and a daily expenses allowance*", see Art 2 lit g of Recast Reception Conditions Directive; see also European Migration Network, 'Asylum and Migration Glossary 7.0' (July 2020) <https://ec.europa.eu/home-affairs/what-we-do/networks/european_migration_network/glossary_search/material-reception-conditions_en> accessed 3 July 2021.

3.3.5.1 Human rights

A Contracting State must grant rights under the aforementioned universal human rights treaties and the ECHR to all individuals as soon as it exercises jurisdiction (see 3.2.1). Resettlement beneficiaries are subject to the jurisdiction of the receiving country when present on the territory of this country. This means that upon arrival of a resettlement beneficiary on a receiving country's territory, the respective human rights treaties apply. This includes economic, social and cultural rights, covering areas such as health, work, education, housing – and more.

Some of these rights set out territorial requirements in addition to jurisdiction. For instance, Art 12 ICCPR affords freedom of movement and the choice of residence only to individuals lawfully on the territory of a Contracting State.[610] "*The question whether an alien is 'lawfully' within the territory of a state is a matter governed by domestic law*".[611] The admission of a resettlement beneficiary arriving on the territory of a receiving country is usually linked to a legal basis under the domestic law of this country. Not all receiving countries explicitly refer to resettlement in their national laws, but by admitting resettlement refugees, they regularly grant them a status grounded in national immigration law. Thus, in the general case, resettlement beneficiaries fulfill the requirement of being lawfully within the territory of the receiving country. Consequently, receiving countries must grant the rights under Art 12 ICCPR to resettlement beneficiaries once they arrive on their territory. In practical terms, this has significant implications; if receiving countries condition resettlement beneficiaries to a particular location in the initial phase, they must justify such interference with Art 12 ICCPR accordingly.

Furthermore, the CRC deserves discussion in this context. Receiving countries who are Contracting States to the CRC must uphold the rights of a child when dealing with unaccompanied and separated children outside their countries of origin (subject to the condition that they exercise jurisdiction; see Art 2 CRC). In terms of reception conditions, the follow-

610 See Walter Kälin and Jörg Künzli, *The Law of International Human Rights Protection*, 523.

611 OHCHR, 'General Comment No 27: Article 12 (Freedom of Movement)', UN Doc CCPR/C/21/Rev1/Add9 (2 November 1999) para 4; see Sarah Joseph and Melissa Castan, *The International Covenant on Civil and Politcal Rights: Cases, Materials and Commentary* (Oxford University Press 3rd ed 2013) 397, para 12.13.

ing obligations under the CRC are particularly relevant: Arts 20[612] and 22 CRC[613] account for special protection and assistance as well as alternative care for unaccompanied or separated children permanently deprived of their family environment, including those outside their home country.[614] Furthermore, under Arts 28, 29 para 1 lit c, 30 and 32 CRC, Contracting States are obligated to ensure access to education during all phases of the displacement cycle.[615] Additionally, Art 27 CRC sets out a right to an adequate standard of living, "*particularly with regard to nutrition, clothing and housing*".[616] Besides, Arts 23, 24 and 39 CRC grant health care protection.

Moreover, when receiving female resettlement beneficiaries, Contracting States to the CEDAW must ensure that the women find themselves in conditions compliant with that Convention. Among others, Contracting States must grant female resettlement beneficiaries equal access to rights like education (Art 10 CEDAW), employment (Art 11 CEDAW), health (Art 12 CEDAW), economic and social benefits (Art 13 CEDAW).

Besides children and women, disabled persons are entitled to special protections, as receiving countries who are Contracting Parties to the UNCRPD face additional obligations under this Treaty. Importantly, the UNCRPD obliges receiving countries to provide reasonable accommodation that accounts for disability-specific needs. Further disability-specific obligations exist, among others, with regard to personal mobility (Art 20 UNCRPD), education (Art 24 UNCRPD), health (Art 25 UNCRPD), habilitation (Art 26 UNCRPD), as well as work and employment (Art 27 UNCRPD). The UNCRPD is even more important against the backdrop

612 "*A child temporarily or permanently deprived of his or her family environment, or in whose own best interests cannot be allowed to remain in that environment, shall be entitled to special protection and assistance provided by the State.*"

613 "*States Parties shall take appropriate measures to ensure that a child who is seeking refugee status or who is considered a refugee in accordance with applicable international or domestic law and procedures shall, whether unaccompanied or accompanied by his or her parents or by any other person, receive appropriate protection and humanitarian assistance in the enjoyment of applicable rights set forth in the present Convention and in other international human rights or humanitarian instruments to which the said States are Parties.*"

614 See Committee on the Rights of the Child, 'General Comment No 6: Treatment of Unaccompanied and Separated Children Outside Their Country of Origin' (1 September 2006) 13f, paras 39f.

615 See ibid 14, para 41. Ibid 14, para 42: "*The unaccompanied or separated child should be registered with appropriate school authorities as soon as possible and get assistance in maximizing leaning opportunities*".

616 Ibid 15, para 44.

that, besides provisions for access to social security (Art 24 para 1 lit b), the Refugee Convention and its *travaux préparatoires* provide little guidance on disability-sensitive interpretation of refugee law.[617]

In addition, from an EU law perspective, EUMS face obligations under the Charter when implementing EU law. Particularly worthy consideration in terms of reception conditions and assistance for resettlement beneficiaries are, amongst others, the right to liberty (Art 6 Charter), the right to education (Art 14 Charter), the freedom to choose an occupation and the right to engage in work (Art 15 Charter), the freedom to conduct a business (Art 16 Charter) and the right to social security and social assistance (Art 34 Charter).

3.3.5.2 Refugee law

Most of the rights under the Refugee Convention demand a further qualification, namely some kind of (legal) relationship to the Contracting State. For example, this is the case for Arts 21 (housing) and 26 (freedom of movement) Refugee Convention. Art 21 Refugee Convention requires lawful stay and Art 26 Refugee Convention demands lawful presence of a refugee on the territory of the receiving country.

According to the prevailing opinion, *lawful stay* can be established through temporary residence status, unless it is not merely a temporary visit.[618] As such, it lies in the very nature of resettlement that resettlement refugees are more than just temporary visitors or refugees in transit. They enter the territory of a receiving country as a consequence of an arranged and controlled transfer, with a view of finding a durable solution to their forced displacement there. It can therefore be deduced that, by definition, resettlement ought to provide a durable solution for refugees.

617 See Clara Straimer, 'Vulnerable or invisible? asylum seekers with disabilities in Europe', Research Paper No 194 (November 2010) 1 <https://www.unhcr.org/4cd9765b9.pdf> accessed 21 June 2021; see also Mary Crock, Laura Smith-Kahn, Ron McCallum and Ben Saul, *The Legal Protection of Refugees with Disabilities, Forgotten and Invisible?* (Elgar Publishing 2017).

618 See Scott Leckie and Ezekiel Simperingham in Andreas Zimmermann (ed), *The 1951 Convention Relating to the Status of Refugees and its 1967 Protocol* (Oxford University Press 2011) Art 21 Refugee Convention, paras 45-47.

In terms of *lawful presence*, Art 26 Refugee Convention applies to "*refugees who were admitted to the country*".[619] Lawful presence must be distinguished from lawful stay in the sense that the former implies admission under national immigration law. Such admission is given in the case of resettlement refugees, who are selected and admitted by receiving countries' authorities based on criteria established under national immigration law.

It results that the required levels of attachment, *lawful stay* as well as *lawful presence*, can be met directly upon arrival of resettlement refugees in a receiving country. Thus, even in the initial period upon arrival, receiving countries' interference in refugee rights whose application depends on such a level (or an even lower level) of attachment requires justification.

3.3.5.3 Concluding remarks

Universal and European human rights treaties set out rights and liberties that a receiving country must grant to resettlement beneficiaries as soon as they arrive on this country's territory. The application of most rights under the Refugee Convention hinges upon a certain level of attachment to the receiving country, whereas it has been shown that resettlement beneficiaries likely fulfill the requirements of *lawful stay* and *lawful presence* immediately upon arrival on the territory of the receiving country.

3.3.6 Naturalization

The UNHCR definition of resettlement highlights the "*opportunity to eventually become a naturalized citizen of the resettlement country*".[620] The following question then arises: does the outlined human rights framework and/or the Refugee Convention oblige receiving countries to provide resettlement beneficiaries access to citizenship?

---

619 Reinhard Marx in Andreas Zimmermann (ed), *The 1951 Convention Relating to the Status of Refugees and its 1967 Protocol* (Oxford University Press 2011) Art 26 Refugee Convention, para 45.

620 Delphine Perrin and Frank McNamara, 'Refugee Resettlement in the EU: Between Shared Standards and Diversity in Legal and Policy Frames', KNOW RESET Research Report 2013/03, 22.

3.3.6.1 Human rights

Art 15 UDHR sets out that "[e]*veryone has the right to a nationality*" and "[n]*o one shall be arbitrarily deprived of his nationality nor denied the right to change his nationality*". As such, the UDHR does not directly create legal obligations for receiving countries, but, for example, the African Court on Human and Peoples' Rights accepted the customary international law nature of Art 15 UDHR.[621] Still, international (human rights) law does not expressly provide for the right to acquire a *particular* nationality, and does not set out specific criteria for the granting of citizenship.[622] The Human Rights Committee clearly asserted "*that neither the Covenant nor international law in general spells out specific criteria for the granting of citizenship through naturalization*".[623] At the same time, the Committee stressed that the principle of equal protection under Art 26 ICCPR implied the prohibition of a denial of citizenship on arbitrary grounds. States may nonetheless refuse citizenship if their decision is based on legitimate grounds, such as national security reasons, even if this entails that the person concerned remains stateless.[624]

In turn, cases of statelessness are particularly protected through the Convention on the Reduction of Statelessness of 30 August 1961. Under this Convention, Contracting States must grant nationality to persons born on their territory. The Convention also regulates the conditions on

621 See African Court on Human and Peoples' Rights, *Robert John Penessis v United Republic of Tanzania* (Judgement) App No 013/2015 (28 November 2019) para 85, which established that the UDHR is part of customary international law, in particular Article 15 on the right to a nationality; see also IACtHR, Advisory Opinion OC-4/84 *Proposed Amendments to the Naturalization Provision of the Constitution of Costa Rica* (January 1984) <https://www.refworld.org/cases,IACRTHR,44e492b74.html> accessed 17 August 2022; ibid para 32: "*It is generally accepted today that nationality is an inherent right of all human beings. Not only is nationality the basic requirement for the exercise of political rights, it also has an important bearing on the individual's legal capacity.*"

622 See Walter Kälin and Jörg Künzli, *The Law of International Human Rights Protection*, 535.

623 OHCHR, 'Communication No 1136/2002: Bozov v Estonia', UN Doc CCPR/C/81/D/1136/2002 (25 August 2004) para 7.4 <http://hrlibrary.umn.edu/undocs/html/1136-2002.html> accessed 21 February 2021.

624 See ibid para 7.4; see also Walter Kälin and Jörg Künzli, *The Law of International Human Rights Protection*, 537.

which nationality should be granted in other cases.[625] Moreover, the CRC contains a provision that aims at preventing children from statelessness. Its Art 7 states that "[t]*he child shall be registered immediately after birth and shall have* [...] *the right to acquire a nationality*".

At the European level, Art 6 para 4 lit g European Convention on Nationality[626] stipulates that each state party shall "*facilitate in its internal law the acquisition of its nationality for* [...] *stateless persons and recognized refugees lawfully and habitually resident on its territory*". However, this is only an obligation to *facilitate* the acquisition of citizenship, rather than to *grant* citizenship. Likewise, the ECtHR made clear that "*a 'right to nationality'* [...] *or a right to acquire or retain a particular nationality, is not guaranteed by the Convention or its Protocols*".[627]

Overall, international and European human rights law does not prevent receiving countries from refusing naturalization of a resettlement beneficiary, unless the decision relies on arbitrary grounds. It results from the interpretation of the Human Rights Committee that a decision is arbitrary if it is discriminatory. A duty to consider equal protection when granting citizenship is also reflected, e.g. in Art 9 para 1 CEDAW, stating that "*States Parties shall grant women equal rights with men to acquire, change or retain their nationality*". It follows that discriminatory citizenship rules are prohibited under international human rights law.

3.3.6.2 Refugee law

Art 34 Refugee Convention stipulates that "[t]*he Contracting States shall as far as possible facilitate the assimilation and naturalization of refugees. They shall in particular make every effort to expedite naturalization proceedings and to reduce as far as possible the charges and costs of such proceedings*". Similar to the aforementioned Art 6 para 4 lit g European Convention on Nationality, this Article sets out an obligation to *facilitate* assimilation and naturalization of refugees but not to *grant* naturalization. The duties under Art 34 Refugee Convention are described as being "*minimalist*".[628] Still, a

---

625 See Convention on the Reduction of Statelessness (adopted 30 August 1961, entered into force 13 December 1975) 989 UNTS 175; see Walter Kälin and Jörg Künzli, *The Law of International Human Rights Protection*, 537.

626 See European Convention on Nationality (signed 6 November 1997, entered into force 1 March 2000) ETS No 166.

627 See *Petropavlovskis v Latvia* App No 44230/06 (ECtHR 13 January 2015) para 73.

628 See James C Hathaway, *The Rights of Refugees Under International Law*[2], 1219.

Contracting State would violate this Article if it refused to provide cogent reasons for denying a refugee access to citizenship. *Grahl-Madsen* pointed out that the wording of Art 34 Refugee Convention ("*shall*") made it clear that this Article imposed a duty on the Contracting States, as opposed to a mere recommendation.[629] In line with this, *Hathaway* purported that it was incumbent upon Contracting States "*at the very least, to provide a good faith justification for the formal or de facto exclusion of refugees from naturalization*".[630]

3.3.6.3 Concluding remarks

In conclusion, there is no international obligation for receiving countries to grant citizenship to resettlement beneficiaries. Still, they must not arbitrarily refuse to naturalize resettlement beneficiaries by discriminating them against others. Furthermore, a child of a resettlement beneficiary born on the receiving country's territory has the "*right to acquire a nationality*" under Art 7 CRC. If no other citizenship comes into consideration, the child would most likely acquire the nationality of the receiving country.

3.3.7 Preliminary conclusion

The analysis of the outlined rights in the respective human rights treaties and the Refugee Convention demonstrated that receiving countries must comply with a firm set of obligations when engaging in resettlement operations.

First, when receiving countries select resettlement beneficiaries on foreign territory, they should consider the principle of *non-refoulement*. There can be exceptional situations where potential resettlement beneficiaries are under their jurisdiction – even in the course of extraterritorial action, and the analyzed implicit and explicit *non-refoulement* provisions allow

629 See Atle Grahl-Madsen, *Commentary on the Refugee Convention 1951: Articles 2-11, 13-37* (Division of International Protection of the UNHCR 1997) Art 34 Refugee Convention, para 2 <https://www.unhcr.org/3d4ab5fb9.pdf> accessed 21 February 2021; see also UNHCR, 'Comments by the United Nations High Commissioner for Refugees (UNHCR) to the Legislative Proposal amending the Citizenship Law', Nr 52/ Lp11 (August 2012)' <https://www.refworld.org/pdfid/57ed07954.pdf> accessed 24 July 2021.

630 James C Hathaway, *The Rights of Refugees Under International Law*², 1219.

for interpretation in favor of extraterritorial obligations where receiving countries exercise jurisdiction.

Besides, when receiving countries implement their resettlement policies in cooperation with countries of (first) refuge, both countries must respect the right to leave of the potential resettlement beneficiaries under their jurisdiction, as this right is acknowledged as independent right in international and European human rights law. There is, however, no right to asylum under international human rights and refugee law that potential resettlement beneficiaries could effectively invoke against receiving countries.[631]

When potential resettlement beneficiaries receive a negative selection decision, they can only rely on their right to an effective review under the ICCPR and the ECHR when there is a claim of violation of rights under the respective Treaty, e.g., this concerns human rights abuses that might occur during the interview process as well as procedural guarantees. The Refugee Convention grants any refugee access to courts in all Contracting States, but refugees are limited to the judicial remedies available under the respective domestic law.

In addition, throughout the resettlement process, resettlement beneficiaries are protected from discrimination by other resettlement beneficiaries and groups of (forced) migrants under general human rights law. The Refugee Convention does not impose a general obligation to equal treatment among refugees, and also not between refugees and nationals of the receiving country.

As soon as resettlement beneficiaries arrive on the receiving country's territory, universal and European human rights treaties as well as the Refugee Convention grant certain rights and liberties that must be reflected in the reception conditions for resettlement beneficiaries on the territory of the receiving country.

Ultimately, receiving countries must not arbitrarily refuse to naturalize resettlement beneficiaries by discriminating them against others.

631 Iris G Lange and Boldizsár Nagy, 'External Border Control Techniques in the EU as a Challenge to the Prnciple of Non-Refoulement' in (2021) European Constitutional Law Review, 1 (6).

3.4 Responsibility for internationally wrongful conduct in relation to resettlement policies

Receiving countries face several obligations under international and European human rights law and international refugee law towards (potential) resettlement beneficiaries. These obligations may arise outside the territory of a receiving country through the exercise of jurisdiction during selection missions or upon arrival of the selected beneficiaries on the receiving country's territory. Breaches of international obligations by receiving countries constitute internationally wrongful conduct, for which the respective country shall bear responsibility. In connection thereto, two legal questions concerning the responsibility for breaches of international law arise: First, what are the requirements to hold the prospective receiving country responsible for its internationally wrongful conduct? Second, are there circumstances where the prospective receiving country incurs responsibility for or in connection with internationally wrongful conduct of other (state) actors involved?[632]

The International Law Commission (ILC) codified rules dealing with state responsibility for internationally wrongful conduct. The so-called Articles on Responsibility of States for Internationally Wrongful Acts (ARSIWA)[633] lack binding effect as a treaty.[634] Nevertheless, the generalized concept of state responsibility has reached the status of customary international law.[635]

632 See Annick Pijnenburg, 'Containment Instead of *Refoulement*: Shifting State Responsibility in the Age of Cooperative Migration Control' in (2020) Human Rights Law Review, 327f.

633 See ILC, 'Draft Articles on Responsibility of States for Internationally Wrongful Acts, with commentaries' (adopted November 2001, ARSIWA Commentary 2001) <http://legal.un.org/ilc/texts/instruments/english/commentaries/9_6_2001.pdf> accessed 21 February 2021; see also James Crawford, *State Responsibility: The General Part* (Cambridge University Press 2013) 45; see also Milka Dimitrovska, 'The Concept of International Responsibility of State in the International Public Law System' in (2015) 1 Journal of Liberty and International Affairs 2, 1 (2).

634 The draft has been recognized by the United Nation's General Assembly in Resolution 56/83. However, the draft itself remains only a means for determining the law but not a source of international law in the sense of Art 38 Statute of the International Court of Justice.

635 See Ilias Bantekas and Lutz Oette, *International Human Rights Law and Practice* (Cambridge University Press 3rd ed 2020) 93; see also James Crawford, 'The ILC's Articles on Responsibility of States for Internationally Wrongful Acts: A Retrospect' in (2002) 96 American Journal of International Law 4, 874 (889f);

Art 1 ARSIWA introduces the essential premise that "[e]*very internationally wrongful act of a State entails the international responsibility of that State*". Accordingly, a state can be held internationally responsible for conduct that (i) is attributable to the state and (ii) constitutes a breach of an international law obligation, (iii) provided that there is no reason precluding unlawfulness.[636]

Attribution comes with conduct, which forms an umbrella term for acts and omissions.[637] A state or international organization is responsible for the conduct of its own organs or agents. Additionally, some occasions require the attribution of the conduct of organs or agents of other states, international organizations, NGOs or private actors. There are also situations of so-called dual attribution, where one single conduct is, amongst others, simultaneously attributed to a state and an international organization (see 3.4.2.1). Eventually, derivative responsibility comprises circumstances where responsibility only arises by dint of a connection with the conduct of another state (see 3.4.1) or international organization (see 3.4.2.2).[638]

The following section assesses whether and how international responsibility of a prospective receiving country can be triggered by the conduct of other states, most prominently the country of (first) refuge, international organizations such as the EU, or the UNHCR as a subsidiary organ of the UN, or other non-state actors involved in the resettlement (selection) process.

3.4.1 Responsibility for complicity with the country of (first) refuge

Given recent policy trends of externalized migration control,[639] it is not unusual that receiving countries promise resettlement but in fact prevent

---

see also *Application of the Convention on the Prevention and Punishment of the Crime of Genocide (Bosnia and Herzegovina v Serbia and Montenegro)* [2007] ICJ Rep 43 (160, para 379): The ICJ referred to "*the rules of customary international law of State responsibility*".

636 See James Crawford, *State Responsibility: The General Part*, 49.

637 See Stian Øby Johansen, 'Dual Attribution of Conduct to both an International Organization and a Member State' in (2019) 6 Oslo Law Review 3, 178 (181).

638 See ibid 182.

639 See Bill Frelick, Ian M Kysel and Jennifer Podkul, 'The Impact of Externalization of Migration Controls on the Rights of Asylum Seekers and Other Migrants' in (2016) 4 Journal on Migration and Security 4, 190-220 <https://www.hrw.org/sites/default/files/supporting_resources/jmhs.pdf> accessed 21 June 2021.

potential resettlement beneficiaries from leaving countries of (first) refuge, inflicting [...] on their rights, most prominently (but not only) the right to leave. As the implementation of such policies is generally based on close cooperation with selected countries of (first) refuge, they may be complicit in internationally wrongful conduct of those countries of (first) refuge. To that effect, the ARSIWA cover instances of derivative responsibility, i.e. situations where states can be held responsible for their contribution to a breach of international law. Such contribution may take the form of aid or assistance (Art 16 ARSIWA), direction and control (Art 17 ARSIWA) or coercion of another state (Art 18 ARSIWA).

When it comes to cooperation for the purpose of migration control, responsibility triggered by aid or assistance demands special attention.[640] According to Art 16 ARSIWA, a state is internationally responsible if it[641]

> *aids or assists another State in the commission of an internationally wrongful act under the condition that it has (a) knowledge of the circumstances of the internationally wrongful act and (b) the act would be internationally wrongful if committed by that same state.*

The application of Art 16 ARSIWA in the context of resettlement operations induces, for example, international responsibility of the country of (first) refuge for a human rights violation, while the prospective receiving country incurs responsibility for its aid or assistance provided.[642]

First, the applicability of this Article depends on whether the conduct of the country of (first) refuge amounts to internationally wrongful conduct. As mentioned above, such internationally wrongful conduct may consist of a violation of the right to leave (see 3.3.2); but also other rights may be violated, for instance, the right to privacy (Art 17 ICCPR)[643], when au-

---

640 See Fabiane Baxewanos in Thomas Gammeltoft-Hansen and Jens Vedsted-Hansen (eds), *Human rights and the dark side of globalisation: Transnational law enforcement and migration control*, 202.

641 Ibid 202.

642 See Annick Pijnenburg, 'Containment Instead of *Refoulement*: Shifting State Responsibility in the Age of Cooperative Migration Control' in (2020) Human Rights Law Review, 328.

643 In its General Comment No 16, the Human Rights Committee set out the requirement under Art 17 ICCPR that the integrity and confidentiality of correspondence should be guaranteed *de jure* and *de facto*; see OHCHR, 'General Comment No 16: Article 17 (Right to Privacy), The Right to Respect of Privacy, Family, Home and Correspondence, and Protection of Honour and Reputation', UN Doc HRI/GEN/1/Rev9 (Vol I) (8 April 1988) para 8 <www.refworld.org/docid/453883f922.html> accessed 21 June 2021.

thorities of countries of (first) refuge track and/or collect data of migrants, sharing them without consent. Notably, the right to privacy is also a particular issue in the course of collaboration between receiving countries and the UNHCR, which is dealt with in 3.4.2.

Second, the prospective receiving country must have provided aid or assistance to the country of (first) refuge. In this context, the ARSIWA Commentary mentions, amongst others, providing an essential facility, or financing the activity in question.[644] *Baxewanos* qualified acts such as "*advice, sponsoring police training, funding detention centers or providing surveillance equipment to third states*" as aid or assistance under Art 16 ARSIWA.[645]

In addition, a causal link must exist between the internationally wrongful conduct committed by the country of (first) refuge and the aid or assistance from the prospective receiving country. Prospective receiving countries indeed support countries of (first) refuge, among others, with surveillance equipment to prevent migrants from leaving the latter. For example, Spain "*provides equipment and training to partner states for border surveillance and enforcement, including the donation of seven patrol boats to Senegal and Mauritania*"[646] for the purpose of impeding irregular migration. In such cases, it must be shown that first, the country of (first) refuge violates, e.g. the right to leave by deterring the migrants, and second, that this breach is causally linked to the equipment and training provided by the prospective receiving country.

Essentially, Art 16 ARSIWA requires "*knowledge of the circumstances of the internationally wrongful act*", meaning that the assisting state must "*be aware of the circumstances making the conduct of the assisted State internationally wrongful*".[647] In order to prove the wrongful intent of a prospective receiving country, it must be shown that this country had actual or near-certain[648] knowledge that the assistance will be used for unlawful purpose

644 See ILC, 'Draft Articles on Responsibility of States for Internationally Wrongful Acts, with commentaries' (ARSIWA Commentary 2001) Art 16 ARSIWA, para 1.

645 See Fabiane Baxewanos in Thomas Gammeltoft-Hansen and Jens Vedsted-Hansen (eds), *Human rights and the dark side of globalisation: Transnational law enforcement and migration control*, 202.

646 Nikolas Feith Tan in Satvinder Singh Juss (ed), *Research Handbook on International Refugee Law*, 173.

647 See ILC, 'Draft Articles on Responsibility of States for Internationally Wrongful Acts, with commentaries' (ARSIWA Commentary 2001) Art 16 ARSIWA, para 4.

648 See James Crawford, *State Responsibility: The General Part*, 408.

by the country of (first) refuge.[649] While the sufficiency of constructive knowledge ('should have known') has remained contested,[650] the knowledge threshold under Art 16 ARSIWA can be met in situations of 'willful blindness', i.e. the "*deliberate effort by the assisting state to avoid knowledge of illegality on the part of the state being assisted, in the face of credible evidence of present or future illegality*".[651] The presumption that an assisting state is turning a blind eye may strengthen over time if the breach continues and information becomes widespread.[652] If a receiving country takes deliberate action to initiate and enter into arrangements with a country of (first) refuge, and conducts eligibility determination and vetting procedures there, valid arguments exist in favor of 'actual' knowledge about the circumstances in that country of (first) refuge. At least when officials are on site, the receiving country cannot simply turn a blind eye and deny its actual knowledge of ongoing human rights violations.

Eventually, Art 16 lit b ARSIWA demands that the main conduct would be internationally wrongful if committed by the prospective receiving country. The vast majority of states are bound by the rights established under the ICCPR, including, for instance, the above-mentioned right to leave, whereby the concrete obligations of a respective state must still be assessed in the particular case. Generally speaking, regarding the rights

649 See Harriet Moynihan, 'Aiding or Assisting: Challenges in Armed Conflict' (November 2016) 15 <https://www.chathamhouse.org/sites/default/files/publications/research/2016-11-11-aiding-assisting-challenges-armed-conflict-moynihan.pdf> accessed 27 August 2022; this might include knowledge about the circumstances and consequences of facilitating the commission of the temporary hosting country's wrongful act, see Maïté Fernandez, 'Multi-stakeholder operations of border control coordinated at the EU level and the allocation of international responsibilities' in Thomas Gammeltoft-Hansen and Jens Vedsted-Hansen (eds), *Human rights and the dark side of globalisation: Transnational law enforcement and migration control* (Routledge 2016) 238 (254f).

650 See Harriet Moynihan, 'Aiding or Assisting: Challenges in Armed Conflict' (November 2016) 13f; a different approach is taken by Gammeltoft-Hansen and Hathaway, who relied on constructive knowledge, namely situations where a state "*knew or should have known*" about its contribution to an internationally wrongful conduct; see Thomas Gammeltoft-Hansen and James C Hathaway, 'Non-Refoulement in World of Cooperative Deterrence' in (2015) 53 Columbia Journal of Transnational Law 2, 235 (280).

651 Harriet Moynihan, 'Aiding or Assisting: Challenges in Armed Conflict' (November 2016) 14. See also Miles Jackson, *Complicity in International Law* (Oxford University Press 2015) 54.

652 See Harriet Moynihan, 'Aiding or Assisting: Challenges in Armed Conflict' (November 2016) 14.

covered by major human rights treaties, such as the ICCPR, this requirement is likely fulfilled.

As a result, migration control practices, which are often linked to unfulfilled resettlement promises, may lead to situations falling under the scope of Art 16 ARSIWA. On the basis of Art 16 ARSIWA, a prospective receiving country can be held responsible in connection with internationally wrongful conduct of a country of (first) refuge. This is subject to a certain knowledge threshold about the occurrence of the wrongful conduct[653] of the country of (first) refuge. In this regard, it is hard to prove that a receiving country *knowingly* assisted the progress of a human rights violation. A receiving country pursuing such policy to control migratory influx could claim that the aid or assistance was intended to stabilize the situation on-site or support the regular migration system rather than to facilitate e.g., violations of the migrants' right to leave.

One specific example is human rights violations committed by the Libyan coast guards. Notably, EU collaboration with Libya has been part of the EU's external migration policy, based on the idea of strengthening external border control through the help of third countries and offering resettlement to the EU as an incentive (see 4.2.7). Instead of increasing their resettlement commitment, EUMS, in this case primarily Italy, have rendered support to the Libyan coast guards preventing departures and intercepting people.[654] In terms of knowledge, *Moreno-Lax* pointed to the fact that malpractices of the Libyan coast guards were widely publicized (e.g. in EUNAVOR MED reports) when Italy donated patrol boats to the Libyan coast guards.[655]

What is more, derivative responsibility in connection with the conduct of another state could be relevant where the refugee resettlement selection process, including security screening and health checks, cannot be conducted in the country of (first) refuge. In such cases, the receiving country may need to reach out to another third country to conduct the necessary interviews and checks there. For example, this is pertinent in the context of Afghan mass displacement, namely US vetting procedures in so-called

653 ILC, 'Draft Articles on Responsibility of States for Internationally Wrongful Acts, with commentaries' (ARSIWA Commentary 2001) Art 16 ARSIWA, para 5.

654 Amnesty International, 'Refugee Rights in 2018' (2018) <https://www.amnesty.org/en/latest/research/2018/12/rights-today-2018-refugees/> accessed 20 June 2021.

655 Violeta Moreno-Lax, 'The Architecture of Functional Jurisdiction: Unpacking Contactless Control – On Public Powers, *SS and Others v Italy*, and the "Operational Model"' in (2020) German Law Journal, 385 (393).

'lily-pad countries' and other third countries.[656] Already earlier in the past, the US established an agreement with the Austrian government to host Iranian refugees destined for the US while they undergo the necessary procedures.[657] Assuming that the US exercises jurisdiction and violates fundamental rights (e.g. right to privacy in the context of data protection or misconduct by US officials) during the vetting processes on foreign territory, third countries who knowingly provide assistance, e.g. technical support or facilities, could incur derivative responsibility in connection with the violation of fundamental rights by the US.

3.4.2 Responsibility for and in connection with international organizations

Besides the cooperation between prospective receiving countries and countries of (first) refuge, international organizations, most prominently the EU, and the UNHCR as a subsidiary organ of the UN, act as intermediaries. The EU and the UNHCR are involved in the resettlement (selection) process whenever prospective receiving countries transfer specific powers to them.[658] Such empowerment can lead to situations where international organizations exercise those powers "*in violation of human rights that Member States have agreed to uphold*".[659] International organizations have a separate international legal personality for the purpose of exercising the transferred powers. As a result, the acts of international organizations are in principle not attributable to their member states.[660] While prospective receiving countries and countries of (first) refuge are bound by human rights treaties and by customary international law, international organizations may not face the same obligations. Most human rights treaties even do not contain a provision allowing international organizations to become

---

656 See Janine Prantl, 'Afghan Mass Displacement: The American Response in Light of International Human Rights and Refugee Law, and the Need for International Cooperation to achieve a Satisfactory Solution' in (2022) ALJ, 17-46.

657 See Molli Fee, 'Pre-resettlement experiences: Iranians in Vienna' in (2017) 54 Forced Migration Review, 23.

658 See Thomas Gammeltoft-Hansen, *Access to asylum: international refugee law and the globalisation of migration control*, 188.

659 Olivier de Schutter, *International Human Rights Law: Cases, Materials, Commentary*, 262.

660 See ibid 262.

contracting parties. Nonetheless, there are a few exceptions to this general rule. For example, the EU ratified the UNCRPD.[661] Furthermore, the Council of Europe Convention on preventing and combating violence against women (Istanbul Convention)[662] provides for EU accession.[663] Besides, the so far failed attempts of an EU accession to the ECHR,[664] which originally intended only states as parties, deserve mention in this context.[665]

Beyond treaty law, international organizations face international obligations, namely under customary international law and derived from peremptory human rights.

First, customary international law can be extended to international organizations.[666] The obligation of an international organization to comply with customary international law rules relevant to the fulfilment of its tasks implicitly derives from the organization's founding treaty. It can be assumed that the member states did not want to create an entity that is outside the international legal order. In addition, the international organization itself creates customary international law through its actions.[667]

Second, *Kälin* and *Künzli* deduced from Art 53 VCLT[668] that international organizations are prohibited from violating peremptory human

---

661 See Council Decision 2010/48 (EC) concerning the conclusion, by the European Community, of the United Nations Convention on the Rights of Persons with Disabilities [2010] OJ L23/35-61.

662 See Council of Europe Convention on preventing and combating violence against women and domestic violence (entered into force 1 August 2014) CETS No 210.

663 The EU has already made attempts with regards to EU's accession to the Istanbul Convention, see Sara de Vido, 'The ratification of the Council of Europe Istanbul Convention by the EU: A step forward in the protection of women from violence in the European legal system' in (2017) 9 European Journal of Legal Studies 2, 69 (69ff).

664 See Opinion 2/13 *Accession of the European Union to the European Convention for the Protection of Human Rights and Fundamental Freedoms* [2014] EU:C:2014:2454.

665 See Walter Kälin and Jörg Künzli, *The Law of International Human Rights Protection*, 78.

666 See Albert Bleckmann, 'Zur Verbindlichkeit des allgemeinen Völkerrechts für internationale Organisationen' in (1977) 37 Zeitschrift für ausländisches öffentliches Recht und Völkerrecht 107 (120).

667 Kirsten Schmalenbach and Christoph Schreuer, 'Die Internationalen Organisationen' in August Reinisch (ed) *Österreichisches Handbuch des Völkerrechts* I (Manz 5th ed 2013) 220f, para 947.

668 "*A treaty is void if, at the time of its conclusion, it conflicts with a peremptory norm of general international law. For the purposes of the present Convention, a*

rights. Accordingly, if the founding treaty of the international organization conflicts with peremptory norms of international law, it becomes void. This means that "*the charter of an international organization cannot under any circumstances explicitly or implicitly permit its organs or agents to disregard peremptory human rights obligations*".[669]

As a matter of fact, the EU Treaties (see Art 3 para 5, Arts 6 and 21 Treaty on European Union, TEU[670]) and the EU Charter, as well as the UN Charter,[671] expressly proclaim commitment to human rights. Consequently, it would not only be in conflict with Art 53 VCLT, but also fundamentally contradictory in itself if these Treaties authorized the EU or the UNHCR to permit their organs or agents to disrespect human rights with *jus cogens* status. As outlined above (see 3.3.1), *jus cogens* status can be assumed for the principle of *non-refoulement*, at least with regard to torture and inhuman or degrading treatment. In addition, several human rights recognized as customary international law[672] are relevant to the EU and/or the UNHCR in fulfilling their tasks under the respective establishing treaties, and are thus binding upon them. To that effect, the EU and/or the UNHCR must bear responsibility for violations of human rights.

The Articles on Responsibility of International Organizations (ARIO)[673], namely Arts 6 to 9 therein, provide a framework for holding an international organization responsible for the conduct of its organs or agents. Specifically, Art 6 para 1 ARIO states that "[t]*he conduct of an organ or agent of an international organization in the performance of functions of that organ*

---

peremptory norm of general international law is a norm accepted and recognized by the international community of States as a whole as a norm from which no derogation is permitted and which can be modified only by a subsequent norm of general international law having the same character."

669 Walter Kälin and Jörg Künzli, *The Law of International Human Rights Protection*, 79.

670 See Consolidated version of the Treaty on European Union [2012] OJ C326/13-390.

671 According to Art 1 para 3 UN Charter, one of the purposes of the United Nations is "[t]*o achieve international co-operation in* [...] *promoting and encouraging respect for human rights and for fundamental freedoms for all* [...]".

672 See e.g., Michael Wood, 'Customary international law and human rights' (Working Paper EUI 2016) <https://cadmus.eui.eu/handle/1814/44445> accessed 10 July 2021.

673 See ILC, Draft Articles on Responsibility of International Organizations (adopted 2011) <http://legal.un.org/ilc/texts/instruments/english/draft_articles/9_11_2011.pdf> accessed 21 February 2021; see also Olivier de Schutter, *International Human Rights Law: Cases, Materials, Commentary*, 270.

or agent shall be considered an act of that organization under international law, whatever position the organ or agent holds in respect of the organization".

In terms of EU involvement in EUMS' resettlement operations, the staff of EU agencies constitute relevant agents whose conduct is attributable to the EU (for a discussion on accountability mechanisms for EU agencies see 4.3.3).

Regarding UNHCR's role in the resettlement (selection) process, UNHCR's staff and the staff of its implementing partners serve as potential agents. Especially, the attribution of the latter to the UNHCR has proven to be a controversial issue.[674] For instance, *Janmyr* raised arguments in favor of attributing the staff of implementing partners to the UNHCR.[675] She argued that considering the staff of UNHCR's implementing partners as agents of the UNHCR was in line with the core understanding of 'agent' under the ARIO. The meaning of agent under the ARIO can in turn be deduced from the ICJ[676] defining 'agent' as follows:[677]

> [I]*n the most liberal sense, that is to say, any person who, whether paid official or not, and whether permanently employed or not has been charged by an organ of the organization with carrying out, or helping to carry out, one of its functions – in short, any person through whom it acts.*

The UNHCR usually charges its partner NGOs to perform specific functions, which suggests considering the staff of UNHCR's partner NGOs as agents of the UNHCR. Strikingly, many agreements between the UNHCR and partner NGOs do not consider the partner as agent or staff member of the UNHCR.[678] Nevertheless, in 2009, Special Rapporteur *Gaja* highlighted[679] that exclusion clauses between subcontractors, similar to those between the UNHCR and partner NGOs, did not dispose of

674 See Maja Janmyr, 'Advancing UNHCR accountability through the Law of International Responsibility' in Kristin Bergtora Sandvik and Katja Lindskov Jacobsen (eds), *UNHCR and the Struggle for Accountability* (Routledge 2016) 46 (53).

675 See ibid 47.

676 See ibid 53f.

677 *Reparation for injuries suffered in the service of the United Nations* (Advisory Opinion) [1949] ICJ Rep 174 (177).

678 See Maja Janmyr in Kristin Bergtora Sandvik and Katja Lindskov Jacobsen (eds), *UNHCR and the Struggle for Accountability*, 55.

679 See ILC, 'Seventh report on the responsibility of international organizations (prepared by G Gaja, Special Rapporteur)', UN Doc A CN4/610 (2009) para 23 <https://legal.un.org/ilc/documentation/english/a_cn4_610.pdf> accessed 21 February 2021.

the question of attribution under international law.[680] Consequently, it appears plausible to not only consider UNHCR's staff but also the staff of partner NGOs as agents of the UNHCR. As a result, the UNHCR should be held responsible for the conduct of these agents. As *Gaja* pointed out, such agents may act independently, which, however, does not rule out attribution if a factual link exists.[681] To that end, Art 15 ARIO refers to effective control, namely direction and control (see 3.4.3 for elaborations on effective control under Art 8 ARSIWA).

Human rights bodies as well as scholars have sought to "*design a regime of international responsibility that would allow for the transfer of powers to international organizations without* [...] *reduced protection of human rights*".[682] Importantly, the ECtHR emphasized that Contracting States may not simply evade their obligations to respect Convention rights by transferring powers to international organizations.[683] Nonetheless, international organizations have a separate legal personality and the so-called veil piercing, i.e. holding a state responsible for any violations merely on the basis of its membership of the international organization, generally lacks support in international law;[684] even in the specific contextual framework of the ARIO.[685] This gives rise to the question whether there are particular situa-

680 See Maja Janmyr in Kristin Bergtora Sandvik and Katja Lindskov Jacobsen (eds), *UNHCR and the Struggle for Accountability*, 55.

681 See Georgio Gaja, 'Articles on the Responsibility of International Organizations' (9 December 2011) <https://legal.un.org/avl/ha/ario/ario.html> accessed 21 June 2021.

682 Olivier de Schutter, *International Human Rights Law: Cases, Materials, Commentary*, 262; see Ilias Bantekas and Lutz Oette, *International Human Rights Law and Practice*, 865ff.

683 See *Matthews v the United Kingdom* App No 24833/94 (ECtHR 18 February 1999); see also *Bosphorus Hava Yollari Turizm ve Tizaret Anonim Şirketi v Ireland* App No 45036/98 (ECtHR 30 June 2004) paras 150-158; see also Walter Kälin and Jörg Künzli, *The Law of International Human Rights Protection*, 83; the ECtHR stated in *Beer and Regan v Germany* App No 28934/95 (ECtHR 18 February 1999) para 59, that the decisive factor on whether to grant international organizations immunity from a Member State's jurisdiction was whether the applicants had reasonable means to protect their rights under the ECHR.

684 "*By virtue of their separate legal personality, the basic position under international law is that the acts of international organizations do not without more give rise to responsibility on the part of its members*", James Crawford, *State Responsibility: The General Part*, 189.

685 Just to name an example in the ARIO: Even if Art 62 ARIO foresees international responsibility of a member state for the international wrongful contact of an international organization, it only envisages such responsibility if the member state has expressly accepted responsibility for a particular course of conduct or

tions where the conduct of an international organization's agent provokes the responsibility of (member) states. To frame it in the resettlement context: for instance, can a prospective receiving country under certain circumstances be held responsible for or due to the conduct of UNHCR's staff (or staff of its partner NGOs) during resettlement pre-selection?

3.4.2.1 Dual attribution

The ARSIWA and the ARIO do not exclude dual attribution of the conduct of an international organization's agent to the international organization and to a state. The ECtHR also acknowledged dual attribution in *Al-Jedda v the United Kingdom*.[686]

In the resettlement pre-selection process, dual attribution occurs when an agent or organ of an international organization is simultaneously instructed by a state; for example, when a prospective receiving country instructs UNHCR's staff or staff of UNHCR's partner NGOs. *Johansen* precisely addressed this constellation:[687]

> *A hypothetical example [...] could be that an UNHCR agent handling resettlement applications from refugees is recruited as spy by a State. The agent in question then copies and transfers sensitive personal data about the refugees whose applications he handles to that State. This irregular collection of personal data is attributable to the UNHCR through organic link, since the agent is acting under apparent authority, while exercising UNHCR*

---

led the injured party to rely on its responsibility; see Stian Øby Johansen, 'Dual Attribution of Conduct to both an International Organization and a Member State' in (2019) 6 Oslo Law Review 3, 196.

686 Although the ECtHR remained reluctant to confirm the possibility of dual attribution in *Behrami and Behrami v France, and Saramati v France, Germany and Norway* App No 71412/01 and 78166/01 (ECtHR 2 May 2007), it adapted its view in favor of the concept of dual attribution in *Al-Jedda v the United Kingdom* App No 27021/08 (ECtHR 7 July 2011); "*The Court does not consider that, as a result of the authorisation contained in Resolution 1511, the acts of soldiers within the Multinational Force became attributable to the United Nations or – more importantly, for the purposes of this case – ceased to be attributable to the troop-contributing nations*", ibid para 80; see also Stian Øby Johansen, 'Dual Attribution of Conduct to both an International Organization and a Member State' in (2019) 6 Oslo Law Review 3, 188f.

687 See Stian Øby Johansen, 'Dual Attribution of Conduct to both an International Organization and a Member State' in (2019) 6 Oslo Law Review 3, 191.

> *functions. At the same time, this irregular data collection is attributable to the State, which exercises effective control over the agent performing it.*

The relevant rule covering such circumstances of dual attribution is Art 8 ARSIWA. It attributes the conduct of international organizations' agents to the prospective receiving country if that country exercises effective control over the agent, as further explained in the broader context of the attribution of conduct of (other) non-state actors and private actors (see 3.4.3).

3.4.2.2 Derivative responsibility

The ARIO address shared[688] responsibility of states in connection with the conduct of international organizations, i.e. the so-called 'derivative responsibility'. The rules under the ARIO deal with derivative responsibility where the conduct of an international organization's agent directly causes the injury, and the state is responsible for its own wrongful conduct due to a connection with the agent's wrongful conduct attributed to the international organization. The ARIO also provide rules for reverse situations where the direct injury is attributed to the state and the international organization is responsible because of a connection with the state's wrongful conduct (Arts 14, 15, 16 and 17 ARIO).[689]

Coming back to those instances of derivative responsibility where the direct injury is attributed to the international organization, Art 58 ARIO extends the above-mentioned Art 16 ARSIWA to international organizations. Accordingly, the state may be held internationally responsible by virtue of aid or assistance in the internationally wrongful conduct of an international organization. It follows that Art 58 ARIO constitutes the pertinent legal basis to hold prospective receiving countries or countries of (first) refuge responsible in connection with internationally wrongful conduct of the UNHCR.

Prospective receiving countries as well as countries of (first) refuge assist the UNHCR in manifold ways. Specifically, they cooperate with the UNHCR for the purpose of fulfilling its mandate (see 2.5.2.1). The *Resettlement Handbook* states that governments of receiving countries "*have the essential role of establishing and maintaining effective resettlement programmes*

688 See ibid 192.
689 See ibid 195.

[...]".[690] Along these lines, the UNHCR constantly exchanges and collaborates with governments of prospective receiving countries regarding the implementation of particular features of national resettlement programs, including selection criteria and preferences.[691]

A noteworthy example in this context is that countries have cooperated with the UNHCR to facilitate the resettlement of particular populations, such as Syrians or Bhutanese. To that effect, state-led 'core' and 'contact' groups were created as a result of the WGR and ATCR forums. While core groups are advocacy-, policy- and operations-oriented, contact groups are mainly operationally focused.[692] Thus, state-led contact groups are in charge of operational support, such as providing technical equipment.[693] This means that derivative responsibility of states can result from aid and assistance provided by their contact groups to the UNHCR.

The inverse case is certainly also practically relevant in the context of cooperation between core groups and the UNHCR, i.e. the UNHCR provides aid and assistance through operational support, incurring derivative responsibility in connection with a direct injury committed by state agents.

Furthermore, it is particularly important to highlight the role of the UNHCR in collecting and distributing data, including highly sensitive information about potential resettlement beneficiaries provided to receiving countries (see 5.2.3.8). The collecting and sharing of data can result in violations of the right to privacy under Art 17 ICCPR (and also other rights). Data could be stolen from a laptop or other device and then sold to human traffickers; it could be shared with home countries, leading to

690 See UNHCR, *Resettlement Handbook* (revised ed July 2011) Chapter XIII, 386.

691 "*It is important for UNHCR field offices to work closely with* [...] *diplomatic representations* [...] *of Governments to understand the specific and unique features of each country's resettlement programme*", ibid 393. See also Natalie Welfens and Yasemin Bekyol, 'The Politics of Vulnerability in Refugee Admissions Under the EU-Turkey Statement' in (2021) Frontiers in Political Science, 5 <https://www.frontiersin.org/articles/10.3389/fpos.2021.622921/full> accessed 13 July 2022: "*To an even greater extent UNHCR needs to address and anticipate admission states' selection priorities and practices, in particular the growing importance of security and integration-related criteria.* [...] *Although UNHCR's frontline staff are well aware that such requirements further marginalize those wh are vulnerable, the fact that admission states have the final say in the process forces UNHCR to incorporate these aspects in its own assessment.*"

692 See Carol Batchelor and Edwina O'Shea, 'The internationalisation of resettlement: lessons from Syria and Bhutan' in (2017) 54 Forced Migration Review, 9.

693 See ibid 9.

the arrest of family members who still find themselves in those countries. Moreover, one could imagine a young refugee being forced into a sexual relationship due to which he or she contracts HIV. His or her sensitive personal information is likely transferred to receiving countries because of health data-sharing requirements. However, if the same information gets into the hands of the refugee's tribe in his or her home country, this could even lead to death of the refugee at the own hands of that tribe.

Next, it should not go unmentioned that – besides the cooperation with receiving countries – cooperation with countries of (first) refuge is requisite for authorizing "*the entry of interviewing and selection missions, and to facilitate refugee departures including the issuance of exit visas*".[694] For example, if a country of (first) refuge provides aid or assistance by allocating facilities and/or technical equipment to enable UNHCR's conduct of pre-selection interviews with prospective resettlement beneficiaries, derivative responsibility could be triggered. In exceptional cases, countries of (first) refuge themselves pre-identify potential resettlement beneficiaries and refer them to the UNHCR.[695] For example, Turkish migration authorities pursue this practice.[696] As in a regular selection process, such pre-selection may result in various human rights violations, triggering derivative responsibility of the UNHCR, especially if the UNHCR keeps on cooperating with those authorities by rendering some form of assistance, despite the knowledge of malpractices.

Overall, as addressed with regard to derivative responsibility in the context of cooperation between receiving countries and countries of (first) refuge, the knowledge criterion constitutes the main obstacle for the establishment of derivative responsibility. The idea that a receiving country or a country of (first) refuge assists the UNHCR, thereby knowingly facilitating human rights violations (or vice versa), is apparently far-fetched. Nevertheless, particularly in the course of data collection and sharing, problematic situations could arise. Receiving countries heavily rely on and assist in the collection and distribution of data through the UNHCR, and vice versa, the UNHCR relies on pre-selection through countries of (first) refuge like Turkey; if any of those actors renders assistance to its counterpart,

694 See UNHCR, *Resettlement Handbook* (revised ed July 2011) 385.

695 See Hanna Schneider, 'Implementing the Refugee Resettlement Process: Diverging Objectives, Interdependencies and Power Relations' in (2021) Frontiers in Political Science, 11.

696 See Natalie Welfens and Yasemin Bekyol, 'The Politics of Vulnerability in Refugee Admissions Under the EU-Turkey Statement' in (2021) Frontiers in Political Science, 4.

albeit being aware of human rights violations, plausible constellations of derivative responsibility arise. Besides the UNHCR, IOM regularly cooperates with receiving countries, for instance Germany, by conducting health checks,[697] which also involves the collection and distribution of sensitive data and might lead to similar scenarios.

Lastly, Art 61 para 1 ARIO contemplates situations where a state, as member of an international organization, transfers competence related to one of its international obligations to an international organization. The state may do so to circumvent that obligation, thereby making the international organization commit an internationally wrongful act.[698] Therefore, Art 61 ARIO stipulates that in such circumstances, the state incurs responsibility, irrespective of "*whether or not the act in question is internationally wrongful for the international organization*". While member states of an international organization are not responsible under Art 61 ARIO when the international organization's internationally wrongful conduct constitutes an unintended result of the state's transfer of competence, the scope of this Article extends beyond situations where member states of an international organization abuse their rights.[699]

Indeed, it remains difficult to prove that prospective receiving countries abuse protection obligations by outsourcing resettlement pre-selection to the UNHCR. Procedural weaknesses in the course of resettlement pre-selection by the UNHCR arguably do not count as a result intended by receiving countries. Even though UNHCR's practice, including its procedural flaws, has met *acquiescence* among receiving countries, it cannot be inferred that procedural flaws are intended. Still, an assessment of the concrete relationship between the specific receiving country and the UNHCR as well as of the individual case is necessary to determine the applicability of Art 61 ARIO.

697 See ibid 9.

698 See Ilias Bantekas and Lutz Oette, *International Human Rights Law and Practice*, 865.

699 See ILC, 'Draft Articles on the Responsibility of International Organizations, with commentaries' (ARIO Commentary 2011) Art 61 ARIO, para 2 <https://legal.un.org/ilc/texts/instruments/english/commentaries/9_11_2011.pdf> accessed 27 March 2021.

3.4.3 Attribution of conduct of other non-state actors and private actors

In addition to agents of international organizations, other non-state actors, namely NGOs and private actors, are involved in the resettlement (selection) process. Their conduct can be attributed to the (prospective) receiving country if a special relationship exists. Such relationship is either derived from legal or governmental authority[700] or from effective control.[701]

The term 'governmental authority' is not explicitly defined in the ARSIWA. Nonetheless, the relevant provision in this regard, Art 5 ARSIWA, indicates requirements for the attribution of a non-state actor exercising governmental authority. It stipulates that

> [t]*he conduct of a person or entity which is not an organ of the State* [...] *but which is empowered by the law of that State to exercise elements of the governmental authority shall be considered an act of the State under international law, provided the person or entity is acting in that capacity in the particular instance.*

The ARSIWA Commentary supports the view that attribution pursuant to Art 5 ARSIWA depends on the precondition of "*empowerment by internal law to exercise governmental authority*".[702] Art 5 ARSIWA does not require a demonstration that a private agent acted on state instructions. It is sufficient that the private agent acts in the "*capacity and pursuit of the governmental functions conferred*".[703] In this light, Art 5 ARSIWA "*was specifically included to take account of the growing number of situations in which governmental functions are outsourced or privatized* [...]. *In such instances, otherwise*

---

700 See Arts 4 to 7 ARSIWA.

701 See Arts 8 to 11 ARSIWA; "[W]*hen the relationship between the subject of international law and the acting entity is not well established by law, or when the apparent legal status of an entity is questionable, international law relies on the notion of control as the basis of a factual link between the subject and the acting entity*". Maïté Fernandez in Thomas Gammeltoft-Hansen and Jens Vedsted-Hansen (eds), *Human rights and the dark side of globalisation: Transnational law enforcement and migration control*, 247; see also Fabiane Baxewanos in Thomas Gammeltoft-Hansen and Jens Vedsted-Hansen (eds), *Human rights and the dark side of globalisation: Transnational law enforcement and migration control*, 202.

702 See ILC, 'Draft Articles on Responsibility of States for Internationally Wrongful Acts, with commentaries' (ARSIWA Commentary 2001) Art 5 ARSIWA, para 7; see also Thomas Gammeltoft-Hansen, *Access to asylum: international refugee law and the globalisation of migration control*, 180.

703 Thomas Gammeltoft-Hansen, *Access to asylum: international refugee law and the globalisation of migration control*, 184.

private actors may be considered as 'para-statal entities' to the extent that they are empowered to exercise specified elements of governmental authority".[704]

Since receiving countries have scarcely incorporated resettlement in their domestic laws, cooperation with NGOs and/or private actors in the resettlement process is regularly not based on any legally sound empowerment. Hence, Art 5 ARSIWA cannot be generally invoked. Notwithstanding, in the case of the US, cooperation with the Volags is expressly anchored in the Refugee Act (see 2.5.3.1). In that case, a special relationship under Art 5 ARSIWA, namely empowerment by domestic law to exercise governmental authority, can be inferred. For the Volags, the empowerment comprises, among other things, reception and placement of core services, and the distribution of funds to refugees (see 2.5.3.1).

Even without conferral of governmental authority by internal law, attribution of a cooperating NGO's or private actor's conduct to a prospective receiving country can arise from the exercise of effective control by this country under Art 8 ARSIWA. This Article states that "[t]*he conduct of a person or group of persons shall be considered an act of a State under international law if the person or group of persons is in fact acting on the instructions of, or under the direction or control of, that State in carrying out the conduct*".

Hobe referred to Art 8 ARSIWA as a "*possibility for achieving NGO accountability*"[705] by attributing the conduct of NGOs to states.[706] Instead of a *de jure* relationship, Art 8 ARSIWA "*depends on* [...] *a 'real link' or the de facto power exercised by a state over the private actor in question*".[707] Such *de facto* power or effective control arises (i) where a specific conduct is in fact *authorized* by a state or (ii) where private agents act under the *direction or control* of a state.[708] Concerning authorization, delegation must not be carried out on the basis of national law but "*some degree of formalized agreement or pre-existing authority must be shown in regard to the specific conduct carried out*".[709] As for direction or control, the ICJ set a rather

---

704 Ibid 180.

705 Stephan Hobe, 'Non-Governmental Organizations' (MPIL, June 2019) para 55.

706 See ibid para 55; see also Fabiane Baxewanos in Thomas Gammeltoft-Hansen and Jens Vedsted-Hansen (eds), *Human rights and the dark side of globalisation: Transnational law enforcement and migration control*, 202.

707 Thomas Gammeltoft-Hansen, *Access to asylum: international refugee law and the globalisation of migration control*, 186.

708 See ibid 186.

709 Ibid 187.

high threshold in the *Nicaragua* case,[710] i.e. the requirement of a specific relation between the control and the action or task leading to an unlawful act.

In practice, EUMS closely cooperate with NGOs in the resettlement process; they do so (indirectly) through external referrals as a basis for the selection process (see 5.2), and also directly for the purpose of departure preparation, as well as pre-departure and post-arrival orientation (see 5.3.1); additionally, private actors may be involved in security and health checks, which could trigger responsibility under Art 8 ARSIWA. It is however difficult to argue that the control of a receiving EUMS is directly related to the specific action of an NGO or a private actor leading to a human rights violation in the course of the resettlement process. Ultimately, the applicability of Art 8 ARSIWA depends on the factual circumstances.

3.4.4 Preliminary conclusion

The analysis revealed that the ARSIWA and the ARIO provide means for the attribution of responsibility for or in connection with human rights violations throughout the resettlement process in the triangular relationship between receiving countries, countries of (first) refuge and the UNHCR.

In principle, Art 16 ARSIWA could be invoked to hold a prospective receiving country responsible in situations where a human rights violation of a country of (first) refuge occurs in connection with the aid or assistance of the prospective receiving country. Nevertheless, a closer observation reveals that certain requirements, in particular the knowledge threshold for the receiving country, are hard to establish.

Furthermore, responsibility of a receiving country in the resettlement pre-selection process could be based on dual attribution when an agent of the UNHCR is simultaneously instructed by a state. Art 8 ARSIWA accounts for such situations but only if the receiving country's instruction directly relates to the action of UNHCR's agent leading to the human rights violation.

What is more, cooperation between the UNHCR and prospective receiving countries as well as between the UNHCR and countries of (first) refuge entails various situations that could trigger derivative responsibility

710 See *Military and Paramilitary Activities in and against Nicaragua Case (Nicaragua v United States of America)* (Merits) [1986] ICJ Rep 14.

under Art 58 ARIO due to aid or assistance. However, in order to invoke Art 58 ARIO, just like Art 16 ARSIWA, the knowledge requirement must be proved, and the above analysis has demonstrated how difficult it is to prove knowledge.

Ultimately, responsibility under Art 8 ARSIWA can be triggered when receiving countries cooperate with NGOs, e.g. in the course of pre-departure and post-arrival orientation. This Article only covers cases where the control of a receiving country is directly related to the action of an NGO or a private actor leading to a specific human rights violation.

4 Resettlement to the EU

4.1 *EU competence and its limits*

The following section outlines the competence and limits under EU law to regulate resettlement at the EU level. Legislative attempts (within the framework of the current EU Treaties) are only possible if they do not go beyond areas where the Treaties give the EU competence to act. This derives from the principle of conferral of powers under Art 5 para 2 TFEU.[711]

EUMS have continuously accepted a loss of sovereignty by transferring competences in the realm of migration and asylum to the EU.[712] So far, the EU has focused on the development of a common asylum policy rather than a common refugee policy.[713] Does that make a (legal) difference? Indeed, there are national law examples, such as in Germany,[714] where asylum and refugee law are legally distinct. Yet, from the perspective of international law, asylum can be considered as legally equivalent to international protection for refugees. *Van Selm* points out that refugee policy can be understood more broadly than asylum policy. In this perspective, asylum policy constitutes an internal matter of a state, generally allocated in the domain of Justice and Home Affairs. It "*frames the procedure for decisions taken as to the status of individuals who, having crossed a state border,*

---

711 Art 5 para 2 TFEU states that "*the Union shall act only within the limits of the competences conferred upon it by the Member States in the Treaties to attain the objectives set out therein. Competences not conferred upon the Union in the Treaties remain with the Member States*".

712 See Albert Bleckmann, 'Das Souveränitätsprinzip im Völkerrecht' in (1985) 23 Archiv des Völkerrechts 4, 450 (463) <https://www.jstor.org/stable/40798156?seq=1> accessed 20 March 2021; see also Konrad Schiemann, 'Europe and the Loss of Sovereignty' in (2007) 56 The International and Comparative Law Quarterly 3, 475 (487).

713 See Joanne van Selm, 'European Refugee Policy: is there such a thing?', UNHCR Research Paper n°115 (May 2005) abstract.

714 See Art 16a para 1 Basic Law for the Federal Republic of Germany [Grundgesetz für die Bundesrepublik Deutschland vom 23. Mai 1949 (BGBl S 1) BGBl III/FNA 100-1]: "*Politically persecuted persons enjoy asylum*" [*Politisch Verfolgte genießen Asylrecht*] versus recognition of refugee status under Section 3 German Asylum Act [Asylgesetz vom 2. September 2008 (BGBl I S 1798)].

arrive spontaneously and request protection and refugee status".[715] Refugee policy, in contrast, "*encompasses a broader view of international or foreign affairs*"[716] and covers a wider range of protection tools, such as resettlement and humanitarian admission.[717]

EU primary law does not literally refer to refugee policy. Art 78 TFEU mentions a "*common policy on asylum, subsidiary protection and temporary protection*".[718] Several commentators took the view that this Article not only covers a competence to make asylum policy, but also refugee policy, including resettlement.[719] This mainly derives from the objective of the provision, which targets persons seeking international protection. Accordingly, resettlement is allocated to the external dimension of EU's asylum policy.[720] Asylum policy, in turn, belongs to the Area of Freedom, Secu-

---

715 Joanne van Selm, 'European Refugee Policy: is there such a thing?', UNHCR Research Paper n°115 (May 2005) 2.

716 Ibid 2.

717 See ibid 1.

718 Art 78 para 1 TFEU states that "[t]*he Union shall develop a common policy on asylum, subsidiary protection and temporary protection with a view to offering appropriate status to any third-country national requiring international protection and ensuring compliance with the principle of non-refoulement. This policy must be in accordance with the Geneva Convention of 28 July 1951 and the Protocol of 31 January 1967 relating to the status of refugees, and other relevant treaties*" (emphasis added).

719 See e.g., Adelheit Rossi in Christian Calliess and Matthias Ruffert (eds), *EUV/AEUV: Das Verfassungsrecht der Europäischen Union mit Grundrechtecharta* (CH Beck 5th ed 2016) Art 78 TFEU, para 12, who expressly refers to a competence covering asylum and refugee law ["*materielles Asyl- und Flüchtlingsrecht*"]; see also Daniel Thym in Eberhard Grabitz, Meinhard Hilf and Martin Nettesheim (eds), *Das Recht der Europäischen Union* (CH Beck 68th supplement October 2019) Art 78 TFEU, para 36: "*Aus den gleichen Gründen kann die Norm konzeptionell eine Resettlement-Politik* [...] *umfassen*" (emphasis as in original); see also Catharina Ziebritzki in Marie-Claire Foblets and Luc Leboeuf (eds), *Humanitarian Admission to Europe*, 320: "*Art 78 para 2 TFEU confers upon the Union the competence to harmonise resettlement rules*"; see also Kay Hailbronner and Daniel Thym in Kay Hailbronner and Daniel Thym (eds), *EU Immigration and Asylum Law: A Commentary* (CH Beck/Hart/Nomos 2nd ed 2016) 1037: "*Such scenarios may include, but are not limited to, a European resettlement scheme*" (emphasis as in original); see also Steve Peers, Violeta Moreno-Lax, Madeline Garlick and Elspeth Guild, *EU Immigration and Asylum Law (Text and Commentary)* (Brill 2nd ed 2015) 629.

720 See Kris Pollet, 'A Common European Asylum System under Construction: Remaining Gaps, Challenges and next Steps', in Vincent Chetail, Philippe de Bruycker and Francesco Maiani (eds), *Reforming the Common European Asylum System: The New European Refugee Law* (Brill 2016) 74 (88ff); see also Steve Peers,

rity and Justice,[721] i.e. a policy field of shared competence,[722] meaning that EUMS take regulatory action where the EU has exercised its competence.[723]

Shared competence implies compliance with the principles of subsidiarity and proportionality.[724] The principle of subsidiarity requires that legislative action on resettlement at the EU level be taken only if action at the national level appears insufficient and the EU is better placed to act (Art 5 para 3 TFEU). The Commission argued in its 2016 Union Resettlement Framework Regulation Proposal that the harmonization of EUMS' resettlement policies would make it "*more likely that persons eligible for resettlement will not refuse to be resettled to one Member State as opposed to another*", and that such harmonization "*would also increase the overall influence of the Union vis-à-vis third countries in policy and political dialogues and sharing the responsibility with third countries to which or within which a large number of persons in need of international protection has been displaced*".[725] By nature, resettlement to the EU has transnational aspects. The admission of resettlement beneficiaries by an EUMS entails access to EU territory, an Area of Freedom, Security and Justice without internal border controls,

---

Violeta Moreno-Lax, Madeline Garlick and Elspeth Guild, *EU Immigration and Asylum Law*, 619; see also Catharina Ziebritzki in Marie-Claire Foblets and Luc Leboeuf (eds), *Humanitarian Admission to Europe*, 326, who discusses whether resettlement forms part of the CEAS or of immigration policy (immigration management) and concludes that resettlement is formally and materially integrated into the CEAS.

721 This area covers the harmonization of private international law, extradition arrangements between EUMS, policies on internal and external border controls, common travel visa, immigration and asylum policies and police and judicial cooperation.

722 Art 4 para 2 lit j TFEU.

723 See Daniel Thym in Eberhard Grabitz, Meinhard Hilf and Martin Nettesheim (eds), *Das Recht der Europäischen Union*, Art 78 TFEU, para 16.

724 The principles of subsidiarity and proportionality require the EU to act only "*if and in so far as the objectives of the proposed action cannot be sufficiently achieved by the Member States, either at central level or at regional and local level, but can rather, by reason of the scale or effects of the proposed action, be better achieved at Union level*" (Art 5 para 3 TFEU); furthermore, "*the content and form of Union action shall not exceed what is necessary to achieve the objectives of the Treaties*" (Art 5 para 4 TFEU). See Kay Hailbronner and Daniel Thym in Kay Hailbronner and Daniel Thym (eds), *EU Immigration and Asylum Law: A Commentary*, 1030, para 12.

725 Commission, Proposal for a Regulation establishing a Union Resettlement Framework and amending Regulation (EU) No 516/2014 of the European Parliament and the Council, COM(2016) 468 final 2016/0225 (COD) 6.

where asylum shopping and secondary migration have been long-term concerns shared among EUMS. Whether, as the Commission argued, harmonization could help to ensure that persons in need for resettlement do not refuse to be resettled in a particular EUMS remains debatable. Basically, this depends on whether resettlement beneficiaries would receive a status that allows them to move freely within the EU and reside in any EUMS of their choice. Moreover, considering that EUMS such as Germany and Sweden – that are by no means considered "*unpopular*" among protection seekers – count among the most active resettlement contributors in the EU, the problem of refusals to be resettled there does not seem to be of large scale. In terms of Treaty objectives, resettlement serves the proclaimed goal of providing international protection to third-country nationals in need (Art 78 para 1 TFEU) and aligns with the principle of solidarity (Art 80 TFEU). The point is whether these objectives would really be distorted if no regulation was made at the EU level. Additionally, one must ask whether a regulation based on voluntariness of EUMS, as proposed in 2016, would really make a significant difference in terms of achieving these objectives, and whether it would produce clear benefits by reason of its scale or effects. In the end, subsidiarity assessment is not purely technocratic since the outcome of such assessment remains highly political and depends on the control through the national parliaments of the EUMS (Art 69 TFEU).

In terms of proportionality, it mainly depends on the Commission's choice of the form of the proposed legal instrument and its content: whether the proposal exceeds what is necessary to achieve its objectives. For the 2016 Union Resettlement Framework Regulation Proposal, the choice of the form of a regulation is remarkable (see 4.2.11.1).[726] By comparison, at the time of writing, most aspects of the CEAS are still regulated through (less intrusive) directives (with the exception of the Dublin system).

726 According to the Commission, a "*higher degree of convergence will allow more synergies in the implementation of the Union Resettlement Framework and contribute to discouraging persons eligible for resettlement from refusing resettlement to a particular Member State as well as discouraging secondary movements of persons resettled*". Ibid 7.

4.1.1 Rules of competence

The Commission based the 2016 Union Resettlement Framework Regulation Proposal on Art 78 para 2 lit d (referring to the establishment of common procedures; see 4.1.1.1) and g TFEU (referring to cooperation with third countries; see 4.1.1.3). The argument of the Commission was that resettlement required international protection.[727] This links resettlement to Art 78 TFEU, which aims at "*offering appropriate status to any third-country national requiring international protection*".

However, as a means for legal entry, resettlement could also be seen from the angle of visa policy. After the Commission had launched the 2016 Proposal, the Court of Justice pointed to Art 79 para 2 lit a TFEU as potential legal basis for future EU legislation on humanitarian (long-term) visas in its judgement in *X and X v État belge*.[728] In that case, the Court decided that the applications at issue fell solely under the scope of Belgium's national law because "*no measure has been adopted, to date, by the EU legislature on the basis of Article 79(2)(a) TFEU, with regard to the conditions governing the issue by Member States of long-term visas and residence permits to third-country nationals on humanitarian grounds*".[729] So far, the Commission has not followed the suggestion of the Court of Justice to propose EU legislation on humanitarian visas on the basis of Art 79 TFEU.[730]

The distinction between Art 78 TFEU and Art 79 TFEU is relevant since visa policy under Art 79 TFEU forms part of immigration policy, as opposed to asylum policy. Indeed, there are aspects of migration policy that reflect the purpose of refugee resettlement. First, migration policy comprises long-term immigration, including permanent residence and citizenship. Second, integration forms an integral part of immigration policy under Art 79 TFEU,[731] along with equal treatment between third-country

727 See ibid 6. See also interview with Dora Schaffrin, Assistant Officer Legal and International Affairs, European Commission (10 July 2019).

728 See Case C-638/16 PPU *X and X v État belge* [2017] EU:C:2017:173.

729 Ibid para 44.

730 See Janine Prantl, ''Lessons to be learned' für ein zukünftiges, gemeinsames EU Resettlement' in (2020) Europarecht Supplement 3, 124f.

731 See Wolfgang Weiß in Rudolf Streinz (ed), *EUV/AEUV Kommentar* (CH Beck 3rd ed 2018) Art 79 TFEU, para 3; see also Adelheit Rossi in Christian Calliess and Matthias Ruffert (eds), *EUV/AEUV: Das Verfassungsrecht der Europäischen Union mit Grundrechtecharta*, Art 79 TFEU, paras 39ff.

nationals and EU citizens.[732] This again mirrors the nature of resettlement as defined by the UNHCR (see 2.2.1). Nevertheless, with its primary target group of particularly vulnerable refugees, refugee resettlement is inherently linked to international protection and should correspondingly be carried out under the special protection regime for refugees. This results from the above-mentioned analysis of additional obligations that receiving countries face under the Refugee Convention (see Chapter 3), and becomes apparent through the specific role of the UNHCR as actor in the resettlement process (see 2.5.2). A shift away from asylum policy could make it more difficult to establish consistency between resettlement and the already well-established protection regime in the internal EU asylum *acquis*. It is recognized that the international and European human rights framework apply in the broader context of migration policy, but there is a risk that EUMS would neglect the special protections set out in international refugee law and in the EU asylum *acquis* if resettlement was detached from international protection.[733]

These considerations ultimately speak in favor of the Commission's approach to locate resettlement within Art 78 TFEU. On that basis, the following analysis elaborates on the specific EU competences under Art 78 TFEU.

4.1.1.1 Centralized assessment

Various stages in the resettlement process, such as the conduct of interviews with potential resettlement beneficiaries and the review of negative selection decisions (see 5.2.3.9), require procedural rules. In this respect, Art 78 para 2 lit d TFEU constitutes the relevant provision, stipulating that the EU legislator is competent to set up "*common procedures for the granting and withdrawing of uniform asylum or subsidiary protection status*; [...]". This rule of competence covers the establishment of a variety of procedural rules, e.g. concerning "*the personal interview, the evaluation by administrative*

732 See Daniel Thym in Eberhard Grabitz, Meinhard Hilf and Martin Nettesheim (eds), *Das Recht der Europäischen Union* (CH Beck 68th supplement October 2019) Art 79 TFEU, para 5. In particular, the status of non-EU nationals who are long-term residents in the EU entails several equal treatment rights (see 5.4.3.3).

733 See ibid Art 79 TFEU, paras 3, 9f; see also Adelheit Rossi in Christian Calliess and Matthias Ruffert (eds), *EUV/AEUV: Das Verfassungsrecht der Europäischen Union mit Grundrechtecharta*, Art 79 TFEU, para 22.

authorities or special rules for vulnerable persons together with guarantees for judicial protection".[734]

The wording of Art 78 para 2 lit d TFEU refers to 'common' instead of 'uniform' procedures. The term 'common' is used under EU law in various contexts, and it does not *per se* rule out the adoption of a uniform procedure by EU legislators. Art 207 para 1 TFEU addresses the 'common' commercial policy, stating that it "*shall be based on uniform principles*", which provides an example in this regard. Nonetheless, the same cannot be automatically implied for asylum policy under Art 78 TFEU. Specifically, when looking at the systematic context of Art 78 TFEU para 2, it is striking that litera a allows for measures to establish "*a uniform status of asylum for nationals of third countries, valid throughout the Union*", and litera b refers to a "*uniform status of international protection*" – litera d, however, does not mention 'uniform' at all. The fact that Art 78 para 2 lit d, in contrast to the other literas of the same paragraph, does not precisely mention 'uniform' suggests that litera d aims at a lower degree of harmonization.[735]

Another question that is slightly distinct from whether the EU legislator is competent to adopt rules on a uniform resettlement procedure concerns the regulation of centralized EU assessment. Against the backdrop that the EU "*shall act only within the limits of the competences conferred upon it by the Member States in the Treaties*" (Art 5 para 2 TEU; principle of conferral of power), it is the prevailing opinion that centralized EU assessment would only be possible if EUMS transferred their competence of assessing claims for international protection to the EU[736] in a Treaty amendment.[737]

---

734 Kay Hailbronner and Daniel Thym in Kay Hailbronner and Daniel Thym (eds), *EU Immigration and Asylum Law: A Commentary*, 1036, para 25; see Gerhard Muzak in Heinz Mayer and Karl Stöger (eds), *Kommentar zu EUV und AEUV* (141st supplement 2012) Art 78 TFEU, para 31.

735 See Daniel Thym in Eberhard Grabitz, Meinhard Hilf and Martin Nettesheim (eds), *Das Recht der Europäischen Union*, Art 78 TFEU, para 34.

736 See Kris Pollet in Vincent Chetail, Philippe de Bruycker and Francesco Maiani (eds), *Reforming the Common European Asylum System: The New European Refugee Law*, 84f; see also Catharina Ziebritzki in Marie-Claire Foblets and Luc Leboeuf (eds), *Humanitarian Admission to Europe*, 321f: "*The EU does not have the competence to decide on individual claims for international protection in territorial asylum procedures. Therefore, it seems that 'replacing' UNHCR with the EU agency with regard to the assessment of the individuals' eligibility for resettlement would be incompatible with Art 78 para 2* [...]".

737 See Kay Hailbronner and Daniel Thym in Kay Hailbronner and Daniel Thym (eds), *EU Immigration and Asylum Law: A Commentary*, 1037, para 27.

Notwithstanding, the current Constitutional Framework allows the EU to "*sponsor the effective application of the EU asylum acquis*".[738] To that effect, Art 78 paras 1 and 2 TFEU have served as legal basis for the establishment of EU agencies, namely the former European Asylum Support Office (EASO),[739] and for today's (better equipped) EU Agency for Asylum (EUAA)[740].[741]

Tsourdi addressed the differences between assisted, common and EU level processing in the context of the CEAS.[742] Accordingly, 'assisted processing' means that officials of the competent EUMS conduct the examination of applications for international protection with support of officials from other EUMS possibly coordinated through the EUAA. A shift from assisted to 'common processing' entails that the competent EUMS grants deployed experts or authorities from other EUMS or the EUAA executive discretion over individuals who would otherwise be outside their decision-making authority. Eventually, 'EU level processing' centralizes the entire decision-making authority at the EU level, which would, as just elaborated, require Treaty amendment. Regarding the *status quo* in terms of examining applications for international protection, *Tsourdi* found that only the stage of assisted processing was reached. The limited mandate

738 Ibid 1037, para 27; "*While there have been calls for 'more EU' in processing asylum claims, direct involvement in assessing claims would necessitate* [...] *that this competence – which presently lies with member states – be transferred to an EU institution* [...]. *In the short term, EU institutions are limited to acting through EASO to support national asylum systems operationally and financially*", Mattia di Salvo et al, 'Flexible Solidarity: A comprehensive strategy for asylum in the EU', MEDAM Assessment Report (15 June 2018) 31f <https://www.medam-migration.eu/fileadmin/Dateiverwaltung/MEDAM-Webseite/Publications/Assessment_Reports/2018_MEDAM_Assessment_Report/MEDAM_Assessment_Report_2018_Full_report.pdf> accessed 20 March 2021; see Catharina Ziebritzki in Marie-Claire Foblets and Luc Leboeuf (eds), *Humanitarian Admission to Europe*, 321.

739 Regulation 2010/439 (EU) establishing a European Asylum Support Office [2010] OJ L132/11-28.

740 Regulation 2021/2303 (EU) on the European Union Agency for Asylum and repealing Regulation (EU) No 439/2010 [2021] OJ L468/1-54.

741 See Daniel Thym in Eberhard Grabitz, Meinhard Hilf and Martin Nettesheim (eds), *Das Recht der Europäischen Union*, Art 78 TFEU, para 37.

742 See Evangelia (Lilian) Tsourdi in Francesca Bignami (ed), *EU Law in Populist Times: Crises and Prospects*, 214; see also Evangelia (Lilian) Tsourdi, 'Holding the European Asylum Support Office Accountable for its role in Asylum Decision-Making: Mission Impossible?' in (2020) 21 German Law Journal, 506 (514ff). This classification is particularly relevant in terms of who holds the final decision-making power, and bears responsibility to ensure compliance with the relevant human rights obligations.

of the then still operative EASO in Art 12 para 2 EASO Regulation[743] reaffirmed her argument.[744] By contrast, the current EUAA Regulation ingrains some elements of 'common processing'. While it appears from the negotiations and the Recitals of the EUAA Regulation that decision-making power on applications for international protection remains without prejudice to the competence of EUMS,[745] the EUAA Regulation provides a basis for the EUAA to potentially handle such applications.[746] Upon request of the competent EUMS or on its own motion (subject to the condition of consent), the EUAA, namely deployed experts, can decide upon applications for international protection if the asylum and reception system of the respective EUMS experiences disproportionate pressure.[747] For further elaboration whether such binding decision-making powers over individuals can be delegated, or rather conferred to the EUAA under the EU Constitutional Order, see 4.3.2.

4.1.1.2 Extraterritorial processing

By its very nature, resettlement includes extraterritorial processing. Therefore, it needs to be assessed whether Art 78 para 2 lit d TFEU provides a

743 "[...] *The documents shall not purport to give instructions to Member States about the grant or refusal of applications for international protection.*"

744 See Evangelia (Lilian) Tsourdi, 'Holding the European Asylum Support Office Accountable for its role in Asylum Decision-Making: Mission Impossible?' in (2020) 21 German Law Journal, 514f; see also Philippe de Bruycker and Evangelia (Lilian) Tsourdi, 'Building the common European asylum system beyond legislative harmonisation: practical cooperation, solidarity and external dimension' in Vincent Chetail, Philippe de Bruycker and Francesco Maiani (eds), *Reforming the Common European Asylum System: The New European Refugee Law* (Brill 2016) 473 (505).

745 See Recital 21 EUAA Regulation. See also Jan Schneider and Anna-Lucia Graff, 'EASO Reloaded: Can The New EU Asylum Agency Guarantee A Standardised System of Protection?' (June 2018) 8 <https://www.svr-migration.de/en/publications/eu_asylum_agency/> accessed 17 July 2022. See also ibid 4, fn 7.

746 Recital 55 EUAA Regulation.

747 This concerns the task of the EUAA under Art 2 para 1 lit i to "*provide effective operational and technical assistance to Member States, in particular when their asylum and reception systems are subject to disproportionate pressure*". See further Art 16ff EUAA Regulation; under Art 16 para 2 lit c EUAA Regulation, the agency may, amongst others, "*facilitate the examination by the competent national authorities of applications for international protection or provide those authorities with the necessary assistance in the procedure for international protection*".

legal basis for the enactment of procedural rules applied outside EU territory. As such, Art 78 para 2 lit d TFEU remains silent on its geographical scope.[748] It does not specify whether the procedures based on this Article necessarily apply within the territory of the EUMS. In that respect, Art 78 para 2 lit d TFEU differs from more restrictive earlier formulations.[749] Art 63 para 1 lit d Treaty of Amsterdam referred to "*procedures in Member States*". In contrast, Art III-266 para 2 lit d Treaty establishing a Constitution for Europe (Constitutional Treaty)[750] did not specify the geographical scope, just like Art 78 para 2 lit d TFEU. Given the political debate on the desirability of external asylum reception centers that took place in parallel to the drafting of the Constitutional Treaty, discussions on the geographical scope of rules on asylum processing came up. The discussions ended with a conscious silence on the territorial scope of Art III-266 Constitutional Treaty. Since the drafters consciously refrained from a territorial restriction, interpretation in light of these discussions suggests that – like its predecessor under the Constitutional Treaty – Art 78 para 2 lit d TFEU covers extraterritorial processing of applications for international protection.[751] In general, therefore, nothing speaks against an extraterritorial resettlement procedure based on Art 78 para 2 lit d TFEU.

4.1.1.3 Cooperation with third countries

Due to the fact that resettlement depends on partnerships between EUMS and third countries, i.e. countries of (first) refuge and home countries, Art 78 para 2 lit g TFEU constitutes another rule of competence worthy of consideration. This provision addresses "*partnership and cooperation with third countries for the purpose of managing inflows of people applying for asylum or subsidiary or temporary protection*". As an explicit EU competence, Art 78 para 2 lit g TFEU allows EU institutions to independently conclude agreements with third countries, even if an implicit external competence

748 See Catharina Ziebritzki in Marie-Claire Foblets and Luc Leboeuf (eds), *Humanitarian Admission to Europe*, 320; see also Daniel Thym in Eberhard Grabitz, Meinhard Hilf and Martin Nettesheim (eds), *Das Recht der Europäischen Union*, Art 78 TFEU, para 36.

749 See Daniel Thym in Eberhard Grabitz, Meinhard Hilf and Martin Nettesheim (eds), *Das Recht der Europäischen Union*, Art 78 TFEU, para 36.

750 OJ [2004] C 310/3.

751 See Daniel Thym in Eberhard Grabitz, Meinhard Hilf and Martin Nettesheim (eds), *Das Recht der Europäischen Union*, Art 78 TFEU, para 36.

under Art 3 para 2 TFEU is missing.[752] This is relevant because financial and operational support for third countries cannot be linked to the EU asylum system in itself.

The primary purpose of Art 78 para 2 lit g TFEU is the establishment of partnerships to control the influx of third country nationals into EU territory, in order to preserve the effectiveness of the CEAS. However, partnerships under this provision can also be understood as "*managing the flow*" to third countries without expecting further migration influx in EU territory.[753] When reflected upon critically, this implies that Art 78 para 2 lit g TFEU could be misused for preventive retention of refugees in third countries, such as Morocco or Libya (see 4.2.7).

Extraterritorial action is generally covered by Art 78 para 2 lit g TFEU.[754] Yet, this does not mean that Art 78 para 2 lit g TFEU provides a basis for extraterritorial *processing*. There is a fundamental legal difference between the promotion of refugee protection by third countries and the rendering of asylum decisions by EU officials abroad and this legal difference must be taken into account.[755] Considering the fact that the EU envisaged reception centers for North Africa[756] in 2018 (see 4.2.5), *Hailbronner* and *Thym* argued that Art 78 para 2 lit g TFEU "*does not, in itself at least, provide a sufficient legal basis for the initiation of such centres*".[757] The key point here is that EU officials cannot simply circumvent the fundamental rights protections under EU law by taking asylum decisions outside the EU. If, on the other hand, authorities of non-EU countries have this decision-making power, they are (only) bound by the fundamental rights obligations that apply under their respective legal regimes. Therefore, a distinction must be made between (mere) cooperation without shifting decision-making

---

752 See Case C-22/70 *Commission v Council* [1971] EU:C:1971:32; see also Catharina Ziebritzki in Marie-Claire Foblets and Luc Leboeuf (eds), *Humanitarian Admission to Europe*, 320.

753 See Daniel Thym in Eberhard Grabitz, Meinhard Hilf and Martin Nettesheim (eds), *Das Recht der Europäischen Union*, Art 78 TFEU, para 45.

754 See ibid Art 78 TFEU, para 47; see also Wolfgang Weiß in Rudolf Streinz (ed), *EUV/AEUV Kommentar* (CH Beck 3rd ed 2018) Art 78 TFEU, para 45.

755 See Daniel Thym in Eberhard Grabitz, Meinhard Hilf and Martin Nettesheim (eds), *Das Recht der Europäischen Union*, Art 78 TFEU, para 47.

756 See Commission, 'Managing migration: Commission expands on disembarkation and controlled centre concepts' (*Press release*, 24 July 2018) <http://europa.eu/rapid/press-release_IP-18-4629_en.htm> accessed 27 February 2021.

757 Kay Hailbronner and Daniel Thym in Kay Hailbronner and Daniel Thym (eds), *EU Immigration and Asylum Law: A Commentary*, 1040f, para 35.

power to the EU, and extraterritorial processing (with EU decision-making power).

More likely, extraterritorial processing, including the extraterritorial resettlement selection process, falls within the scope of Art 78 para 2 lit d TFEU. Art 78 para 2 lit g TFEU can be used in a complementary manner for third-country support to ensure the effective application of international protection obligations.

4.1.2 Principles governing the exercise of EU competences

Besides rules of competence, on which EU legislative action on resettlement must be based, EU legislators are also bound by general principles underlying the EU legal order.[758]

In the external dimension of the CEAS, where resettlement is located, three principles deserve particular consideration, namely (i) the principle of solidarity and fair sharing of responsibility, (ii) adherence to international refugee law and international and European human rights as well as (iii) consistency between internal and external action. The following section elaborates on the specific characteristics of these principles.

4.1.2.1 Solidarity and fair sharing of responsibility

Already in 1973 the Court of Justice made clear that "[i]*n permitting Member States to profit from the advantages of the Community, the Treaty imposes on them also the obligation to respect its rules*".[759] The Court of Justice saw a "*failure in the duty of solidarity*"[760] when an EUMS, following its own conception of national interest, unilaterally breaks the equilibrium

758 The function of these principles is threefold: (i) They enable the CJEU to fill normative gaps and ensure the autonomy and coherence of the EU legal system; (ii) they serve as a source for interpretation, and (iii) they may be relied upon as grounds for judicial review; see Koen Lenaerts and José A Gutiérrez-Fons, 'The Role of General Principles of EU Law' in Anthony Arnull et al (eds), *A Constitutional Order of States? Essays in EU Law in Honour of Alan Dashwood* (Hart 2011) 179 (179ff).

759 Case C-39/72 *Commission of the European Communities v Italian Republic* [1973] EU:C:1973:13, para 24

760 Ibid para 25.

between advantages and obligations.[761] From this follows that solidarity is not a one-way street.[762] In 1979, the Court of Justice defined solidarity as a general principle of EU law, flowing from the particular nature of the (then existing) communities.[763] In this vein, Art 2 TEU refers to a society "[...] *in which pluralism, non-discrimination, tolerance, justice, solidarity and equality between women and men prevail*".[764]

Yet, EU law does not establish a general legal definition of solidarity.[765] Art 80 TFEU stipulates the most concrete primary law provision anchoring the principle of solidarity in relation to the CEAS.[766] It states that the CEAS and its implementation "*shall be governed by the principle of solidarity and fair sharing of responsibility, including its financial implications, between the Member States. Whenever necessary, the Union acts adopted pursuant to this Chapter shall contain appropriate measures to give effect to this principle*".[767] Art 80 TFEU links solidarity to responsibility sharing. A close reading of this Article suggests "*that solidarity and fair sharing of responsibilities are one single principle. Otherwise, the drafters would have opted for the plural*".[768]

761 See ibid para 24.

762 Christian Calliess, '"In Vielfalt geeint" – Wie viel Solidarität? Wie viel nationale Identität?' in Christian Calliess (ed), *Europäische Solidarität und nationale Identität. Überlegungen im Kontext der Krise im Euroraum* (Mohr Siebeck 2013) 5 (17).

763 See Case 128/78 *Commission of the European Communities v United Kingdom of Great Britain and Northern Ireland* [1979] EU:C:1979:32.

764 Emphasis added; see Joined Cases C-715/17, C-718/18 and 719/17 *European Commission v Republic of Poland, Hungary and Czech Republic* [2019] EU:C:2019:917, Opinion of AG Sharpston, para 248.

765 See Herbert Rosenfeldt, 'The European Border and Coast Guard in Need of Solidarity: Reflections on The Scope and Limits of Article 80' in Valsamis Mitsilegas, Violeta Moreno-Lax and Niovi Vavoula (eds), *Securitising Asylum Flows: Deflection, Criminalisation and Challenges for Human Rights* (Brill 2020) 169 (170).

766 See Andreas Th Müller, 'Solidarität in der gemeinsamen europäischen Asylpolitik' in (2015) Zeitschrift für öffentliches Recht, 486.

767 By addressing "*financial implications*", this Article has served as a basis for financial support measures for over-indebted EUMS in the past. Recalling, for instance, the financial crises in Greece and the opposition of some EUMS as well as the emotional reactions among EU citizens claiming to be saddled with the debt burden of the Greeks shows how sensitive it is to achieve support and commitment by invoking solidarity. Christian Calliess in Christian Calliess (ed), *Europäische Solidarität und nationale Identität. Überlegungen im Kontext der Krise im Euroraum*, 10f.

768 Herbert Rosenfeldt in Valsamis Mitsilegas, Violeta Moreno-Lax and Niovi Vavoula (eds), *Securitising Asylum Flows: Deflection, Criminalisation and Challenges for Human Rights*, 178.

That link between solidarity and responsibility sharing fosters the relevance of Art 80 TFEU in the resettlement context because, as elaborated, resettlement not only constitutes a sign of international solidarity with countries of (first) refuge, but also a responsibility-sharing mechanism (see 2.1.1).

The wording of Art 80 TFEU expressly refers to solidarity between EUMS.[769] Notwithstanding, Art 80 TFEU is not limited to solidarity within the EU. Against the backdrop that resettlement concerns solidarity with third countries, it is relevant that solidarity in the CEAS context has indeed been extended to third countries outside the EU, as indicated in Art 78 para 2 lit g TFEU.[770]

In terms of the means to implement solidarity, Art 80 TFEU goes beyond the expressly stated financial solidarity (compensation for overburdened EUMS/third states) by including normative solidarity (common rules), operational solidarity (EU agencies), and, eventually, solidarity in the form of physical relocation or resettlement of refugees.[771]

Implementing resettlement to effectuate solidarity and responsibility sharing implies fairly-divided resettlement contributions of all EUMS. A potential duty of EUMS to participate in resettlement presupposes that normative force is vested in the principle of solidarity and responsibility sharing under Art 80 TFEU. When examining the normative force of Art 80 TFEU, two issues need to be considered: First, whether individuals can take legal action against EU institutions and EUMS not complying

769 Solidarity in EU law refers either to the relationship between human beings and groups of people, or to the relationship between EUMS or more broadly to the relationship between states, whereas the context and wording of a specific Treaty provision dealing with solidarity determines which of the mentioned relationships is addressed; see Herbert Rosenfeldt in Valsamis Mitsilegas, Violeta Moreno-Lax and Niovi Vavoula (eds), *Securitising Asylum Flows: Deflection, Criminalisation and Challenges for Human Rights*, 171.

770 See Wolfgang Weiß in Rudolf Streinz (ed), *EUV/AEUV Kommentar* (CH Beck 3rd ed 2018) Art 80 TFEU, para 1; see also Daniel Thym in Eberhard Grabitz, Meinhard Hilf and Martin Nettesheim (eds), *Das Recht der Europäischen Union* (CH Beck 68th supplement October 2019) Art 80 TFEU, para 4.

771 See Daniel Thym in Eberhard Grabitz, Meinhard Hilf and Martin Nettesheim (eds), *Das Recht der Europäischen Union*, Art 80 TFEU, para 5; see also Obiora Chinedu Okafor, 'Cascading toward "De-Solidarity"? The Unfolding of Global Refugee Protection' in (30 August 2019) TWAILR Reflections 2, 2 <https://twailr.com/cascading-toward-de-solidarity-the-unfolding-of-global-refugee-protection/> accessed 27 February 2021.

with this principle; and second, which obligations, if any, arise out of Art 80 TFEU between EUMS.

As regards potential legal action taken by individuals invoking Art 80 TFEU, it must be noted that this Article is generally conceived as state-centered.[772] Moreover, individuals can only invoke EU-law provisions before domestic courts if these provisions have direct effect. Direct effect demands a precise, clear and unconditional obligation, not calling for additional national or European measures.[773] Consequently, scholars raised doubts about the legislative effectiveness of Art 80 TFEU. They claimed that Art 80 TFEU is too imprecise and unclear to have a direct effect.[774] Hence, the prevailing legal opinion does not consider Art 80 TFEU to be justifiable by itself. Consequently, individuals cannot rely on this Article as a basis for a challenge under Art 263 TFEU or for an action for failure to act under Art 265 TFEU. As opposed to individuals, EUMS are privileged claimants and do not have to prove "*direct and individual concern*"; thus, they could indeed invoke Arts 263 and 265 TFEU.

In light of the second perspective on obligations between EUMS, Art 80 TFEU frames an attitude of working together, namely an obligation of means where "*policies are yet to be adopted*".[775] Essentially, this Article impacts the interpretation of EU secondary law in the field of asylum and migration, including a prospective Union Resettlement Framework Regulation.[776] Beyond that, it compels EUMS to follow a specific course of action and to adopt and implement defined measures. *Thym* compared the principle of solidarity with the federal aim [*Staatszielbestimmung*] in the German Constitution.[777] What is more, *Kotzur* put forward that Art 80 TFEU included concrete obligations to act.[778] *Peers et al* confirmed that the

772 See Evangelia (Lilian) Tsourdi in Francesca Bignami (ed), *EU Law in Populist Times: Crises and Prospects*, 202.

773 See Case C-26/62 *Van Gend en Loos v Administratie der Belastingen* [1963] ECLI:EU:C:1963:1.

774 See Herbert Rosenfeldt in Valsamis Mitsilegas, Violeta Moreno-Lax and Niovi Vavoula (eds), *Securitising Asylum Flows: Deflection, Criminalisation and Challenges for Human Rights*, 181.

775 Ibid 173.

776 See Andreas Th Müller, 'Solidarität in der gemeinsamen europäischen Asylpolitik' in (2015) Zeitschrift für öffentliches Recht, 486f (with further references).

777 See Daniel Thym in Eberhard Grabitz, Meinhard Hilf and Martin Nettesheim (eds), *Das Recht der Europäischen Union*, Art 80 TFEU, para 4.

778 See Markus Kotzur in Rudolf Geiger, Daniel Erasmus-Khan and Markus Kotzur (eds), *European Union Treaties: Treaty on the European Union, Treaty on the Functioning of the European Union* (CH Beck/Hart 2015) Art 80 TFEU, para 2.

principle of solidarity created a series of positive obligations, namely an obligation to adopt legal measures for the management of refugee influx. In the same vein, *Tsourdi* affirmed that Art 80 TFEU "*in fact requires the adoption of concrete measures, whenever necessary*".[779]

Eventually, the ECtHR approved that Art 80 TFEU imposes direct obligations on EUMS. The Court stated in its judgement on the violation of relocation decisions by Poland, Hungary, and the Czech Republic that the obligations under "*the provisional measures provided for in Decisions 2015/1523 and 2015/1601,* [...] *adopted under Article 78(3) TFEU* [...] *must, in principle, be divided between all the other Member States, in accordance with the principle of solidarity and fair sharing of responsibility between the Member States, which, in accordance with Article 80 TFEU, governs the Union's asylum policy*".[780] There can indeed be reasons, such as national security and public policy, that justify EUMS' refusal of admission. However, as Advocate General (AG) *Sharpston* aptly concluded in the infringement proceedings against the Czech Republic, Hungary, and Poland: Allowing EUMS to reject commitment *in toto* would run counter to the principle of solidarity and fair sharing of responsibilities. She made clear that even if the defendant EUMS "*were really confronting significant difficulties*", unilateral absolute suspension was not "*the appropriate course of action to pursue in order to respect the principle of solidarity*".[781] As a result, the past effort to impose a mandatory quota for *intra*-EU relocation demonstrates that such quota did not attain the anticipated relocation contributions.

The politically contentious question consists of whether EUMS enjoy discretion as to the means to be employed to implement solidarity and responsibility sharing under Art 80 TFEU. Considering this issue, the concept of so-called 'flexible solidarity' arose. Already in 2012, the Council of the EU affirmed that "*the framework for genuine and practical solidarity is a flexible and open 'tool box' compiled of both existing and possible new measures*".[782] In 2016, when EUMS lacked consensus on concrete actions, numbers and what kind of refugees to take, the Visegrád group proposed

779 Evangelia (Lilian) Tsourdi in Francesca Bignami (ed), *EU Law in Populist Times: Crises and Prospects*, 203 (emphasis as in original).

780 Joined Cases C-715/17, C-718/17 and C-719/17 *Commission v Republic of Poland, Hungary and Czech Republic*, para 181.

781 Joined Cases C-715/17, C-718/18 and 719/17 *European Commission v Republic of Poland, Hungary and Czech Republic*, Opinion of AG Sharpston, para 235.

782 Council of the EU, 'Council Conclusions on a common framework for genuine and practical solidarity towards Member States facing particular pressures due to mixed migration flows', 7115/12 ASIM 20 FRONT 30 (8 March 2012) <https:/

flexible solidarity as an alternative to mandatory quotas. The underlying argument is that flexible solidarity would enable EUMS to contribute according to their experience and potential,[783] allowing them to volunteer on the *how* of burden sharing. This concept is not about forcing EUMS to admit refugees, it rather deals with what an EUMS can offer as an alternative. After all, the enforceability of flexible contributions remains debatable.

Four years after the Visegrád group's demand for flexible solidarity, the Commission brought the topic back on the political agenda. With the New Pact on Asylum and Migration, the Commission proposed a 'flexible' solidarity mechanism as part of a prospective Asylum and Migration Management Regulation.[784] At the same time, it expressly referred to the above-mentioned judgement of the Court of Justice[785] in the infringement proceedings concerning unfulfilled obligations under the 2015 relocation scheme (see 2.1.2), highlighting that "[s]*olidarity implies that all Member States should contribute*".[786] From this statement, it can be inferred that the Commission does indeed – perhaps unlike some EUMS – deduce a positive obligation to act from the principle of solidarity and fair sharing of responsibilities.

Ultimately, any kind of flexible solidarity must not unburden EUMS from binding international obligations.[787] In this context, *Schmalz* aptly stated that while the law did not restrict the scope of political actions

---

/www.consilium.europa.eu/uedocs/cms_data/docs/pressdata/en/jha/130731.pdf> accessed 27 February 2021.

783 See Markus Kotzur, 'Flexible Solidarity – Effective Solidarity?' (*Völkerrechtsblog*, 16 November 2016) <https://voelkerrechtsblog.org/flexible-solidarity-effective-solidarity/> accessed 27 February 2021; see also Milan Nič, 'The Visegrád Group in the EU: 2016 as a turning-point?' in (2016) European View, 281 (286f); see also Heads of Government of the V4 Countries, 'Joint Statement of the Heads of Governments of the V4 Countries' (16 September 2016) 3 <https://www.euractiv.com/wp-content/uploads/sites/2/2016/09/Bratislava-V4-Joint-Statement-final.docx.pdf> accessed 20 March 2021.

784 See Commission, Proposal for a Regulation on asylum and migration management and amending Council Directive 2003/109 and the proposed Regulation (EU) XXX/XXX [Asylum and Migration Fund], COM(2020) 610 final; see also Communication on a New Pact on Migration and Asylum, 5.

785 See Joined Cases C-715/17, C-718/17 and C-719/17 *Commission v Republic of Poland, Hungary and Czech Republic.*

786 Commission, Communication on a New Pact on Migration and Asylum, 5.

787 See Markus Kotzur, 'Flexible Solidarity – Effective Solidarity?' (*Völkerrechtsblog*, 16 November 2016).

to zero, some legal stipulations were just not freely negotiable politically, including the protection of human rights.[788]

4.1.2.2 A policy in accordance with international refugee law and international and European human rights

With a view to adopting future EU resettlement legislation that complies with the Refugee Convention and relevant human rights treaties, it needs to be questioned whether the EU is bound by these treaties.

From a general international law perspective, the EU – unlike the EUMS – is not bound to comply with the Refugee Convention and its Protocol because the EU has never acceded to these Treaties. It is also not bound by way of functional succession. The doctrine of functional succession in EU law considers that the EU is bound by an international treaty to which it is not formally a party if all EUMS are contracting parties and the treaty falls within an area in which the EU has assumed exclusive competence.[789] All EUMS are Contracting Parties to the Refugee Convention, but the Convention does not fall within an area where the EU has assumed exclusive competence. Consequently, the EU is not bound by the Refugee Convention and its Protocol by way of functional succession.[790]

Nevertheless, or rather for this very reason, the references in Art 78 para 1 TFEU and Art 18 Charter to the Refugee Convention are of significant relevance. Art 78 para 1 TFEU makes it clear that EU's policy to develop a CEAS "*must be in accordance with the Geneva* [Refugee] *Convention* [...] *and the Protocol* [...] *relating to the status of refugees, and other relevant treaties*". In addition, Art 18 Charter stipulates that "[t]*he right to asylum shall be guaranteed with due respect for the rules of the Geneva* [Refugee] *Convention* [...] *and the Protocol* [...] *relating to the status of refugees and in accordance with the Treaty on European Union and the Treaty on the Functioning of the European Union* [...]". Even in the absence of a formal obligation under

788 See Dana Schmalz, 'Am Ende der Kraft' (*Verfassungsblog*, 14 September 2020) <https://verfassungsblog.de/am-ende-der-kraft/> accessed 27 February 2021.

789 See Robert Schütze, *Foreign Affairs and the EU Constitution: Selected Essays* (Cambridge University Press 2014) 109ff.

790 See Andreas Th Müller, 'Solidarität in der gemeinsamen europäischen Asylpolitik' in (2015) Zeitschrift für öffentliches Recht, 470; see also Martin Nettesheim in Eberhard Grabitz, Meinhard Hilf and Martin Nettesheim (eds), *Das Recht der Europäischen Union* (CH Beck 68th supplement October 2019) Art 4 TFEU, para 7.

international law, EU primary law incorporates the Refugee Convention as legally binding. Consequently, EU legal instruments must respect international refugee law, which can be understood as 'international supplementary constitution' of the CEAS.[791] In line with this, the Court of Justice confirmed that "*although the European Union is not a contracting party to the Geneva* [Refugee] *Convention, Article 78(1) TFEU and Article 18 of the Charter nonetheless require it to observe the rules of that convention*".[792] The EU legislator must "*adopt measures on asylum, in accordance with the Geneva* [Refugee] *Convention and other relevant treaties*".[793] An infringement of the Refugee Convention constitutes an infringement of Art 78 para 1 TFEU and Art 18 Charter, invalidating EU secondary law or requiring an interpretation in conformity with the Refugee Convention.[794] The Court of Justice has jurisdiction "*to examine the validity* [...] *in the light of Article 78(1) TFEU and Article 18 of the Charter and, in the context of examination, to verify whether* [...] *provisions* [...] *can be interpreted in a way which is in line with the level of protection guaranteed by the rules of the Geneva Convention*".[795]

Hence, the Court of Justice would have jurisdiction to examine whether a future Union Resettlement Framework Regulation was developed and interpreted in conformity with the Refugee Convention.

What is more, Art 78 para 1 TFEU refers to "*other relevant treaties*". According to the prevailing opinion, all treaties related in content to the provision of international protection are considered to be relevant, including at least the ECHR,[796] and also other pertinent universal human rights treaties.[797] It follows that the human rights treaties analyzed in Chapter 3

---

791 See Catharina Ziebritzki in Marie-Claire Foblets and Luc Leboeuf (eds), *Humanitarian Admission to Europe*, 332 with further references.

792 Joined Cases C-391/16, C-77/17 and C-78/17 *M v Ministerstvo vnitra, X and X v Commissaire général aux réfugiés et aux apatrides* [2019] EU:C:2019:403, para 74.

793 Case C-175/08 *Aydin Salahadin Abdulla v Bundesrepublik Deutschland* [2010] EU:C:2010:105, para 51.

794 See Daniel Thym in Eberhard Grabitz, Meinhard Hilf and Martin Nettesheim (eds), *Das Recht der Europäischen Union*, Art 78 TFEU, para 16.

795 The high threshold of compliance with the Refugee Convention was confirmed by the Court of Justice in Joined Cases C-391/16, C-77/17 and C-78/17 *M v Ministerstvo vnitra, X and X v Commissaire général aux réfugiés et aux apatrides*, para 75, where the validity of the Qualification Directive with regards to Art 78 para 1 TFEU was assessed.

796 The binding relationship to the ECHR already arises from Art 6 para 3 TEU.

797 See Daniel Thym in Eberhard Grabitz, Meinhard Hilf and Martin Nettesheim (eds), *Das Recht der Europäischen Union*, Art 78 TFEU, para 19; see also Gerhard

– ICESCR, ICCPR, CAT, CRC, CEDAW, UNCRPD, as well as the ECHR – are covered by the reference in Art 78 para 1 TFEU. This means that future secondary law on resettlement must be developed and interpreted not only in conformity with the Refugee Convention, but also with international and European human rights.[798] As a result, the international law obligations outlined in Chapter 3 are relevant in the EU law context, as they inform the development and interpretation of EU law.[799]

Besides international human rights and refugee law, EUMS as well as the EU as such are bound to guarantee the rights under the Charter, which observe the meaning and scope of the rights under the ECHR.[800] Art 51 para 1 Charter addresses these rights to the EUMS "*only when they are implementing Union law*" – without territorial restriction.[801] At present, refugee resettlement is not attached to any binding EU law obligation, posing the question whether discretionary provisions can trigger implementation of EU law.

Case law of the CJEU suggests that even if a prospective Union Resettlement Framework Regulation failed to determine mandatory quotas and relied on EUMS' discretion, the Charter could apply. According to the

---

Muzak in Heinz Mayer and Karl Stöger (eds), *Kommentar zu EUV und AEUV*, Art 78 TFEU, para 6.

798 In contrast to earlier provisions, Art 78 para 1 TFEU "*clarifies, however, that the necessary respect for the Geneva Convention and corresponding human rights guarantees applies to all instruments building the EU asylum acquis*", Kay Hailbronner and Daniel Thym in Kay Hailbronner and Daniel Thym (eds), *EU Immigration and Asylum Law: A Commentary*, 1029, para 9.

799 Given that resettlement comprises extraterritorial action, it is important to highlight commentators agreeing that the EU cannot bypass these obligations when acting outside EU territory. See Daniel Thym in Eberhard Grabitz, Meinhard Hilf and Martin Nettesheim (eds), *Das Recht der Europäischen Union*, Art 78 TFEU, paras 36, 47; see also Kay Hailbronner and Daniel Thym in Kay Hailbronner and Daniel Thym (eds), *EU Immigration and Asylum Law: A Commentary*, 1037, para 26; see also Wolfgang Weiß in Rudolf Streinz (ed), *EUV/AEUV Kommentar*, Art 78 TFEU, para 45.

800 At least, the meaning and scope of the Charter rights shall be the same as those laid down by the ECHR. See Art 52 para 3 Charter.

801 See Stephanie Law, 'Humanitarian Admission and the Charter of Fundamental Rights' in Marie-Claire Foblets and Luc Leboeuf (eds), *Humanitarian Admission to Europe: The Law between Promises and Constraints* (Hart/Nomos 2020) 77 (99): "*As regards the existence of a territorial requirement, the CFR is silent*"; see also Koen Lenaerts and Piet van Nuffel, *European Union Law* (Sweet & Maxwell 3rd ed 2011) 837, paras 22-27.

judgement of the Court of Justice in *Florescu and others*,[802] implementation of EU law can be assumed when an EUMS adopts measures based on discretion conferred upon it by an act of EU law. This also applies in the specific context of the CEAS, which the Court of Justice already approved earlier in *NS and ME and Others*.[803] Indeed, *de Boer* and *Zieck* asserted that EUMS were implementing EU law when conducting resettlement, namely by claiming the lump sum reserved by the AMIF. Although the AMIF Regulation does not oblige EUMS to resettle at all, EUMS are implementing EU law when conducting resettlement under the terms of the AMIF.[804] However, the Court of Justice has not consistently followed this approach. For example, in its order in *Demarchi Gino*,[805] the Court recalled that the application of fundamental EU rights required an EU law obligation in the subject area with regard to the situation at issue.

In conclusion, CJEU case law indicates that EUMS can be bound by the Charter when exercising discretion conferred upon them by an act of EU law. This speaks in favor of EUMS facing Charter obligations when conducting AMIF-funded resettlement. The AMIF Regulation does not set out strict obligations but imposes several requirements on EUMS to get funding (see 4.3.1). EUMS hence do not entirely act under their national laws when conducting resettlement according to the requirements set out in the AMIF – they arguably implement EU law triggering the application of the Charter.[806]

The implementation of EU law giving rise to Charter obligations can equally be assumed for resettlement under a prospective Union Resettle-

---

802 See Case C-258/14 *Eugenia Florescu and others v Casa Județeană de Pensii Sibiu and others* [2017] EU:C:2017:448, para 48.

803 See *NS and ME and Others*, paras 64-69.

804 See Tom de Boer and Marjoleine Zieck, 'The Legal Abyss of Discretion in the Resettlement of Refugees: Cherry-Picking and the Lack of Due Process in the EU' in (2020) 32 International Journal of Refugee Law 1, 80.

805 See Joined Cases C-177/17 and C-178/17 *Demarchi Gino Sas and Graziano Garavaldi v Ministero della Giustizia* [2017] EU:C:2017:656, paras 21ff.

806 Against the backdrop that AMIF-funded resettlement triggers the application of the Charter, funding could be a tool to strengthen compliance with both human rights and refugee rights. To wit, the 2018 report on the EU Charter highlighted "*the need to use funds in full compliance with Charter rights and principles. Actions implemented with the support of EU funds should take particular account of the fundamental rights of children, migrants, refugees and asylum seekers and ensure the full respect of* [...] *the rights of those in need of international protection* [...]". Commission, '2018 report on the application of the EU Charter of Fundamental Rights' (2019) 12 <https://ec.europa.eu/info/sites/info/files/2018_annual_report_charter_en_0.pdf> accessed 28 February 2021.

ment Framework Regulation – irrespective of whether such Regulation would set out a binding obligation to resettle. As a result, the conduct of resettlement under the proposed Union Resettlement Framework Regulation would trigger Charter obligations.

The situation is again different for EU agencies, such as the EUAA. In this regard, Art 51 para 1 Charter states that the provisions of the Charter are addressed "*to the institutions, bodies, offices and agencies of the Union*". Unlike EUMS, EU institutions and agencies would not only be bound by the Charter in situations of implementing EU law. For instance, if the EUAA engages in the decision-making of the resettlement of an individual to an EUMS, it is bound by the Charter – regardless of whether it applies EU law or national law of that EUMS.

4.1.2.3 Consistency

As clarified above, EU secondary law developing a CEAS must uphold the protection standards in international refugee law and international and European human rights. That is why these standards are incorporated in the firm set of secondary legislation forming the *internal* EU asylum *acquis*. Resettlement is, however, located in the *external* CEAS, which still lacks such a firm set of legislative acts and overlaps with the external action of the EU.

In this light, the principle of consistency becomes relevant. Consistency in EU law primarily aims at ensuring that concepts of EU law which have already been determined, e.g. by CJEU case law, are properly interpreted and applied.[807] This implies a sense of attachment or entanglement among EU policy areas – as aptly depicted in the French term "*cohérence*".[808] Hence, consistency concerns whether the protection standards set out in the Directives of the internal EU asylum *acquis* "*should be understood to prevent the EU from engaging extra-territorially in the promotion of less protective*

807 For elaborations on the distinction between unity and consistency of EU law see Sandra Hummelbrunner, 'The Unity and Consistency of Union Law: The Core of Review under Article 256(2) and (3) TFEU' in (2018) 73 Zeitschrift für öffentliches Recht, 295 (307).

808 See Hans-Joachim Cremer in Christian Calliess and Matthias Ruffert (eds), *EUV/AEUV: Das Verfassungsrecht der Europäischen Union mit Grundrechtecharta* (CH Beck 5th ed 2016) Art 21 TEU, para 13.

standards".[809] In concrete terms, the question to be addressed is whether the principle of coherence prevents the EU or its EUMS from observing a lower standard of protection in the resettlement context than in the internal EU asylum *acquis*.

Art 7 TFEU, the general rule on consistency, states that "[t]*he Union shall ensure consistency between its policies and activities, taking all of its objectives into account and in accordance with the principle of conferral of powers*". This Article demands consistency between different EU policy fields, i.e. in the case of resettlement the CEAS and the external action of the EU. In terms of the latter, Art 21 para 3 TEU constitutes the more specific rule on consistency, namely that "[t]*he Union shall ensure consistency between the different areas of its external action and between these and its other policies*". The wording of this provision makes it clear that it addresses not only external action but also overlapping policy areas,[810] such as the *external* CEAS, including resettlement.

Art 7 TFEU is directed to "[t]*he Union*". The primary addressees are the Commission, the Council of the EU and the Common Foreign and Security Policy (CFSP) High Representative, but not the EUMS.[811] Yet, resettlement procedures are implemented at the national rather than at the EU level. Here, Art 24 para 3 subpara 2 sentence 2 TEU comes into play. It clarifies that "[t]*hey* [EUMS] *shall refrain from any action which is contrary to the interests of the Union or likely to impair its effectiveness as a cohesive force in international relations*". In addition, under the principle of loyalty (Art 4 para 3 TEU), EUMS face a duty to act consistently with the EU.[812]

As with the principle of solidarity and responsibility sharing (see 4.1.2.1), the normative force of the principle of consistency depends on justiciability. In that respect, it is important to note that the assessment of consistency within actions under the CFSP is outside the scope of CJEU's jurisdiction due to the non-effectuation clause in Art 40 TEU. Notwithstanding the CJEU's power to review the internal consistency of measures in policy areas outside the CFSP, even if they affect external

809 Steve Peers, Violeta Moreno-Lax, Madeline Garlick and Elspeth Guild, *EU Immigration and Asylum Law*, 632f; from the Directives of the internal asylum *acquis*, only the scope of application of the Qualification Directive is not restricted to the territory of EUMS; see Art 3 paras 1 and 2 Asylum Procedures Directive; Art 3 paras 1 and 2 Reception Conditions Directive.

810 See Elfriede Regelsberger and Dieter Kugelmann (ed), *EUV/AEUV Kommentar* (CH Beck 3rd ed 2018) Art 21 TEU, para 17.

811 See ibid Art 21 TEU, para 18.

812 See ibid Art 21 TEU, para 19.

action.[813] Furthermore, the principle of loyalty in Art 4 para 3 TEU as well as Art 7 TFEU, the general provision on the principle of consistency, fall within the scope of CJEU's jurisdiction. This means that the consistency of resettlement measures with the internal asylum *acquis* (amongst others, this concerns consistency with the Asylum Procedures Directive[814], the Qualification Directive and the Reception Conditions Directive[815], as well as their interpretation in line with international refugee and international and European human rights) can be subject to review – albeit that such measures affect external action.

From the perspective of individuals, they can hardly rely on the principle of consistency by itself. Similar to the principle of solidarity and responsibility sharing, the rules on consistency in Art 7 TFEU and Art 21 para 3 TEU are considered to be vague,[816] thus not precise enough to confer rights on individuals.

Eventually, consistency under EU law is well-established, and it provides valid arguments for a formal procedure of resettlement measures in compliance with the internal EU asylum *acquis*.[817] Such consistent approach would necessarily prohibit EUMS from distinguishing rights of individuals on the basis of their means of entry, i.e. through a resettlement program or irregular border-crossing. Since EU's internal asylum *acquis* establishes a firm set of rights for persons eligible for international protection, it would only be consistent to equally apply those rights in the resettlement context.

---

813 See ibid Art 21 TEU, para 19; see also Andreas Th Müller, 'Das Individuum im auswärtigen Handeln der Union' in Andreas Kumin, Julia Schimpfhuber, Kirsten Schmalenbach and Lorin-Johannes Wagner (eds), *Außen- & sicherheitspolitische Integration im Europäischen Rechtsraum – Festschrift Hubert Isak* (Jan Sramek 2020) 51 (71).

814 See Directive 2013/32 (EU) on common procedures for granting and withdrawing international protection [2013] OJ L180/60-95.

815 See Directive 2013/33 (EU) laying down standards for the reception of applicants for international protection [2013] OJ L180/96-116.

816 See Matthias Ruffert in Christian Calliess and Matthias Ruffert (eds), *EUV/AEUV: Das Verfassungsrecht der Europäischen Union mit Grundrechtecharta* (CH Beck 5th ed 2016) Art 7 TFEU, para 5; see also Kirsten Schmalenbach in Thomas Jaeger and Karl Stöger (eds), *Kommentar zu EUV und AEUV* (238th supplement June 2020) Art 21 TEU, para 16; see also Hans-Joachim Cremer in Christian Calliess and Matthias Ruffert (eds), *EUV/AEUV: Das Verfassungsrecht der Europäischen Union mit Grundrechtecharta*, Art 21 TEU, para 13.

817 See Philippe de Bruycker and Evangelia (Lilian) Tsourdi in Vincent Chetail, Philippe de Bruycker and Francesco Maiani (eds), *Reforming the Common European Asylum System: The New European Refugee Law*, 533.

4.1.3 Preliminary conclusion

The relevant rules of competence for resettlement are Art 78 para 2 lit d and lit g TFEU. Art 78 para 2 lit d TFEU allows for the establishment of procedural rules on various aspects of the resettlement process, but does not go as far as to allow for procedures on centralized EU assessment. Furthermore, Art 78 para 2 lit d TFEU accounts for the extraterritorial aspects of resettlement since it covers the establishment of procedural rules that apply outside EU territory. While extraterritorial processing falls within the scope of Art 78 para 2 lit d TFEU, Art 78 para 2 lit g TFEU can be used in a complementary manner for third-country support to ensure the effective application of international protection obligations.

Besides, EU legislators must consider the principle of solidarity and responsibility sharing (Art 80 TFEU), international refugee law and international and European human rights (Art 78 para 1 TFEU) as well as the principle of consistency when regulating resettlement (Art 21 para 3 TEU and Art 7 TFEU).

The principle of solidarity and responsibility sharing impacts interpretation and requires EUMS to take concrete measures. However, it grants EUMS discretion on what those measures look like. Resettlement as a form of physical solidarity would be a measure to implement this principle.

Even if the implementation of resettlement is based on a discretionary choice, EUMS must conduct resettlement within the limits set by international law. In this light, Art 78 para 1 TFEU requires resettlement to be developed and interpreted in conformity with the Refugee Convention as well as with the ECHR and the Charter (in the European context), and with universal human rights treaties pertinent to the provision of international protection.

Finally, consistency between EU's internal asylum *acquis* and external action demands that the protection standards incorporated in EU asylum law, namely the regulations and directives established as part of the CEAS, including their required interpretation in conformity with international refugee law and international and European human rights, must equally be observed in the resettlement context.

4.2 Evolution of an EU resettlement policy

Over the decades, the EU has shaped the definition of resettlement and gained influence over the resettlement policies of EUMS. Even though

EU law does not oblige EUMS to resettle an imposed number of persons, it sets out priorities on whom to resettle from where, and it offers financial and operational support to EUMS. The following section evinces the evolvement of EU's resettlement policy.[818] It provides the basis for subsequent evaluation in light of the above-elaborated principles of the EU Constitutional Framework (see 4.4).

4.2.1 Intergovernmental rapprochement by three Conventions

All EUMS signed and ratified the 1951 Refugee Convention. In addition, the Refugee Convention is incorporated in EU primary law under Art 78 para 1 TFEU (see 4.1.2.2). Hence, this Convention constitutes the common denominator for the evolution of EU legislation to protect refugees and other force migrants. Thereby, the initial focus was on asylum, and resettlement was considered later on (see 4.2.3). The coordination of EUMS' asylum and visa policies began in 1985, when EUMS decided to abolish internal border controls in order to realize a Common European Market, including the free movement of persons. The White Paper on Completing the Internal Market announced in its paragraph one that "[u]*nifying this market* [...] *presupposes that Member States will agree on the abolition of barriers of all kinds, harmonisation of rules, approximation of legislation* [...]".[819] Moreover, the growing numbers of asylum applications at that time triggered the endeavor to resolve the asylum issue at the EU (at that time EC) level.[820]

818 In this regard, Ziebritzki referred to the 'emerging EU resettlement law'; see Catharina Ziebritzki in Marie-Claire Foblets and Luc Leboeuf (eds), *Humanitarian Admission to Europe*, 298ff; see also Marie-Claire Foblets and Luc Leboeuf in Marie-Claire Foblets and Luc Leboeuf (eds), *Humanitarian Admission to Europe*, 26.

819 Commission, White Paper 'Completing the Internal Market', COM(85) 310 final <https://eur-lex.europa.eu/legal-content/EN/TXT/PDF/?uri=CELEX:51985DC0310&from=DE> accessed 21 February 2021; see Ulrich Haltern, *Europarecht: Dogmatik im Kontext* Vol I (Mohr Siebeck 3rd ed 2017) para 284f.

820 See Joanne van Selm, 'European Refugee Policy: is there such a thing?', UNHCR Research Paper n°115 (May 2005) 9f; see also Timothy J Hutton, 'Asylum Policy in the EU: The Case for Deeper Integration' in (2015) 61 CESifo Economic Studies 3, 605 (612).

The 1985 Schengen Agreement[821] anchored the then EC Member States' willingness to "*move the entry checks from the door of the apartment to the door of the building*".[822] The focus on EU's external borders implicated two main issues, namely asylum shopping and refugees *in orbit*. Asylum shopping refers to "*the phenomenon where a third-country national applies for international protection in more than one EU Member State with or without having already received international protection in one of those EU Member States*".[823] A refugee *in orbit* is a refugee "*who, although not returned directly to a country where* [he or she] *may be persecuted, is denied asylum or unable to find a State willing to examine* [his or her] *request, and* [is] *shuttled from one country to another in a constant search for asylum*".[824] Both topics were addressed in the 1990 Dublin Convention.[825]

Under the 1990 Dublin Convention, an asylum claim was supposed to be assessed only once, normally by the country of first entry.[826] This

---

821 See The Schengen *acquis* – Convention implementing the Schengen Agreement of 14 June 1985 between the Governments of the States of the Benelux Economic Union, the Federal Republic of Germany and the French Republic on the gradual abolition of checks at their common borders [2000] OJ L239/19-62.

822 First President of the Executive Committee of the 1990 Convention Implementing the 1985 Schengen Agreement, cited in Francesco Cherubini, 'Uniformity, Responsibility and solidarity in the Common European Asylum System (CEAS): A 'Constitutional' Solution' in Valsamis Mitsilegas, Violeta Moreno-Lax and Niovi Vavoula (eds), *Securitising Asylum Flows: Deflection, Criminalisation and Challenges for Human Rights* (Brill 2020) 236.

823 European Migration Network, 'Asylum and Migration Glossary 7.0' (July 2020) < https://ec.europa.eu/home-affairs/what-we-do/networks/european_migration_network/glossary_en> accessed 17 August 2021; see Kay Hailbronner and Daniel Thym in Kay Hailbronner and Daniel Thym (eds), *EU Immigration and Asylum Law: A Commentary*, 1024, para 1.

824 European Migration Network, 'Asylum and Migration Glossary 7.0' (July 2020) < https://ec.europa.eu/home-affairs/what-we-do/networks/european_migration_network/glossary_search/refugee-orbit_en> accessed 17 August 2021.

825 See Convention determining the State responsible for examining applications for asylum lodged in one of the Member States of the European Community – Dublin Convention [1997] OJ C254/1-12; the Dublin Convention was signed on 15 June 1990 and came into force on 1 September 1997; see also Moritz Baumgärtel, *Demanding Rights: Europe's Supranational Courts and the Dilemma of Migrant Vulnerability* (Cambridge University Press 2019) 47.

826 Art 3 para 2 Dublin Convention stipulated that only one EUMS should be responsible for examining an asylum application; see Moritz Baumgärtel, *Demanding Rights: Europe's Supranational Courts and the Dilemma of Migrant Vulnerability*, 47; see also Timothy J Hutton, 'Asylum Policy in the EU: The Case for Deeper Integration' in (2015) 61 CESifo Economic Studies 3, 612.

Dublin mechanism was not immediately incorporated in Community legislation, instead it was an international treaty (because in 1990, the then European Community was not competent to adopt Community legislation in the field of asylum or migration). From its initial phase,[827] the Dublin system was criticized to be non-effective.[828] The problem with Dublin has been that under this system, the allocation of responsibility for examining an asylum application to a specific EUMS does not take account of the map of Europe. The geographic location of some EUMS entails that they are more exposed to migration flows than others. Dublin has failed to unburden these EUMS.[829] There have been reformational efforts, namely the Commission's proposal to adopt a Dublin IV Regulation[830], as well as

---

827 "*An evaluation was carried out into the working of the* [...] *1990 Dublin Convention. That showed that in 6.00 percent of asylum cases a request was made to another Member State to take back an asylum seeker for determination procedures. In total of 4.20 percent of all asylum requests, states agreed to take back an asylum seeker as a result of a Dublin claim by the second Member State. In only 1.70 percent of cases did the asylum seeker actually move*", Joanne van Selm, 'European Refugee Policy: is there such a thing?', UNHCR Research Paper n°115 (May 2005) 14.

828 In the 1998/1999 period (ten years after the agreement) 95% of asylum applications took place outside the Dublin system, see Kay Hailbronner and Daniel Thym in Kay Hailbronner and Daniel Thym (eds), *EU Immigration and Asylum Law: A Commentary*, 1024, para 1; recent figures of 2019 show that the failure of Dublin persisted: Germany made about 27,000 take-back requests but only 3,500 transfers actually took place, see Daniel Thym, 'Secondary Movements: Overcoming the Lack of Trust among the Member States?' (*Eumigrationlawblog.eu*, 29 October 2020) <http://eumigrationlawblog.eu/secondary-movements-overcoming-the-lack-of-trust-among-the-member-states/> accessed 21 February 2021; see also 2017 figures: "[A]*ccording to Eurostat, 100.254 outgoing requests (across Europe) compare to only 23.670 actual transfers in 2017*", Moritz Baumgärtel, *Demanding Rights: Europe's Supranational Courts and the Dilemma of Migrant Vulnerability*, 50; see also Francesco Cherubini in Valsamis Mitsilegas, Violeta Moreno-Lax and Niovi Vavoula (eds), *Securitising Asylum Flows: Deflection, Criminalisation and Challenges for Human Rights*, 238.

829 See Joined Cases C-490/16 and 646/16 *AS v Republic of Slovenia* and *Jafari* [2017] EU:C:2017:443, Opinion of AG Sharpston, paras 3f; see also Marcello Di Filippo, 'The Dublin Saga and the Need to Rethink the Criteria for the Allocation of Competence in Asylum Procedures' in Valsamis Mitsilegas, Violeta Moreno-Lax and Niovi Vavoula (eds), *Securitising Asylum Flows: Deflection, Criminalisation and Challenges for Human Rights* (Brill 2020) 196 (200).

830 See Commission, Proposal for a Regulation establishing the criteria and mechanisms for determining the Member State responsible for examining an application for international protection lodged in one of the Member States by a third-country national or a stateless person (recast), COM(2016) 270 final.

the currently proposed Asylum and Migration Management Regulation,[831] to ensure just that, but agreement on such a reform has not yet been reached.

4.2.2 First attempts on solidarity and responsibility sharing

The EU made its first steps towards solidarity and responsibility sharing in the course of the Kosovo crisis. In 1994, the German Presidency of the Council of the EU suggested a refugee distribution key,[832] inspired by the refugee distribution mechanism among the federal states of Germany.[833] Some members of the Council, however, raised concerns about potential human rights violations when transferring refugees among EUMS without their consent.[834] The French Presidency followed up with the Resolution on burden sharing, where a compulsory distribution mechanism was not mentioned.[835] Instead, it referred to voluntary commitment in mass influx situations. This exemplifies that voluntary *ad hoc* burden sharing remained the limit of what was politically feasible.[836]

---

831 Commission, Proposal for a Regulation on asylum and migration management and amending Council Directive 2003/109 and the proposed Regulation (EU) XXX/XXX [Asylum and Migration Fund], COM(2020) 610 final.

832 See German Presidency, Draft Council Resolution on burden-sharing with regard to the admission and residence of refugees of 1 July 1994, Council Document 7773/94 ASIM 124; the distribution key was based on three criteria of equal weight, i.e. (i) population size, (ii) size of EUMS' territory and (iii) the Gross Domestic Product (GDP).

833 "*Where the numbers admitted by a Member State exceed its indicative figure* [...], *other Member States which have not yet reached their indicative figure* [...] *will accept persons from the first state*", ibid 8, para 10; see Eiko R Thielemann, 'Between Interests and Norms: Explaining Burden-Sharing in the European Union' in (2003) 16 Journal of Refugee Studies 3, 253 (259); the so-called 'Königsteiner Schlüssel' is currently enshrined in Art 45 of the German Asylum Act as of 8 September 2008, BGBl I 2008, 1798.

834 See Eiko R Thielemann, 'Between Interests and Norms: Explaining Burden-Sharing in the European Union' in (2003) 16 Journal of Refugee Studies 3, 260.

835 See Council Resolution on burden-sharing with regard to the admission and residence of displaced persons on a temporary basis [1995] OJ C262/1.

836 See Eiko R Thielemann, 'Between Interests and Norms: Explaining Burden-Sharing in the European Union' in (2003) 16 Journal of Refugee Studies 3, 260.

The Treaty of Amsterdam[837] revived responsibility sharing discussions.[838] Its Art 63 para 2 proclaimed the promotion of "*a balance of effort between Member States in receiving and bearing the consequences of receiving refugees and displaced persons*". In addition, the Tampere Conference in 1999 addressed the external dimension of the CEAS and cooperation with countries outside the EU.[839] In particular, the Temporary Protection Directive[840] and the European Refugee Fund (ERF)[841] were adopted to reinforce the principle of solidarity and responsibility sharing.[842] Accordingly, EUMS "*shall receive persons who are eligible for temporary protection in a spirit of Community solidarity*".[843] Until 2022, political disputes and disagreement about 'burden sharing' in mass influx situations, such as in 2015/16, blocked the activation of the Directive.[844] Unprecedently, when facing mass influx of individuals fleeing the Russian invasion of Ukraine, unanimous agreement resulted in a Council Decision to implement the

837 See Treaty of Amsterdam amending the Treaty on European Union, the Treaties establishing the European Communities and certain related acts [1997] OJ C340/1-144.

838 See Ségolène Barbou des Places, 'Burden Sharing in the Field of Asylum: Legal Motivations and Implications of a Regional Approach' (2012) 1, fn 2 <https://hal.archives-ouvertes.fr/hal-01614068/document> accessed 21 February 2021.

839 See Christina Boswell, 'The 'External Dimension' of EU Immigration and Asylum Policy' in (2003) 79 International Affairs, 619-638.

840 See Directive 2001/55 (EC) on minimum standards for giving temporary protection in the event of a mass influx of displaced persons and on measures promoting a balance of efforts between Member States in receiving such persons and bearing the consequences thereof [2001] OJ L212/12-23.

841 See Decision 2000/596 (EC) establishing a European Refugee Fund [2000] OJ L252/12-18. Pursuant to Art 24 Temporary Protection Directive, relocation measures are to be funded by the ERF.

842 See Ségolène Barbou des Places, 'Burden Sharing in the Field of Asylum: Legal Motivations and Implications of a Regional Approach' (2012) 3, 11.

843 Art 25 Temporary Protection Directive. This Article also expressly mentions the UNHCR, as it states that EUMS shall indicate their capacity to receive persons eligible for temporary protection and that "[t]*his information shall be passed on swiftly to UNHCR*".

844 See Meltem İneli Ciğer, '5 Reasons Why: Understanding the reasons behind the activation of the Temporary Protection Directive in 2022' (*Eumigrationlawblog.eu*, 7 March 2022) <https://eumigrationlawblog.eu/5-reasons-why-understanding-the-reasons-behind-the-activation-of-the-temporary-protection-directive-in-2022/> accessed 18 July 2022; see also Timothy J Hutton, 'Asylum Policy in the EU: The Case for Deeper Integration' in (2015) 61 CESifo Economic Studies 3, 614.

Temporary Protection Directive.[845] Politically speaking, negotiations on this Implementing Decision were not hampered by disputes over quotas. While the Temporary Protection Directive sets out a basis to specify which EUMS will accommodate how many people (Art 5 para 3 lit c, Art 25 paras 1 and 3 Temporary Protection Directive), EUMS refrained from incorporating such specification in the Implementing Decision. Instead, they relied on the free of choice of the protection seekers.[846]

4.2.3 Calling upon resettlement

The Commission made its first reference to resettlement in its Communication of 2000[847]. It referred to resettlement schemes as a means to facilitate refugee arrivals on EUMS' territory and offer rapid access to protection. In this Communication, the Commission made reference to the US and its "*two-tier asylum procedure: one for spontaneous arrivals and one, very different, based on a resettlement scheme*".[848] The US conducts asylum and refugee resettlement in a complementary manner.[849] The Commission followed the US approach in its Communication of March 2003[850] by clarifying that "*resettlement complements a fair and efficient territorial asylum*

845 See Council Implementing Decision 2022/382 (EU) establishing the existence of a mass influx of displaced persons from Ukraine within the meaning of Article 5 of Directive 2001/55/EC, and having the effect of introducing temporary protection [2022] OJ L71/1-6.

846 See Daniel Thym, 'Temporary Protection for Ukrainians: the Unexpected Renaissance of 'Free Choice'' (*Eumigrationlawblog.eu*, 7 March 2022) <https://eumigrationlawblog.eu/temporary-protection-for-ukrainians-the-unexpected-renaissance-of-free-choice/> accessed 18 July 2022.

847 See Commission, Communication 'Towards a common asylum procedure and a uniform status, valid throughout the Union, for persons granted asylum', COM(2000) 755 final.

848 Ibid 9; see Joanne van Selm et al, Study on 'The Feasibility of setting up resettlement schemes in EU Member States or at EU Level, against the background of the Common European Asylum system and the goal of a Common Asylum Procedure', 28; see also Steve Peers, Violeta Moreno-Lax, Madeline Garlick and Elspeth Guild, *EU Immigration and Asylum Law*, 620.

849 See Statement of L Francis Cissna cited in Nayla Rush, 'The FY 2020 Refugee Ceiling? 15,000 could cover all UNHCR urgent and emergency submissions worldwide next year' (*Center for Immigration Studies*, 27 August 2019) <https://cis.org/Rush/FY-2020-Refugee-Ceiling> accessed 21 February 2021.

850 See Commission, Communication on the common asylum policy and the Agenda for protection (Second Commission Report on the implementation of

system. However, it is not part of the asylum system: rather both asylum and resettlement are part of a protection system".[851] The Commission further acknowledged that the complementary function of resettlement implied overall compliance of a comprehensive protection system with international obligations.[852]

It appears that the Commission's original intention was to provide (territorial) asylum and resettlement in a complementary manner. However, the Commission was less clear on complementary protection through (territorial) asylum and resettlement in the 2016 Proposal for a Union Resettlement Framework Regulation, where it pointed to resettlement as "*the preferred avenue to international protection*", which "*should not be duplicated by an asylum procedure*".[853] In the same vein, the Commission stated in the Dublin IV Proposal that refugee resettlement "*should become the model for the future*".[854]

In the following, the Commission initiated a study to evaluate the feasibility of setting up resettlement schemes in EUMS or at the EU level.[855] The evaluation showed that a common approach was necessary as a political and operational basis in order (i) to produce beneficial effects and (ii) to use resettlement for strategic purposes as well as (iii) to attain

---

Communication, COM(2000) 755 final of 22 November 2000), COM(2003) 152 final.

851 Joanne van Selm et al, Study on 'The Feasibility of setting up resettlement schemes in EU Member States or at EU Level, against the background of the Common European Asylum system and the goal of a Common Asylum Procedure', 32.

852 See Commission, Communication on the common asylum policy and the Agenda for protection, COM(2003) 152 final, 15; see also Joanne van Selm et al, Study on 'The Feasibility of setting up resettlement schemes in EU Member States or at EU Level, against the background of the Common European Asylum system and the goal of a Common Asylum Procedure', 28.

853 Proposal for a Union Resettlement Framework, 13; see Catharina Ziebritzki in Marie-Claire Foblets and Luc Leboeuf (eds), *Humanitarian Admission to Europe*, 309.

854 See Commission, Proposal for a Regulation establishing the criteria and mechanisms for determining the Member State responsible for examining an application for international protection lodged in one of the Member States by a third-country national or a stateless person (recast), COM(2016) 270 final, 2.

855 See Joanne van Selm et al, Study on 'The Feasibility of setting up resettlement schemes in EU Member States or at EU Level, against the background of the Common European Asylum system and the goal of a Common Asylum Procedure'.

UNHCR's objectives.[856] Notwithstanding these findings, in its 2004 Communication[857], the Commission shifted its focus from a common approach to a situation-specific approach on resettlement, namely *ad hoc* schemes with flexible EUMS participation.[858]

4.2.4 Protection in the region

In parallel, the European Council formally introduced the external dimension of the CEAS with the approval of the Hague Program in November 2004. The envisaged externalization involved "*the development of EU-Regional Protection Programmes (RPP) which included a joint resettlement programme for Member States willing to participate in such a programme*"[859]. The first two RPPs "*geared to finding durable solutions for refugees in selected regions that had strategic importance for the EU*"[860]. They were implemented by EUMS on a voluntary basis and located in the Great Lakes Area (Tanza-

856 See Commission, Communication on the common asylum policy and the Agenda for protection, COM(2003) 152 final, 12; see also Steve Peers, Violeta Moreno-Lax, Madeline Garlick and Elspeth Guild, *EU Immigration and Asylum Law*, 620.

857 See Commission, Communication on the Managed Entry in the EU of Persons in Need of International Protection and the Enhancement of the Protection Capacity of the Regions of Origin 'Improving Access to Durable Solutions', COM(2004) 410 final.

858 See Lyra Jakulevičiené and Mantas Bileišis, 'EU refugee resettlement: Key challenges of expanding the practice into new Member States' in (2016) 9 Baltic Journal of Law & Politics 1, 103; the 2004 Communication resulted from a seminar of the Italian Presidency held in Rome where advantages, such as immediate access to durable solutions, were identified and resettlement became recognized as an indispensable and essential part of the international protection system; see Steve Peers, Violeta Moreno-Lax, Madeline Garlick and Elspeth Guild, *EU Immigration and Asylum Law*, 620.

859 Delphine Perrin and Frank McNamara, 'Refugee Resettlement in the EU: Between Shared Standards and Diversity in Legal and Policy Frames', KNOW RESET Research Report 2013/03, 4.

860 Tom de Boer and Marjoleine Zieck, 'The Legal Abyss of Discretion in the Resettlement of Refugees: Cherry-Picking and the Lack of Due Process in the EU' in (2020) 32 International Journal of Refugee Law 1, 64; see Commission, Communication 'Regional Protection Programmes', COM(2005) 388 final.

nia).[861] The European Refugee Fund III (ERF III),[862] and subsequently the AMIF, provided financial support, which was criticized for being "*insignificant in comparison to the scale of the needs to be addressed*".[863] A 2010 evaluation of RPPs revealed limited flexibility, funding, visibility and coordination with other EU humanitarian and development policies as well as insufficient third-country engagement.[864]

Although the European Council claimed to provide "*better access to durable solutions*"[865], the focus was on migration control, return and readmission. The return issue relates to compliance of third countries hosting RPPs with their human rights obligations. Scholarly writing and ECtHR case law support an obligation under the ECHR and the Charter not to re-

861 See Philippe de Bruycker and Evangelia (Lilian) Tsourdi in Vincent Chetail, Philippe de Bruycker and Francesco Maiani (eds), *Reforming the Common European Asylum System: The New European refugee law* (Brill 2016) 481.

862 See Decision of the European Parliament and of the Council (EC) 573/2007 of 23 May 2007 establishing the European Refugee Fund for the period 2008 to 2013 as part of the General programme 'Solidarity and Management of Migration Flows' [2007] OJ L144/1-21; "*The EU decision establishing the European Refugee Fund for the years 2008 to 2013 (ERF III)* [...] *entailed an EU definition of refugee resettlement and provisions for financial support to EU member-states resettling refugees on the basis of this definition*", Adèle Garnier, 'Narratives of accountability in UNHCR's refugee resettlement strategy' in Kristin Bergtora Sandvik and Katja Lindskov Jacobsen (eds), *UNHCR and the Struggle for Accountability* (Routledge 2016) 64 (72); "*The ERF (EUR 630 million over the period 2008-13) support*[ed] [...] *resettlement programmes and actions related to the integration of persons whose stay is of a lasting and stable nature*", Commission, 'Refugee Fund' <https://ec.europa.eu/home-affairs/financing/fundings/migration-asylum-borders/refugee-fund_en> accessed 21 February 2021.

863 Steve Peers, Violeta Moreno-Lax, Madeline Garlick and Elspeth Guild, *EU Immigration and Asylum Law*, 638; see Tom de Boer and Marjoleine Zieck, 'The Legal Abyss of Discretion in the Resettlement of Refugees: Cherry-Picking and the Lack of Due Process in the EU' in (2020) 32 International Journal of Refugee Law 1, 64; see also Philippe de Bruycker and Evangelia (Lilian) Tsourdi in Vincent Chetail, Philippe de Bruycker and Francesco Maiani (eds), *Reforming the Common European Asylum System: The New European Refugee Law*, 485.

864 See Steve Peers, Violeta Moreno-Lax, Madeline Garlick and Elspeth Guild, *EU Immigration and Asylum Law*, 639f.

865 European Council, 'The Hague Programme – Strengthening Freedom, Security and Justice in the European Union' [2005] OJ C53/1 (5); see also Steve Peers, Violeta Moreno-Lax, Madeline Garlick and Elspeth Guild, *EU Immigration and Asylum Law*, 619.

turn individuals to RPP countries unless a comparable level of protection is accessible there.[866]

4.2.5 Proposal for extraterritorial processing and third-country partnerships

The Stockholm Program[867] of 2009 emphasized legal pathways and access to efficient asylum procedures for those in need of protection. At the same time, it prioritized external border controls to stop irregular migration.[868] This Program triggered the most detailed proposal to date for an EU offshore processing scheme to resolve the migration situations of the Mediterranean and the Eastern migration routes. It was based on US experience, namely the Caribbean Interdiction Program and US agreements with Jamaica and the Turks and Caicos Islands. The suggested approach for the EU was to build partnerships with countries of origin and transit countries, such as Libya and Turkey.[869] In the end, human rights concerns, such as about arbitrary detention, torture and ill-treatment as well as violations of the *non-refoulement* principle in the course of automatic returns to partnership countries, prevented the establishment of reception centers.[870] In 2018, similar concerns led to the rejection of setting up so-called regional disembarkation platforms, including the possibility of resettlement to the EU.[871]

---

866 See Steve Peers, Violeta Moreno-Lax, Madeline Garlick and Elspeth Guild, *EU Immigration and Asylum Law*, 642f; see also *Amuur v France* App No 19776/92 (ECtHR 20 May 1996) para 48.

867 See European Council, 'Stockholm Programme – An Open and Secure Europe Serving and Protecting Citizens' [2010] OJ C115/1-38.

868 See Steve Peers, Violeta Moreno-Lax, Madeline Garlick and Elspeth Guild, *EU Immigration and Asylum Law*, 617.

869 The proposal included two alternatives, i.e. (i) either *ad hoc* protection in Libya with the participation of the UNHCR, the IOM and financial support by the EU or (ii) the possibility of lodging asylum applications at EUMS' embassies there; see ibid 655ff.

870 See ibid 659f; see also UNHCR, 'Protection Policy Paper: Maritime interception operations and the processing of international protection claims: legal standards and policy considerations with respect to extraterritorial processing' (November 2010) <https://www.refworld.org/docid/4cd12d3a2.html> accessed 21 February 2021.

871 See European Council meeting of 28 June 2018 – Conclusions EUCO 9/18 (28 June 2018) para 5 <https://www.consilium.europa.eu/media/35936/28-euco-final-conclusions-en.pdf> accessed 21 February 2021; see also Cathari-

4.2.6 A Joint EU Resettlement Program

In 2009, only ten EUMS had regular annual resettlement schemes[872] with limited contributions in comparison to traditional resettlement countries such as the US or Canada.[873] Against this backdrop, the Commission responded with a Communication on the establishment of a Joint EU Resettlement Program.[874] This was a voluntary program that "*did not determine any common European resettlement quota or other mechanisms for coordinating MS actions*".[875] During the subsequent period from 2009 to 2014, resettlement to the EU still failed in large parts. In 2012, EUMS accounted for "[...] *just above 5% of the total number of refugees resettled in the world and 9% of the number of asylum applicants that were granted refugee status in the EU that year*".[876] Moreover, the Joint Resettlement Program was criticized for focusing on cooperation with selected partner countries instead of actual protection needs.[877] The focus on selected partners was further pursued in the GAMM (see 4.2.7) and the later Proposal for a Union Resettlement Framework (see 4.2.11).

na Ziebritzki in Marie-Claire Foblets and Luc Leboeuf (eds), *Humanitarian Admission to Europe*, 297f; see also Francesco Maiani, '"Regional Disembarkation Platforms" and "Controlled Centres": Lifting Drawbridge, Reaching out Across The Mediterranean, or Going Nowhere?' (*Eumigrationlawblog.eu*, 18 September 2018) <http://eumigrationlawblog.eu/regional-disembarkation-platforms-and-controlled-centres-lifting-the-drawbridge-reaching-out-across-the-mediterranean-or-going-nowhere> accessed 21 February 2021.

872 The Czech Republic Denmark, Finland, France, Ireland, the Netherlands, Portugal, Romania, Sweden, and the United Kingdom.

873 See Steve Peers, Violeta Moreno-Lax, Madeline Garlick and Elspeth Guild, *EU Immigration and Asylum Law*, 622.

874 See Commission, Communication 'Establishment of a joint EU resettlement programme', Communication 'Establishment of a joint EU resettlement programme', COM(2009) 447 final.

875 Lyra Jakulevičiené and Mantas Bileišis, 'EU refugee resettlement: Key challenges of expanding the practice into new Member States' in (2016) 9 Baltic Journal of Law & Politics 1, 103.

876 Jesus Férnandez-Huertas Moraga and Hillel Rapoport, 'Tradable Refugee-admission Quotas and EU Asylum Policy' in (2015) 61 CESifo Economic Studies 3, 638 (644).

877 See Steve Peers, Violeta Moreno-Lax, Madeline Garlick and Elspeth Guild, *EU Immigration and Asylum Law*, 624.

4.2.7 Global Approach to Migration and Mobility (GAMM)

The EU has benefited from cooperation with third countries to strengthen external border control and readmission of irregular migrants. In turn, the EU has offered resettlement, trade benefits and financial support.[878]

In 2011, the Global Approach to Migration and Mobility (GAMM)[879] fostered the partnership between the EU and Africa. On this basis, a new Partnership Framework followed in 2016. It prioritized solutions for irregular and uncontrolled movement. Under this Framework, the Commission considered returns to Africa and resettlement to Europe for an integrable part of third-country nationals or stateless persons.[880]

A progress report of 16 May 2018[881] showed intensified cooperation with several African partners, including Morocco and Libya.[882] In 2018, the EU supported increased funding to Morocco, Spain's preferred partner in migration management.[883] Major criticism pointed to insufficient assessment of the human rights situations in the partner countries,[884] with a lack of respective monitoring.[885] In fact, the situation required resettlement efforts, as migrants and refugees complained about lacking durable prospects in Morocco.[886] Especially, Lesbian, Gay, Bisexual, and Transgender (LGBT) refugees depend on resettlement since they can neither repatriate nor stay in Morocco, where homosexuality is criminalized and refugee cards for LGBT refugees are refused, depriving them of their core refugee

878 See Tineke Strik, 'The Global Approach to Migration and Mobility' in (2017) 5 Groningen Journal of International Law 2, 310.

879 See Commission, Communication 'The Global Approach to Migration and Mobility', COM(2011) 743 final.

880 See Tineke Strik, 'The Global Approach to Migration and Mobility' in (2017) 5 Groningen Journal of International Law 2, 323.

881 See Commission, Communication 'Progress report on the Implementation of the European Agenda on Migration', COM(2018) 301 final.

882 See ibid 13f.

883 See Sabrina Ardalan in Valsamis Mitsilegas, Violeta Moreno-Lax and Niovi Vavoula (eds), *Securitising Asylum Flows: Deflection, Criminalisation and Challenges for Human Rights*, 295.

884 Afghanistan, Algeria, Bangladesh, Eritrea, Ethiopia, Ghana, Ivory Coast, Mali, Morocco, Niger, Nigeria, Pakistan, Senegal, Somalia, Sudan, Tunisia; see Commission, Communication on establishing a new Partnership Framework with third countries under the European Agenda on Migration, COM(2016) 385 final, 8.

885 See Tineke Strik, 'The Global Approach to Migration and Mobility' in (2017) 5 Groningen Journal of International Law 2, 310.

886 See ibid 301.

and human rights.[887] Also in the cooperation between Libya and Italy,[888] actual resettlement efforts remained scarce while on-site assistance to the Libyan coast guards was emphasized. This facilitated push-back operations, and raised concerns about *non-refoulement* violations (see 3.3.1).

4.2.8 The Lisbon Treaty, mutual trust, and Dublin III

The 2009 Lisbon Treaty consolidated EU law in the Area of Freedom, Security and Justice (Art 67 TFEU). Its goal was to further develop a CEAS based on solidarity and responsibility sharing, including external asylum and migration policy as well as border control.[889] In furtherance of the proclaimed goals, the Commission issued a package of proposals, including the revision of Eurodac, Dublin II, the Reception Conditions Directive and the proposal to establish EASO.[890] The lack of agreement on the revision of Dublin II initially blocked the envisaged reform.[891] Eventually, the Dublin III Regulation[892] was adopted,[893] whereas its Art

887 "[F]*ew refugees are resettled to each year from Morocco, since refugees are generally expected either to integrate or repatriate, not resettle*", ibid 305.

888 See Commission, Communication 'Progress report on the Implementation of the European Agenda on Migration', 10.

889 See Art 67 para 2 TFEU.

890 See Patricia Van de Peer, 'Negotiating the Second Generation of the Common European Asylum System Instruments: A Chronicle' in Vincent Chetail, Philippe de Bruycker and Francesco Maiani (eds), *Reforming the Common European Asylum System: The New European Refugee Law* (Brill 2016) 55 (56); see also Kris Pollet in Vincent Chetail, Philippe de Bruycker and Francesco Maiani (eds), *Reforming the common European asylum system: The New European Refugee Law*, 82.

891 See Council Regulation No 343/2003 (EC) establishing the criteria and mechanisms for determining the Member State responsible for examining an asylum application lodged in one of the Member States by a third-country national [2003] OJ L50/1–10; see also Patricia Van de Peer in Vincent Chetail, Philippe de Bruycker and Francesco Maiani (eds), *Reforming the Common European Asylum System: The New European Refugee Law*, 59f.

892 See Regulation 2013/604 (EU) establishing the criteria and mechanisms for determining the Member State responsible for examining and application for international protection lodged in one of the Member States by a third-country national or a stateless person [2013] OJ L180/31-59.

893 "*Where it is impossible to transfer an applicant to the Member State primarily designated as responsible because there are substantial grounds for believing that there are systemic flaws in the asylum procedure and in the reception conditions for applicants in that Member State, resulting in a risk of inhuman or degrading treatment within*

3 para 2 accounts for derogation in case of systemic deficiencies in the asylum procedure and the reception conditions in the responsible EUMS. This provision was a necessary response to ECtHR and CJEU rulings that some EUMS did not comply with human rights standards.[894]

Systemic deficiencies in EUMS also impact resettlement to the EU. First, divergent protection standards impede a fair distribution of resettlement beneficiaries among all EUMS. Second, resettlement to a receiving EUMS with serious systemic deficiencies runs counter the purpose of resettlement, since a resettlement beneficiary would face (a threat of) human rights violations in the receiving EUMS – possibly similar to the situation in the country of (first) refuge. Such circumstances likely lead to secondary migration from EUMS with systemic deficiencies to EUMS with higher protection standards. Thus, diverging protection standards, namely systemic deficiencies in some EUMS, are not only Dublin issues. Systemic deficiencies implicate that a durable solution might not be available in certain EUMS, and thereby exert a negative impact on resettlement to the EU.

4.2.9 The 2015 European Resettlement Scheme

The 2015 Recommendation on a European Resettlement Scheme[895] was referred to as "*the first attempt to develop an EU-wide resettlement scheme based on common criteria*".[896] The Commission recommended to resettle "*20,000 people in need of international protection on the basis of the condi-*

---

the meaning of Article 4 of the Charter of Fundamental Rights of the European Union, the determining Member State shall continue to examine the criteria set out in Chapter III in order to establish whether another Member State can be designated as responsible."

894 See *MSS v Belgium and Greece*; see also *Tarakhel v Switzerland*; see also Joined cases C-411/10 and C-493/10 *NS v Secretary of State for the Home Department and ME and Others v Refugee Applications Commissioner and Minister for Justice, Equality and Law Reform* [2011] EU:C:2011:865; see also Case C-578/16 PPU *CK, HF and AS v Republic of Slovenia Reform* [2017] EU:C:2017:127.

895 See Commission, Recommendation on a European resettlement scheme, C(2015) 3560 final.

896 Lyra Jakulevičienė and Mantas Bileišis, 'EU refugee resettlement: Key challenges of expanding the practice into new Member States' in (2016) 9 Baltic Journal of Law & Politics 1, 104; see Arne Niemann and Natascha Zaun, 'EU Refugee Policies and Politics in Times of Crisis: Theoretical and Empirical Perspectives' in (2018) 56 Journal of Common Market Studies 1, 7.

tions and the distribution key laid down in this Recommendation".[897] The Recommendation set out the following definition of resettlement, which resembles the UNHCR definition (see 2.2.1) – with the exception of not explicitly addressing refugees:[898]

> *'Resettlement' means the transfer of individual displaced persons in clear need of international protection, on request of the United Nations High Commissioner for Refugees, from a third country to a Member State, in agreement with the latter, with the objective of protecting against refoulement and admitting and granting the right to stay and any other rights similar to those granted to a beneficiary of international protection.*

Accordingly, the scope of resettlement beneficiaries was not limited to refugees but also allowed for resettlement of other forcibly displaced persons, including IDPs.[899] What status the beneficiaries would receive remained vague, as the Commission only defined that they should receive similar rights as beneficiaries of international protection. Also, the Commission did not distinguish between resettlement and other forms of (shorter-term) humanitarian admission.[900]

Moreover, the Commission intended the scheme to cover all EUMS.[901] Their contributions should be based on a formal procedure following the EU asylum *acquis*.[902] Yet, EUMS refused to define a binding distribution key and opted for voluntary pledging instead.[903] In their Conclusions of July 2015, the Representatives of the Governments of the EUMS did not mention the conducting of formal procedures in accordance with the EU asylum *acquis*.[904]

---

897 Commission, Recommendation on a European resettlement scheme, para 1.

898 Ibid para 2.

899 The Commission specified its attempts to include IDPs in the scope of resettlement beneficiaries in the 2016 Proposal for a Union Resettlement Framework (see 4.2.11.4).

900 This remained a contentious point in the negotiations on the Proposal for a Union Resettlement Framework Regulation.

901 See Commission, Recommendation on a European resettlement scheme, para 3.

902 See ibid para 8; see also Philippe de Bruycker and Evangelia (Lilian) Tsourdi in Vincent Chetail, Philippe de Bruycker and Francesco Maiani (eds), *Reforming the Common European Asylum System: The New European Refugee Law*, 531.

903 See Philippe de Bruycker and Evangelia (Lilian) Tsourdi in Vincent Chetail, Philippe de Bruycker and Francesco Maiani (eds), *Reforming the Common European Asylum System: The New European Refugee Law*, 532.

904 See Council of the EU, 'Conclusions of the Representatives of the Governments of the Member States meeting within the Council on resettling through mul-

Still, the Council of the EU agreed on the admission of 22,504 people from the Middle East, the Horn of Africa, and Northern Africa during the period 2015-2017.[905] The 2015 resettlement scheme achieved 19,432 resettlements to Europe, i.e. 86% of the initial pledge.[906] Upon the expiration of the Scheme covering the period from 2015 to 2017, the Commission recommended a second *ad hoc* scheme for at least 50,000 refugees.[907] By March 2018, 19 EUMS pledged 40,000 places.[908] Due to the missing agreement on a permanent EU resettlement framework before the European Parliament elections in May 2019, the second *ad hoc* program was prolonged[909] and EUMS increased their pledges to 50,039 places. The second scheme actually achieved 43,827 resettlements in total, i.e. 88% of the increased pledge.[910] A new pledge followed for 2020 (see 4.2.12).

4.2.10 EU-Turkey Statement

The EU-Turkey Statement of 18 March 2016 constituted an agreement between the EU and Turkey to address migratory pressure by means of

tilateral and national schemes 20,000 persons in clear need of international protection', Council Doc 11130/15 (22 July 2015) <https://data.consilium.europa.eu/doc/document/ST-11130-2015-INIT/en/pdf> accessed 21 February 2021; see also Philippe de Bruycker and Evangelia (Lilian) Tsourdi in Vincent Chetail, Philippe de Bruycker and Francesco Maiani (eds), *Reforming the Common European Asylum System: The New European Refugee Law*, 533.

905 See for the exact participation of EUMS, ibid 532f, fn 239-244.

906 See Commission, Recommendation on legal pathways to protection in the EU: promoting resettlement, humanitarian admission and other complementary pathways, 2, Recital 8; see also Commission, 'European Agenda on Migration: Continuous efforts needed to sustain progress' (*Press release*, 14 March 2018) <http://europa.eu/rapid/press-release_IP-18-1763_en.htm> accessed 21 February 2021.

907 See Commission, Recommendation (EU) 2017/1803 on enhancing legal pathways for persons in need of international protection [2017] OJ L259/21-24 [notified under the document C(2017)6504].

908 See Commission, 'European Agenda on Migration: Continuous efforts needed to sustain progress' (*Press release*, 14 March 2018).

909 See Commission, 'Delivering on resettlement' (16 October 2019) <https://ec.europa.eu/commission/presscorner/detail/en/FS_19_6079> accessed 21 February 2021; see also Janine Prantl, ''Lessons to be learned' für ein zukünftiges, gemeinsames EU Resettlement' in (2020) Europarecht Supplement 3, 117 (130).

910 See Commission, Recommendation on legal pathways to protection in the EU: promoting resettlement, humanitarian admission and other complementary pathways, 2f, Recital 9.

resettlement.[911] Originally, it was agreed that irregular migrants crossing from Turkey into Greek islands should be returned to Turkey. For any Syrian returned to Turkey from Greece, the EU would, in turn, resettle another Syrian from Turkey to the EU. The major purpose was to prevent Syrian migrants from taking dangerous boat journeys between Turkey and Greece.[912]

The EU-Turkey Statement made resettlement dependent on returns of those refugees who reached the Greek border to Turkey. It thereby implemented the 'safe third country' principle. Greece could only refrain from full examination when returning applicants for international protection if Turkey met the requirements of a safe third country. This is problematic because it has been disputed whether Turkey qualifies as a safe third country.[913] The Asylum Procedures Directive sets out the thresholds for the determination of a safe third country. It thereby distinguishes between safe third countries under Art 38 and European safe third countries under Art 39 Asylum Procedures Directive. It remains questionable whether Turkey satisfies Art 39 Asylum Procedures Directive because this Article demands ratification and observation of the Refugee Convention without any geographical limitations. While Turkey is party to the Refugee Convention, it does not apply the geographical changes introduced through the Protocol to the Convention. This means that Turkey has maintained the initial geographical limitation of the Refugee Convention,[914] i.e. "*only people from the*

---

911 See European Council, 'EU-Turkey statement, 18 March 2016' (*Press Release*, 18 March 2016) <https://www.consilium.europa.eu/en/press/press-releases/2016/03/18/eu-turkey-statement/> accessed 21 February 2021.

912 See Arne Niemann and Natascha Zaun, 'EU Refugee Policies and Politics in Times of Crisis: Theoretical and Empirical Perspectives' in (2018) 56 Journal of Common Market Studies 1, 8.

913 See Thomas Spijkerboer, 'Bifurcation of people, bifurcation of law: externalization of migration policy before the EU Court of Justice' in (2017) 31 Journal of Refugee Studies 2, 216 (221); see also Sergio Carrera, *An Appraisal of the European Commission of Crisis: Has the Juncker Commission delivered a new start for EU Justice and Home Affairs?* (Centre for European Policy Studies 2018) 35; see also Mattia di Salvo et al, 'Flexible Solidarity: A comprehensive strategy for asylum in the EU', MEDAM Assessment Report (15 June 2018) 32.

914 Turkey made the following declaration: "*The instrument of accession stipulates that the Government of Turkey maintains the provisions of the declaration made under section B of article 1 of the Convention relating to the Status of Refugees, done at Geneva on 28 July 1951, according to which it applies the Convention only to persons who have become refugees as a result of events occurring in Europe, and also the reservation clause made upon ratification of the Convention to the effect that no provision of this Convention may be interpreted as granting to refugees greater rights*

Council of Europe are allowed to seek refugee status in Europe".[915] Although, theoretically, non-European asylum seekers could have access to alternative forms of protection in Turkey, those forms of protection are more limited than the refugee status accessible to people from the Council of Europe.[916]

As an example of reference, the 2011 refugee swap agreement between Australia and Malaysia, deserves mentioning.[917] The Australian High Court invalidated this Agreement "*due to inadequate legal guarantees that refugees in Malaysia would receive the protection required by Australian law*".[918] As opposed to the Australian High Court, the CJEU avoided to rule on whether the legal guarantees for protection seekers in Turkey are adequate in light of the requirements under EU law. Both the General Court[919] and the Court of Justice[920] confirmed that the EU-Turkey Statement qualified as an 'extra Treaty' instrument. The General Court denied jurisdiction to hear and determine the actions against the EU-Turkey Statement, since the Statement was not an 'EU-product' but rather emerged under authorship of the Heads of Government and State of EUMS.[921] Con-

than those accorded to Turkish citizens in Turkey." UN Treaty Collection, Chapter V Refugees and Stateless Persons: Protocol relating to the Status of Refugees (as of 19 September 2020) <https://treaties.un.org/pages/ViewDetails.aspx?src=TREATY&mtdsg_no=V-5&chapter=5#EndDec> accessed 21 February 2021.

915 Evelien Wauters and Samuel Cogolati in Valsamis Mitsilegas, Violeta Moreno-Lax and Niovi Vavoula (eds), *Securitising Asylum Flows: Deflection, Criminalisation and Challenges for Human Rights*, 123.

916 See ibid 123f.

917 See Nikolas Feith Tan in Satvinder Singh Juss (ed), *Research Handbook on International Refugee Law*, 175: "*In July 2011 the Australian government signed a non-binding agreement with Malaysia to resettle, on an annual basis 4,000 refugees in exchange for Malaysia accepting 800 asylum seekers intercepted at sea*".

918 Ibid 175; see Naoko Hashimoto, 'Refugee Resettlement as an Alternative to Asylum' in (2018) 37 Refugee Survey Quarterly, 178f; see also *M70 v Minister for Immigration and Citizenship*, 244 CLR 144 (2011).

919 See Cases T-192/16, T-193/16 and T-257/16 *NF, NG and NM v European Council* [2017] EU:T:2017:128, Orders of the General Court.

920 See Joined Cases C-208/17 P to C-210/17 *P NF and Others v European Council* [2018] EU:C:2018:705, Order of the Court (First Chamber).

921 See ibid para 23f; see also Sergio Carrera, *An Appraisal of the European Commission of Crisis: Has the Juncker Commission delivered a new start for EU Justice and Home Affairs?* (Centre for European Policy Studies 2018) 33; see also Thomas Spijkerboer, 'Bifurcation of people, bifurcation of law: externalization of migration policy before the EU Court of Justice' in (2017) 31 Journal of Refugee Studies 2, 223.

sequently, the EU institutions could not be held accountable for human rights violations while implementing this Statement.[922]

For the implementation of the EU-Turkey Statement, the Commission trusted in EUMS' willingness to resettle "*once the irregular flows from Turkey have come to an end*".[923] Actually, the implementation of the resettlement targets happened very slowly. "*At this pace, it would take the EU around 13 years to resettle all the Syrians it promised to.*"[924] Against the backdrop of 3.7 million Syrian registered refugees in Turkey as of December 2019,[925] the actual mid-September 2020 resettlement number of 27,000[926] justifies doubts on the Commission's promotion of the EU-Turkey Statement as a success and role model.[927]

4.2.11 The Proposal for a Union Resettlement Framework

Beyond the EU-Turkey Statement, resettlement was used as a major tool to address the migration crisis of 2015/16. The Commission put resettlement on its 'European Agenda on Migration'.[928] Consequently, its legislative

922 See Ulrich Haltern, *Europarecht: Dogmatik im Kontext* Vol I, para 315; see also Daniela Vitiello in Valsamis Mitsilegas, Violeta Moreno-Lax and Niovi Vavoula (eds), *Securitising Asylum Flows: Deflection, Criminalisation and Challenges for Human Rights*, 143.

923 Lyra Jakulevičiené and Mantas Bileišis, 'EU refugee resettlement: Key challenges of expanding the practice into new Member States' in (2016) 9 Baltic Journal of Law & Politics 1, 103.

924 Arne Niemann and Natascha Zaun, 'EU Refugee Policies and Politics in Times of Crisis: Theoretical and Empirical Perspectives' in (2018) 56 Journal of Common Market Studies 1, 9.

925 See UNHCR, '2020 Planning Summary' (20 December 2019) <http://reporting.unhcr.org/sites/default/files/pdfsummaries/GA2020-Turkey-eng.pdf> accessed 21 February 2021.

926 See Commission, Recommendation on legal pathways to protection in the EU: promoting resettlement, humanitarian admission and other complementary pathways, Recital 11.

927 See Darla Davitti, 'Biopolitical Borders and the State of Exception in the European Migration 'Crisis'' in (2018) 29 European Journal of International Law 4, 1193.

928 See Commission, Communication 'A European Agenda on Migration', COM(2015) 240 final; see also Kay Hailbronner and Daniel Thym in Kay Hailbronner and Daniel Thym (eds), *EU Immigration and Asylum Law: A Commentary*, 1026, para 4; see also Catharina Ziebritzki in Marie-Claire Foblets and Luc Leboeuf (eds), *Humanitarian Admission to Europe*, 295f.

reform packages of July 2016[929] comprised the Proposal for a Regulation establishing a Union Resettlement Framework (Proposal). The proposed Regulation signifies a remarkable step towards the harmonization of resettlement policy because it would introduce a common resettlement definition, criteria to determine (potential) non-EU countries from where resettlement would occur, as well as eligibility criteria to select resettlement beneficiaries.[930]

4.2.11.1 The legal nature of the Proposal

The Commission chose to harmonize resettlement through a regulation, i.e. a legal instrument binding in its entirety and directly applicable in all EUMS (see Art 288 TFEU). At the same time, the Commission refrained from making resettlement mandatory. Instead of a mandatory resettlement mechanism, the proposed Regulation would introduce a two-stage procedure (Arts 7f Proposal), that means voluntary pledging by EUMS followed by the Commission's adoption of an implementing act.[931] According to this procedure, the Council would first adopt an annual Union resettlement plan under Art 7 Proposal, including the total number of persons to be resettled, the contributions to this number by each EUMS, and overall geographical priorities. As a second step, the Commission would adopt implementing acts under Art 8 Proposal consistent with the Council's annual Union resettlement plan under Art 7 Proposal.

Besides, the discretion of EUMS is reflected in the fact that refugees would not have a subjective right to be resettled under the proposed Regulation (Recital 19).[932]

---

929 See Commission, 'Completing the reform of the Common European Asylum System: towards an efficient, fair and humane asylum policy' (*Press release*, 13 July 2016) <http://europa.eu/rapid/press-release_IP-16-2433_en.htm> accessed 21 February 2021.

930 See Sergio Carrera, *An Appraisal of the European Commission of Crisis: Has the Juncker Commission delivered a new start for EU Justice and Home Affairs?* (Centre of European Policy Studies 2018) 24.

931 See Janine Prantl, ''Lessons to be learned' für ein zukünftiges, gemeinsames EU Resettlement' in (2020) Europarecht Supplement 3, 129.

932 See Tom de Boer and Marjoleine Zieck, 'The Legal Abyss of Discretion in the Resettlement of Refugees: Cherry-Picking and the Lack of Due Process in the EU' in (2020) 32 International Journal of Refugee Law 1, 60.

4.2.11.2 Resettlement definition

The Commission did not explicitly refer to the role of resettlement as a durable solution in the Proposal's resettlement definition (see 2.2.2). In addition, the Council urged for the inclusion of (temporary) humanitarian admissions "*on an equal footing to resettlement*".[933] The determination whether a refugee is considered for resettlement or for humanitarian admission impacts the legal status of the refugee in the receiving EUMS. Regularly, the rights and length of residence of those admitted through the channel of humanitarian admissions are more limited.[934] While resettlement aims at offering a durable solution to refugees, EUMS have adopted humanitarian admission programs under the expectation that the beneficiaries would return to their home country after the end of the conflict, war, or crisis.[935] During the negotiations, the European Parliament accepted the Council of the EU's demand to include humanitarian admission in the Proposal under the condition of separate quotas for resettlement and humanitarian admission.[936]

4.2.11.3 Criteria to determine countries of (first) refuge

The Commission followed up on the approach taken in the GAMM to prioritize and foster partnership with selected third countries. To that effect, the proposed Art 4 Union Resettlement Framework Regulation would set out criteria for regions or third countries from which resettlement is to occur. Decisive factors would be, amongst others, overall relations between the third country and the EU as well as a third country's effective cooperation with the EU in the area of migration and asylum, including the reduction of irregular migration.

933 Katharina Bamberg, 'The EU Resettlement Framework: From a humanitarian pathway to a migration management tool?', Discussion Paper European Migration and Diversity Programme (26 June 2018) 7.

934 In Germany, for example, refugees who are admitted by means of humanitarian admission receive fewer rights than resettlement refugees.

935 See Eva Lutter, Vanessa Zehnder and Elena Knežević, 'Resettlement und humanitäre Aufnahmeprogramme' in (2018) Asylmagazin, 29 (30).

936 See Katharina Bamberg, 'The EU Resettlement Framework: From a humanitarian pathway to a migration management tool?', Discussion Paper European Migration and Diversity Programme (26 June 2018) 7.

In this regard, the most contentious point is that the protection of vulnerable individuals would depend on the effective cooperation of the country of (first) refuge or the home country of that individual. In its comments from November 2016, the UNHCR expressed concerns about blurring the distinction between resettlement as a protection and migration management tool.[937] UNHCR's comments highlighted that "*resettlement is, by design, a tool to provide protection and a durable solution to refugees rather than a migration management tool*".[938] Also, civil society actors denounced the management control approach.[939]

4.2.11.4 Eligibility criteria

Regarding the eligibility criteria to select resettlement beneficiaries, the proposed Regulation would not limit resettlement to Convention Refugees. Compared to the 2015 Scheme, which did not literally rule out resettlement of IDPs, the proposed Regulation would expressly allow for resettlement of third-country nationals in need for international protection "*from a third country to which or within which they have been displaced*" (Art 2 Proposal). This means that the scope of the proposed Regulation would include the resettlement of IDPs.[940] Generally, the proposed Regulation would recognize the UNHCR resettlement submission criteria for the assessment of resettlement needs (see 5.2.1).

In addition, the proposed Regulation would count "*family members of third-country nationals or stateless persons or Union citizens legally residing in*

---

937 See UNHCR, 'Proposal for a Regulation of the European Parliament and of the Council establishing a Union Resettlement Framework and amending Regulation (EU) No 516/2014 of the European Parliament and the Council, COM(2016) 468 final 2016/0225 (COD): UNHCR's Observations and Recommendations' (November 2016) <https://www.refworld.org/pdfid/5890b1d74.pdf> accessed 21 February 2021.

938 Ibid 1; see Sergio Carrera, *An Appraisal of the European Commission of Crisis: Has the Juncker Commission delivered a new start for EU Justice and Home Affairs?* (Centre of European Policy Studies 2018) 25.

939 See Caritas Europa, Churches' Commission for Migrants in Europe, ECRE, International Refugee Committee and Red Cross EU Office, 'Recommendations on a Union Resettlement Framework' (14 November 2016) <https://redcross.eu/positions-publications/recommendations-on-a-union-resettlement-framework> accessed 27 February 2021.

940 See European Parliament, 'Resettlement of refugees: EU framework' (*Briefing*, April 2017) 11.

a Member State" among the persons eligible for resettlement (Art 5 lit b point ii Proposal). During the negotiations, the European Parliament critically pointed out that family reunification should take place irrespective of the inclusion of family members as a category of persons eligible for resettlement. Finally, the institutions agreed that close family members shall form a category of individuals to be resettled (see 5.2.3.4).[941] Criticism remained due to a problematic overlap between the legal schemes of resettlement and family reunification:[942]

> *For example, both pieces of legislation target the spouse or partner of the applicant and their minor unmarried children. The family reunification directive already covers these cases. Their mention in the Resettlement Framework proposal would enable member states to select candidates for resettlement that would have had a right to come to the EU under the family reunification directive anyway. <u>The resettlement spaces allocated to family reunification would be taken away from individuals that do not have family links in the EU, which would limit the overall number of people eligible for resettlement</u>.*

Furthermore, similar to the EU-Turkey Statement, Art 6 para 1 lit d Proposal states that persons who have irregularly stayed in or attempted to irregularly enter the territory of an EUMS "*shall be excluded*". Critically speaking, this Article would open up a source of discrimination among refugees, and it would run counter to Art 31 Refugee Convention, which prohibits Contracting States to penalize refugees on account of their illegal entry or presence.[943] Against the backdrop of the above elaborations on the reference to the Refugee Convention in Art 78 para 1 TFEU (see 4.1.2.2), Art 6 para 1 lit d Proposal would be in contradiction with EU primary law.

Another issue in the context of the proposed scope of resettlement beneficiaries was the inclusion of the beneficiaries' integration potential, namely their "*social or cultural links, or other characteristics that can facilitate integration in the participating Member State*" (Art 10 para 1 lit b Propos-

941 See Katharina Bamberg, 'The EU Resettlement Framework: From a humanitarian pathway to a migration management tool?', Discussion Paper European Migration and Diversity Programme (26 June 2018) 7.

942 Ibid 7 (emphasis added).

943 See Tom de Boer and Marjoleine Zieck, 'The Legal Abyss of Discretion in the Resettlement of Refugees: Cherry-Picking and the Lack of Due Process in the EU' in (2020) 32 International Journal of Refugee Law 1, 68.

al).[944] While the EU has not been in a position to condition the access to international protection on the potential to integrate, some EUMS have applied the potential to integrate either as a formal or implicit selection criterion (see 5.2.3.5). For instance, *Bamberg* criticized this approach to rely on integration related selection criteria as a potential source of discrimination:[945]

> *Including this as a criterion could give preference to certain individuals over some of the most vulnerable in resettlement processing, especially since it is not clearly defined in the Commission proposal how this would relate to vulnerability and other eligibility criteria. In the end, the integration potential criterion could lead to discriminatory practices in selecting candidates for resettlement and potentially undermine member states' need to resettle those that are the most vulnerable.*

4.2.12 Current resettlement policy

The new Commission, led by President *Ursula von der Leyen*, is expected to further spur the development of a more harmonized EU resettlement policy:[946]

> *We need to allay the legitimate concerns of many and look at how we can overcome our differences. We need a new way of burden sharing, we need a fresh start.*

944 Art 10 para 1 lit b Proposal for a Union Resettlement Framework refers to social and cultural links; "*The Council was in favour of including a lack of integration prospects, such as a refusal to participate in pre-departure orientation, as a reason for ineligibility for resettlement in Article 6. The Parliament has vigorously opposed this, stressing the universality of the right to asylum and arguing that protection should not be made conditional on one's integration potential*", Katharina Bamberg, 'The EU Resettlement Framework: From a humanitarian pathway to a migration management tool?', Discussion Paper European Migration and Diversity Programme (26 June 2018) 8.

945 Ibid 8 (emphasis added).

946 Ursula von der Leyen, 'A Union that strives for more: My agenda for Europe' (Political guidelines for the next European Commission 2019-2024) 15 <https://ec.europa.eu/info/sites/info/files/political-guidelines-next-commission_en_0.pdf> accessed 20 March 2021.

In the agenda for Europe, *von der Leyen* announced a New Pact on Migration and Asylum and expressed commitment to resettlement:[947]

> *We need diplomacy, economic development, stability and security. This would help stop smugglers and bring a stronger commitment to resettlement, as well as pathways for legal migration to help us bring in the people with the skills and talents we need.*

For the year of 2020, EUMS collectively pledged more than 30,000 resettlement places at the first Global Refugee Forum in Geneva. The Commission offered them financial support, i.e. EUR 10,000 per resettled refugee will be provided from the EU budget.[948] In fact, the outbreak of the COVID-19 pandemic impeded the implementation of the 2020 target. Several EUMS, the UNHCR and the IOM temporarily suspended their resettlement operations.[949] Countries of (first) refuge, in turn, responded with access restrictions for refugees and other forced migrants. The Commission was alarmed that the impact of COVID-19 on the countries of (first) refuge could render resettlement needs even more pressing. It released a Communication to provide guidance and to encourage EUMS "*to continue showing solidarity with persons in need of international protection and third countries hosting large numbers of refugees*". In terms of the 2020 pledges, the Commission declared to "*be flexible as regards the implementation period beyond 2020 to ensure that Member States have enough time to implement fully the pledges made under the 2020 pledging exercise*".[950]

In September 2020, the Commission launched the previously announced New Pact on Migration and Asylum,[951] including a recommenda-

947 Ibid 14 (emphasis added); see Commission, 'Delivering on Resettlement', 2.

948 See Commission, 'Resettlement: EU Member States' pledges exceed 30,000 places for 2020' (*Press release*, 18 December 2019).

949 See IOM, 'UNHCR announce temporary suspension of resettlement travel for refugees' (*Press release*, 17 April 2020) <https://www.iom.int/news/iom-unhcr-announce-temporary-suspension-resettlement-travel-refugees> accessed 27 February 2021; see also UN, 'COVID-19: Agencies temporarily suspend refugee resettlement travel' (17 March 2020) <https://news.un.org/en/story/2020/03/1059602> accessed 27 February 2021.

950 Commission, Communication 'COVID-19: Guidance on the implementation of relevant EU provisions in the area of asylum and return procedures and on resettlement', OJ [2020] C126/12 (22).

951 See Commission, Communication on a New Pact on Migration and Asylum; see also Commission, 'A fresh start on migration: Building confidence and striking a new balance between responsibility and solidarity' (*Press release*, 23 September 2020) <https://ec.europa.eu/commission/presscorner/detail/en/i

tion to formalize the 2020 target and to extend it to the two-year period 2020-2021.[952] According to IOM, 16 states in the European region resettled and admitted 21,828 refugees in 2021, which is still low compared to 30,264 resettlements in 2019.[953]

At the time of writing, the Union Resettlement Framework Regulation has not been adopted.[954] A partial provisional agreement on the 2016 Proposal between the Council of the EU and the European Parliament was reached on 13 June 2018. However, COREPER did not finally endorse it, and subsequent negotiations remained at the technical level within the Council. In December 2022, the European Parliament and the Council made progress and agreed on an updated text of the Resettlement Framework Regulation. The updated text of the EU Resettlement Framework Regulation is much more diluted than the text of the 2016 Proposal in terms of the degree of establishing a common approach on resettlement to the EU. The link between resettlement and the reduction of irregular migration, through collaboration with third countries, became less obvious in the updated text. Still, there is no change in the approach that resettlement remains voluntary and that EUMS only have few obligations under the proposed Regulation towards the resettlement beneficiaries.[955]

---

p_20_1706> accessed 27 February 2021; see also Daniel Thym, 'Mehr Schein als Sein?: Legislative Unklarheiten und operative Fallstricke des EU-Asylpakets' (Verfassungsblog, 24 September 2020) <https://verfassungsblog.de/mehr-schein-als-sein/> accessed 27 February 2021.

952 See Commission, Communication on a New Pact on Migration and Asylum, 22; see also Commission, Recommendation on legal pathways to protection in the EU: promoting resettlement, humanitarian admission and other complementary pathways, 8, para 2.

953 See IOM, 'Resettlement' <https://eea.iom.int/resettlement> accessed 11 September 2022.

954 See Petra Bendel, 'Neustart oder Fehlstart? Zum neuen EU-Pakt für Migration und Asyl' (*Fluchtforschungsblog*, 26 September 2020) <https://blog.fluchtforschung.net/neustart-oder-fehlstart-zum-neuen-eu-pakt-fur-migration-und-asyl/> accessed 27 February 2021.

955 For an analysis of the updated text, see Emiliya Bratanova van Harten, 'The new EU Resettlement Framework: the Ugly Duckling of the EU asylum acquis?' (*EU Law Analysis*, 3 February 2023) <http://eulawanalysis.blogspot.com/2023/02/the-new-eu-resettlement-framework-ugly.html> accessed 2 May 2023.

4.2.13 Preliminary conclusion

As of today, the EU has shaped some aspects of EUMS' resettlement policies, which has led to increased contributions by EUMS to the global resettlement needs. EU's share of global resettlement increased from below 9% before 2016 to 41% in 2018.[956] This increase mainly traces back to the increase in the number of EUMS contributing to resettlement in the course of the refugee crisis in 2016.[957] How sustainable and significant the increase in EU contributions to global resettlement needs will actually be remains unclear.

Despite EU involvement in national resettlement policies, the voluntary nature of resettlement has been preserved. Resettlement from third countries to the EU has remained a voluntary act under the discretion of states. While the Commission introduced a permanent resettlement framework in the form of a regulation, the proposed Regulation would not impose binding resettlement quota.

The Proposal for a Resettlement Framework Regulation as well as the EU-Turkey Statement reveal two major contentious points where EU resettlement policy has departed from international refugee law and human rights. Potential violations of the principle of non-discrimination constitute the first issue. For instance, the EU-Turkey Statement only covered the resettlement of Syrians. Furthermore, the proposed Resettlement Framework Regulation would prioritize resettlements from selected countries of (first) refuge, whereas those countries are chosen on the basis of specific criteria that do not reflect actual resettlement needs. In addition, the proposed Regulation would support the application of the integration potential as a selection criterion, which again prioritizes certain individuals for resettlement irrespective of their vulnerability or actual need to be resettled. This is not prohibited *per se*, but it could result in a violation of international human rights law, namely discrimination between and among (groups) of refugees, and thus result in an EU primary law violation of Art 78 para 1 TFEU. The second issue traces back to the focus on penalizing those who tried to enter the EU in an irregular manner by excluding them

956 See Commission, Recommendation on legal pathways to protection in the EU: promoting resettlement, humanitarian admission and other complementary pathways, 2, Recital 7.

957 See Hanna Schneider, 'Implementing the Refugee Resettlement Process: Diverging Objectives, Interdependencies and Power Relations' in (2021) Frontiers in Political Science, 4.

from resettlement eligibility. Specifically, the EU-Turkey Statement and the Proposal for a Resettlement Framework Regulation introduced such approach, albeit running counter to Art 31 Refugee Convention.

However, the Proposal for a Resettlement Framework Regulation not only unveiled restrictions, but also an expansion of the scope of resettlement beneficiaries. The Commission committed to the resettlement of IDPs.

Beyond the addressed discrepancies with international law, EU resettlement policy raises more general issues of effective protection for those in need, such as (i) managing migration flows externally, (ii) favoring resettlement over territorial asylum and (iii) mixing up humanitarian admission with resettlement.

The focus on external migration management is rooted in the policy approach to prevent irregular migration through co-operation with selected third countries. The EU has offered resettlement together with on-site assistance to persuade third countries to hold back migrants in their territory. Such approach can be found in the GAMM, the EU-Turkey Statement and the Proposal for a Resettlement Framework Regulation. The conditions in selected partnership countries are, however, regularly incomparable to the conditions in the EU. This raises questions about the notion of a safe third country and concerns about potential *refoulement* violations resulting from automatic returns, namely returns without taking into account the actual conditions that the individual would face upon return.

The prevention of irregular migration is closely related to the preference of resettlement over (territorial) asylum. In its first Recommendations dealing with resettlement, the Commission recognized that resettlement and (territorial) asylum should be used in a complementary manner, but it then departed from this position in the Resettlement Framework Regulation. Neglecting (territorial) asylum overlooks the reality that the offered resettlement places do not cover the global resettlement needs. Merely relying on resettlement would therefore not amount to effective international protection for those in need, which is the proclaimed goal of the EU asylum *acquis* (see Art 78 para 1 TFEU).

Lastly, the analysis showed that EU resettlement policy failed to make a clear commitment towards resettlement as a durable solution. Instead, the proposed Resettlement Framework Regulation would include humanitarian admission besides resettlement. With this comes the risk of blurring the line between resettlement as a durable solution and humanitarian admission, a measure perceived as temporary because beneficiaries are expected to return to their home countries in the foreseeable future.

4.3 Institutional involvement in resettlement

It has already been clarified that under the current Constitutional Order, EU's institutional involvement cannot amount to centralized conduct of resettlement procedures at EU level (see 4.1.1.1). Notwithstanding, the EU has gained increasing influence over EUMS' resettlement policies through financial and operational support. Indeed, the funding of resettlement under the AMIF and the operational support provided by the EUAA (and the former EASO) deserve attention. Moreover, with the EU's increased influence on EUMS' resettlement policies comes increased responsibility for the EU. It is therefore necessary to take into consideration the accountability mechanisms.

4.3.1 Support through funding

Since 2014, financial incentives for resettlement have been provided under the AMIF Regulation.[958] The initial total amount for the seven-year period from 2014 to 2020 was EUR 3.137 billion. The largest share (88%) of the AMIF was channeled through shared management, i.e. the implementation of EUMS' multiannual national programs. Thereof, around 11% were allocated to actions implemented under EUMS' national programs responding to specific EU priorities and to EU resettlement programs.[959] In total numbers based on the initial EUR 3.137 billion, these 11% amount to about EUR 0.304 billion.

Concretely, the 2014 AMIF Regulation influenced national resettlement policies by (i) introducing a binding definition of EU-funded resettlement

958 See Regulation 2014/516 (EU) establishing the Asylum, Migration and Integration Fund [2014] OJ L150/168-195. At the time of writing, the most current version of the AMIF Regulation is the consolidated version of 12 April 2022 of Regulation 2021/1147 (EU) OJ [2022] L112/1.

959 See Commission Directorate-General Home Affairs, 'Asylum, Migration and Integration Fund (AMIF)' <https://ec.europa.eu/home-affairs/financing/fundings/migration-asylum-borders/asylum-migration-integration-fund_en> accessed 28 February 2021.

(Art 2 lit a of the 2014 AMIF Regulation;[960] see also 2.2.2 for a comparison with other resettlement definitions introduced by the Commission) and (ii) making funding dependent on the implementation of EU resettlement priorities and adherence to certain requirements.

Art 17 of the 2014 AMIF Regulation set out the resources for the Union Resettlement Program. It addressed "*common Union resettlement priorities*" such as the admission of persons identified to be in need for resettlement by the UNHCR and the implementation of RPPs (see 4.2.4).[961] EUMS received funding every two years "*on the basis of their pledges, and in accordance with EU resettlement priorities*".[962]

Furthermore, the 2014 AMIF Regulation imposed requirements that had to be upheld by EUMS in order to receive the lump sum. For example, an EUMS had to ensure that a resettlement beneficiary qualifying for refugee or subsidiary protection status was granted such status upon arrival. Apart from these requirements, the 2014 AMIF Regulation did not include procedural or substantive rights for individuals in the resettlement process. It could merely be inferred from the resettlement definition in Art 2 lit a AMIF Regulation, which demanded residence based either on refugee status, subsidiary protection status or "*any other status which offers similar rights and benefits under national and Union law*", that post-resettlement rights of resettlement beneficiaries should not significantly differ from the rights of those who crossed the border irregularly and were accepted by virtue of their application for international protection.[963] In the future, equal legal status for refugees admitted through resettlement and other refugees could be stimulated by making funding dependent on granting such status without discrimination (for elaborations on equal treatment among refugees see 3.3.4).

---

960 The current definition of resettlement can be found in Art 2 lit 8 of the 2021 AMIF Regulation. Accordingly, resettlement means "*the admission following a referral from the UNHCR of third-country nationals or stateless persons from a third country to which they have been displaced, to the territory of the Member States, and who are granted international protection and have access to a durable solution in accordance with Union and national law*".

961 See European Parliament, 'Resettlement of refugees: EU framework' (*Briefing*, April 2017) 3.

962 Ibid 3.

963 See Tom de Boer and Marjoleine Zieck, 'The Legal Abyss of Discretion in the Resettlement of Refugees: Cherry-Picking and the Lack of Due Process in the EU' in (2020) 32 International Journal of Refugee Law 1, 65.

The new budget for 2021-2027 significantly increased compared to the 2014-2020 budget. The Commission under *von der Leyen* committed to "*reinforcing the Asylum and Migration Fund and Integrated Border Management Fund to reach a level of EUR 22 billion*",[964] compared to EUR 12.4 billion of the previous period 2014-2020.[965] Eventually, the Multiannual Financial Framework (MFF) Regulation was adopted on 17 December 2020,[966] and allocated EUR 25.7 billion to the category Migration and Border Management, as well as EUR 110.6 billion to the category Neighborhood and the World, which can also be used, amongst others, for migration purposes.[967]

Notably, the Commission amended the 2018 Proposal for the MFF Regulation 2021-2027 in response to the COVID-19 crisis.[968] The amendment introduced an enhanced Solidarity and Emergency Reserve that may be used as a response to specific emergency needs "*within the Union or in third countries*"[969], including "*situations of particular pressure at the Union's external borders resulting from migratory flows, where circumstances so require*". The COVID-19 crisis underpinned the relevance of funding to ensure continued resettlement efforts and immediate responses in emergency situations. Continued resettlement in exceptional circumstances is crucial to avoid exposure of vulnerable forced migrants in countries of (first) refuge to worsened and even life-threatening conditions, as these countries likely face greater difficulties to cope with the crisis than prospective receiving EUMS. As an example, in September 2020, Lebanon hosted 900,000

964 Commission, Communication 'The EU budget powering the recovery plan for Europe', COM(2020) 442 final, 12.

965 See Commission, Communication 'A Modern Budget for a Union That Protects, Empowers and Defends: The Multiannual Financial Framework for 2021-2027', COM(2018) 321 final, 14f; see also Philippe de Bruycker, 'Towards a New European Consensus on Migration and Asylum' (*Eumigrationlawblog.eu*, 2 December 2019) <http://eumigrationlawblog.eu/towards-a-new-european-consensus-on-migration-and-asylum/> accessed 28 February 2021.

966 Council Regulation 2020/2093 (EU, Euratom) laying down the multiannual financial framework for the years 2021 to 2027 [2020] OJ L433/11-22.

967 Commission, 'Headings: spending categories' <https://ec.europa.eu/info/strategy/eu-budget/long-term-eu-budget/2021-2027/spending/headings_en#heading-6-neighbourhood-and-the-world> accessed 23 June 2021.

968 "*The enhanced reserve will be able to reinforce swiftly EU action, as and when needed, through EU instruments which provide for such emergency mechanisms, such as* [...] *the Asylum and Migration Fund*", Commission, Amended proposal for a Regulation laying down the multiannual financial framework for the years 2021 to 2027, COM/2020/443 final, 3f.

969 Emphasis added.

refugees among 6.8 million nationals, with half of the local population living below the poverty line. COVID-19 exacerbated this dire situation.[970]

Furthermore, an extended EU budget for resettlement would offer the opportunity to reinforce the function of resettlement as a *durable* solution. In this regard, an acknowledgement of resettlement as durable solution can now be found in the resettlement definition set out in Art 2 para 8 of the current 2021 AMIF Regulation (see 2.2.2). Resettlement beneficiaries and receiving EUMS would both benefit from the funding for pre-departure and post-arrival assistance (see 5.3), as well as assistance for community sponsorship programs (see 2.5.3), and for resettlement beneficiaries to enter the labor market in the receiving EUMS. Initially, the Commission refrained from including 'integration' in the 2018 Proposal for an Asylum and Migration Fund Regulation,[971] indicating an exclusion of integration measures. These measures would have had to be covered by other budget lines instead.[972] The Commission adopted an Action Plan on integration and inclusion[973] in 2020, with support for EUMS to ensure the provision of "*meaningful opportunities* [...] *for all*"[974] to participate in economy and society, thereby promoting a European way of life. In particular, the Commission pointed out that EUMS should "*set up and expand pre-departure integration measures (e.g. training, orientation courses), and effectively link them with post-arrival measures to facilitate and speed up the integration process, including in the context of resettlement and community sponsorship*".[975]

4.3.2 Support through agencies

Operational cooperation and support in resettlement have been strengthened through the EUAA (and former EASO). EU agencies are generally involved in cooperative or joint administrative interactions between

970 See International Rescue Committee et al, 'Joint Resettlement: Resettlement Can't Wait' (23 September 2020).

971 See Commission, Proposal for a Regulation establishing the Asylum and Migration Fund, COM(2018) 471 final 2018/0248 (COD).

972 See Evangelia (Lilian) Tsourdi in Francesca Bignami (ed), *EU Law in Populist Times: Crises and Prospects*, 222f.

973 See Commission, Communication 'Action plan on Integration and Inclusion 2021-2027', COM(2020) 758 final.

974 Commission, Communication on a New Pact on Migration and Asylum, 27.

975 Commission, Communication 'Action plan on Integration and Inclusion 2021-2027', 7.

EUMS.[976] Hence, they are crucial actors to spur harmonization in future EU resettlement.

EU agencies are not mentioned in the EU Treaties. They are established on the basis of separate regulations.[977] Within the Area of Freedom, Security and Justice, three core EU agencies were established, namely the European Border and Coast Guard (EBCG)[978] (border management), EUAA (asylum), and Europol (police cooperation).

The EUAA is tasked to assist EUMS with their actions on resettlement (Art 2 para 1 lit s EUAA Regulation). Already the EUAA's predecessor, the EASO, provided a hub for cooperation of EUMS in resettlement matters. Specific resettlement-related activities of EASO included, amongst others, selection and fact-finding missions, pre-departure orientation programs, medical screenings, travel or visa arrangements, joint training, reception and integration tools, identification of best practice and the launch of pilot projects.[979]

The mandate of EASO was, however, limited. Art 12 para 2 EASO Regulation stated that EASO "*should have no direct or indirect powers in relation to the taking of decisions by Member States' asylum authorities on individual applications for international protection*".[980] Consequently, the Commission proposed to expand EASO's mandate, including its decision-making powers.[981] The result was the establishment of the EUAA, operational since

976 See Maïté Fernandez in Thomas Gammeltoft-Hansen and Jens Vedsted-Hansen (eds), *Human rights and the dark side of globalisation: Transnational law enforcement and migration control*, 241.

977 See ibid 241; see also Miroslava Scholten and Marloes van Rijsbergen, 'The ESMA-Short Selling Case: Erecting a New Delegation Doctrine in the EU upon the *Meroni-Romano* Remnants' in (2014) 41 Legal Issues of Economic Integration 4, 389 (402).

978 See Regulation 2016/1624 (EU) on the European Border and Coast Guard and amending Regulation (EU) 2016/399 and repealing Regulation (EC) No 863/2007, Regulation (EC) No 2007/2004 and Decision 2005/267/EC [2016] OJ L251/1-76.

979 See Steve Peers, Violeta Moreno-Lax, Madeline Garlick and Elspeth Guild, *EU Immigration and Asylum Law*, 625.

980 Art 12 para 2 Regulation 2010/439 (EU) establishing a European Asylum Support Office [2010] OJ L132/11-28 (emphasis added).

981 See Proposal for a Regulation on the European Union Agency for Asylum and repealing Regulation (EU) No 439/2010, COM(2016) 271 final; see also Amended Proposal for a Regulation on the European Union Agency for Asylum and repealing Regulation (EU) No 439/2010: A contribution from the European Commission to the Leaders' meeting in Salzburg on 19-20 September 2018 COM/2018/633 final; national Greek law already granted EASO powers that

19 January 2022.[982] Upon request or with the consent of the competent EUMS, the EUAA is empowered to, among others, decide on applications for international protection (Art 16 para 2 lit c EUAA Regulation). Furthermore – most relevant for resettlement selection –, the EUAA can engage in vulnerability assessments. It may "*assist Member States in identifying applicants in need of special procedural guarantees or applicants with special reception needs, or other persons in a vulnerable situation, including minors, in referring those persons to the competent national authorities for appropriate assistance on the basis of national measures and in ensuring that all the necessary safeguards for those persons are in place*" (Art 16 para 2 lit k EUAA Regulation). In addition, for the purpose of resettlement procedures, the EUAA may transfer the personal data of identified third country nationals to third countries, third parties or international organizations (subject to the individual's consent; Art 30 para 5 EUAA Regulation). Furthermore, the EUAA shall analyze the situation and reception capacities in third countries (Art 5 EUAA Regulation), which can in turn impact resettlement priorities of EUMS and resettlement eligibility.

Against the backdrop of this extended mandate, the EUAA could conduct personal interviews[983] to determine the vulnerability (and eligibility)

---

exceeded its mandate; see Evangelia (Lilian) Tsourdi, 'Holding the European Asylum Support Office Accountable for its role in Asylum Decision-Making: Mission Impossible?' in (2020) 21 German Law Journal, 516f; see also Evangelia (Lilian) Tsourdi, 'The New Pact and EU Agencies: an ambivalent approach towards administrative integration' (*Eumigrationlawblog.eu*, 6 November 2020) <http://eumigrationlawblog.eu/the-new-pact-and-eu-agencies-an-ambivalent-approach-towards-administrative-integration/> accessed 28 February 2021. In terms of the proposed expansion of decision-making powers, see Art 21 para 2 lit b Proposal for a Regulation on the European Union Agency for Asylum and repealing Regulation (EU) No 439/2010, which refers to operational and technical enforcement, including "*the registration of applications for international protection and, where requested by Member States, the examination of such applications*".

982 See EUAA, 'New EU Agency for Asylum starts work with reinforced mandate' (19 January 2022) <https://euaa.europa.eu/news-events/new-eu-agency-asylum-starts-work-reinforced-mandate> accessed 19 July 2022.

983 See Joanne van Selm et al, Study on 'The Feasibility of setting up resettlement schemes in EU Member States or at EU Level, against the background of the Common European Asylum system and the goal of a Common Asylum Procedure', 172, 175; e.g., in 2018 and 2019 EASO's involvement in interview-tasks as part of Greek border procedures was significant: "*EASO conducted 8,958 interviews in the fast-track border procedure during 2018. During the first half of 2019, EASO conducted 2,955 interviews in the fast-track border procedure, mainly covering applicants from Afghanistan, Palestine, Iraq, Syria and Cameroon*", Evangelia (Lil-

of prospective resettlement beneficiaries, and, by transferring the respective data of identified individuals, e.g. to the UNHCR, it could play a role as referral entity.

From a constitutional perspective, the extended mandate of EUAA implies that binding decision-making powers over individuals can be delegated, or rather conferred to an EU agency. Prominently, the *Meroni* doctrine[984] sets out criteria for the delegation or conferral of executive powers. These criteria are that (i) no one can delegate more rights than he or she possesses, (ii) delegation can never be presumed but must be explicit, (iii) only clearly defined executive powers can be delegated; and (iv) the principle of conferral of powers must be respected.[985]

While the first two criteria are largely undisputed, the third criterion that only clearly defined executive powers can be delegated remains unclear. The Court of Justice made the following distinction in *Meroni*:[986]

> *The consequences resulting from a delegation of powers are very different depending on whether it involves clearly defined executive powers the exercise of which can, therefore, be subject to strict review in the light of objective criteria determined by the delegating authority, or whether it involves a discretionary power, implying a wide margin of discretion which may, according to the use which is made of it, make possible the execution of actual economic policy.*

Clearly defined executive powers that do not entail a large margin of discretion can in principle be subject to delegation. Conversely, unrestricted discretionary decision-making powers should not be delegated. Yet, the Court did not clarify the demarcation line between restricted and unrestricted decision-making powers in *Meroni*.[987]

What is more, there was a long debate about whether the *Meroni* criteria applied to EU agencies. The *Meroni* case concerned a body governed by

---

ian) Tsourdi, 'The New Pact and EU Agencies: an ambivalent approach towards administrative integration' (*Eumigrationlawblog.eu*, 6 November 2020).

984 See Cases C-9/56 and C-10/56 *Meroni & Co, Industrie Metallurgiche, SpA v High Authority of the European Coal and Steel Community* [1958] EU:C:1958:7; for subsequent case law see e.g., Case 98/80 *Giuseppe Romano v Institut national d'assurance maladie-invalidité* [1981] EU:C:1981:104.

985 See Andreas Orator, *Möglichkeiten und Grenzen der Einrichtung von Unionsagenturen* (Mohr Siebeck 2017) 230.

986 Cases C-9/56 and C-10/56 *Meroni & Co, Industrie Metallurgiche, SpA v High Authority of the European Coal and Steel Community*, 173.

987 See Andreas Orator, *Möglichkeiten und Grenzen der Einrichtung von Unionsagenturen*, 232f.

private law without any basis in EU legislation.[988] In contrast, EU agencies are based on individual EU regulations, but without being expressly mentioned in EU Treaties.

In greater detail, it has been argued that the *Meroni* case concerned the delegation of powers from the Commission, while vesting competences in the EU agencies constitutes a conferral of powers by the EU legislators. To be clear, in the case of *Meroni*, the explicit powers of the Commission were formally delegated to bodies governed by private law, instead of by EU law.[989] In contrast, EU legislators conferred powers to the EUAA on the basis of a regulation. However, *Orator* argued that in both cases practically the same results were achieved.[990] Without the establishment of an agency, the Commission would be exceptionally responsible for the direct implementation of [...] at the EU level (see Arts 17 para 1 TEU and 291 para 2 TFEU) within the limits of rules laid down by EU legislation (Art 291 para 3 TFEU). If the Commission then delegated this power, we would face a situation similar to *Meroni*. So, it is irrelevant for the application of the *Meroni* criteria whether the origin of the power is understood as power conferral (by the EU legislator) or delegation (by the Commission). As a result, the *Meroni* judgement has been interpreted to apply to EU agencies.

The Court of Justice confirmed the application of the *Meroni* criteria to EU agencies.[991] In its reasoning in *ESMA-short selling*,[992] the Court applied the *Meroni* criteria for the first time to EU agencies.[993] It concluded that the powers conferred to the European Securities and Markets Authority (ESMA) "*comply with the requirements laid down in Meroni v High Authori-*

988 See ibid 229; see also Miroslava Scholten and Marloes van Rijsbergen, 'The ESMA-Short Selling Case: Erecting a New Delegation Doctrine in the EU upon the *Meroni-Romano* Remnants' in (2014) 41 Legal Issues of Economic Integration 4, 394.

989 See Case C-270/12 *The United Kingdom of Great Britain and Northern Ireland v European Parliament and the Council of the European Union* [2014] EU:C:2014:18, para 43.

990 See Andreas Orator, *Möglichkeiten und Grenzen der Einrichtung von Unionsagenturen*, 265f.

991 See ibid 243.

992 See Case C-270/12 *The United Kingdom of Great Britain and Northern Ireland v European Parliament and the Council of the European Union*, paras 41ff.

993 See Miroslava Scholten and Marloes van Rijsbergen, 'The ESMA-Short Selling Case: Erecting a New Delegation Doctrine in the EU upon the *Meroni-Romano* Remnants' in (2014) 41 Legal Issues of Economic Integration 4, 390.

ty"[994] because ESMA's exercise of powers "*is circumscribed by various conditions and criteria which limit ESMA's discretion*".[995] In the case of ESMA, decision-making powers did not undermine the rules governing the delegation of powers, namely Arts 290 (delegated acts) and 291 TFEU (implementing acts). The provision equipping ESMA with decision-making powers formed part of a series of rules designed to uphold financial stability and market confidence within the EU, and ESMA's empowerment was necessary to follow an essential objective of the EU financial system.[996]

What is more, the Court pointed to Arts 263[997] and 277 TFEU,[998] stating that the competence of EU legislators to empower EU agencies to issue acts of general application could implicitly be derived from these provisions that ensure the reviewability of EU agencies' decisions.[999]

With its liberal decision in ESMA, the Court of Justice did not actually depart from the core findings of the *Meroni* judgement, i.e. the delegation of powers could not go so far as to alter policy choices, bringing about an actual transfer of responsibility.[1000] The Court rather suggested a more flexible approach to the conferral of powers, on the basis that unlike in *Meroni*, the exercise of powers in ESMA's case was circumscribed by various conditions and criteria which limited ESMA's discretion.[1001]

It cannot automatically be inferred that the liberal approach regarding ESMA, an agency within the EU financial system, equally applies to cases where binding decision-making powers would be conferred upon the EU-

994 Case C-270/12 *The United Kingdom of Great Britain and Northern Ireland v European Parliament and the Council of the European Union*, para 53.

995 Ibid para 45.

996 See Case C-270/12 *The United Kingdom of Great Britain and Northern Ireland v European Parliament and the Council of the European Union*, paras 73, 85.

997 "*It shall also review the legality of acts of bodies, offices or agencies of the Union intended to produce legal effects vis-à-vis third parties*."

998 "[A]*ny party may, in proceedings in which an act of general application adopted by an institution, body, office or agency of the Union is at issue, plead the grounds specified in Article 263, second paragraph, in order to invoke before the Court of Justice of the European Union the inapplicability of that act*."

999 See Case C-270/12 *The United Kingdom of Great Britain and Northern Ireland v European Parliament and the Council of the European Union*, para 65; see also Miroslava Scholten and Marloes van Rijsbergen, 'The ESMA-Short Selling Case: Erecting a New Delegation Doctrine in the EU upon the *Meroni-Romano* Remnants' in (2014) 41 Legal Issues of Economic Integration 4, 401.

1000 See Case C-270/12 *The United Kingdom of Great Britain and Northern Ireland v European Parliament and the Council of the European Union*, paras 41f.

1001 See ibid para 45; see Andreas Orator, *Möglichkeiten und Grenzen der Einrichtung von Unionsagenturen*, 244.

AA, an EU agency active in the field of migration and asylum.[1002] Still, essential requirements for the delegation or conferral of executive powers on the EUAA can be derived from the rulings of the Court of Justice in *Meroni* and ESMA. First, any conferral of such powers must be based on an explicit decision of the EU legislators. In this regard, the EUAA Regulation can be considered as sufficient.[1003] Second, the restriction not to confer executive powers that would allow for policy alterations by EU agencies does not preclude the EUAA from making decisions that affect an individual's legal position, as long as there are sufficient conditions and criteria that define EUAA's decision-making power. In this light, *Tsourdi* pointed out that "*executive discretion to decide, for example, whether an individual fulfils criteria of the legal definition of a refugee, does not amount to the prohibited discretion of formulating policy*".[1004] In addition, in the case of the EUAA, such power remains contingent on the consent of the competent EUMS. Ultimately, any delegated power must be subject to judicial review and other accountability mechanisms, which will be elaborated in the following.

4.3.3 Accountability and legal protection

The EU operates in the resettlement process through the EUAA. Therefore, the following elaborations focus on accountability mechanisms addressing actions of the EUAA.

Tsourdi examined the accountability processes in the former EASO Regulation in greater detail.[1005] She thereby identified several political accountability processes, not only before EASO's own Management Board (Art 29 EASO Regulation), but also before the Council of the EU, the Commission and the European Parliament (Arts 7 para 1, 12 para 2, 30

1002 The questions remain "*what powers (and how much discretion) can be conferred upon an entity, when and how the conferral takes place (within what procedural and substantive limits) and who holds the recipients of the conferred powers to account and how*", Miroslava Scholten and Marloes van Rijsbergen, 'The ESMA-Short Selling Case: Erecting a New Delegation Doctrine in the EU upon the *Meroni-Romano* Remnants' in (2014) 41 Legal Issues of Economic Integration 4, 402.

1003 See Andreas Orator, *Möglichkeiten und Grenzen der Einrichtung von Unionsagenturen*, 231.

1004 Evangelia (Lilian) Tsourdi, 'Holding the European Asylum Support Office Accountable for its role in Asylum Decision-Making: Mission Impossible?' in (2020) 21 German Law Journal, 521.

1005 See ibid 523ff.

para 1 and 31 para 3 EASO Regulation). Regarding social accountability, civil society preferences influenced the establishment process of EASO.[1006] However, beyond the establishment process, EASO did not have to report or explain its conduct to the civil society.[1007] Similar provisions can be found in the EUAA Regulation, for example Art 47 EUAA Regulation deals with accountability to the Management Board. The EUAA Regulation introduced significant additional accountability developments. Most notable are the EUAA's obligations to appoint a Fundamental Rights Officer (Art 49 EUAA Regulation) and to establish and implement a complaints mechanism (Art 51 EUAA Regulation). In that respect, EUAA's compliance with fundamental rights is currently under review by the European Ombudswoman.[1008] Eventually, social accountability is fostered through EUAA's Consultative Forum (Art 50 EUAA Regulation) where civil society organizations have gained an enhanced role.

With regard to legal accountability in the form of judicial review, the essential question is whether EUAA's mandate comprises measures that have legal effects vis-à-vis third parties as required under Art 263 TFEU para 1. It remained contested if, for example, (non-binding) advisory opinions of EASO produced such effects.[1009] By contrast, EUAA's extended mandate implicates binding decisions with legal effect upon individuals (upon request or with consent of the EUMS that would otherwise have the final decision-making power). With regard to such decisions, Art 263 TFEU can serve as a basis for CJEU review. In addition, for the sake of transparency in the form of public access to documents, Art 63 para 5 EUAA Regulation states that decisions taken by the EUAA "*pursuant to Article 8 of Regulation (EC) No 1049/2001 may give rise to* [...] *action before the CJEU, under the conditions laid down in Articles 228 and 263 TFEU respectively*". Another avenue to achieve judicial review would be a preliminary ruling under Art

1006 See Satoko Horii, 'Accountability, Dependency, and EU Agencies: The Hotspot Approach in the Refugee Crisis' in (2018) 37 Refugee Survey Quarterly 2, 204 (211f).

1007 See Evangelia (Lilian) Tsourdi, 'Holding the European Asylum Support Office Accountable for its role in Asylum Decision-Making: Mission Impossible?' in (2020) 21 German Law Journal, 523.

1008 See European Ombudsman, 'How the EU Asylum Agency complies with its fundamental rights obligations and ensures accountability for potential fundamental rights violations', Case SI/4/2022/MHZ (opened on 11 July 2022) <https://www.ombudsman.europa.eu/en/case/en/61991> accessed 19 July 2022.

1009 See Evangelia (Lilian) Tsourdi, 'Holding the European Asylum Support Office Accountable for its role in Asylum Decision-Making: Mission Impossible?' in (2020) 21 German Law Journal, 525 (with further references).

267 TFEU. In the course of a preliminary ruling, the CJEU can also review the validity of non-binding acts.[1010] This, however, depends on whether a national court makes a referral to the CJEU. It results that overall, EU law remains limited when it comes to legal accountability.

Moreover, Art 67 EUAA Regulation read in combination with Art 228 TFEU offers the possibility to hold the EUAA accountable for its actions before the European Ombudswoman.[1011] Somewhat difficult in this context is that the Ombudswoman's jurisdiction *ratione personae* excludes non-EU citizens not having their residence in the EU. This, however, does not render the Ombudswoman ineffective in the resettlement context since she can initiate inquiries (Art 228 para 1 TFEU). Indeed, the Ombudswoman "*has used this tool to circumvent the restrictions on its complaints-based jurisdiction*",[1012] meaning that "*the Ombudsman has formally dismissed the complaint for lack of jurisdiction ratione personae and then immediately opened an own-initiative inquiry into the same facts*".[1013] Moreover, the Ombudswoman's jurisdiction *ratione materiae* covers the entirety of EU's actions, thus is not limited to the enforcement and review of legally binding acts. Despite the non-binding nature of her decisions, the Ombudswoman has made a substantial contribution to good governance, namely "*a strong track-record in getting Union bodies and agencies to comply*".[1014] For that reason, her involvement could have a positive impact on the hitherto legally undefined resettlement process.

1010 See ibid 525f; for the reviewability of non-binding acts see Case C-322/88 *Salvatore Grimaldi v Fonds des Maladies Professionnelles* [1989] EU:C:1989:646, para 8.

1011 See Evangelia (Lilian) Tsourdi, 'Holding the European Asylum Support Office Accountable for its role in Asylum Decision-Making: Mission Impossible?' in (2020) 21 German Law Journal, 523.

1012 Stian Øby Johansen, 'Human Rights Accountability of CSDP Missions on Migration' (*Eumigrationlawblog.eu*, 8 October 2020) <http://eumigrationlawblog.eu/human-rights-accountability-of-csdp-missions-on-migration/#more-2839> accessed 28 February 2021.

1013 Ibid.

1014 Ibid; see Evangelia (Lilian) Tsourdi, 'Holding the European Asylum Support Office Accountable for its role in Asylum Decision-Making: Mission Impossible?' in (2020) 21 German Law Journal, 528.

4.3.4 Preliminary conclusion

The EU has financially supported resettlement operations of EUMS, and support by means of EU funding has increased. The AMIF makes funding dependent on certain status requirements, but it does not comprehensively address refugee and human rights. In the future, EU funding could be structured to foster those rights in the resettlement process. Furthermore, funding could reinforce the character of resettlement as a durable solution if funds were restricted to those EUMS offering meaningful opportunities for resettlement beneficiaries to participate in the economy and society of the receiving EUMS.

Besides, the EU has provided operational support through the EUAA (and the former EASO). The limited mandate of EASO was expanded through the establishment of the EUAA. The conferral of powers by the EU legislator that made the EUAA competent to take binding decisions upon individuals are covered by the criteria set out by the Court of Justice in the *Meroni* case. The powers are based on an explicit decision of the EU legislators in the form of an EUAA Regulation. In addition, EUAA's decision-making power is subject to the consent of the competent EUMS. Furthermore, discretion to decide whether an individual fulfills the criteria of eligibility for resettlement, such as the qualification for refugee or subsidiary protection status, does not amount to the prohibited discretion of formulating policy.

In terms accountability mechanisms to address potential misconduct, the means for individuals to take judicial action have significantly increased with EUAA's expanded mandate. EASO was limited to generating non-binding advisory opinions, and it was difficult to claim that such opinion produce legal effects, which is required for a review under Art 263 TFEU. By contrast, the mandate of the EUAA includes the potential competence to take binding decisions upon individuals, meaning that Art 263 TFEU has become a viable means for the individuals concerned to have these decisions reviewed by the CJEU.

In addition, the European Ombudswoman could take up a substantial role to unveil misconduct in the resettlement process by initiating inquiries pursuant to Art 228 para 1 TFEU. Her decisions are, however, not binding, rendering them less effective than court decisions.

4.4 Analysis: Status quo of EU resettlement

The above elaborations on EU's institutional involvement in resettlement have raised various questions about potential developments, which can only be answered by first assessing the *status quo* of EU resettlement. Therefore, the following analysis addresses the *status quo* of EU resettlement policy from three perspectives: The first perspective shows where we stand in terms of EU involvement in processing resettlement cases. Second, the analysis evinces the degree of national commitment to implement the principle of solidarity and responsibility sharing through resettlement. Finally, it puts resettlement in the context of EU's proclaimed goal to offer effective protection to those in need.

4.4.1 Resettlement processing – national or EU level?

The EUAA Regulation ingrains elements of common processing, including the possibility for EUAA deployed experts to decide upon applications for international protection. Eventually, the expanded EUAA mandate could also cover decisions on resettlement selection that have legal effect upon potential resettlement candidates, as the EUAA might take over the function of a (pre-)referral entity. In 2016, the Commission even contemplated one step further towards EU-level processing by announcing (as a long-term goal) an "*EU-level first-instance decision-making Agency, with national branches in each Member State, and establishing an EU appeal structure*".[1015] So far, this idea has not been taken up in legal reforms.[1016]

As elaborated in 4.1.1.1, centralized assessment at the EU level would require a Treaty amendment under Art 48 TEU, which demands, among others, a 'Convention' and 'common accord' (intergovernmental conference), as well as ratification by all EUMS in accordance with their respective constitutional requirements. From a political perspective, the high requirements for a Treaty amendment make the shift to EU-level processing difficult to achieve. On the other hand, *Cherubini* considered a shift of re-

1015 Commission, Communication 'Towards a Reform of the Common European Asylum System and Enhancing Legal Avenues to Europe', COM(2016) 197 final.

1016 See Francesco Cherubini in Valsamis Mitsilegas, Violeta Moreno-Lax and Niovi Vavoula (eds), *Securitising Asylum Flows: Deflection, Criminalisation and Challenges for Human Rights*, 247.

sponsibility from EUMS to the EU to be favorable for EUMS.[1017] Through such responsibility shift, EUMS "*would be alleviated from the burden*",[1018] while the EU would be internationally responsible, and its actions could be challenged directly before the CJEU.[1019]

Another issue in terms of centralized EU assessment concerns funding. Realizing the (necessary) substantial allocation of resources from EUMS to EU bodies would be linked to strict procedural rules. The process to decide on the MFF requires, amongst others, unanimity in the Council (Art 311 para 3 TFEU states that "[t]*he Council, acting in accordance with a special legislative procedure, shall unanimously and after consulting the European Parliament adopt a decision*").

While legally speaking, the Treaty amendment process as well as decisions on funding could introduce centralized EU assessment, the political hurdles likely hamper such development.

4.4.2 Implementation of the principle of solidarity and fair sharing of responsibilities – discretion or mandatory quota?

In the long term, the EU can only ensure continuing resettlement contributions by creating a permanent framework beyond *ad hoc* responses. Likewise, the Commission asserted in its Recommendation of September 2020 that the EU "*needs to move from ad hoc resettlement schemes to schemes that operate on the basis of a stable framework that ensures that Union resettlement schemes are sustainable and predictable*".[1020] Scholarly debate in political science remains divided on whether such permanent resettlement framework should be based on mandatory quotas or whether the voluntary nature of resettlement should be preserved. *Thielemann* emphasized that Europe would need a clear, binding legal framework to strengthen resettlement.[1021] In contrast, *Suhrke* considered that a binding resettlement quota would only be accepted by receiving countries if it did not require them

1017 See ibid 248f.
1018 See ibid 249.
1019 See ibid 249.
1020 Commission, Recommendation on legal pathways to protection in the EU: promoting resettlement, humanitarian admission and other complementary pathways, 3, Recital 12.
1021 See Eiko R Thielemann, 'Why Refugee Burden-Sharing Initiatives Fail: Public Goods, Free-Riding and Symbolic Solidarity in the EU' in (2018) 56 Journal of Common Market Studies 1, 63-82.

to do more than they were already doing.[1022] From a legal perspective, CJEU case law on mandatory *intra*-EU relocation suggests that Art 80 TFEU prevents EUMS from generally refusing admission on the basis of responsibilities with regard to the maintenance of law and order and the safeguarding of internal security concerns when implementing a quota-based resettlement framework (Art 72 TFEU). Instead, such refusal would be limited to temporary suspension and case-by-case assessments.

Eventually, the aforementioned concept of 'flexible solidarity' could be a way out of the political deadlock. Flexible solidarity militates against mandatory resettlement quotas, thus confirming the current approach in the 2016 Proposal for a Union Resettlement Framework Regulation. A cynical note nevertheless lingers in flexible solidarity, considering, among others, the position of the Visegrád states in the relocation infringement proceedings. This experience leads to AG *Sharpston*'s prediction that, for at least some EUMS, 'flexible' could be taken to mean "*if we think there may be a problem then we don't need to show solidarity*".[1023] Whether EUMS will finally understand that flexibility does not imply free riding remains pie in the sky.

4.4.3 A comprehensive CEAS – protection or migration management tool?

Pursuant to Art 78 para 1 TFEU, the EU shall develop a CEAS with a view to offering international protection to those in need in conformity with international refugee law and international and European human rights. However, it seems that the current EU resettlement policy is not in line with this legally anchored goal. Recent EU policy trends, i.e. initiatives such as the GAMM (see 4.2.7), the EU-Turkey Statement (see 4.2.10), and the Proposal for a Union Resettlement Framework Regulation (see 4.2.11), have raised doubts about the protection focus. From a legal perspective, these initiatives show contradictions with international human rights and refugee law and (thus) EU primary law.

1022 See Astri Suhrke, 'Burden-sharing during Refugee Emergencies: The Logic of Collective versus National Action' in (1998) 11 Journal of Refugee Studies 4, 412f; see also Adèle Garnier, Kristin Bergtora Sandvik and Amanda Cellini, 'The COVID-19 Resettlement Freeze: Towards a Permanent Suspension?' (14 April 2020) <https://www.kaldorcentre.unsw.edu.au/publication/covid-19-resettlement-freeze-towards-permanent-suspension> accessed 28 February 2021.

1023 Email from Eleanor Sharpston (10 June 2020).

In the course of partnerships under the GAMM, and also along with the EU-Turkey Statement, the EU followed a 'return for resettlement' policy, namely cooperation with countries of (first) refuge to avoid irregular migration flows to the EU. For example, under the EU-Turkey Statement, the EU departed from international refugee law because those who had not previously entered or tried to enter the EU irregularly were prioritized for resettlement to the EU. This runs counter the prohibition of penalties for illegal entry or the presence of refugees pursuant to Art 31 Refugee Convention.[1024] Such policy focus is retrieved in the Proposal for a Union Resettlement Framework Regulation, where the Commission set out criteria for selected partnership countries from where resettlement should preferably take place.

Regarding returns of irregular migrants to partnership countries, regularly forming part of the political deal in exchange for resettlement, concerns were, among others, raised by *Peers et al.* They claimed that automatic returns could result in violations of EU law and international obligations, most prominently the *non-refoulement* principle. The EU and EUMS could not shift responsibility for violating obligations under the ECHR and the Charter[1025] to third countries and/or the UNHCR, the IOM or Frontex[1026] on the basis of cooperation agreements.[1027]

In terms of the GAMM, *Moreno-Lax* pointed out that "*Italian (and EU) authorities have invested vastly, to establish a Libyan SAR* [search and rescue] *and interdiction capacity so they can assume responsibility for rescue*

1024 See Tom de Boer and Marjoleine Zieck, 'The Legal Abyss of Discretion in the Resettlement of Refugees: Cherry-Picking and the Lack of Due Process in the EU' in (2020) 32 International Journal of Refugee Law 1, 67; see also European Council, 'EU-Turkey statement, 18 March 2016' (18 March 2016) para 2; see also Daniela Vitiello, 'Legal Narratives of the EU External Action in the Field of Migration and Asylum: From the EU-Turkey Statement to the Migration Partnership Framework and Beyond' in Valsamis Mitsilegas, Violeta Moreno-Lax and Niovi Vavoula (eds), *Securitising Asylum Flows: Deflection, Criminalisation and Challenges for Human Rights* (Brill 2020) 130 (147f).

1025 See Steve Peers, Violeta Moreno-Lax, Madeline Garlick and Elspeth Guild, *EU Immigration and Asylum Law*, 659f.

1026 See *Bosphorus v Ireland*, para 154.

1027 See *TI v UK* App No 43844/98 (ECtHR 7 March 2000) 15; "*Where States establish* [...] *international agreements to pursue cooperation in certain fields of activities, there may be implications for the protection of fundamental rights. It would be incompatible with the purpose and object of the* [ECHR] *if Contracting States were thereby absolved from their responsibility under the Convention in relation to the activity covered by such* [agreements]", *KRS v UK* App No 32733/08 (ECtHR 2 December 2008) 16.

(and disembarkation) and stymie irregular migration across the Central Mediterranean".[1028] It was argued that the Libyan Coast Guard brought migrants back to Libyan camps where they faced inhuman and degrading treatment. From there, they were usually not resettled but rather *"returned to Nigeria after agreeing to 'voluntary repatriation' as the only alternative to indefinite detention they were offered"*.[1029]

The example of Libya demonstrates a reality that the EU has not reached its proclaimed political objectives to re-establish a more stable situation and reduce human rights abuses in third countries. To say it in *Agamben*'s[1030] words, the EU and its MS aimed at saving lives of migrants but at the same time suspended them.[1031] The problem seems to be that the EU has promoted two sets of contradicting objectives. On the one hand, the EU announced in the GAMM and its subsequent Partnership Framework to pursue foreign policy objectives such as the promotion of peace, human rights and the rule of law. On the other hand, EU's migration policy aimed at strengthening external borders through migration control. These objectives apparently clash with each other. For instance, withholding funds to sanction a country of (first) refuge for non-cooperation in terms of border control exacerbates poverty, conflicts, and human rights abuses in this country.[1032]

The departure from international law is also relevant in the light of the principle of consistency. Applying the principle of consistency entails that a violation of international refugee law or international and/or European human rights law in EU's external action in the course of resettlement operations also violates EU primary law, namely Art 78 para 1 TFEU. This Article demands that development and interpretation of the (internal) EU asylum *acquis* be in compliance with the Refugee Convention as well as the ECHR and pertinent universal human rights treaties. Against this

---

1028 Violeta Moreno-Lax, 'The Architecture of Functional Jurisdiction: Unpacking Contactless Control – On Public Powers, *SS and Others v Italy*, and the "Operational Model"' in (2020) German Law Journal, 390f.

1029 Ibid 390.

1030 See Giorgio Agamben, *Homo Sacer Sovereign Power and Bare Life* (Stanford University Press 1998).

1031 See Giorgio Agamben cited in Darla Davitti, 'Biopolitical Borders and the State of Exception in the European Migration 'Crisis'' in (2018) 29 European Journal of International Law 4, 1181; see also Arne Niemann and Natascha Zaun, 'EU Refugee Policies and Politics in Times of Crisis: Theoretical and Empirical Perspectives' in (2018) 56 Journal of Common Market Studies 1, 4.

1032 See Tineke Strik, 'The Global Approach to Migration and Mobility' in (2017) 5 Groningen Journal of International Law 2, 323.

backdrop, consistency means that the same must hold true for the external CEAS, including resettlement.

Moreover, the proclaimed goal to effectively offer international protection to those in need is linked to the relationship between resettlement and (territorial) asylum. Effective international protection suggests balancing these two distinct policy tools in order to establish a comprehensive refugee policy. The UNHCR addressed "*the concern that some countries exhibited a tendency to control their total refugee intake by balancing between refugees who arrive through resettlement and those who apply directly for asylum*".[1033] Accordingly, resettlement should not be used to block admission of those who seek international protection on shore, "*since this would undermine the right to seek asylum*".[1034]

Commentators affirmed that it was a misconception to assume that resettlement could replace (territorial) asylum. For instance, *Hashimoto* argued against a one-sided approach because resettlement would never be able to replace asylum.[1035] *Ziebritzki* also raised concerns about an EU approach where resettlement would replace asylum. She concluded that such approach would contradict the political goals underlying the EU asylum *acquis*, since at that point in time, effective international protection for those in need could not be ensured by merely relying on discretionary resettlement offers.[1036] Evidently, the global protection needs cannot be covered by resettlement only. In addition, *Ziebritzki* pointed to international law as the benchmark for the EU asylum *acquis* and warned that abolishing territorial asylum could result in serious *non-refoulement* violations.[1037] Notwithstanding, when the Commission promoted resettlement as the preferred avenue in its 2016 Proposal for a Union Resettlement Framework Regulation, that reality was neglected.

Overall, only if EU resettlement policy complied with international and European human rights and international refugee law, it could serve to achieve a comprehensive CEAS in line with Art 78 para 1 TFEU. This must

---

1033 Haruno Nakashiba, 'Postmillennial UNHCR refugee resettlement: New developments and challenges', UNHCR Research Paper n°265 (November 2013) 7.

1034 Ibid 7.

1035 See Naoko Hashimoto, 'Refugee Resettlement as an Alternative to Asylum' in (2018) 37 Refugee Survey Quarterly, 184.

1036 See Catharina Ziebritzki in Marie-Claire Foblets and Luc Leboeuf (eds), *Humanitarian Admission to Europe*, 310; see also ibid 330: "[T]*he 'replacement argument' is a hypothetical scenario in which global resettlement needs would be met by global resettlement capacity*".

1037 See ibid 332f.

not lead to a replacement of (territorial) asylum since such replacement would undermine EU's proclaimed political – and legally anchored – goal to offer effective international protection to those in need.

5 The resettlement process

5.1 European and US resettlement practice in comparison

The following section offers a comparative analysis of European and US resettlement practice. The purpose of this comparison is to identify legal issues throughout the resettlement process that demand solutions *de lege ferenda*. First, this section discusses how EUMS and the US select potential resettlement beneficiaries. Second, it sheds light on the transfer of selected resettlement beneficiaries to the EU and the US, including pre-departure and post-arrival orientation as well as placement. Third, the analysis shows whether and how (long-term) integration of resettled individuals is fostered within the EU and in the US. This also includes the possibilities for the resettled individuals to become citizens of an EUMS, and thereby obtain EU citizenship, compared to possibilities to become US citizens.

Recent attempts to conceptualize the resettlement process, i.e. "*the entire implementation process, starting with the resettlement programs and its resettlement goals*"[1038], were made by *Schneider*. Similarly, the following analysis sheds light on the operational level, namely the implementation of the resettlement process, but it goes beyond *Schneider*'s contribution by adding a legal perspective to practical and policy questions. The following analysis focuses on those stages of the resettlement process where legal questions arise, in other words, where the rights of (potential) resettlement beneficiaries are likely to be affected. For this reason, the analysis starts with the pre-selection by the UNHCR and ends with the naturalization and its potential legal implications for re-resettlement, namely a right to return to the initial home country.

1038 Hanna Schneider, 'Implementing the Refugee Resettlement Process: Diverging Objectives, Interdependencies and Power Relations' in (2021) Frontiers in Political Science, 6.

5.2 Selection

Selecting resettlement beneficiaries means "*identifying refugee applicants based on protection principles*",[1039] such as equal treatment, *non-refoulement* and due process. In the majority of cases, the UNHCR pre-selects persons in need for resettlement, subsequently referring them to national authorities, who take the final selection decision. As a general rule, individuals seeking protection in a third country have neither a right to apply nor to be selected for resettlement.[1040]

5.2.1 Selection procedures and practices of the UNHCR and EUMS

While EUMS follow diverse national selection practices, they work together with the UNHCR, who identifies and interviews persons in need for resettlement.[1041] The UNHCR pre-selects refugees and other forced migrants based on objective needs and refers them to prospective receiving countries.[1042] Eligibility for a referral to a prospective receiving country requires: firstly, the recognition as a refugee or as a person of concern to the UNHCR;[1043] secondly, a general assessment of the prospects for

---

1039 Haruno Nakashiba, 'Clarifying UNHCR Resettlement: A few considerations from a legal perspective', UNHCR Research Paper n°264 (November 2013) 2.

1040 See Annelisa Lindsay, 'Surge and selection: power in the refugee resettlement regime' in (2017) 54 Forced Migration Review, 11 <https://www.refworld.org/docid/58cbcb314.html> accessed 28 February 2021; see also Recital 19 Proposal for a Union Resettlement Framework: "*There is no subjective right to be resettled*"; see also Luc Leboeuf and Marie-Claire Foblets in Marie-Claire Foblets and Luc Leboeuf (eds), *Humanitarian Admission to Europe*, 27: "*EU resettlement programmes do not allow individuals to directly petition European authorities to obtain humanitarian admission to Europe on grounds relating to protection*".

1041 See European Migration Network, 'Resettlement and Humanitarian Admission Programmes in Europe – what works' (9 November 2016) 22 <https://ec.europa.eu/home-affairs/sites/homeaffairs/files/what-we-do/networks/european_migration_network/reports/docs/emn-studies/emn-studies-00_resettlement_synthesis_report_final_en.pdf> accessed 28 February 2021.

1042 See UNHCR, *Resettlement Handbook* (revised ed July 2011) 216; see also Annelisa Lindsay, 'Surge and selection: power in the refugee resettlement regime' in (2017) 54 Forced Migration Review, 11.

1043 Besides refugees, persons of concern to the UNHCR include returnees, stateless persons and, under certain circumstances, IDPs; exceptions can also be made for certain non-refugee dependent family members to retain family unity; see UNHCR, *Resettlement Handbook* (revised ed July 2011) 76.

durable solutions in favor of resettlement as the most appropriate solution; and thirdly, a match with one of the seven submission categories of the UNHCR.[1044]

The seven UNHCR submission categories target particularly vulnerable groups and refer to (i) legal and/or physical protection needs, (ii) survival of violence and torture, (iii) medical needs, (iv) special risk faced by women and girls, (v) family reunification, (vi) special needs of children and adolescents and (vii) the lack of foreseeable alternative durable solutions.[1045] These categories are coupled with priority levels, i.e. emergency, urgent and normal priority.[1046]

According to UNHCR's resettlement data from 2018, UNHCR referrals were primarily based on legal and/or physical protection needs (28%), followed by survival of violence and torture (27%). In 2019 (between January and October), the categories legal and/or physical protection needs, and survival of violence and torture constituted the most relevant categories (31%).[1047] These two categories remained the major submission categories in 2020. In 2022 (from January to June), the legal and/or physical protection needs category was again the category with the most submissions (39%).[1048] The overall trend within the last four years shows that legal and/or physical protection needs constituted the most common reason for being identified as in need for resettlement. In order to be assigned to the legal and/or physical protection needs category, a refugee or person of concern to the UNHCR must, among other things, be facing an immediate or long-term threat of *refoulement* to the country of origin or expulsion to another country from where he or she may be refouled.[1049] It follows that the criteria for this important submission category particularly reflect the role of resettlement as a means "[...] *to guarantee protection when refugees*

1044 See Eva Lutter, Vanessa Zehnder and Elena Knežević, 'Resettlement und humanitäre Aufnahmeprogramme' in (2018) Asylmagazin, 31; see also UNHCR, *Resettlement Handbook* (revised ed July 2011) 3, 173; see also Garry G Troeller, 'UNHCR Resettlement: Evolution and Future Direction' in (2002) 14 International Journal of Refugee Law 1, 87.

1045 See UNHCR, *Resettlement Handbook* (revised ed July 2011) Chapter VI.

1046 See ibid 246-250; see also Tom de Boer and Marjoleine Zieck, 'The Legal Abyss of Discretion in the Resettlement of Refugees: Cherry-Picking and the Lack of Due Process in the EU' in (2020) 32 International Journal of Refugee Law 1, 62.

1047 See UNHCR, 'Resettlement Data' (as of 19 December 2019).

1048 See UNHCR, 'Resettlement Data' (as of 20 July 2022).

1049 See UNHCR, *Resettlement Handbook* (revised ed July 2011) 248.

are faced with threats which seriously jeopardize their continued stay in a country of refuge".[1050]

Ideally, selection is "*associated with entitlements under law and* [...] *mechanisms to vindicate claims in respect of those entitlements*".[1051] Such ideal situation has not been perfected in the UNHCR pre-selection process, though. In fact, UNHCR's *Resettlement Handbook* only addresses a few rights available to refugees and other potential resettlement beneficiaries by express reference, such as the right to object to a particular interpreter and to stop the interview if the refugee feels that he or she is being misunderstood or needs a break.[1052] Some rights are further derived from the so-called Resettlement Registration Form (RRF). The UNHCR submits this form to a prospective receiving country. Accordingly, during the interview with UNHCR officials, the prospective resettlement beneficiary must be given an opportunity to correct or clarify information that will later appear in the RRF. However, if the RRF review determines that the individual is not eligible, he or she has no possibility of appeal and will not be referred to any prospective receiving country.[1053] Otherwise, a positive RRF review leads to further examination by the authorities of the prospective receiving country obtaining the RRF. Prior to such examination, the identified individual must consent[1054] to the referral of the RRF to that country.[1055] In practice, lacking consent will likely interrupt further processing of a case for resettlement to the prospective receiving country suggested to obtain the RRF. At the same time, withholding consent does not entail that the potential resettlement beneficiary has a legal claim to be referred to another receiving country.

According to a 2016 study of the European Migration Network (EMN), the majority of EUMS required that the UNHCR had previously recog-

---

1050 Ibid 247.

1051 Arthur C Helton, 'What Is Refugee Protection' in (1990) 2 International Journal of Refugee Law, 119.

1052 See UNHCR, *Resettlement Handbook* (revised ed July 2011) 318.

1053 See Tom de Boer and Marjoleine Zieck, 'The Legal Abyss of Discretion in the Resettlement of Refugees: Cherry-Picking and the Lack of Due Process in the EU' in (2020) 32 International Journal of Refugee Law 1, 62.

1054 See UNHCR, *Resettlement Handbook* (revised ed July 2011) 124, 238; notably, this 'right to consent' is established in the *Resettlement Handbook*, which constitutes a guideline that has not reached the status of binding international custom (see 2.2.1).

1055 See Tom de Boer and Marjoleine Zieck, 'The Legal Abyss of Discretion in the Resettlement of Refugees: Cherry-Picking and the Lack of Due Process in the EU' in (2020) 32 International Journal of Refugee Law 1, 62.

nized potential resettlement beneficiaries as refugees. Notwithstanding, most EUMS re-assessed the status of the prospective resettlement beneficiaries referred by the UNHCR.[1056] In the face of EUMS doubting the credibility of UNHCR's interviews, they have preferred selection missions with personal interviews over dossier-only selection (see 2.5.1).[1057]

Inconsistent interpretation and application of the refugee definition further complicate cooperation between the UNHCR and receiving countries in the resettlement selection process. While UNHCR's resettlement definition uses the term 'refugee' without explicit reference to the Refugee Convention, the *Resettlement Handbook* emphasizes the application of the Convention's refugee definition.[1058]

Adherence to the Refugee Convention is not only an issue in terms of selection criteria ('positive' or 'inclusion' criteria that have to be met in order to *include* an individual in the scope of eligible persons), but also in terms of exclusion grounds (negative or 'exclusion' criteria that *exclude* eligibility – mostly assessed during security and medical screening) (see 5.2.3.7). For the latter, it has been shown that exclusion from resettlement due to prior attempts to enter the EU illegally under the EU-Turkey Statement contravenes Art 31 Refugee Convention (see 4.2.10).[1059] In any event, the application of selection criteria and/or exclusion grounds beyond the realms of the Refugee Convention likely leaves Convention refugees without recognized legal status and rights resulting therefrom. The Refugee Convention not only protects refugees arriving spontaneously

1056 See European Migration Network, 'Resettlement and Humanitarian Admission Programmes in Europe – what works' (9 November 2016) 23.

1057 It has been claimed that UNHCR's interviews do not provide a sufficient basis for adequate decision-taking; see Joanne van Selm et al, Study on 'The Feasibility of setting up resettlement schemes in EU Member States or at EU Level, against the background of the Common European Asylum system and the goal of a Common Asylum Procedure', 174.

1058 "*Although UNHCR applies both the 1951 Convention definition and the broader refugee definition when examining eligibility for refugee status, it is important for resettlement consideration to seek to identify the basis for eligibility under the 1951 Convention. In practice, it may be more challenging for UNHCR to resettle a refugee recognized only under the broader refugee definition, as many States do not have provisions to accept refugees who do not meet the 1951 Convention criteria*", UNHCR, *Resettlement Handbook* (revised ed July 2011) 21.

1059 See ibid 89-103.

and seeking asylum, but also (resettlement) refugees arriving with prior authorization in a more controlled manner.[1060]

In practice, EUMS have applied selection criteria beyond vulnerability and objective protection needs, including their integration potential,[1061] i.e. selection on the basis of, amongst others, "*age, education, work experience and language skills*".[1062] The use of such criteria implies that receiving EUMS draw distinctions between (groups of) refugees. Against this backdrop, obligations of equal treatment must be taken into account. The potential for integration is usually (at least implicitly) based on an enumerated ground under Art 2 ICCPR, such as language or national and social origin, meaning that the threshold for justification is particularly high. Accordingly, when differentiating in their treatment, receiving EUMS must show that their differentiation is reasonable and objective, and that they are following a legitimate purpose.[1063] The positive impact of integration for the receiving country as well as the individual concerned could indeed be considered as an important reason. However, when invoking such reason, EUMS face a heavy burden[1064] to explain it, and the reasons must be "very weighty"[1065]. Moreover, distinctions based on race are in any case prohibited under international law (see 3.3.4.1). In this light, the *Resettlement Handbook* states that selection "*should not be based on the desire of any specific actors, such as the host State, resettlement States, other partners or UNHCR staff themselves*"[1066] and that resettlement should take account of

1060 See Marjoleine Zieck in Vincent Chetail and Céline Bauloz (eds), *Research Handbook on International Law and Migration*, 579.

1061 Denmark has even incorporated this into legislation; see Delphine Perrin and Frank McNamara, 'Refugee Resettlement in the EU: Between Shared Standards and Diversity in Legal and Policy Frames', KNOW RESET Research Report 2013/03, 28.

1062 Margret AM Piper, Paul Power and Graham Thom, 'Refugee Resettlement: 2012 and Beyond', UNHCR Research Paper n°253 (February 2013) 23.

1063 See OHCHR, 'General Comment No 18: Non-discrimination', UN Doc HRI/GEN/1/Rev9 (Vol I) (10 November 1989) para 13.

1064 The Human Rights Committee stated that "*different treatment based on one of* [the enumerated grounds] [...] *places a heavy burden on the State party to explain the reason.*" OHCHR, 'Communication No 919/2000: Mr. Michael Andreas Müller and Imke Engelhard v Namibia', UN Doc CCPR/C/74/D/919/2000 (26 March 2022) para 6.7.

1065 See *Gayusuz v Austria* App No 17371/90 (ECtHR 16 September 1996) para 42; *Koua Poirrez v France* App No 40892/98 (ECtHR 30 December 2003) para 46; *Andrejeva v Latvia* App No 55707/00 (ECtHR 18 February 2009) para 87.

1066 UNHCR, *Resettlement Handbook* (revised ed July 2011) 216.

"*the prohibition of racial discrimination* [which] *is part of general international law*"[1067].

EUMS have followed divergent approaches to whether to consider persons eligible for subsidiary protection for resettlement. A majority of EUMS "*include the possibility to resettle persons who would meet the conditions to be granted subsidiary protection*" (for instance, Denmark, Finland, Sweden), whereas some EUMS, such as the Czech Republic, Hungary and Romania, firmly rely on the Refugee Convention's refugee definition.[1068] Furthermore, the resettlement of IDPs constituted a contentious issue between EUMS and the Commission in the course of the negotiations for the Resettlement Framework Regulation Proposal (see 4.2.11.4).

Similar to UNHCR's pre-selection decision, there are examples of (prior) EUMS where selection decisions cannot be challenged through an appeal. As of 2020, the Czech Republic, Denmark, Finland, France, the Netherlands, Norway, Portugal, Sweden and the United Kingdom expressly refrained from providing remedies against a negative resettlement selection decision.[1069] Likewise, the Proposal for a Union Resettlement Framework Regulation falls short of granting a prospective resettlement beneficiary the right to appeal against a negative decision (Art 10 para 6 Proposal).[1070]

As shown in 3.3.3.1, rejected resettlement candidates cannot invoke Art 14 ICCPR and Art 6 para 1 ECHR for access to courts to appeal against a negative selection decision. In this light, *de Boer* and *Zieck* addressed the lack of means to appeal resettlement selection decisions and reiterated that the right to a fair trial pursuant to Art 6 ECHR was not violated because the resettlement selection process fell outside the scope of this Article.[1071] Notwithstanding, the right to an effective review under the ECHR and the ICCPR cannot be denied when there is an arguable claim of violation of rights under the respective treaty. As elaborated in 3.3.3.1, this is relevant

---

1067 Vincent Chetail, *International Migration Law*, 143; see e.g., International Convention on the Elimination of All Forms of Racial Discrimination (adopted 21 December 1965, entered into force 4 January 1969) 660 UNTS 195.

1068 See Delphine Perrin and Frank McNamara, 'Refugee Resettlement in the EU: Between Shared Standards and Diversity in Legal and Policy Frames', KNOW RESET Research Report 2013/03, 22; see also European Migration Network, 'Resettlement and Humanitarian Admission Programmes in Europe – what works' (9 November 2016) 23.

1069 See Tom de Boer and Marjoleine Zieck, 'The Legal Abyss of Discretion in the Resettlement of Refugees: Cherry-Picking and the Lack of Due Process in the EU' in (2020) 32 International Journal of Refugee Law 1, 71.

1070 See ibid 60.

1071 See *MN and Others v Belgium*, para 137.

in case of abuses by field officers during selection interviews that amount, e.g. to a violation of Art 3 ECHR.

Furthermore, in terms of EU law, *de Boer* and *Zieck* pointed to Art 47 Charter (right to an effective remedy and to a fair trial).[1072] Unlike Art 6 ECHR, Art 47 Charter does not only refer to court proceedings related to civil rights and obligations or criminal charges.[1073] This Article is, however, restricted to disputes which have their basis in EU law. It follows that Art 47 Charter would only apply if resettlement became an established right under EU law.[1074]

Ultimately, *de Boer* and *Zieck*[1075] addressed Art 41 Charter. This Article provides the right to good administration, including a right to be heard and to be treated impartially and fairly.[1076] Art 41 Charter does not require resettlement to become a well-established right under EU or national law. Although the wording of Art 41 Charter refers to EU institutions, bodies and agencies, the Court of Justice[1077] applied the right to good administration as a general principle of EU law also to EUMS' actions.[1078] Given that the Charter may apply extraterritorially (subject to the condition that EUMS are implementing EU law; see 4.1.2.2), EUMS are bound to guarantee the right to good administration when interviewing potential resettlement beneficiaries during selection missions.

1072 See Tom de Boer and Marjoleine Zieck, 'The Legal Abyss of Discretion in the Resettlement of Refugees: Cherry-Picking and the Lack of Due Process in the EU' in (2020) 32 International Journal of Refugee Law 1, 79, 81.

1073 See Rudolf Streinz in Rudolf Streinz (ed), *EUV/AEUV Kommentar* (CH Beck 3rd ed 2018) Art 47 Charter, para 2.

1074 See Hermann-Josef Blanke in Christian Calliess and Matthias Ruffert (eds), *EUV/AEUV: Das Verfassungsrecht der Europäischen Union mit Grundrechtecharta* (CH Beck 5th ed 2016) Art 47 Charter, para 3.

1075 See Tom de Boer and Marjoleine Zieck, 'The Legal Abyss of Discretion in the Resettlement of Refugees: Cherry-Picking and the Lack of Due Process in the EU' in (2020) 32 International Journal of Refugee Law 1, 79, 81.

1076 See Rudolf Streinz in Rudolf Streinz (ed), *EUV/AEUV Kommentar* (CH Beck 3rd ed 2018) Art 41 Charter, para 8f; see also Matthias Ruffert in Christian Calliess and Matthias Ruffert (eds), *EUV/AEUV: Das Verfassungsrecht der Europäischen Union mit Grundrechtecharta* (CH Beck 5th ed 2016) Art 41 Charter, para 13ff.

1077 See Case C-277/11 *MM v Minister for Justice Equality and Law Reform* [2012] EU:C: 2012:744, paras 81-89.

1078 See Matthias Ruffert in Christian Calliess and Matthias Ruffert (eds), *EUV/AEUV: Das Verfassungsrecht der Europäischen Union mit Grundrechtecharta*, Art 41 Charter, para 9; see also Rudolf Streinz in Rudolf Streinz (ed), *EUV/AEUV Kommentar*, Art 41 Charter, para 7.

Finally, in the case of a positive selection decision, most EUMS do not require the selected beneficiaries to sign a formal agreement stating their commitment and willingness to be resettled. Only the Czech Republic, Slovakia and Italy have demanded resettlement beneficiaries to confirm their commitment.[1079] In a similar vein, Section 8 para 5 Danish Aliens (Consolidation) Act stipulates that the Alien "*signs a declaration concerning the conditions for resettlement in Denmark*". Still, it needs to be contemplated whether these approaches amount to a genuine right to consent. As mentioned with regard to consenting to the submission of the RFF to a specific receiving country, the individual concerned will generally have no alternative because he or she has no right to negotiate or change the conditions. If he or she does not agree to the conditions, there might be no resettlement at all.

5.2.2 US procedure and practice

In the US, the 1980 Refugee Act sets out a permanent framework for refugee resettlement. Accordingly, the US President annually determines a total number of refugees to be admitted. This determination requires mandated consultations with the US Congress, and unforeseen emergencies can implicate an increase of admissions.[1080] The Immigration and Nationality Act (INA)[1081] specifies that – within the scope of these presidential determinations – the Secretary of Homeland Security may admit any refugee who is (i) not firmly resettled in any foreign country, (ii) of special humanitarian concern to the US and (iii) admissible (see Section 207 INA).[1082]

Admission for resettlement to the US depends on *refugee* status determination. The definition of refugee in the 1980 Refugee Act corresponds to the definition in the Refugee Convention (see 2.5.4.2). Contrary to this, various Attorneys General, in their powerful role as head of the US Justice Department, continued to invoke their parole authority "*on a blanket*

1079 See European Migration Network, 'Resettlement and Humanitarian Admission Programmes in Europe – what works' (9 November 2016) 27.

1080 See Daniel J Steinbock, 'The Qualities of Mercy: Maximizing the Impact of US Refugee Resettlement' in (2003) 36 University of Michigan Journal of Law Reform, 957.

1081 See Immigration and Nationality Act 1952 <https://www.uscis.gov/laws-and-policy/legislation/immigration-and-nationality-act> accessed 13 February 2021.

1082 See Stephen H Legomsky and David B Thronson, *Immigration Law and Policy* (The Foundation Press 7th ed 2019) 1149.

basis", paroling groups in the US that did not qualify as refugees under the Convention. The parole authority under Section 212 lit d para 5 INA was eventually amended by Section 602 lit a Illegal Immigration Reform and Immigrant Responsibility Act of 1996 (IIRIRA).[1083] This amendment introduced a limitation to use parole authority only "*for emergent reasons or for reasons deemed strictly in the public interest*". Furthermore, parole authority must be exercised "*on a case-by-case basis for urgent humanitarian reasons or significant public benefit*" (Section 602 lit a IIRIRA). Due to this limitation of parole authority, "*the executive branch today has no clearly-defined statutory authority to bring into the United States a large group of people who face dangers other than persecution*".[1084]

As a general rule, an individual is only eligible for resettlement to the US if he or she cannot be considered as *firmly resettled* in another country.[1085] This requirement accounts for situations where the person concerned received an offer of permanent resettlement in another country before arriving in the US, eliminating the need for resettlement in the US (see 2.2.3). Substantially and consciously restricted conditions of residence in that other country, however, preclude a situation of firm resettlement. Furthermore, firm resettlement must not be confused with the safe third-country concept. According to the latter, US law permits the Department of Homeland Security (DHS) to remove asylum applicants to third countries – irrespective of whether they will be firmly resettled there.[1086]

Regarding the *admissibility* requirement, it is notable that exclusion grounds such as labor certification, public charge or certain documentation requirements do not apply to refugees. In addition, the Attorney General has discretionary power to waive most other admissibility requirements (see Section 207 lit c para 3 INA).[1087] This means that US law addresses the special situation of refugees who are, for example, regularly unable to meet documentation requirements because they had to leave

1083 See Immigrant Responsibility Act 1996 <https://www.govinfo.gov/content/pkg/PLAW-104publ208/pdf/PLAW-104publ208.pdf> accessed 27 March 2021.

1084 Stephen H Legomsky and David B Thronson, *Immigration Law and Policy*, 1391.

1085 See Section 208.15 Title 8 Code of Federal Regulations 2018.

1086 The requirements under US law for removing an applicant to a safe third country are the existence of a bilateral or multilateral agreement and certain minimum safeguards (Section 604 lit a IIRIRA; Section 208 lit a para 2 INA); see Stephen H Legomsky and David B Thronson, *Immigration and Refugee Law and Policy*, 1292.

1087 See ibid 1149.

their documents behind, lost them while fleeing or because their home country no longer issues them documents. Also, it comes naturally that refugees would find it difficult to meet the criterion of not being a public charge, given that they regularly come unprepared and have yet to navigate through the US labor market.

The annual presidential allocation includes admission numbers by region, but it does not set out specific criteria for the refugees to be admitted within the regions. Since the designated numbers per region hardly cover all refugees in need, further criteria are necessary. Selection is therefore based on the so-called processing priorities,[1088] i.e. categories of prioritized individuals or groups eligible to enter the US under the USRAP.[1089]

Priority one covers *Individual Referrals*, i.e. refugees with compelling protection needs referred by the UNHCR, a designated NGO or a US embassy.[1090] The cases under this priority align with the aforementioned UNHCR submission categories,[1091] and indeed most of the individual referrals are made by the UNHCR.[1092]

Priority two deals with *Group Referrals*. It allows specific groups of special concern to the US to directly access the USRAP, including groups of IDPs.[1093] Each year, the specific groups are listed by the Department

---

1088 See Daniel J Steinbock, 'The Qualities of Mercy: Maximizing the Impact of US Refugee Resettlement' in (2003) 36 University of Michigan Journal of Law Reform, 957f.

1089 Traditionally, there are four main categories. For Fiscal Year 2023, a fourth category for privately sponsored refugees has been introduced for the first time. Its implementation remains to be seen and depends on the launch of a private sponsorship pilot program expected for the end of calendar year 2022. See US Department of State, Department of Homeland and Security, Department of Health and Human Services, 'Report to Congress on Proposed Refugee Admissions for Fiscal Year 2023' (8 September 2022).

1090 See Daniel J Steinbock, 'The Qualities of Mercy: Maximizing the Impact of US Refugee Resettlement' in (2003) 36 University of Michigan Journal of Law Reform, 959.

1091 See Jessica H Darrow, 'Working It Out in Practice: Tensions Embedded in the US Refugee Resettlement Program Resolved through Implementation' in Adèle Garnier, Liliana Lyra Jubilut and Kristin Bergtora Sandvik (eds), *Refugee Resettlement: Power, Politics, and Humanitarian Governance* (Berghahn 2018) 95 (102f).

1092 See Daniel J Steinbock, 'The Qualities of Mercy: Maximizing the Impact of US Refugee Resettlement' in (2003) 36 University of Michigan Journal of Law Reform, 959.

1093 Exceptionally, in-country processing is also available for individual UNHCR referrals under priority 1. As the annual Report for 2023 lays out: "*In El Salvador, Guatemala, and Honduras, UNHCR refers to the USRAP cases of vulnerable*

of State's Bureau of Population, Refugees, and Migration (PRM) after consultation with NGOs and other entities.[1094] In the fiscal years 2020 and 2021, direct access was granted to (i) certain members of religious minority groups in Eurasia and the Baltics, and to (ii) certain Iraqis associated with the US.[1095] In addition, as a response to the taking over of Afghanistan by the Taliban regime after US group withdrawal, Afghan nationals were designated as a priority group in August 2021.[1096]

Priority three encompasses *Family Reunification*, namely "*access to members of designated nationalities who have immediate family members in the United States who entered as refugees or were granted asylum (even if they subsequently gained LPR status* [lawful permanent resident status] *or naturalized as US citizens)*".[1097] Participation is open to parents, spouses and unmarried children under the age of 21 of a US-based asylee or refugee. As additional avenue for family reunification, within two years of admission, a refugee admitted to the US may request so-called "*following-to-join benefits*" for his or her spouse and/or unmarried children under the age of 21 who were not previously granted refugee status.[1098]

The US, like most EUMS, does not merely rely on UNHCR's pre-screening interviews. In order to ensure that the referred refugees meet one of the US admission priorities, potential resettlement refugees are once more pre-screened overseas in US Resettlement Support Centers (RSCs). Besides re-checking UNHCR's pre-selection, i.e. referrals under priority one, individuals who do not meet the criteria of priorities two or three

---

individuals identified by a consortium of NGOs. Cases with the most extreme protection needs may be transferred to Costa Rica for refugee processing under a tripartite Memorandum of Understanding between the Government of Costa Rica, UNHCR, and IOM; all other cases are eligible for in-country processing for resettlement to the United States." US Department of State, Department of Homeland and Security, Department of Health and Human Services, 'Report to Congress on Proposed Refugee Admissions for Fiscal Year 2023' (8 September 2022) 13.

1094 See Daniel J Steinbock, 'The Qualities of Mercy: Maximizing the Impact of US Refugee Resettlement' in (2003) 36 University of Michigan Journal of Law Reform, 979.

1095 See US Department of State, 'US Refugee Admissions Program Access Categories' <https://2017-2021.state.gov/refugee-admissions/u-s-refugee-admissions-program-access-categories/index.html> accessed 20 July 2022.

1096 US Department of State, 'US Refugee Admissions Program Priority 2 Designation for Afghan Nationals' (2 August 2021) <https://www.state.gov/u-s-refugee-admissions-program-priority-2-designation-for-afghan-nationals/> accessed 20 July 2022.

1097 US Department of State, 'US Refugee Admissions Program Access Categories'.

1098 See ibid.

are removed without an interview with Refugee Officers from DHS' US Citizenship and Immigration Services (USCIS).[1099]

Following pre-screening, USCIS assesses the eligibility of potential resettlement beneficiaries for resettlement through personal interviews. A USCIS officer's decision cannot be appealed. Reconsideration of the case can only be requested if new or previously unavailable information is present, and it is at the discretion of the USCIS officer who conducted the original screening interview to grant a new interview. The DHS/USCIS provides a so-called Request for Review Tip Sheet[1100] that assists in this process. If the resettlement candidate successfully passes the interview process, he or she becomes formally recognized as refugee by DHS/USCIS; but this only entails conditional approval for resettlement. The prospective resettlement refugee still has to undergo medical examination and pass multiple security checks. Moreover, the US Customs and Border Protection (CBP) must confirm admissibility to the US. It performs initial vetting based on documentation of resettlement candidates already approved and scheduled to travel to the US by air. The CBP also conducts additional background checks upon arrival at a US port of entry. Only after passing these series of security checks, an individual is finally admitted to the US as a refugee.[1101]

5.2.3 Analysis

The depiction of European and US resettlement selection showed the following points of issue: The first question concerns UNHCR's credentials as referral entity. Second, the comparison revealed differences in the national approaches among EUMS, and between EUMS and the US, regarding status determination. Third, the US priority system means prioritizing certain groups with ties to the US. Fourth, the prerogative of family reunification entails legal issues, e.g. the scope of family, that need to be clarified for future EU resettlement. Fifth, EUMS have applied the integration potential as additional selection criterion that goes beyond vulnerability and the objective resettlement needs. Sixth, the outlined US con-

1099 See Refugee Council USA, 'Resettlement Process' <https://rcusa.org/resettlement/resettlement-process/> accessed 27 March 2021.

1100 See USCIS, 'Request for Review Tip Sheet' <https://www.uscis.gov/humanitarian/refugees-asylum/refugees/request-review-tip-sheet> accessed 27 March 2021.

1101 See USCIS, 'Refugee Processing and Security Screening' <https://www.uscis.gov/refugeescreening#Enhanced%20Review> accessed 27 March 2021.

cept of firm resettlement raises the question whether an individual's firm resettlement in a third country should bar that individual from further resettlement. Seventh, exclusion grounds from resettlement deserve particular attention in terms of their compatibility with international refugee law. Eighth, extensive screening practices need to be assessed because they may trigger (unjustified) interferences with individual rights of the persons concerned. Ninth, there are lacking or insufficient means to appeal a negative selection decision, and lastly, the legal value of a resettlement beneficiary's right to consent deserves further reflection.

5.2.3.1 Referral entities

The US and EUMS both operate on the premise that the UNHCR plays a major role in the identification of resettlement cases. EUMS generally rely on referrals by the UNHCR, similar to what the US does in its priority one. Several EUMS, namely Austria, France, Hungary, Slovakia and Luxembourg (until 1997) have additionally relied on NGOs as referral entities.[1102] Correspondingly, the US' priority one also covers individual referrals by NGOs. This makes the UNHCR an important but not singular referral entity.

The UNHCR must comply with the refugee law and human rights framework outlined in Chapter 3 – particularly the principles of *non-refoulement* (see 3.3.1) and equal treatment (see 3.3.4), as well as procedural rights (see 3.3.3). The fact that the UNHCR itself is not a state actor does not relieve the UNHCR from responsibility to comply with obligations under international law (see 3.4.2).

To ensure the required legal standard, the UNHCR shall not be "*the only referral entity, or the only body preparing dossiers*".[1103] Allowing NGOs and other non-state actors to make referrals in addition to those provided by the UNHCR opens up resources and offers a diversified and more comprehensive case identification, namely capacity to properly assess the specific situation of and conditions faced by potential resettlement benefi-

1102 See European Migration Network, 'Resettlement and Humanitarian Admission Programmes in Europe – what works' (9 November 2016) 27.

1103 Joanne van Selm et al, Study on 'The Feasibility of setting up resettlement schemes in EU Member States or at EU Level, against the background of the Common European Asylum system and the goal of a Common Asylum Procedure', 10.

ciaries. This is necessary to guarantee compliance with the aforementioned human rights and refugee rights. For example, the principle of *non-refoulement* demands a careful risk assessment, which is enhanced by first-hand information through NGOs' direct field work. Also, compliance with the principle of non-discrimination is fostered by direct engagement with potential resettlement refugees. NGO involvement helps to ensure more comprehensive case identification because they regularly visit refugee camps or other refugee accommodations and can identify cases at place that may otherwise be overlooked. Eventually, procedural rights could be strengthened, which are likely at odds if there is scarce capacity and time for engagement with the potential resettlement beneficiaries.

Overall, NGOs regularly have more capacity to closely engage with refugees in the field because they do not have to deal with global migration issues at large. They rather concentrate on certain regions. Moreover, the cooperation between the UNHCR and NGOs, specifically staff loaning from NGOs, has already become established practice. In terms of responsibility, it has been shown that the conduct of the staff of NGOs may be attributed to the UNHCR (see 3.4.2).

In addition to NGOs, the EUAA could become a crucial actor in case identification and function as (pre-)referral entity for future EU resettlement. Compared to its predecessor EASO, EUAA's decision-making power and overall mandate are expanded. Specifically, the EUAA can engage in vulnerability assessments, which is important for the identification of resettlement candidates (see 4.3.2). However, the actual effectiveness of additional accountability mechanisms under the EUAA Regulation has yet to be tested (see 4.3.3). From the perspective of international law, namely the ARSIWA and ARIO, the conduct of the EUAA experts could – depending on the specific circumstances – be attributed to the EU and/or the responsible state in the event of rights violations (see 3.4.3).

5.2.3.2 Status determination

With regard to (refugee) status determination, EUMS as well as the US have insisted on re-assessment of UNHCR's pre-determination on the basis of their national practices. It follows that prospective resettlement beneficiaries must undergo a more or less rigorous status determination process, depending on the prospective receiving country which they are referred to by the UNHCR.

Harmonization of EUMS' national practices - namely the requirements, contents, reporting and recording of selection interviews – would enable a more objective analysis, thereby establishing comparably high procedural standards among EUMS. Harmonization efforts on the conduct of personal interviews have already been made for the internal EU asylum *acquis*, namely in Arts 15 to 17 Asylum Procedures Directive. This means that already *de lege lata*, the principle of consistency between external and internal EU asylum policy (Art 7 TFEU and Art 21 para 3 TEU; see 4.1.2.3) demands that EUMS guarantee the threshold set under Arts 15 to 17 Asylum Procedures Directive for interviews in the resettlement selection process.

Moreover, harmonization of EUMS' divergent scopes of resettlement beneficiaries would streamline the eligibility criteria for resettlement to the EU. *De lege ferenda*, harmonization in favor of including persons eligible for subsidiary protection would be the solution that most consistently reflects the internal EU asylum *acquis*. The subsidiary protection status constitutes an EU law specificity to fill protection gaps and to refine the restrictive refugee definition of the Refugee Convention (see 2.5.4.1). Moreover, protection gaps could be filled by further pursuing the current attempts of the Commission to include IDPs in the scope of resettlement beneficiaries (see 2.2.2), as IDPs might be equally in need for resettlement, even though they do not meet the definition of refugee under the Refugee Convention.

With a view to filling protection gaps in the global refugee regime, US scholars proposed an expansion of the refugee definition. One inspiring approach was taken in the so-called Model International Mobility Convention. It goes beyond the concept of a refugee and defines a broader group of 'forced migrants', "*including any individual who, owing to the risk of serious harm, is compelled to leave or unable to return to her or his country of origin*"[1104]. 'Harm' would not only cover generalized armed conflict and mass violations of human rights, but also threats resulting from environmental disasters, enduring food insecurity, acute climate change or other events seriously disturbing public order.[1105] In light of the considerations on groups that are potentially in need for resettlement (see 2.5.4.3), this broadened definition of forced migrants reflects the realities of persons having to leave their home countries more comprehensively than the restrictive refugee definition of the Refugee Convention. It would thus

1104 Kiran Banerjee, 'Rethinking the Global Governance of International Protection' in (2018) 56 Columbia Journal of Transnational Law, 319.

1105 See ibid 319.

be an apt starting point to reconsider and adjust the scope of resettlement beneficiaries *de lege ferenda*.

5.2.3.3 Resettlement of prioritized groups

The US Priority Two for Group referrals is not based on criteria that comprehensively reflect individual vulnerability and objective humanitarian needs. In the last fiscal years, the US prioritized a few selected religious groups, such as Jews, and certain categories of one specific nationality, Iraqis. The additional designation of Afghan Nationals in 2021 is largely limited to certain Afghans who worked with the US. In fact, the US has designated groups that rely heavily on resettlement, and also represent a response to acute humanitarian crises and mass displacements such as from Afghanistan. However, distinctions are obviously made on grounds of religion and nationality. Additionally, distinctions are based on the former work for, or other ties to the US. Overall, the prioritization reflects US foreign policy interests.

Indeed, preferential treatment by a State Party for its own citizens was acknowledged by the Human Rights Committee. This does not mean that foreigners can be treated differently because of their national origin, religion, or nationality without justification. As outlined, the distinctions on grounds such as of religion or national origin require a particularly high threshold for justification, because these grounds count among the enumerated grounds under the ICCPR. Also, for nationality, State Parties must base justification of differential treatment on reasonable and objective criteria.[1106]

In terms of the US prioritization, a legitimate goal could be, for example, the benefit of faster self-sufficiency and integration of individuals that already have ties to the US. One could also imagine (more complex) reasons, such as special moral obligations towards those who served the US.[1107] Even if such reasons would be weighty, it appears unreasonable to rely, for example, solely on the Afghan nationality. Specifically, it is not plausible to exclude non-Afghans who are equally affected by the

---

1106 OHCHR, 'Communication No 196/1985: Gueye v France' (1989) para 9.4.

1107 In this light, *Tendayi Achiume* pointed to compelling claims to national admission based on colonialism. See E Tendayi Achiume, 'Migration as Decolonialization' in (2020) 71 Stanford Law Review, 1509-1574.

humanitarian situation in Afghanistan and served for or have ties to the US, just like their counterparts with Afghan citizenship.

Moreover, the US policy of including groups of IDPs in Priority Two is remarkable, but this extended beneficiary scope is – again – limited to designated groups or individuals who find themselves in a particular country, thus likely opening up another source for discriminatory treatment. By comparison, the Commission attempted to include IDPs generally in its 2016 Proposal for a Union Resettlement Framework Regulation (see 4.2.11.4). With a view to including IDPs in the scope of EU resettlement *de lege ferenda*, Art 78 para 1 TFEU requires the EU to adopt an approach that complies with the principle of equal treatment as incorporated in the ECHR, ICCPR and other pertinent universal human rights treaties. Distinctions between IDPs from different countries would only comply with the principle of non-discrimination if the mentioned justification requirements were met.

5.2.3.4 Family reunification

Until 2021, the US Priority Three for family reunification followed the approach of Priority Two, i.e. prioritizing certain groups from designated countries. By comparison, the 2016 Commission Proposal includes a new category of family members of third-country nationals, stateless persons or EU citizens legally residing in an EUMS, making them potentially eligible for resettlement (Art 4 lit b number ii). As such, this category would be more inclusive than the (former) US approach.

As a general rule, international law protects the family as a "*fundamental group unit of society*", namely under Art 23 para 1 ICCPR – this is also stated in the non-binding Art 16 para 3 UDHR. In terms of the scope of Art 23 ICCPR, the Human Rights Committee highlighted in General Comment No 13 that the right to found a family implies "*the possibility to procreate and live together*". The possibility to live together, in turn, necessitates the adoption of appropriate measures, "*both at the internal level and as the case may be, in cooperation with other States, to ensure the unity or reunification of families, particularly when their members are separated for political, economic or similar reasons*".[1108] Applying the Committee's view results in a positive

1108 OHCHR, 'General Comment No 19: Article 23 (The Family) Protection of the Family, the Right to Marriage and Equality of the Spouses' (27 July 1990) para 5 <https://www.refworld.org/pdfid/45139bd74.pdf> accessed 21 July 2022.

duty of Contracting States, including EUMS and the US, to ensure the reunification of resettlement beneficiaries with their family members who are left behind, without "*any discriminatory treatment*".[1109]

Under Art 78 para 1 TFEU, the EU legally committed to develop its policy in accordance with relevant universal human rights treaties. Against this backdrop, a non-discriminatory approach in family reunification must be pursued for future EU resettlement. A non-discriminatory approach requires that family reunification must not be limited to specific groups of individuals with a certain nationality or religious belief, unless distinction on such ground is justified. For example, one could imagine prioritized family reunification with family members who find themselves in certain countries where they are exposed to a serious risk of harm (amounting, e.g. to violations of Art 3 ECHR); also, the above-mentioned integration considerations as well as ties based on decolonialization could be invoked. Otherwise, however, differential treatment based *purely* on grounds of nationality must be justified by reasonable and objective criteria.

Consistently, EU policy promotes the right to family life (Art 7 Charter) and takes into consideration the thresholds set by the internal EU asylum *acquis*, especially the Family Reunification Directive.[1110] The standard requirements for family reunification under this Directive are (i) a residence permit valid for at least one year, (ii) reasonable prospects of obtaining permanent residence, (iii) residence of the family members outside the territory when the application is made (although EUMS can derogate from that rule), and (iv) no grounds for rejection, such as public policy, security or health (see Arts 3, 5 and 6 Family Reunification Directive). In addition, EUMS may demand integration measures (Art 7 para 2 Family Reunification Directive).

Under the Family Reunification Directive, a waiting period of two years of lawful stay of the sponsor may be required before family reunion takes place (Art 8 Family Reunification Directive). This waiting period of two years is similar to the two-year waiting period for the US 'following-to-join benefits'. Effective application of the right to family life would be facilitated by reducing the waiting period *de lege ferenda*. Aside from formal waiting periods, this entails that receiving countries must avoid circumvention through informal waiting periods as, for example, Ireland did. It introduced a one-year waiting period after status recognition, which was

1109 Ibid para 9.

1110 See Directive 2003/86 (EC) on the right to family reunification [2003] OJ L251/12-18.

problematic according to a 2017 issue paper published by the Council of Europe because "*status determination is often protracted in Ireland, and sometimes takes years*".[1111] In addition, other procedural hurdles like onerous evidential requirements or tight deadlines are likely to interfere with the right to family reunification.[1112]

Moreover, subsidiary protection status is regularly linked to waiting periods for family reunification longer than two years.[1113] This means differential treatment between refugees and individuals with subsidiary protection status. As explained in 2.5.4.1, subsidiary protection status comes with the expectation that the stay of the individual concerned will be limited in time, i.e. that the individual will return once the danger in the home country no longer exists. As opposed to refugees, persons eligible for subsidiary protection do not flee because of persecution on account of a protected ground; rather, they flee harmful situations, such as civil war, where the duration is difficult to estimate and which can end relatively fast, in the sense that safe conditions prevail again in their home country. This is also why subsidiary protection status depends on the regular review of the situation in the home country. It follows that, while there are similarities, the positions of refugees and persons eligible for subsidiary protection are not identical. Yet, whether a situation constitutes a comparable situation for purposes of establishing discrimination is both fact-specific and contextual. The ECtHR does not require identical situations, but relative similarities.[1114] The Human Rights Committee has likewise suggested the fact-specific nature of evaluating whether two groups are *de facto* the same or different for purposes of evaluating discrimination.[1115] Against this backdrop, it seems more correct from the perspective of international

1111 Council of Europe, 'Realising the right to family reunification of refugees in Europe' (7 February 2017) 40 <https://familie.asyl.net/fileadmin/user_upload/pdf/PREMS_052917_GBR_1700_Realising_Refugees_160x240_Web.pdf-1.pdf> accessed 27 March 2021.

1112 See ibid 41.

1113 See Commission, 'EMN Ad-Hoc Query on BE AHQ on the waiting period for family reunification for beneficiaries of subsidiary protection' (requested on 10 August 2016) <https://ec.europa.eu/home-affairs/sites/homeaffairs/files/2016.1096_-_be_ahq_on_the_waiting_period_for_family_reunification.pdf> accessed 27 March 2021.

1114 See *Fábián v Hungary* App No 78117/13 (ECtHR 5 September 2017) para 121; see also *Clift v the United Kingdom* App No 7205/07 (ECtHR 22 November 2010) para 66.

1115 See OHCHR, 'Communication No 864/1999: Alfonso Ruiz Agudo v Spain', UN Doc CCPR/C/76/D/864/1999 (31 October 2002) para 7.2 <http://www.w

non-discrimination law not to make a blanket distinction on the basis of refugee or subsidiary protection status when it comes to the future regulation of waiting periods for family reunification in the course of EU resettlement. Rather, it would be more appropriate to take into account the factual situation in the home country and the likeliness of a return to that country.

A resettlement beneficiary's interest in family reunification must be balanced with conflicting public interests of the receiving environment, namely the reception capacity. A complete abolishment of the waiting period seems to be the ideal solution in light of the right to family life, but such ideal solution is prone to lack practical feasibility; particularly in situations where receiving countries and communities are already overwhelmed by the number of those who have actually arrived, not to mention having to host all their family members. Within this framing, Art 8 Family Reunification Directive includes the possibility for EUMS to derogate from the two-year waiting period and set a longer period of no more than three years, provided that their national legislation takes account of their reception capacity. Correspondingly, in a 2011 Green Paper addressing the right to family reunification, the Commission acknowledged that the reception capacity may be one of the factors to consider when deciding upon an application for family reunification. Still, by way of derogation, receiving EUMS must not ignore the factual circumstances of a specific case.[1116]

Waiting periods are inevitable from a practical point of view. Once this period has elapsed, a different question concerns the concept of family, i.e. whether only the nuclear family or also additional family members should be considered for family reunification by means of resettlement. *Di Filippo* deals with this issue in the context of the Dublin system. He argues in favor of a wide notion of family:[1117]

> *In contrast to some European countries, in many countries of origin, relatives are as important in family life as the core family members, due to*

orldcourts.com/hrc/eng/decisions/2002.10.31_Ruiz_Agudo_v_Spain.htm> accessed 21 July 2022.

1116 See Commission, Green Paper on the right to family reunification of third-country nationals living in the European Union (Directive 2003/86/EC), COM(2011) 735 final, 5.

1117 Marcello Di Filippo in Valsamis Mitsilegas, Violeta Moreno-Lax and Niovi Vavoula (eds), *Securitising Asylum Flows: Deflection, Criminalisation and Challenges for Human Rights*, 212.

> *the cultural concept of family and the related moral obligations of mutual assistance and care. Moreover, on occasions when the original nuclear family may be dispersed or deceased, the only form of family life available to the asylum seeker may be represented by a cousin, an aunt or an uncle, a nephew or a grandparent. Finally* [...] *the closeness to persons coming from the same familiar milieu – regardless of how old individuals at stake are – may prove to be fundamental for psychological welfare and propensity to establish a collaborative and fruitful relationship* [...] *with the surrounding environment.*

Apparently, the Commission acknowledged the need for a broadened notion of family in the resettlement context. The 2016 Proposal for a Union Resettlement Framework Regulation includes couples who are not married as well as minor children of unmarried couples. Furthermore, the Proposal expressly refers to siblings (Art 5 lit b number ii Proposal, first and second bullet point). The Commission also included the possibility to resettle family members "*who are dependent on their child or parent for assistance as a result of pregnancy, a newborn child, serious illness, severe disability or old age*" (Art 5 lit b number ii Proposal, fifth bullet point). This proposed scope of family goes beyond US law.

In this context it is important to point to the risk of circumventing a broad notion of family by simultaneously restricting the scope of care givers for a 'dependent person'. For example, in Art 24 Migration Management Regulation Proposal as part of the 2020 New Pact on Migration and Asylum, the Commission did not mention spouses and siblings as care-giving supporters for dependent applicants. Such approach could lead to situations where those dependent on family support would be deprived of enlarged reunification possibilities.[1118]

Politically speaking, broadening its definition of family in future EU legislation on resettlement involves persuading EUMS that a broad notion of family is beneficial rather than burdensome. The benefit consists of faster and more sustainable integration. Resettlement beneficiaries will more likely become active contributors to the community of a receiving EUMS if their demand for family life is satisfied. Indeed, some restrictions might be necessary to achieve political support, such as prioritizing the

1118 See Francesco Maiani, 'A "Fresh Start" or One More Clunker? Dublin and Solidarity in the New Pact' (*Eumigrationlawblog.eu*, 20 October 2020) <http://eumigrationlawblog.eu/a-fresh-start-or-one-more-clunker-dublin-and-solidarity-in-the-new-pact/> accessed 27 March 2021.

nuclear family before other relatives and/or requiring proof of the capacity to take care of the respective family member or relative.[1119]

Moreover, as a specific issue, it needs to be taken up *de lege ferenda* what happens when a child comes of age during the resettlement (selection) process. While the determination of the age of majority is left to EUMS, the Family Reunification Directive does not refer to national law regarding the date when the condition of majority must be satisfied. This means that EU law should have a uniform interpretation on how to determine that date. In *BMM*, the Court of Justice considered the date of submission of the application for entry and residence as the date to be taken into account to determine whether a family member of a sponsor is a 'minor child'.[1120] However, there is no date equivalent to the date of submission of the application for entry and residence in the resettlement context, because individuals generally cannot apply for resettlement. Under the internal EU asylum *acquis*, a minor irregularly arriving in the receiving country can apply for entry and residence immediately upon arrival or already at the border (see Art 3 para 1 Asylum Procedures Directive). Accordingly, in the resettlement context, the arrival on the territory of the receiving country could be the relevant point in time for the determination whether resettlement beneficiary has reached the age of majority.

5.2.3.5 Potential to integrate

The Commission and EUMS have both considered integration-related criteria to select resettlement beneficiaries. The Commission included the integration potential in the 2016 Proposal for a Union Resettlement Framework Regulation (see 4.2.11.4).

According to *Bamberg*, the inclusion of the integration potential as selection criterion "*is part of an ongoing shift from a value-based to an interest-based approach*".[1121] Such a shift is not merely a European phenomenon. In the US, the 1980 Refugee Act was originally intended to abolish integra-

1119 See Marcello Di Filippo in Valsamis Mitsilegas, Violeta Moreno-Lax and Niovi Vavoula (eds), *Securitising Asylum Flows: Deflection, Criminalisation and Challenges for Human Rights*, 212.

1120 See Joined Cases C-133/19, C-136/19 and C-137/19 *BMM, BS, BM and BMO v État belge* [2020] EU:C:2020:577.

1121 Katharina Bamberg, 'The EU Resettlement Framework: From a humanitarian pathway to a migration management tool?', Discussion Paper European Migration and Diversity Programme (26 June 2018) 12.

tion-based selection. Admission to the US "*has not been predicated on the extent to which individual refugees are work ready*"[1122] even though, upon arrival, the US program has forced self-sufficiency and rapid labor market entry. Notwithstanding, for its referrals to the US, the UNHCR "[…] *may also take into account certain criteria that enhance a refugee's likelihood of successful assimilation and contribution to the United States*".[1123] For example, the Report to Congress on Proposed Refugee Admissions for Fiscal Year 2018 proclaimed close cooperation with the UNHCR "*to ensure that, in addition to referrals of refugees with compelling protection needs, referrals may also take into account certain criteria that enhance a refugee's likelihood of successful assimilation and contribution to the United States.*"[1124] It highlighted that "[s]*uccessful assimilation of refugees into US society directly benefits refugees, asylees, and communities, while it also serves the national interest of the United States by helping to establish a safe and secure homeland. Assimilation facilitates the ability of refugees and asylees to make positive contributions to the United States and the communities where they live.*"[1125] Particularly remarkable here is the usage of 'assimilation' (absorbing into the mainstream culture), as opposed to 'integration' (joining of cultures). By contrast, previous US refugee guidelines used 'integration',[1126] which underscores the shift from value to interest-based selection.

The above stated language used by the US points out valid arguments in favor of the integration potential from the perspective of receiving countries, and even from the perspective of resettlement beneficiaries. One main consideration is that enhanced integration of resettlement beneficiaries in the receiving community serves the interest of the resettlement

1122 Jessica H Darrow in Adèle Garnier, Liliana Lyra Jubilut and Kristin Bergtora Sandvik (eds), *Refugee Resettlement: Power, Politics, and Humanitarian Governance*, 102.

1123 Ibid 113.

1124 US Department of State, Department of Homeland and Security, Department of Health and Human Services, 'Report to Congress on Proposed Refugee Admissions for Fiscal Year 2018', 8 <https://s3.documentcloud.org/documents/4063604/Report-to-Congress-Proposed-Refugee-Admissions.pdf> accessed 22 July 2022.

1125 Ibid 52.

1126 See The World staff, 'Refugees to be assessed on ability to 'assimilate'' (*The World*, 18 October 2017) <https://theworld.org/stories/2017-10-18/refugees-be-assessed-ability-assimilate> accessed 22 July 2022. See also Lauren Wolfe, 'The Trump Administration Wants Refugees to Fit In or Stay Out' (*Foreign Policy*, 12 October 2017) <https://foreignpolicy.com/2017/10/12/the-trump-administration-wants-refugees-to-fit-in-or-stay-out/> accessed 22 July 2022.

beneficiaries, as well as the receiving countries. It allows resettlement beneficiaries to contribute and positively impact their social and professional environment. Moreover, successful integration is in the interest of national security and the maintenance of public order in the receiving country.

Legally speaking, the potential to integrate has no basis in the Refugee Convention, thus constituting an additional requirement to the existing requirements of the refugee definition. Its assessment comes with large discretion. What this means in terms of practical implementation is exemplified by German authorities, who themselves admitted that there are no fixed criteria when determining the "*prospect*"[1127] of integration. As such, the lack of clearly established criteria raises the risk of discrimination in the course of arbitrary decisions (see 3.3.4.1). In addition, the determination of the potential to integrate may involve that potential resettlement beneficiaries are confronted with uncomfortable questions like, how often do you pray, or, would you save the life of a terrorist? Such questions may trigger further interferences with human rights, such as the right to privacy (Art 17 ICCPR) or/and the right to freedom of thought, conscience and religion (Art 18 para 1 ICCPR).

Overall, the views on the integration potential remain controversial, and there are plausible arguments from both sides. Notwithstanding this controversy, if the integration potential criterion is applied, the limits under human rights and refugee law and in particular the principle of equal treatment (see 3.3.4) must be upheld. The main challenge for future EU resettlement therefore consists of reducing discrimination resulting from integration-based selection of resettlement beneficiaries. To that end, improvements *de lege lata* could be made through the introduction of clearly defined criteria and adoption of guidance for assessment.

The UNHCR plays an important role in this regard. The above-quoted US language exemplifies that receiving countries work closely with the UNHCR to assess the likelihood of integration of resettlement candidates. Notwithstanding the receiving countries' interests in the admission of individuals who are more likely to integrate, the UNHCR must uphold the humanitarian purpose of its work – in accordance with its Statute (see 2.5.2.1). Consistently, in its *Resettlement Handbook*, the UNHCR states that the usage of the integration potential "*should not negatively influence the se-*

1127 Hanna Schneider, 'Implementing the Refugee Resettlement Process: Diverging Objectives, Interdependencies and Power Relations' in (2021) Frontiers in Political Science, 15.

lection and promotion of resettlement cases."[1128] In the end, many vulnerable forced migrants have no other option than to resettle and to demonstrate their willingness to cope with integration challenges.[1129]

5.2.3.6 Firm resettlement

As opposed to the European approach, US law bars individuals from protection if they are firmly resettled in any other country. By comparison, EU law and national laws of EUMS rely on the safe third country principle for accelerated returns. The safe third country principle, however, does not make returns conditional on a third country's former offer of permanent settlement, or a durable solution.

The following practical example illustrates the difference between firm resettlement as applied in the US, and the safe third country condition under EU law: An Egyptian, having fled to Turkey, would likely be denied international protection in the EU without individual assessment of his claim. In contrast, in the US, he would not be barred from refugee status on the basis of firm resettlement if he could, for instance, prove that he only lived in Turkey on a tourist visa without any legal avenue or prospect of indefinite residence in that country.

It has been shown that individual assessment is essential especially with regard to the *non-refoulement* principle (see 3.3.1). In contrast to the safe third country principle, the firm resettlement bar is less prone to automatic returns without assessment.[1130] In light of the *non-refoulement* principle, it would thus be more consistent to reconsider the third country principle *de lege ferenda* and rely on firm resettlement instead. This would allow EUMS to refuse admission in situations where an applicant has access to a durable solution elsewhere, while at the same time following an approach that is more consistent with the *non-refoulement* principle.

1128 UNHCR, *Resettlement Handbook* (revised ed July 2011) 245.

1129 See Hanna Schneider, 'Implementing the Refugee Resettlement Process: Diverging Objectives, Interdependencies and Power Relations' in (2021) Frontiers in Political Science, 14f.

1130 For guidance on the application of the firm resettlement bar, see USCIS, 'RAIO Combined Training Program: Firm Resettlement' (20 December 2019) <https://www.uscis.gov/sites/default/files/document/foia/Firm_Resettlement_LP_RAIO.pdf> accessed 24 August 2022.

5.2.3.7 Exclusion grounds

Another contentious issue is where a receiving EUMS excluded individuals in need for international protection from admission to their territory on the basis of their previous irregular entry. Specifically, the EU-Turkey Statement prioritized individuals for resettlement who had not irregularly stayed in or attempted to irregularly enter the territory of an EUMS (see 4.2.10). In the same vein, the 2016 Proposal for a Union Resettlement Framework Regulation excludes such irregular migrants from resettlement (see 4.2.11.4).

US law as such does not set out a similar exclusion ground.[1131] Yet, when the number of irregular crossings at the US-Mexican border reached a peak in fall 2022, the US launched a private sponsorship program for displaced Venezuelans that excludes, among others, individuals who have crossed irregularly into the US, or unlawfully crossed the Mexican or Panamanian borders after the program's announcement.[1132]

Excluding refugees from international protection for reasons that are not covered by international refugee law, namely the exclusion grounds in the Refugee Convention (Art 1 F), interferes with the principle of equal treatment among and between (groups of) refugees under international human rights law, unless such exclusion is justified on the basis of reasonableness, objectivity and proportionality to achieve a legitimate aim. From the Commission's and the EUMS' standpoint, the legitimate aim behind such exclusion is to prevent smuggling and trafficking.

Indeed, the Refugee Convention does not obligate a state to admit an individual from a third country merely because this individual meets the refugee definition. However, it explicitly prohibits punishment on account of illegal entry (Art 31 Refugee Convention) – and exactly such punish-

---

1131 In effect, the system established by the US and Mexico has blocked access in the US to international protection. For instance, asylum seekers have been required to make an appointment with Mexican immigration officials in order to meet CBP requirements. See Sabrina Ardalan in Valsamis Mitsilegas, Violeta Moreno-Lax and Niovi Vavoula (eds), *Securitising Asylum Flows: Deflection, Criminalisation and Challenges for Human Rights*, 282, 303; "*Through a bilateral security program, called Merida Initiative, the US has already contributed millions of dollars to the development of technology, personnel training and infrastructure for border security at both the northern and southern borders, as well as airports and ports*", ibid 285 and 289.

1132 See USCIS, 'Process for Venezuelans' (as of 19 October 2022) <https://www.uscis.gov/venezuela> accessed 15 November 2022.

ments which would be effectuated by excluding refugees from resettlement on account of their prior illegal entry. Under EU law, it constitutes a primary law violation (Art 78 para 1 TFEU) to develop and interpret secondary law contrary to Art 31 Refugee Convention (see 4.1.2.2).

5.2.3.8 Security screening and health checks

Security screening implies interferences with fundamental rights of the individual concerned, as it affects the private sphere of this individual, most prominently protected by European human rights law under Art 8 ECHR and Art 7 Charter. While interferences with ECHR rights may be justified on the basis of a limited number of legitimate interests of a Contracting State such as national security and public order, the Charter is not limited in this regard. Art 52 para 1 Charter contains a general clause stating that any limitation of a Charter right "*must be provided for by law and respect the essence of those rights and freedoms. Subject to the principle of proportionality, limitations may be made only if they are necessary and genuinely meet objectives of general interest recognised by the Union or the need to protect the rights and freedoms of others*". So, for Charter rights, EUMS may invoke further legitimate interests, such as the interest not to admit individuals who committed criminal offenses like tax fraud or individuals with a record that indicates that they are prone to abuse the social welfare system of the receiving country as well as individuals who might engage in political radicalization in the receiving country.

In any case, a measure pursuing such interest must be proportionate to the associated interference with individual rights. First, proportionality requires that the checks are suited to uphold the invoked legitimate interest of the state. Second, it demands that the legitimate interest of the state cannot be maintained through less intrusive measures. Lastly, the extent of the checks must be overall appropriate in relation to the interferences with the rights of the potential resettlement beneficiary being checked.

The Refugee Convention takes account of security interests of the receiving country as it provides "*a system of checks and balances that take into account both the security interests of states and the protection of refugees*".[1133] Refugees and asylum seekers must abide by the laws of the receiving country and may be prosecuted there. Where due process is followed,

1133 Volker Türk, 'Prospects for Responsibility Sharing in the Refugee Context' in (2016) 4 Journal on Migration and Human Security 3, 51.

refugees posing a risk to national security or public order may be subject to detention,[1134] cancellation or revocation of refugee status, extradition or even expulsion,[1135] provided that they would not be at risk of facing serious harm in the country to which they are returned.[1136] Consequently, the Refugee Convention equips Contracting States with tools to protect national security and public order even after a resettlement refugee has been admitted.

From a political point of view, increased security checking constitutes a manifestation of an overall policy shift to prioritize national security. In this regard, *Davitti* raised concerns that the language used by EU officials contributed to the creation of an image of the arriving refugees as potential terrorists. She pointed out that "*whilst the situation at the southern borders was depicted as a humanitarian emergency demanding immediate intervention, those same refugees* [...] *were simultaneously portrayed as a potential security threat*".[1137] Accordingly, the superficial usage of humanitarian and emergency language provided the EU with the opportunity to engage in externalized migration control.[1138]

In terms of health screening, medical examinations allow for a comprehensive picture of the prospective resettlement beneficiary's health status, which is not only important for the assessment of the respective individual's vulnerability. In essence, it enables preparedness for special needs and treatment during the journey as well as upon arrival. Similar to security screening, health screening involves interferences with fundamental rights of the individual concerned and such interferences must be justified and proportionate. In the context of health screening, justification can be based on the right to health. The crucial point is whether the specific measure is proportionate, namely that the interference in the private sphere is not excessive in relation to the health protection that it enables.

1134 Restrictions on the movement of asylum seekers are allowed, including detention, if necessary in circumstances prescribed by law and subject to due process safeguards; e.g. in case of strong reasons for suspecting links with terroristic acts or violence; see Volker Türk, 'Prospects for Responsibility Sharing in the Refugee Context' in (2016) 4 Journal on Migration and Human Security 3, 51.

1135 See Art 32 Refugee Convention.

1136 See Volker Türk, 'Prospects for Responsibility Sharing in the Refugee Context' in (2016) 4 Journal on Migration and Human Security 3, 51.

1137 Darla Davitti, 'Biopolitical Borders and the State of Exception in the European Migration 'Crisis'' in (2018) 29 European Journal of International Law 4, 1179.

1138 See ibid 1179.

One particular issue in the context of screening concerns the protection of personal data. A remarkable example in this regard is a Memorandum of Understanding of 2019 between UNHCR and DHS, where the UNHCR agrees to directly transfer biometric and associated biographic data of those refugees who it refers to the US for resettlement into the DHS's automated Biometric Identification System (IDENT). It is a matter of concern that, as DHS recognizes, under this scheme, the US could come in the possession of data from individuals that will, for various reasons, eventually never set foot in the US.[1139]

For EUMS (subject to the condition that they are implementing EU law), an obligation to protect personal data derives, amongst others, from Art 8 Charter. This Article demands the fair processing of data "*for specified purposes and on the basis of the consent of the person concerned*". Denmark can be considered as a best-practice example. Section 8 para 5 Danish Aliens (Consolidation) Act expressly requires an alien's consent to the health information being transmitted.

5.2.3.9 Right to appeal the selection decision

Eventually, future EU resettlement legislation should ensure that negative decisions of the UNHCR in the pre-selection phase, as well as selection decisions of national authorities of the receiving country, can be appealed. Incorporating the right to appeal when there is an arguable claim of violation of rights under the ICCPR and/or the ECHR constitutes an act of compliance with international law (see 3.3.3.1). This means that appeal options must go beyond the current US approach, i.e. allowing for review in cases where unknown circumstances arise and where the officer who conducted the previous interview grants such review at his or her discretion. This approach would violate international law if, for instance, a potential resettlement beneficiary was deprived of effective review despite having experienced (other) human rights abuses in the course of his or her selection interview, exceeding, for example, the required threshold under Art 7 ICCPR. An officer who conducted the interview and abused human

---

1139 See US Department of Homeland and Security, 'Privacy Impact Assessment for the United Nations High Commissioner for Refugees (UNHCR) Information Data Share', DHS/USCIS/PIA-081 (13 August 2019) <https://www.dhs.gov/sites/default/files/publications/privacy-pia-uscis081-unhcr-august2019.pdf> accessed 11 July 2021.

rights of the potential resettlement beneficiary during the interview will most likely be biased in his or her review decision.

Furthermore, it is relevant for resettlement to the EU that the right to good administration, which is stipulated in Art 41 Charter and established as a general principle of EU law, demands that EU agencies as well as EUMS grant prospective resettlement beneficiaries several procedural safeguards, including the right to be heard (see 5.2.1).

5.2.3.10 Resettlement contract

Lastly, the practice of some EUMS to ask for express consent of selected beneficiaries to be resettled to their territory, deserves further consideration.

The Refugee Convention acknowledges the relevance of the refugee's will. In this regard, *Moreno-Lax* claimed that the Refugee Convention endorsed a refugee's discretion about whether and where to seek international protection.[1140] For instance, Art 31 para 2 Refugee Convention sets out an obligation of Contracting States to "*allow* [...] *refugees a reasonable period and all the necessary facilities to obtain admission into another country*". Moreover, Art 1 C Refugee Convention repeatedly uses the term 'voluntary' in relation to the cessation of refugee status. Accordingly, such cessation regularly involves a discretionary choice of the refugee. Against this backdrop, *Moreno-Lax* concluded that refugees enjoy certain discretion regarding where they may properly claim international protection.[1141]

In terms of EU law, the Temporary Protection Directive accounts for the will of refugees. Its Art 25 para 2 stipulates that "[t]*he Member States concerned* [...] *shall ensure that the eligible persons* [...] *who have not yet arrived in the Community have expressed their will to be received onto their territory*".[1142] Eventually, Art 9 Commission Proposal on a Union Resettlement Framework Regulation expressly refers to the consent of resettlement beneficiaries. It states that "[t]*he resettlement procedures* [...] *shall apply to*

1140 See Violeta Moreno-Lax, 'The Legality of the "Safe Third Country" Notion Contested: Insights from the Law of the Treaties' in Guy S Goodwin-Gill and Philippe Weckel (eds), *Migration & Refugee Protection in the 21st Century: Legal Aspects – The Hague Academy of International Centre for Research* (Martinus Nijhoff 2015) 665 (691-695).

1141 See ibid 692.

1142 See Ségolène Barbou des Places, 'Burden Sharing in the Field of Asylum: Legal Motivations and Implications of a Regional Approach' (2012) 16f.

third-country nationals or stateless persons who have given their consent to be resettled and have not subsequently withdrawn their consent, including refusing resettlement to a particular Member State". These provisions confirm that the consent of resettlement beneficiaries has legal weight. Specifically, under the proposed Resettlement Framework Regulation, resettlement beneficiaries would have a right not to be resettled to a particular EUMS without their consent.

In practice, the right to consent must not amount to a so-called *pactus diabolic*, limiting the beneficiary's rights by imposing certain conditions on the beneficiary that he or she cannot refuse due to fear of not being resettled at all. The legal standard that most closely describes such a situation is duress. Here analogies could be drawn from contract law.

5.2.4 Preliminary conclusion

The UNHCR constitutes the major referral entity for resettlement to the US as well as to the EU, but increased involvement of NGOs would offer additional resources for a comprehensive case identification in the future. Differences in status determination are a source of discrimination among and between (groups of) refugees. Applying different standards to refugees and persons eligible for subsidiary protection status does not amount to discrimination, provided that their situations are factually not comparable. From a policy perspective, harmonization efforts *de lege ferenda* are desirable. For example, only a few EUMS account for persons eligible for subsidiary protection. Additionally, IDPs should generally be included in the scope of resettlement beneficiaries as opposed to the US approach of prioritizing only some groups of IDPs. Eventually, extending the scope of resettlement beneficiaries to 'forced migrants' would include "*any individual who, owing to the risk of serious harm, is compelled to leave or unable to return to her or his country of origin*".[1143] In terms of family reunification, the Commission proposed a broadened scope of family in the Proposal for a Union Resettlement Framework Regulation, which goes beyond the US approach. In the light of Art 7 Charter, it is consistent to follow the Commission's broadened understanding of family *de lege ferenda*. Considering the potential to integrate when assessing eligibility for future EU resettlement can result in discrimination among and between

1143 Kiran Banerjee, 'Rethinking the Global Governance of International Protection' in (2018) 56 Columbia Journal of Transnational Law, 319.

(groups of) refugees if such assessment is arbitrary. It has been shown that the application of the integration potential remains controversial, and that there are reasonable arguments from the perspective of states in favor of its application. Next, the US approach that firm resettlement in a third country bars individuals from being eligible for resettlement to the US, deserves consideration *de lege ferenda*. As regards exclusion grounds for resettlement to the EU, it is, from a legal perspective, not prohibited *per se* to go beyond the grounds allowing for exclusion of refugee status under the Refugee Convention. However, penalizing refugees who attempted to enter the EU irregularly by excluding them from resettlement violates Art 31 Refugee Convention. Security and medical screening entail interferences with fundamental rights of those who are screened. This requires justification, i.e. a legitimate aim in the interest of the state and a proportionality test. The analysis showed that several EUMS do not provide the possibility for potential resettlement beneficiaries to appeal a negative selection decision. Such approach likely violates international law, namely in cases where the resettlement beneficiary has an arguable claim of a violation of another right under the ICCPR and/or the ECHR. The current US approach does not sufficiently account for this requirement under international law. In terms of EU law, the Charter, which applies during selection missions outside the EU when an EUMS implements EU law, grants the right to good administration and includes a right to be heard for the prospective resettlement beneficiary. Moreover, a right to consent to resettlement to a specific receiving country can be deduced from the Refugee Convention. As regards EU law, the Commission envisaged a right to consent in the Proposal for a Resettlement Framework Regulation.

5.3 Pre-departure, arrival and placement

Forced migrants identified as in need for resettlement cannot choose their receiving country.[1144] The only choice they have is denying resettlement outright by withholding their consent to be referred to a specific receiving country (see 5.2.1). For this reason, it is important to equip selected resettlement beneficiaries with accurate information about the process and

1144 See Annelisa Lindsay, 'Surge and selection: power in the refugee resettlement regime' in (2017) 54 Forced Migration Review, 12.

the receiving country to which they are admitted.[1145] *Fratzke* and *Kainz* emphasized that "[p]*redeparture orientation programmes ... are intended to build refugees' confidence and feelings of control, as well as their ability to cope with unfamiliar situations and to navigate everyday life in the resettlement country*".[1146] The majority of resettlement programs include pre-departure and post-arrival services, usually under the guidance of the IOM.[1147]

5.3.1 Programs of EUMS

Correspondingly, most European resettlement programs encompass pre-departure orientation. According to a 2019 Migration Policy Institute (MPI) report, thirteen out of twenty-one European countries[1148] conducting resettlement through the UNHCR in 2017 provided some form of pre-departure orientation.[1149]

The content of orientation programs typically comprises travel information and guidance regarding the rights and obligations of refugees in the resettlement process. The 2019 MPI report carried out that beyond this core content, Norway and Finland launched language training sessions and Germany prepared skill profiles to facilitate employment after arrival.[1150]

Most EUMS offer pre-departure orientation after having made their selection decision, prior to departure. According to the 2019 MPI report, Sweden was the only EUMS delivering the full pre-departure program already during selection interviews.[1151] Furthermore, there are significant differences between EUMS regarding the length of their orientation programs, ranging from a few hours to several days.[1152] The Netherlands stand out as they split pre-departure orientation in three separate courses: an

1145 See William Lacy Swing, 'Practical considerations for effective resettlement' in (2017) 54 Forced Migration Review, 4 <https://www.refworld.org/docid/58cbcb314.html> accessed 27 March 2021.

1146 Susan Fratzke and Lena Kainz, 'Preparing for the unknown: Designing effective predeparture orientation for resettling refugees' (May 2019) 1.

1147 See ibid 1; see also William Lacy Swing, 'Practical considerations for effective resettlement' in (2017) 54 Forced Migration Review, 5.

1148 Including EUMS and states of the European Economic Area (EEA).

1149 See Susan Fratzke and Lena Kainz, 'Preparing for the unknown: Designing effective predeparture orientation for resettling refugees' (May 2019) 6.

1150 See ibid 14, 17.

1151 See ibid 17f.

1152 See ibid 16.

initial course taking place about twenty weeks before departure; a second course twelve weeks before departure focusing, among other things, on the municipality where the refugee will live; and finally, a third session three weeks before departure explaining characteristics of accommodation and housing.[1153] These sessions are typically held in-person. In addition, the Netherlands has supplied MP3 players for their one-hour-per-day 12-day language training sessions.[1154] As opposed to the Netherlands, Finland used online seminars as early as in 2016.[1155]

EU level funding for pre-departure orientation is provided through the AMIF. For example, the AMIF Implementing Decision of April 2017 explicitly mentioned "[p]*re-departure and post-arrival support for the integration of persons in need for international protection in particular when having been resettled from a third country*".[1156] This reference implies that funding of pre-departure programs and subsequent measures enhancing the integration of resettlement beneficiaries counted among the Commission's priorities for the AMIF. The Commission continued in this vein and pointed to pre-departure integration measures and post-arrival measures in the Action plan on Integration and Inclusion 2021-2027.[1157]

On-site pre-departure assistance and the subsequent transfer to the receiving country are commonly carried out by the IOM, based on bilateral agreements or contracts with EUMS.[1158] Only the Netherlands solely tasked national authorities with the design and the delivery of its pre-departure and post-arrival programs. Some EUMS used blended programs involving manifold actors, such as subnational authorities, civil-law societies and higher education institutions alongside the IOM. For example, Norway collaborated with so-called 'cross-cultural trainers' being

---

1153 See Dutch Country Chapter to the UNHCR *Resettlement Handbook* <https://www.unhcr.org/3c5e5925a.pdf> accessed 30 July 2020.

1154 See Susan Fratzke and Lena Kainz, 'Preparing for the unknown: Designing effective predeparture orientation for resettling refugees' (May 2019) 14.

1155 See European Migration Network, 'Resettlement and Humanitarian Admission Programmes in Europe – what works' (9 November 2016) 27f.

1156 Commission, Implementing Decision on the adoption of the work programme for 2017 and the financing of Union actions in the framework for the Asylum, Migration and Integration Fund, C(2017) 2572 final, 20 <https://ec.europa.eu/research/participants/data/ref/other_eu_prog/home/wp/amif-awp-2017_en.pdf> accessed 27 March 2021.

1157 See Commission, Communication 'Action plan on Integration and Inclusion 2021-2027', 7.

1158 See Susan Fratzke and Lena Kainz, 'Preparing for the unknown: Designing effective predeparture orientation for resettling refugees' (May 2019) 28.

former resettlement beneficiaries themselves or having an immigration background.[1159]

For the internal placement of resettlement beneficiaries, several EUMS, such as the Czech Republic, Estonia, Finland, Germany, the Netherlands or Poland, adopted dispersal schemes among their respective components to avoid concentration in certain areas.[1160] By contrast, Austria, Belgium, Bulgaria, France, Hungary, Italy and Luxembourg have refrained from reverting to any form of internal geographical distribution to accommodate protection seekers within their territory.[1161] Despite geographical distribution, placement criteria applied by EUMS include the commitment of municipalities, availability of housing, preferences of admitted resettlement refugees (only acknowledged by Bulgaria) as well as economic considerations and personal circumstances of the specific resettlement beneficiary.[1162]

Several – but not all – EUMS equally offer immediate support after arrival to resettlement beneficiaries and other beneficiaries of international protection, but specific measures of some EUMS prioritize resettlement beneficiaries. For instance, according to the 2019 MPI report, Belgium provided tailor-made assistance and intensive support for up to twenty-four months for particularly vulnerable resettlement beneficiaries only. Finland prioritized resettlement beneficiaries in terms of housing assignments.[1163] The overall range of immediate support from EUMS was similar, from food supplies and interpretation services to medical examinations. Several EUMS granted financial support through a weekly or monthly allowance for varying durations.[1164] Noteworthy, in the two crucial areas of housing and freedom of movement, some EUMS imposed significant restrictions.[1165] What is more, age-appropriate protection and care deserve special attention.[1166]

1159 See ibid 20, 27f.

1160 See Philippe de Bruycker and Evangelia (Lilian) Tsourdi in Vincent Chetail, Philippe de Bruycker and Francesco Maiani (eds), *Reforming the Common European Asylum System: The New European Refugee Law*, 506.

1161 See European Migration Network, 'Resettlement and Humanitarian Admission Programmes in Europe – what works' (9 November 2016) 31.

1162 See ibid 31.

1163 See ibid 29.

1164 Ranging from a minimum of 6 weeks in Ireland to as long as needed e.g. in Belgium, Germany and the Netherlands; see ibid 30f.

1165 See ibid 32f.

1166 In this regard, The UN Committee on the Rights of the Child announced in October 2021 that Spain had violated the rights of unaccompanied migrant

5.3.2 US program and practice

The US has conducted overseas Cultural Orientation (CO) programs in RSCs in more than forty countries of (first) refuge.[1167] PRM provides funding and contracts with intergovernmental, international and US-based agencies[1168] to conduct the CO. As opposed to EUMS, predominantly relying on the IOM for the delivery of pre-departure programs, the US primarily works with two Volags, the International Rescue Committee and Church World Service.[1169] In addition, US embassies and other government entities provide CO.

All refugees older than 15 years and conditionally approved for resettlement to the US are eligible to receive CO. However, childcare obligations, logistical problems, and class size regularly hinder participation or make CO attendance possible for only one family member. Refugees may attend CO at any point in time between their approval for resettlement and their departure for the US. The length of CO differs. For example, in 2014, it varied between six and 36 hours, depending on the location.[1170] Currently, according to the Report to Congress on Proposed Refugee Admissions for FY 2023, CO takes place "*usually one week to three months before departure*" and "*generally lasts from one to five days*".[1171]

---

and asylum-seeking children in 14 cases since 2019. OHCHR, 'Spain's age assessment procedures violate migrant children's rights, UN committee finds' (13 October 2020) <https://ohchr.org/EN/NewsEvents/Pages/DisplayNews.aspx?NewsID=26375&LangID=E> accessed 21 June 2021.

1167 For fifteen years (until 2015), the Cultural Orientation Resource (COR) Center served as the national technical assistance provider on overseas as well as domestic refugee orientation. Its activities comprised the training of trainers, development of print, audiovisual, and web resources, outreach to receiving communities, assessment of orientation, research on impact and results of pre-departure and post-arrival refugee orientation as well as pre-departure English language instruction and exchange of information; see Center for Applied Linguistics, 'Immigrant & Refugee Integration' <http://www.cal.org/areas-of-impact/immigrant-refugee-integration> accessed 27 March 2021.

1168 The International Catholic Migration Commission, the IOM, and the International Rescue Committee, HIAS and Church World Service.

1169 See Susan Fratzke and Lena Kainz, 'Preparing for the unknown: Designing effective predeparture orientation for resettling refugees' (May 2019) 22.

1170 See Cultural Orientation Resource Center, 'Overseas CO' <http://50.116.32.248/index.php/providing-orientation/overseas> accessed 22 August 2020.

1171 US Department of State, Department of Homeland and Security, Department of Health and Human Services, 'Report to Congress on Proposed Refugee Admissions for Fiscal Year 2022' (20 September 2021) 22.

The content of overseas CO was manifested in the Overseas Cultural Orientation Objectives and Indicators,[1172] a multi-year joint effort of governmental agencies, Volags and other stakeholders. The Cultural Orientation Resource Exchange (CORE),[1173] a technical assistance program, works to ensure consistent messages, trains resettlement staff to deliver CO and provides additional material for resettlement beneficiaries to engage in self-learning. Above all, the US pre-departure orientation puts emphasis on communicating the expectation that the resettlement beneficiaries seek and obtain rapid employment to become self-sufficient, reflecting the overall goal of the USRAP.[1174] In order to achieve that goal, the US expanded on English language training, which has proven successful since "*tests with participants in the US predeparture English programme show that refugees improved their knowledge of English and retained what they learned after they were resettled, even if their departure was delayed*".[1175]

In parallel with the CO, the preparation of the actual transfer to the US starts with the RSC sending a request for confirmation of placement capacity. The Refugee Processing Center, a part of the State Department, manages the assessment of placement capacity in coordination with the nine Volags.

The responsible Volag determines where in the US a resettlement beneficiary will live.[1176] "*Factors considered as part of the process include health, age, family make up, and language of the refugee, as well as the cost of living and the availability of job opportunities, housing, education, and health services*".[1177] The responsible Volag makes all necessary arrangements for the reception of resettlement beneficiaries in the local community, while the IOM, in cooperation with the RSCs, takes care of travel coordination and medical checks. In countries of (first) refuge where the IOM is not present, US embassies or the UNHCR organize the travel. Upon receipt of the IOM travel notification, the responsible Volag prepares the welcome of

1172 See ibid.

1173 See <https://coresourceexchange.org/> accessed 2 May 2023.

1174 See Susan Fratzke and Lena Kainz, 'Preparing for the unknown: Designing effective predeparture orientation for resettling refugees' (May 2019) 5.

1175 Ibid 13f.

1176 See James Y Xi, 'Refugee Resettlement Federalism' in (2017) Stanford Law Review 69, 1205.

1177 Michael Fix, Kate Hooper and Jie Zong, 'How Are Refugees Faring: Integration at US and State Levels' (June 2017) 5 <https://www.migrationpolicy.org/research/how-are-refugees-faring-integration-us-and-state-levels> accessed 27 March 2021.

a resettlement beneficiary at the airport and transportation to housing at their final destination.

Post-arrival CO is provided by staff at local resettlement agencies. "*For example, state health care coverage is explained as refugees learn how to access and pay for health services; refugees are introduced to the local public school system and learn about customary student behavior and expectations of parental involvement; and refugees learn about the amenities and services available in their new communities.* [...] *Laws and responsibilities are also a focus.*"[1178] The so-called Reception and Placement (R&P) period, where resettlement beneficiaries receive initial core services from resettlement agencies (including housing, furnishings, clothing, and food, as well as assistance with access to medical, employment, educational, and social services) is limited to three months after arrival.[1179] Regarding financial assistance, the Volags receive a one-time grant from the federal government for each resettlement refugee under their responsibility, which they then distribute to the resettlement beneficiaries.[1180]

To pay for the travel costs to the US, resettlement beneficiaries receive an interest-free travel loan from the PRM in a program administered by the IOM. Six months after arrival in the US, loan repayment starts.[1181]

5.3.3 Analysis

The treatment of selected resettlement beneficiaries before and during the transfer to the receiving country as well as upon arrival constitutes a key factor impacting the resettlement beneficiaries' opportunities of setting up

1178 US Department of State, Department of Homeland and Security, Department of Health and Human Services, 'Report to Congress on Proposed Refugee Admissions for Fiscal Year 2022' (20 September 2021) 23.

1179 See US Department of State, 'Reception and Placement', <https://www.state.gov/refugee-admissions/reception-and-placement/> accessed 17 September 2022. See Michael Fix, Kate Hooper and Jie Zong, 'How Are Refugees Faring: Integration at US and State Levels' (June 2017) 7. See also Gregor Noll and Joanne van Selm, 'Rediscovering Resettlement' in (2003) 3 Migration Policy Institute Insight, 22.

1180 See Michael Fix, Kate Hooper and Jie Zong, 'How Are Refugees Faring: Integration at US and State Levels' (June 2017) 7.

1181 See American Immigration Council, 'An Overview of US Refugee Law and Policy' (8 January 2020) <https://www.americanimmigrationcouncil.org/research/overview-us-refugee-law-and-policy> accessed 27 March 2021; see also Refugee Council USA, 'Resettlement Process'.

their new lives in this country. US and European resettlement programs comprise divergent orientation services, placement and reception processes.

5.3.3.1 Pre-departure orientation

The pre-departure orientation programs offered by EUMS differ from the US CO program. At the same time, pre-departure orientation varies among EUMS themselves. The differences affect manifold aspects of pre-departure orientation. Specifically, divergent contents, lengths, formats, and actors of EUMS' pre-departure orientation programs create unequal opportunities for resettlement beneficiaries to set up their new lives in the EU. Multiple external and specific refugee-related factors impact the practical feasibility and implementation of pre-departure orientation.[1182] Even if these factors require national programs to remain flexible, common reference points are indispensable to create a more equal starting situation for resettlement beneficiaries destined to the EU *de lege ferenda*. For that matter, it stands to reason that the extensive cooperation between EUMS and the IOM in the wake of pre-departure orientation makes the IOM a promising actor to implement further harmonization of the divergent national programs. It is worth mentioning that as a general principle under EU law, the principle of subsidiarity must be considered when harmonizing pre-departure programs of EUMS at the EU level. Apparently, not all decisions about the content and design of pre-departure orientation for resettlement in a specific EUMS can better be taken at the EU level than by the EUMS themselves. That being said, it would be mistaken in the light of the subsidiarity principle to anticipate detailed harmonization of country-specific content of cultural orientation.

When harmonizing the content of future pre-departure orientation, the following points should be considered: Travel information is crucial since many resettlement beneficiaries are taking a plane for the first time; a clear description of the living conditions in the receiving country is equally important to avoid frustration emerging from unfulfilled expectations; and intensive language training sessions as included in the US, and also in some of EUMS' pre-departure programs have proven successful. Other means to foster integration of resettlement beneficiaries are the prepara-

1182 See Susan Fratzke and Lena Kainz, 'Preparing for the unknown: Designing effective predeparture orientation for resettling refugees' (May 2019) 20.

tion of skill profiles for job applications and guidance on access to further education in the receiving country.

Concerning the format of pre-departure orientation, the example of Finland offering online courses, as well as self-learning through the US CORE program, induce considerations *de lege ferenda* on remote pre-departure preparation. What is more, the CORE stands out as it offers translations of its Welcome Guide Textbook in various languages.[1183] Remote preparation and self-learning could be of value in emergency cases and/or where time and capacities are limited.[1184] The 2020 COVID-19 outbreak demonstrated the relevance of remote learning during public health crises. Conversely, there are valid reasons not to generally switch to remote pre-departure orientation. As such, it deprives resettlement beneficiaries of personal contacts with trainers and case workers, as well as other resettlement beneficiaries destined to the same receiving country. Besides, practical issues concerning, amongst others, electricity, stable internet access and appropriate hardware render remote pre-departure orientation less practical or even impossible in some countries of (first) refuge. This means that online courses are a valuable format for pre-departure orientation if technically feasible and used in an appropriate manner, or rather in emergency or crisis situations. Overall, they should not replace in-person courses at large.

In the light of the principle of equal treatment (see 3.3.4), future EU legislation on resettlement must ensure equal access to orientation programs for all resettlement beneficiaries. As mentioned, Art 2 para 1 ICCPR prohibits discrimination among refugees on grounds such as language or national origin. It follows that receiving EUMS would have to justify access restrictions to pre-departure orientation on such grounds, namely, they would have to justify differential treatment between resettlement beneficiaries coming from a specific country or speaking a particular language.

Equal access to pre-departure orientation is particularly relevant in case of families to be resettled. For example, Austria's past resettlement efforts comprised two-day trainings with childcare available during the sessions.[1185] Especially mothers could be deprived of participation if no childcare service was offered during pre-departure training. The resulting

---

1183 These include Amharic, Arabic, Burmese, Chin, Dari, Farsi, French, Karen, Kinyarwanda, Kirundi, Nepali, Russian, Somali, Spanish, Swahili, Tigrinya and Vietnamese. The Welcome Guide Textbook is available at: <https://coresourceexchange.org/welcome-guides/> accessed 23 November 2022.

1184 See European Migration Network, 'Resettlement and Humanitarian Admission Programmes in Europe – what works' (9 November 2016) 27f.

1185 See ibid 27f.

lack of pre-departure information would arguably weaken their starting position when arriving in the receiving country.

Another worthwhile future policy goal consists of establishing continuity between pre-departure and post-arrival assistance. A means to achieve continuity would be, for instance, engaging the same institution for language sessions in the course of pre-departure orientation and in the receiving country upon arrival. In addition, cooperation of workers at place in the countries of (first) refuge with the receiving community is crucial to avoid disruption in the resettlement process. This can be achieved by collecting and sharing detailed information about the prospective resettlement beneficiaries.

5.3.3.2 Placement

Empirical data confirms that the placement of resettlement beneficiaries has a significant impact on integration outcomes. For example, a 2018 study on the determinants of refugee naturalization in the US revealed that "*refugees are systematically more likely to naturalize when initially placed in locations with low unemployment rates and dense urban settings*".[1186]

In addition, the resettlement beneficiaries themselves contribute to sustainable integration. Empirical evidence showed that not involving refugees in the placement process and resettling them in communities where they had no intention to live increased the likeliness of failure in areas such as education and employment.[1187] "*A frustrated, poorly integrated and under-employed refugee is a problem not only for the person involved, but also for the host community: Such situation is a lose-lose one* [...]".[1188] Consequently, neglecting preferences of resettlement beneficiaries encourages secondary migration instead of sustainable integration.[1189]

In fact, placement decision-making and internal distribution systems substantially differ between EUMS and the US. In 2010, *Thielemann et*

1186 Nadwa Mossaad et al, 'Determinants of refugee naturalization in the United States' in (11 September 2018) 115 PNAS 37, 9175 (9178).

1187 See Will Jones and Alexander Teytelboym, ''Matching' refugees' in (2017) 54 Forced Migration Review, 25.

1188 Marcello Di Filippo in Valsamis Mitsilegas, Violeta Moreno-Lax and Niovi Vavoula (eds), *Securitising Asylum Flows: Deflection, Criminalisation and Challenges for Human Rights*, 201.

1189 See ibid 200f.

al compared EUMS' internal distribution systems with the US system as follows:[1190]

> *Compared to the USA, EU Member States base their decision on governmental directives, may they be federal, regional, or municipal level. In the USA, however, non-governmental organizations (nine agencies plus the State of Iowa) decide how to disperse the resettled refugees across the States.*

In the US, the nine Volags determine the placement of resettlement refugees. *De lege ferenda*, policy considerations towards the inclusion of voluntary agencies in the placement process are promising for future resettlement to the EU. The US example demonstrates that the staff of Volags has experience with a huge range of profiles of resettlement beneficiaries and, at the same time, they engage in close contact with host communities within a well-established network throughout the US. This experience and network confirm the ability of Volags to match the resettlement-beneficiary-profiles with the conditions in the receiving communities. Overall, the US concept of assigning Volags to support self-sufficiency encourages resettlement beneficiaries to become active contributors, who positively impact the receiving community.

Against this backdrop, it follows for future EU resettlement that the establishment and expansion of a network of voluntary non-governmental agencies would be a desirable policy objective. Such agencies could contribute to the placement process to improve the matching of profiles of resettlement beneficiaries with the respective receiving communities. Additionally, community engagement, including the involvement of private sponsors in referral and placement processes, constitutes a model that has gained increased attention, both in Europe and the US.[1191] Ultimately, it is desirable to strengthen the resettlement beneficiaries as valuable actors in these communities.

1190 Eiko R Thielemann et al cited in Jesus Férnandez-Huertas Moraga and Hillel Rapoport, 'Tradable Refugee-admission Quotas and EU Asylum Policy' in (2015) 61 CESifo Economic Studies 3, 646; see Eiko R Thielemann et al 'What system of burden-sharing between Member States for the reception of asylum seekers?' (European Parliament 22 January 2010) <http://www.europarl.europa.eu/RegData/etudes/etudes/join/2010/419620/IPOL-LIBE_ET(2010)419620_EN.pdf> accessed 27 March 2021.

1191 See Janine Prantl and Stephen Yale-Loehr, 'Let Private Citizens Sponsor Refugees' (*NY Daily News*, 15 October 2022) <https://www.nydailynews.com/opinion/ny-oped-let-private-citizens-sponsor-refugees-20221015-dtepnanthfegnpf6anjirwt3by-story.html> accessed 23 November 2022.

5.3.3.3 Cooperation with local governments and receiving communities

The work of voluntary agencies depends on political and civic commitment at the local level. In this light, the US federal government has been criticized for undermining local needs, conditions and concerns on multiple tiers. First, pre-resettlement information provided by the federal government to receiving communities has proven insufficient. As a result, the receiving communities could not adequately prepare for the resettlement beneficiaries' arrivals. Second, federal funding is reactive, i.e. dictated by the number of refugee arrivals over the last two years. Hence, in case of sudden influx, communities lack adequate resources. Third, federal assistance for receiving communities does not consider the education level, health condition and/or psychological background of a resettlement beneficiary allocated to this community.[1192]

To counter these policy issues, *Xi* recommended giving states and local communities more weight in the placement decision.[1193] With a view to increasing EU involvement in the field of resettlement, the two most significant takeaways from *Xi*'s contribution are that enhanced information sharing between the EU and the local level as well as proactive and tailor-made allocation of EU funding should become a priority *de lege ferenda*.

It also deserves a mention that in 2015, European local governments played a substantial role in filling gaps in the national provision of reception services for individuals in need for protection, which renders *Xi*'s arguments to better account for local communities' concerns even more relevant. Indeed, European cities and municipalities have called for further involvement in migration policy, including at the EU level. There are prominent examples of local government initiatives for the reception of refugees in Europe, amongst other things transnational city partnerships, such as Eurocities and Solidarity Cities. Also, the cooperation between local regions and networks of church associations, civil society and NGOs has proven successful, for instance in Italy, the Community of Sant'Egidio.[1194]

1192 See James Y Xi, 'Refugee Resettlement Federalism' in (2017) Stanford Law Review 69, 1229.

1193 See ibid 1234.

1194 See Tihomir Sabchev and Moritz Baumgärtel, 'The path of least resistance? EU cities and locally organised resettlement' in (February 2020) 63 Forced Migration Review, 38-40 <https://citiesofrefuge.eu/sites/default/files/2020-02/sabchev-baumgartel-fmr.pdf> accessed 27 March 2021.

De lege ferenda, supporting local government initiatives through direct EU funding "*could represent the path of least resistance to more far-reaching reforms of the EU migration governance system*".[1195] On that basis, *Sabchev* and *Baumgärtel* identified two main driving factors designed to minimize political tensions in and among EUMS. First, security concerns of central governments have to be satisfied before authorization of resettlement. Second, central governments will more likely agree with local resettlement initiatives if they do not have to bear the costs of initial reception and short to medium-term integration into local communities. So, it was suggested that municipalities should receive direct EU funding to realize their initiatives.[1196] Given that significant EU funds were channeled to central governments, who failed to meet their commitments in the end, it appears that channeling EU funds to the municipalities who are able and willing to admit refugees could be a promising tool to empower the local actors and gain additional reception capacity.

To take it one step further, is it politically desirable to grant local governments a right to veto, i.e. to refuse admission, or to select whom they want to admit? Concerns that a veto would drastically reduce the number of admissions, e.g. because local governments would refuse admission for security reasons, were refuted by the continued commitment of US governors to admit refugees in response to the former President *Trump*'s Executive Order of 26 September 2019 (see 2.3.15).

In the EU context, the numerous pro-admission initiatives show that local support in favor of admission exists. Legally speaking, EU law demands considerations in terms of the subsidiarity principle. Indeed, situations are conceivable where local entities are better suited to assess how many people/refugees in need of protection they can accommodate and who could best integrate in the particular environment. Nevertheless, human rights and refugee law set limits to a potential right to refuse admission: e.g. such approach must comply with the *non-refoulement* principle, and it must not lead to unjustified discrimination. Eventually, the idea of solidarity supports that not one community can bear the whole burden alone. As elaborated in 4.1.2.1, a right to generally refuse all admissions would not be permissible under Art 80 TFEU.

1195 See ibid 39.
1196 See ibid 40.

5.3.3.4 Reception conditions

Interaction with local governments and receiving communities constitutes an essential prerequisite to establishing the reception conditions required under international law for resettlement beneficiaries in due time. Even though resettled refugees cannot rely on a right to long-term integration, they have several rights under international human rights law and refugee law concerning their sojourn in the receiving country. As shown in 3.3.5, these rights apply immediately after arrival in the receiving country.

This is also required under EU law. As outlined above, EUMS are bound to the Charter when implementing EU law – irrespective of whether they are acting outside their territory. In this light, the implementation of the AMIF Regulation arguably triggers the applicability of the Charter in the resettlement selection process (see 4.1.1.2). It follows that in the course of AMIF funded resettlements, EUMS must grant the Charter rights even before and during the travel as well as immediately upon arrival of a resettlement beneficiary on their territory. Therefore, the point in time when a particular EUMS starts to implement resettlement under the conditions of the AMIF is crucial; when an EUMS at a certain point in time acts outside the AMIF, and ceases to implement EU law, the applicability of the Charter is not given.

5.3.4 Preliminary conclusion

The current differences in pre-departure orientation programs of EUMS demonstrate that policy efforts are necessary *de lege ferenda* to establish equal opportunities for resettlement beneficiaries coming to the EU. This is even more important since equal treatment among and between (groups of) refugees must be granted under international law. From an EU law perspective, Art 78 para 1 requires compliance with prohibitions of discrimination under the Refugee Convention and other pertinent human rights treaties. Moreover, the principle of subsidiarity sets legal limits in the sense that detailed EU-level harmonization of pre-departure programs would not align with this principle. What is more, it derives from international refugee law and EU law that the will of refugees has legal weight when it comes to the decision where he or she will actually be placed. A lesson to be learned from the US is that the receiving community should be involved in the resettlement process through enhanced information sharing between the EU and the local level as well as proactive and tailor-made EU funding. The efforts to include the receiving community are also necessary to achieve compliance with international law by providing the required reception conditions to resettlement beneficiaries immediately upon arrival. Finally, integration policy considerations and considerations in light of the principle of subsidiarity suggest granting local governments a right to refuse admission and/or select whom they want to admit. Yet, the EU law principle of solidarity (Art 80 TFEU) speaks against a right to generally refuse admission (as laid out by the CJEU addressing incompliances with EU's internal relocation scheme; see 4.1.2.1).

5.4 Long-term integration and naturalization

Receiving countries are not obligated to offer long-term integration to individuals whom they have granted international protection.[1197] This stems from the fact that the Refugee Convention does not include a right to permanently integrate[1198] as refugee status is meant to be temporary.[1199] The temporary nature of refugee status emanates from clear cessation rules under the Refugee Convention. Accordingly, the refugee status ceases to exist when the circumstances in the country of origin allow for return (Art 1 C paras 5 and 6 Refugee Convention). On the other hand, refugee status can also end by naturalization in the receiving country (Art 1 C para 3 Refugee Convention).[1200]

As a matter of fact, EUMS pursue different approaches in granting refugees long-term residency and citizenship. Likewise, the political views of scholars on how fast refugees should gain permanent residence status and/or access to citizenship have been divided.[1201] For example, *Miller* opposed the immediate award of long-term residence status and fast access

---

1197 See Guy S Goodwin-Gill, *The Refugee in International Law* (Oxford University Press 1983) 225.

1198 See Joanne van Selm, 'European Refugee Policy: is there such a thing?', UNHCR Research Paper n°115 (May 2005) 8.

1199 See Marjoleine Zieck, 'Refugees and the Right to Freedom of Movement: From Flight to Return' in (2018) 39 Michigan Journal of International Law 1, 104.

1200 See Marjoleine Zieck in Vincent Chetail and Céline Bauloz (eds), *Research Handbook on International Law and Migration*, 579.

1201 See David Owen, 'Refugees, EU Citizenship and the Common European Asylum System A Normative Dilemma for EU Integration' in (2019) Ethical Theory and Moral Practice, 347 (348f).

to citizenship. In his view, it could not be assumed that all refugees chose to "*identify politically with the society that takes them in*".[1202] By contrast, *Owen* opted in favor of rapid naturalization. He purported that refugees were *de facto* stateless since they were effectively unable to exercise their right of diplomatic protection and their right to return (to their home country). Accordingly, the receiving country "*stands in loco civitatis to them and must reflect this standing in its treatment of their claims*".[1203] Otherwise, refugees would be deprived of the ability "*to conduct their lives against the background of a right to secure residence of a state*"[1204] and plan their future in the long run, which in turn would discourage them from becoming self-sufficient.

5.4.1 EU law and practice of EUMS

Similar to the Refugee Convention, EU (secondary) law does not set out a duty to achieve long-term integration of refugees or persons eligible for subsidiary protection. While focusing on the definition of basic rights and obligations arising from refugee and subsidiary protection status, EU law remains silent on *how* to accomplish integration in the receiving EUMS. On that account, EU level harmonization of the legal status of protection seekers in EUMS has brought about extensive but not complete equality within the EU.[1205] In particular, resettlement beneficiaries face inequalities regarding their legal status. The two contrasting approaches of EUMS are to either treat resettlement refugees as refugees with only the *prospect* of permanent residency, or as migrants with immediate permanent residency.[1206]

1202 David Miller, *Strangers in our midst* (Harvard University Press 2016) 135f.

1203 David Owen, 'Refugees, EU Citizenship and the Common European Asylum System A Normative Dilemma for EU Integration' in (2019) Ethical Theory and Moral Practice, 349.

1204 Ibid 350.

1205 See Martin Nettesheim, 'Migration im Spannungsfeld von Freizügigkeit und Demokratie' in (2019) Archiv des öffentlichen Rechts, 358 (398, 401).

1206 E.g. refugees who are resettled to Sweden immediately receive a permanent residence permit irrespective of their status; Denmark and Finland grant a five-year stay permit to resettled refugees; see Marjoleine Zieck in Vincent Chetail and Céline Bauloz (eds), *Research Handbook on International Law and Migration*, 577.

Significant inequalities exist between resettlement beneficiaries and protection seekers admitted through humanitarian admission programs. In terms of the latter, EUMS admit persons in need for international protection under the assumption that they will likely return to their home country within a short period of time (probably not exceeding two years). Consequently, beneficiaries of humanitarian admission programs regularly obtain residence permits with limited duration. By contrast, protection seekers admitted under traditional resettlement schemes are granted a longer period of residence or even immediate permanent residence status.

Moreover, some EUMS apply different waiting periods for permanent resident status to resettlement refugees and other refugees (having crossed the border irregularly).[1207] Beyond waiting periods, refugees in many receiving EUMS face the hurdle of additional requirements, such as language proficiency or cultural and/or historical knowledge ('civic knowledge') about their receiving country in order to obtain a permanent residence permit and/or maintain residency. For example, the CJEU ruled in *A v Staatssecretaris van Veiligheid en Justitie* on the validity of a Dutch law provision requiring a civic integration examination. The Court found that the Dutch law provision did not contradict the Long-term Residents Directive,[1208] meaning that the examination of civic knowledge is not forbidden *per se*. However, such examination must not exceed the level of basic knowledge and costs must remain reasonable. Also, the specific circumstances of the third-country national at issue must be considered.[1209]

Differences among EUMS arise regarding integration assistance and social welfare, with treatment in Ireland constituting a prominent example.[1210] While the Irish Government made considerable efforts to provide Syrian resettlement beneficiaries with housing, financial aid, education and health services, only marginal support was given to asylum seekers.[1211]

1207 See Delphine Perrin and Frank McNamara, 'Refugee Resettlement in the EU: Between Shared Standards and Diversity in Legal and Policy Frames', KNOW RESET Research Report 2013/03, 31-34; see also European Migration Network, 'Resettlement and Humanitarian Admission Programmes in Europe – what works' (9 November 2016) 29f.

1208 See Case C-257/17 *C, A v Staatssecretaris van Veiligheid en Justitie* [2018] EU:C:2018:876, paras 63f.

1209 See ibid paras 63f.

1210 See Natalia Pestova, 'Differential treatment of refugees in Ireland' in (2017) 54 Forced Migration Review, 45-47.

1211 Asylum seekers in Ireland "*are awaiting decisions on their protection claims and are accommodated in open prison conditions under the system called Direct Provision*

Still, EMN reported in 2016 that integration and welfare support in twelve EUMS was "*overall the same*" for resettlement refugees and other refugees.[1212] It was common practice in most EUMS that resettlement refugees received, amongst others, permanent access to mainstream health services on the same scale as other refugees. Furthermore, the 2016 EMN study revealed that all EUMS engaging in resettlement provided educational support and/or vocational training to resettlement refugees just like they did for other refugees. Hungary and Poland stood out as they offered specialized services such as support for elderly or disabled people only to resettlement refugees and not to other refugees.[1213]

There is a general awareness of EUMS that the pursuit of a durable solution implies equal treatment between resettlement beneficiaries and their own nationals. Pursuant to *Perrin* and *McNamara*, in 2013, several EUMS provided the same rights to resettlement refugees and national citizens in terms of health care, social welfare, access to education and employment.[1214] Yet, international law does not require equality between foreigners and own nationals with regard to all rights (see 3.3.4). After all, pursuing a policy of equal treatment between natives and foreigners promotes integration.

A significant step towards equality with citizens of the receiving EUMS is achieved by long-term residence status under the Long-term Residents Directive, which includes resettlement beneficiaries with refugee or subsidiary protection status. They can access long-term residence status under this Directive after five years of legal residence in the receiving EUMS.[1215]

---

under which asylum seekers are not allowed to work, study or cook for themselves", ibid 45.

1212 See European Migration Network, 'Resettlement and Humanitarian Admission Programmes in Europe – what works' (9 November 2016) 34.

1213 See ibid 34f.

1214 E.g. Belgium, the Czech Republic, Denmark, Finland, France, Germany, Ireland, the Netherlands, Portugal, Romania, Slovenia, Spain, Sweden, UK; see Delphine Perrin and Frank McNamara, 'Refugee Resettlement in the EU: Between Shared Standards and Diversity in Legal and Policy Frames', KNOW RESET Research Report 2013/03, 57ff.

1215 In order to acquire long-term residence status, the Long-term Residents Directive expressly "*requires the presence of the person concerned in the relevant territory to go beyond a mere physical presence and that it be of a certain duration or have a certain stability*", namely to "*reside…legally and continuously for five years immediately prior to the submission of* [his or her] *application, subject to the periods of absence permitted under Article 4(3) of that directive*" Case C-432/20, *Landeshauptmann von Wien* [2022] EU:C:2022:39, para 33.

This status is essential for the integration of resettlement beneficiaries because it guarantees a degree of equal treatment with citizens of the receiving EUMS, amongst others, in terms of employment, education, social security, assistance and protection, and housing. It also facilitates the prospect of moving to another EUMS, and protects long-term residents against expulsion.

Under the Long-term Residents Directive, resettlement beneficiaries could lose their long-term residence status due to absence from the EU territory or the territory of the receiving EUMS. First, Art 9 para 1 Long-term Residents Directive sets forth that long-term residence status can be lost or withdrawn, amongst others, "*in the event of absence from the territory of the Community for a period of 12 consecutive months*".[1216] Second, according to Art 9 para 4 Long-term Residents Directive, long-term residents can lose their status after six years of absence from the EUMS that granted it.[1217] In a case concerning absence from EU territory, the CJEU ruled that in order to interrupt such absence, "*it is sufficient for the long-term national concerned to be present* [...] *in the territory of the European Union, even if such presence does not exceed a few days.*"[1218] Given that the two instances of loss of status due to absence are regulated under the same Article and subject to the same exceptions, systematic interpretation suggests that the CJEU ruling on the meaning of absence equally applies to cases where the potential loss of status traces back to six years absence from the EUMS that granted the status is at issue.

Regarding integration in the specific receiving EUMS, the liberal stance of the CJEU on the absence rule remains questionable. It seems to conflict with the idea that resettlement beneficiaries should establish self-sufficiency and a durable solution in the receiving EUMS that admitted them. On the other hand, when considering integration in the EU as a form of (gradual) equality with EU citizens, it seems consistent to enable resettlement beneficiaries with long-term residence status to reside in another EUMS or leave the EU without having to fear the loss of legal status. Yet, absence

1216 EUMS *may* stipulate in their national laws that "*absences exceeding 12 consecutive months or for specific or exceptional reasons*" do not lead to loss or withdrawal.

1217 Long-term residence status from one EUMS is also lost once it is obtained from another EUMS after residing there.

1218 Case C-432/20, *Landeshauptmann von Wien* [2022] EU:C:2022:39, para 45. See Steven Peers, 'Residents of everywhere?' (*EU Law Analysis*, 26 January 2022) <http://eulawanalysis.blogspot.com/2022/01/residents-of-everywhere-cjeu-rules-on.html?m=1> accessed 24 July 2022.

from the territory of the receiving EUMS can also not be completely disregarded in the context of citizenship. Indeed, some EUMS provide for the loss of national citizenship, and thus EU citizenship, due to absence (together with additional factors). For developments *de lege ferenda*, the judgment of the CJEU must be followed and implemented by EUMS. In addition, from the perspective of legal certainty, there is a need to clarify the meaning of "*a few days*". What is more, situations of abuse of short interruption of absence should be regulated in future legislation, as the CJEU has not yet taken a concrete position on this.[1219]

Aside from the loss of long-term residence status, resettlement beneficiaries could face involuntary cessation of refugee status in the receiving EUMS. For instance, refugees from Somalia who were resettled to Denmark via UNHCR's resettlement program lost their protection status when conditions in Somalia changed. In this case, it was criticized that the loss of refugee status was based on the changed conditions in Somalia *in general* rather than on a specific assessment of the circumstances in connection with the particular refugee at issue (Art 1 C para 5 Refugee Convention).

Notwithstanding the demand to apply the status cessation rules under the Refugee Convention on a case-by-case basis, the preliminary question is whether these rules cover resettlement refugees at all.[1220] *O'Sullivan* approached the issue by pointing to the already mentioned tension, i.e. on the one hand refugee status is temporary, on the other hand, the aim is to achieve durable solutions for refugees, such as resettlement. Concerning future EU resettlement, Art 78 para 1 TFEU requires the EU legislators at least not to impose stricter rules than the cessation rules of the Refugee Convention – also with regard to resettlement refugees.

By way of successful long-term integration, refugee and long-term residence status ends with naturalization in the receiving EUMS, although resettlement beneficiaries have no right to attain citizenship under international law (see 3.3.6). Over the course of past resettlement programs, all EUMS granted resettlement beneficiaries a right to apply for naturalization according to the requirements and procedures under national law.[1221] Generally, these national requirements include a certain "*residential time*

1219 See Steven Peers, 'Residents of everywhere?' (*EU Law Analysis*, 26 January 2022).

1220 See Maria O'Sullivan, 'Can States cease the protection status of resettled refugees?' (*Asylum Insight*, November 2019) <https://www.asyluminsight.com/maria-osullivan#.Xd0yrndFzt4> accessed 27 March 2021.

1221 See European Migration Network, 'Resettlement and Humanitarian Admission Programmes in Europe – what works' (9 November 2016) 35f.

plus a combination of language, character and finance conditions which may be more or less demanding".[1222] *Owen* compared ordinary naturalization procedures with those for refugees and concluded that EUMS facilitated access to citizenship for refugees compared to other migrants. First, while some EUMS required renunciation of prior nationality in their ordinary naturalization procedures, they acknowledged that this was not justified in the case of refugees. Second, there was a tendency among EUMS to reduce or even remove waiting periods for refugees.[1223] Third, while fourteen EUMS applied a residency requirement of more than six years in their ordinary naturalization procedure, seven thereof reduced that requirement for refugees to six years or less.[1224]

Naturalization in an EUMS encompasses EU citizenship. According to Art 20 para 1 TFEU "[e]*very person holding the nationality of a Member State shall be a citizen of the Union. Citizenship of the Union shall be additional to and not replace national citizenship*".[1225] In fact, the competence to set the requirements for granting and terminating citizenship has remained a national competence of EUMS. Notwithstanding, the relationship between national and EU citizenship implies obligations for EUMS. In this light, EUMS must comply with the principle of sincere cooperation under Art 4 para 3 TEU. It contains a positive obligation for EUMS to take "*any appropriate measure, general or particular, to ensure fulfilment of the obligations arising out of the Treaties or resulting from the acts of the institutions of the Union*". EU citizenship rights are rights "*arising out of the Treaties*" that must be granted by the EUMS. The last sentence of Art 20 TFEU para 2 states that [t]*hese rights shall be exercised in accordance with the conditions and limits defined by the Treaties and by the measures adopted thereunder*".[1226]

1222 David Owen, 'Refugees, EU Citizenship and the Common European Asylum System A Normative Dilemma for EU Integration' in (2019) Ethical Theory and Moral Practice, 350.

1223 E.g. Bulgaria, Czech Republic, France, Ireland and Sweden.

1224 See David Owen, 'Refugees, EU Citizenship and the Common European Asylum System A Normative Dilemma for EU Integration' in (2019) Ethical Theory and Moral Practice, 351f; see also Delphine Perrin and Frank McNamara, 'Refugee Resettlement in the EU: Between Shared Standards and Diversity in Legal and Policy Frames', KNOW RESET Research Report 2013/03, 57ff.

1225 See Yuval Dvir, Paul Morris and Miri Yemini, 'What kind of citizenship for whom? The 'refugee crisis' and the European Union's conceptions of citizenship' in (2019) 17 Globalization, Societies and Education 2, 208 (211).

1226 E.g. Directive 2004/38 (EC) on the right of citizens of the Union and their family members to move and reside freely within the territory of the Member States [2004] OJ L158/77-123.

Against this backdrop, the CJEU interfered in the national policy field of citizenship and invoked the direct relationship between EU citizenship and national citizenship. The most prominent case of CJEU interference in this regard is the *Tjebbes* case. *Tjebbes* concerned the issue of cessation (as opposed to initial denial) of national citizenship, but it also underscored the overall need for EUMS authorities to consider the direct impact on the status of the individual as EU citizen when deciding upon national citizenship. The Court affirmed former case law by stressing that[1227]

> *while it is for each Member State, having due regard to international law, to lay down the conditions for acquisition and loss of nationality, the fact that a matter falls within the competence of the Member States does not alter the fact that, in situations covered by EU law, the national rules concerned must have due regard to the latter.*

Subsequently, the Court set out a requirement for competent national authorities and courts to "*determine whether the loss of the nationality of the Member State concerned, when it entails the loss of citizenship of the Union and the rights attaching thereto, has due regard to the principle of proportionality so far as concerns the consequences of that loss for the situation of the person concerned*".[1228] With this in mind, the Court went further than in its previous rulings by specifying that competent authorities had to undertake an individual assessment, taking account of a "*serious risk, to which the person concerned would be exposed, that his or her safety or freedom to come and go would substantially deteriorate because of the impossibility for that person to enjoy consular protection*".[1229] Remarkably the wording used by the Court resembles the *raison* behind the principle of *non-refoulement* – even if in an attenuated way.

By applying the considerations of the CJEU in *Tjebbes* to the resettlement context (this is only an analogy, because in the resettlement context the granting of citizenship constitutes the initial focus – only after that, a potential withdrawal could come into question), the following conclusions can be deduced: The competent authorities of the receiving country must carry out an individual assessment when granting citizenship. In other words, automatic refusal of national citizenship would contradict CJEU case law. Furthermore, in their assessment, EUMS must consider

1227 Case C-221/17 *Tjebbes and others v Minister van Buitenlandse Zaken* [2019] EU:C:2019:189, para 30.

1228 Ibid para 40.

1229 Ibid para 46.

various aspects of the specific situation of the resettlement beneficiary, in particular the risks for safety and freedom to which the individual concerned would be exposed in case of refusal of citizenship.

5.4.2 US law and practice

In the US, long-term integration measures are scarce. This traces back to the US resettlement program that pressures resettlement beneficiaries to rapidly enter the labor market and achieve self-sufficiency.[1230] While Volags track short-term employment indicators of resettlement beneficiaries within the first 90 to 180 days upon their arrival, there is hardly any documentation on whether resettlement beneficiaries succeed in integrating in the US in the long-term.[1231] After eight months, resettlement beneficiaries are expected to transition to (economic) self-sufficiency.[1232]

Legislation evidences the pressure on refugees to find and accept work, as Section 412 lit e para 2 subpara C Refugee Act determines sanctions in case of resistance:[1233]

> *In the case of a refugee who—*
> *(i) refuses an offer of employment which has been determined to be appropriate either by the agency responsible for the initial resettlement of the refugee under subsection (b) or by the appropriate State or local employment service,*
> *(ii) refuses to go to a job interview which has been arranged through such agency or service, or*
> *(iii) refuses to participate in a social service or targeted assistance program referred to in subparagraph (A)(ii) which such agency or service determines to be available and appropriate,*

1230 See Jessica H Darrow in Adèle Garnier, Liliana Lyra Jubilut and Kristin Bergtora Sandvik (eds), *Refugee Resettlement: Power, Politics, and Humanitarian Governance*, 105.

1231 See Nadwa Mossaad et al, 'Determinants of refugee naturalization in the United States' in (11 September 2018) 115 PNAS 37, 9175.

1232 The Volags "*work with the refugees to ensure that within eight months they are employed*", Joanne van Selm, 'Public-Private Partnerships in Refugee Resettlement: Europe and the US' in (2003) 4 Journal of International Migration and Integration 2, 169f.

1233 Section 412 lit e para 2 subpara C Refugee Act (emphasis added); see also Jessica H Darrow in Adèle Garnier, Liliana Lyra Jubilut and Kristin Bergtora Sandvik (eds), *Refugee Resettlement: Power, Politics, and Humanitarian Governance*, 104.

> *cash assistance to the refugee shall be terminated (after opportunity for an administrative hearing) for a period of three months (for the first such refusal) or for a period of six months (for any subsequent refusal).*

To elucidate the purpose and impact of the self-sufficiency target, *Darrow* used the following quote of a Volag refugee worker:[1234]

> *The amount is not enough for you to live. They know you cannot survive on this money; this is temporary. After a short time they will be asking you, "Why is it taking so long to find a job?" The money is small because the government has no money to pay everyone to sit at home and do nothing, so you must work hard.*

From a legal standpoint, pressuring refugees to achieve independence from governmental funds by minimizing the timeframe for funding contradicts the 1980 Refugee Act. This Act initially stated that "*the federal government would cover all public assistance program costs incurred by states for the first 36 months a refugee was in the United States*".[1235] The thirty-six months mentioned therein have gradually been decreased to today's limit of eight months for Refugee Cash Assistance and Refugee Medical Assistance.

After that period, refugees are subject to the limited regular US welfare system. Accordingly, only needy families obtain assistance up to five years (Temporary Assistance for Needy Families) and low-income individuals, who are aged, blind, or disabled are eligible for up to seven years of assistance (Supplemental Security Income).[1236] An aggravating factor is that, in practice, sources of federal funding have proven insufficient for resettlement beneficiaries to cover their living. Hence, there is a growing reliance on state and local sources, resulting in differential treatment due to the significant differences among the public benefit programs of individual states. For example, in 2017, a refugee family of three in New York received about USD 500 less in Temporary Assistance for Needy Families per month than in Texas.[1237] Nevertheless, it was claimed that the extensive network of the nine Volags helped to redress state-to-state inequalities.[1238] Overall, the extent of federal and state funding programs remains subject to political debate, but it becomes legally relevant if refugees

1234 Ibid 108.

1235 Michael Fix, Kate Hooper and Jie Zong, 'How Are Refugees Faring: Integration at US and State Levels' (June 2017) 10.

1236 See ibid 8.

1237 See ibid 11.

1238 See ibid 20.

face discrimination, and/or are forced to live below the standards required under international law.

Besides the short period of assistance, a lack of insurance coverage has barred refugees from accessing health care in the US. In this regard, the 2014 Affordable Care Act,[1239] known as Obamacare, represented a significant regulatory overhaul, expanding health insurance coverage. In particular, Medicaid and the State Children's Health Insurance Program introduced coverage for individuals with limited incomes.[1240] Between 2014 and 2017 in which the Affordable Care Act was in force, it had caused a significant decrease of immigrants without health insurance;[1241] for example, in 2015 there were 16% less uninsured non-citizens than in 2010.[1242] This notwithstanding, the percentage of immigrants without health insurance remained much higher than among US citizens. Compared to 9.1% of US citizens, 53.5% of immigrants did not benefit from health insurance in 2015.[1243]

Moreover, becoming self-sufficient within eight months comes with the challenge that resettlement beneficiaries have to apply for adjustment to lawful permanent resident (LPR) status after being physically present in the US for one year,[1244] as stipulated in the INA and in certain other federal laws.[1245] The adjustment to LPR status is informally referred to as

1239 This Act was challenged by former Republican-lead states and the former *Trump* administration. On June 17, 2021 the US Supreme Court dismissed the challenge meaning that Obama Care remains in place; see *California et al v Texas et al* 593 US __ (2021) <https://www.supremecourt.gov/opinions/20pdf/19-840_6jfm.pdf> accessed 18 July 2021.

1240 See Michael Fix, Kate Hooper and Jie Zong, 'How Are Refugees Faring: Integration at US and State Levels' (June 2017) 8.

1241 See ibid 18.

1242 See Jim P Stimpson and Fernando A Wilson, 'Medicaid Expansion Improved Health Insurance Coverage For Immigrants, But Disparities Persist' in (2018) 37 Health Affairs 10, 1656.

1243 See Adam Gaffney and Danny McCormick, 'The Affordable Care Act: implications for health-care equity' in (2017) 389 The Lancet 10077, 1442 (1445).

1244 See USCIS, 'I am a refugee or asylee... How do I become a US permanent resident?' (October 2013) <https://www.uscis.gov/sites/default/files/USCIS/Resources/D3en.pdf> accessed 27 March 2021.

1245 See Section 209 INA – Adjustment of Status of Refugees; Section 212 INA – Excludable Aliens; Section 209.1 Title 8 Code of Federal Regulations – Adjustment of status of refugees; USCIS Policy Manual, Volume 7, Part A, Adjustment of Status Policies and Procedures; USCIS Policy Manual, Volume 7, Part L, Refugee Adjustment.

applying for a 'Green Card'.[1246] In this process, refugees are exempted from several grounds of inadmissibility, including inadmissibility due to public charge.[1247] Yet, obtaining a Green Card constitutes a costly and lengthy process.[1248] The fee for adjustment of status amounts to over USD 1,000.[1249] Exemptions only exist for younger and elderly applicants.[1250] As of July 2022, the processing of an application for adjustment of status could take up to 39 months.[1251]

On the one hand, the US offer resettlement beneficiaries access to permanent residency after only one year and exempt them from grounds of inadmissibility that they may not be able to fulfill in their special situation as a refugee. On the other hand, however, the precondition of paying

---

1246 The following requirements must be met by a refuge to be eligible for a Green Card: (i) proper file of Application to Register Permanent Residence or Adjust Status (Form I-485); (ii) admission into the US as a refugee under Section 207 of the INA; (iii) physical presence in the US at the time when filing the application (generally, if a refugee has a pending application and leaves the US without an advance parole document, he or she will have abandoned his or her application); (iv) physical presence in the US for at least one year after admission as a refugee at the time of filing the application; (v) no termination of refugee status; (vi) no former grant of permanent resident status;(vii) admissibility for LPR or eligibility for a waiver of inadmissibility or other form of relief (the reasons for inadmissibility are listed in Section 212 lit a INA; certain grounds of inadmissibility do not apply to refugee adjustments); see USCIS, 'I-485, Application to Register Permanent Residence or Adjust Status' <https://www.uscis.gov/i-485> accessed 27 March 2021; see also USCIS, 'Green Card for Refugees' <https://www.uscis.gov/greencard/refugees> accessed 27 March 2021.

1247 This ground of inadmissibility involves that an alien is inadmissible to the US under Section 212 lit a para 4 INA because he or she is likely at any time to become a public charge. In other words, the use of public benefits could pose a barrier to the adjustment of the legal status. "*Inadmissibility on Public Charge Grounds*" has been subject to debate and was blocked by preliminary injunction. Ultimately, it applies since February 2020; see USCIS, 'Inadmissibility on Public Charge Grounds' (14 August 2019) <https://www.govinfo.gov/content/pkg/FR-2019-08-14/pdf/2019-17142.pdf> accessed 27 March 2021; see also USCIS, 'I-485, Application to Register Permanent Residence or Adjust Status'.

1248 See International Rescue Committee, 'How immigrants and refugees become US citizens' (3 July 2018) <https://www.rescue.org/article/how-immigrants-and-refugees-become-us-citizens> accessed 27 March 2021.

1249 See Citizen Path, 'Adjustment of Status Package Fees' <https://citizenpath.com/adjustment-of-status-fee/> accessed 27 July 2022.

1250 See USCIS, 'I-485, Application to Register Permanent Residence or Adjust Status'.

1251 See USCIS, 'Check Case Processing Times' <https://egov.uscis.gov/processing-times/> accessed 27 July 2022.

a relatively high fee after that short period in the US and the lengthy processing time pose substantial obstacles undermining the access to LPR status. First, it is difficult to imagine that resettlement beneficiaries have generally become self-sufficient after only one year and can afford a fee of more than USD 1,000 dollars without facing a considerable financial setback. Second, they likely have to live in uncertainty for up to two and a half years, neither being allowed to leave the country nor knowing whether they can stay there in the long run, which, in effect prolongs the one-year waiting period.

Once LPR status has been obtained and integration has been solidified, the US recognizes the opportunity for refugees to apply for naturalization. In its original understanding, naturalization means the conferral of "*citizenship to proud and thankful immigrants*"[1252] in a courtroom by a judge. According to Art I Section 8 para 4 US Constitution, Congress is competent to "*establish an uniform Rule of Naturalization*". The Immigration Act of 1990 transferred the authority to grant citizenship from the courts to the Attorney General, i.e. the USCIS acting on behalf of the Secretary of Homeland Security. Still, most applicants are required to take the final oath in court, and courts maintain jurisdiction to review naturalization denials (Section 310 INA).[1253]

Currently, Green Card holders upon the age of eighteen are eligible to apply for citizenship after five consecutive years in the US as LPR or three years if married to a US citizen[1254] (Sections 316 lit a, 318, 319 lit a INA).[1255] Resettlement refugees enjoy facilitated access to citizenship because their five-year-waiting period already starts running when they

1252 Stephen H Legomsky and David B Thronson, *Immigration Law and Policy*, 1539.

1253 See ibid 1539.

1254 The LPR must meet the following conditions: (i) age of at least 18 years; (ii) good moral character; (iii) ability to read, write and speak basic English; (iv) understanding of the principles and ideals of the US Constitution; (v) basic understanding of US history and government; (vi) oath of allegiance to the US; see International Rescue Committee, 'How immigrants and refugees become US citizens' (3 July 2018); see also Stephen H Legomsky and David B Thronson, *Immigration Law and Policy*, 1545ff.

1255 "*The applicant must 'reside' continuously in the United States during the five-year period immediately preceding the filing of the application, all after admission as LPR; must be 'physically present' in the United States for at least half that period; and must 'reside' continuously in the United States from the filing of the application to the grant of naturalization*", Stephen H Legomsky and David B Thronson, *Immigration Law and Policy*, 1546.

enter the US (instead of when they adjust to LPR status). In other words, their first year counts toward the five-year-waiting period even though their status can be adjusted to LPR only after one year.[1256]

Like the adjustment of status, the naturalization procedure is lengthy and costly. For 2022, the filing fee for citizenship amounted to USD 1,170[1257] and the estimated processing time was about 12.5 months.[1258] The fees can be halved for certain low-income naturalization applicants.[1259] Strikingly, the costs for naturalization are similar (and may even be slightly lower) than for adjustment to LPR status. With this comes the following contradiction: While resettlement beneficiaries pay about the same amount to apply for naturalization, which is based on their voluntary decision, they have to pay a relatively high fee for the Green Card, i.e. a requirement to maintain their legal status in the US and prevent involuntary return after only one year. On that account, the US fees for LPR status appear to be disproportionately high.

At the beginning of the naturalization process, applicants must give their fingerprints and take photographs for the purpose of multiple background checks. Those passing these checks are invited to an in-person interview with an USCIS officer. This interview includes an examination of civic knowledge and language.

The required civic knowledge is described as "*knowledge and understanding of the fundamentals of the history, and form of the government, of the United States*" (Section 312 lit a para 2 INA). The USCIS officer typically asks applicants up to ten questions (from a list of one hundred), covering principles of American democracy, systems of government, geography, rights and responsibilities, and history. Applicants must answer six of the ten questions correctly to pass the test.[1260]

In terms of language, Section 312 lit a para 1 INA requires the applicant to demonstrate "*an understanding of the English language, including an ability*

1256 See Nadwa Mossaad et al, 'Determinants of refugee naturalization in the United States' in (11 September 2018) 115 PNAS 37, 9176.

1257 See USCIS, 'N-600K, Application for Citizenship and Issuance of Certificate Under Section 322' <https://www.uscis.gov/n-600k > accessed 27 July 2022.

1258 See USCIS, 'Check Case Processing Times' <https://egov.uscis.gov/processing-times/> accessed 27 July 2022.

1259 See USCIS, 'Our Fees' <https://www.uscis.gov/forms/our-fees> accessed 27 March 2021.

1260 See International Rescue Committee, 'How immigrants and refugees become US citizens' (3 July 2018).

to read, write, and speak words in ordinary usage".[1261] Certain applicants are exempted from the English requirement because of age or/and length of permanent residency (Section 312 lit a para 2 INA). However, this waiver does not affect the civic knowledge requirement.[1262] Only physical or mental disability may allow for waiving both the English and the civic knowledge test (Section 312 lit b para 1 INA). Finally, successful applicants must take an oath of allegiance to the US at a public ceremony before receiving their certificates of naturalization.[1263]

The value of US citizenship goes beyond freedom from immigration laws, the right to be in the US and diplomatic protection. Citizenship enables naturalized resettlement beneficiaries to petition for the admission of certain family members as immigrants. Petition rights can also be derived from LPR status, but only with limitations, including numerical quotas. Beyond that, federal and state laws restrict the status of non-citizens in various ways. For instance, LPRs cannot obtain certain state professional licenses.[1264] This shows that the US does not guarantee comprehensive equality between resettlement beneficiaries and its own citizens – even the LPR status does not change this. Again, such differential treatment arguably complies with US non-discrimination obligations under the ICCPR, because the Human Rights Committee has accepted citizenship as an inherently reasonable basis upon which individuals may be treated differently (see 3.3.4.1).

Eventually, naturalized resettlement beneficiaries may want to return to their home country. In this light, the question arises whether and how returning to the initial home country impacts US citizenship. In *Afroyim v Rusk*, the US Supreme Court interpreted Section 1 of the Fourteenth Amendment to the US Constitution as giving every citizen "*a constitutional right to remain a citizen* [...] *unless he voluntarily relinquishes that citizenship*".[1265] Still, Section 349 lit a INA lists specific reasons for expatriation. These reasons were subject of the 1990 Announcement of the US Department of State. The State Department declared in its Announcement that the expatriation grounds did not entail a loss of citizenship *ex lege*.

1261 Stephen H Legomsky and David B Thronson, *Immigration Law and Policy*, 1547.

1262 See ibid 1547.

1263 See International Rescue Committee, 'How immigrants and refugees become US citizens' (3 July 2018).

1264 See Stephen H Legomsky and David B Thronson, *Immigration Law and Policy*, 1622.

1265 Ibid 1605.

Rather, all individuals would be presumed to "*intend to retain United States citizenship when they obtain naturalization in a foreign state, subscribe to routine declarations of allegiance to a foreign state, or accept non-policy level employment with a foreign government*". With that Announcement, the State Department clarified that in order to surrender US citizenship, individuals either had "*to affirm that intention in writing to a US consular officer or to formally renounce* [...]".[1266] This reflects a general discomfort of the US government towards expatriation, not only in cases where it would result in statelessness.[1267]

5.4.3 Analysis

Laws and practice in Europe and the US indicate that resettlement beneficiaries face various challenges to access and maintain long-term residence and citizenship status. On that basis, there are three key challenges to stimulate long-term integration *de lege ferenda*: First, the reduction of differential treatment where there is no objective and reasonable justification; second, the elimination of excessive examination requirements and/or fees; third, the reconsideration of rules on the loss of legal status.

5.4.3.1 Temporary approach versus long-term integration

It is evident from the outlined European and US resettlement policies that long-term integration approaches significantly differ among EUMS and even amongst American states. The major issue comprises the conceptualization of resettlement either as a temporary protection tool versus a long-term integration measure, or durable solution.

The issue is of political nature and can be explained as follows: Governments are seemingly more prone to justify temporary admissions towards their electorate, i.e. the receiving community, than long-term integration and naturalization of third-country nationals. This traces back to the fact that the electorate feels less threatened by foreigners when they are only temporarily admitted.[1268] Furthermore, governments appear to disregard

1266 Ibid 1614.
1267 See ibid 1614f.
1268 See Jürgen Fijalkowski, 'Optionen und Spielraum europäischer Zuwanderungspolitik — Ein Essay' in Alfredo Märker and Stephan Schlothfeldt

the negative impacts of temporary protection on the lives of protection seekers who might suffer from a so-called warehouse effect. This was critically addressed by *Bruce-Jones*:[1269]

> *To keep newly arrived people separate from the labour economy and other facets of social citizenship and participation, is ultimately a form of warehousing. Temporary protection, whilst it arguably coaxes states to provide certain forms of relief up-front, would trap refugees into lives 'on hold'. The eventual forced return of migrants to countries of origin would threaten to break apart supportive networks and family bonds accrued in host countries, which will have, in the meantime, become home for these people.*

As some governments became aware of these negative impacts, High Commissioner *Grandi* expressed hope for a decisive shift towards a sustainable long-term approach in the course of the Global Refugee Forum in Geneva in December 2019.[1270]

5.4.3.2 Economic benefits

Beneficial aspects of long-term integration in the receiving country are predominantly linked to an economic rationale. In other words, from the receiving country's perspective, economic arguments speak in favor of long-term integration. The US practice relies on self-sufficiency and labor market entry, which has proven to be economically beneficial. For example, in 2016, labor force participation and employment rates of resettle-

(eds), *Was schulden wir Flüchtlingen und Migranten?: Grundlagen einer gerechten Zuwanderungspolitik* (Springer 2002) 19-44; see also e.g. call by Chancellor Angela Merkel for asylum seekers and refugees to return to their home country, Marcel Leubecher, 'Warum die meisten Flüchtlinge Merkels Appell nicht folgen werden' (*Die Welt*, 1 February 2016) <https://www.welt.de/politik/deutschland/article151744427/Warum-die-meisten-Fluechtlinge-Merkels-Appell-nicht-folgen-werden.html> accessed 27 March 2021.

1269 Eddie Bruce-Jones in Satvinder Singh Juss (ed), *Research Handbook on International Refugee Law*, 77.

1270 See UNHCR, 'Global Refugee Forum pledges collective action for better refugee inclusion, education, jobs' (*Press release*, 18 December 2019) <https://www.unhcr.org/news/press/2019/12/5dfa56b54/global-refugee-forum-pledges-collective-action-better-refugee-inclusion.html> accessed 27 March 2021.

ment refugees in the US exceeded those of the overall US population.[1271] Furthermore, a 2015 study conducted in the area of Ohio revealed that added economic value emerged from high self-employment rates among refugees.[1272] Nonetheless, the short period of assistance and the related time pressure to enter the labor market deprived refugees of the opportunity to search for jobs matching their qualifications. Even though past employment rates showed that refugees were more likely to be employed than US-born people, refugees were also more likely to accept low-skilled jobs despite holding a bachelor's degree.[1273]

From the US experience, the following conclusion can be drawn for future EU resettlement legislation: Granting resettlement beneficiaries a more relaxed transition period would allow them to prepare for and take job opportunities according to their profile, which would in turn result in an overall more beneficial outcome – not only for the resettlement beneficiaries themselves but also for the economy of the receiving country and EU's internal market as a whole – thus creating a win-win situation. This corresponds to the previous statement of the Commission that the aim should be to enable economic productivity of migrants.[1274] The Com-

1271 See Donald Kerwin, 'The US Refugee Resettlement Program – A Return to First Principles: How Refugees Help to Define, Strengthen, and Revitalize the United States' in (2018) 6 Journal on Migration and Human Security 3, 213.

1272 See US Together, Community Refugee & Immigration Services, World Relief Columbus and City of Columbus, 'Impact of Refugees in Central Ohio' (2015) <https://www.crisohio.org/wp-content/uploads/2016/04/IMPACT-OF-REFUGEES-ON-CENTRAL-OHIO_2015-SP_I.pdf> accessed 27 March 2021; see also Initiative of the Harvard Immigration and Refugee Clinical Program, 'Fulfilling US Commitment to Refugee Resettlement: Protecting Refugees, Preserving National Security, & Building the US Economy through Refugee Admissions' in (2017) 5 Texas A&M Law Review, 183.

1273 See Michael Fix, Kate Hooper and Jie Zong, 'How Are Refugees Faring: Integration at US and State Levels' (June 2017) 18.

1274 See Yuval Dvir, Paul Morris and Miri Yemini, 'What kind of citizenship for whom? The 'refugee crisis' and the European Union's conceptions of citizenship' in (2019) 17 Globalization, Societies and Education 2, 214. Specifically, in its 2016 Action Plan on the Integration of Third Country Nationals, the Commission made it clear that social integration had to be realized by offering migrants meaningful opportunities to participate in the economy and society of the receiving EUMS. See Commission, Communication 'Action Plan on the Integration of Third Country Nationals', COM(2016) 377 final, 5.

mission re-emphasized this goal in the 2020 Recommendation in a New Pact on Migration and Asylum.[1275]

5.4.3.3 Harmonization of permanent residence status

De lege lata, Art 4 Long-term Residents Directive states that EUMS shall grant long-term residence status to third-country nationals, including refugees and persons eligible for subsidiary protection,[1276] after five years of legal and uninterrupted stay in an EUMS. Five years are a comparatively long period given that in the US, refugees have to (or may) apply for an adjustment to LPR status already after one year. As regards consistency within EU law, the five-year requirement under the Long-term Residents Directive aligns with the requirements for EU citizens to gain permanent residency in another EUMS under Art 16 para 1 EU Citizenship Directive.

De lege ferenda, valid arguments speak in favor of introducing a waiting period shorter than five years for resettlement beneficiaries to become permanent residents of an EUMS. First, earlier recognition of long-term residence status corresponds to the very character of resettlement as a durable solution. Second, refugees, unlike EU citizens, do not usually have social support from their home country. Thus, they depend on the long-term residence status because this status usually implies social rights. Finally, the prospect of earlier long-term residence status can be an incentive for beneficiaries of international protection to refrain from unauthorized secondary movement. To that effect, the Commission proposed in its New Pact on Migration and Asylum to amend the Long-term Residents Directive so that beneficiaries of international protection would obtain long-term residence status after three years of legal and continuous residence instead of the usual five years.[1277]

Furthermore, Art 5 Long-term Residents Directive sets out additional requirements for permanent residence status, such as a stable and regular source of income, health insurance and, if so required by an EUMS, inte-

1275 See Commission, Communication on a New Pact on Migration and Asylum, 27.

1276 In 2011, the Long-term Residents Directive was amended to include persons eligible for international protection.

1277 See Commission, Communication on a New Pact on Migration and Asylum, 6.

gration measures.[1278] As indicated above, the CJEU upheld the Dutch law provision requiring a civic integration examination[1279] (see 5.4.1). By comparison, refugees in the US do not have to undergo examination to obtain an adjustment of their residence status to LPR. They only have to do so for naturalization. Still, there is no compelling reason for condemning the CJEU's approach to accept examination of *basic* civic and/or language knowledge as a requirement for permanent residence status, hence before naturalization – unless costs are excessive.

In terms of costs, the US fees of more than USD 1,000 for adjusting to LPR status are relatively high compared to the EU average, although the fees to apply for permanent residency significantly vary throughout the EU; by the end of 2019, costs for citizenship applications varied from less than EUR 100 (Hungary, Spain, Latvia, Estonia, Luxembourg, the Czech Republic, Portugal, and Slovenia) up to EUR 1,100 in Lithuania – the fees in the former EUMS UK even amounted to EUR 1,345.[1280] Given these variations among EUMS, the question of EU harmonization arises. Such harmonization must be reflected in light of the principle of subsidiarity. Is the EU really in a better position than the EUMS to determine these costs than EUMS? Very strong arguments against EU regulation are the differences in social assistance, living costs, and the general economic situations in the EUMS. The EUMS themselves are arguably in the best position to determine the application costs according to these specifics.

To conclude, valid policy arguments speak in favor of (i) shortening the waiting period for resettlement beneficiaries to become permanent residents of an EUMS to less than five years; and (ii) harmonizing the requirements to obtain long-term residence status through future EU resettlement legislation. Concerning the latter, the CJEU has already established that there are limits for national particularities. Accordingly, examination must be kept to a basic level, must not involve excessive costs and must account for the individual situation of the applicant.

1278 Art 5 para 2 Long-term Residents Directive states: "*Member States may require third-country nationals to comply with integration conditions, in accordance with national law*", Koen Lenaerts and Piet van Nuffel, *European Union Law*, 325, para 10-014.

1279 See Case C-257/17 C, *A v Staatssecretaris van Veiligheid en Justitie*, paras 63f.

1280 See Andrew Henderson, '5 Most Expensive Residency Applications in Europe' (last updated 26 December 2019) <https://nomadcapitalist.com/2017/11/06/most-expensive-residency-applications/> accessed 27 July 2022.

5.4.3.4 Naturalization

In the ideal case, the long-term residence status of a resettlement beneficiary ends with his or her naturalization in the receiving country. As highlighted above, international refugee law, namely Art 34 Refugee Convention, instructs states to facilitate access to citizenship for refugees. The refugees' special need for access to citizenship is rooted in the very definition of a refugee as being unable or unwilling to avail him or herself of the protection of his or her home country.

It follows from *Owen*'s findings that in general, EUMS facilitate the access to citizenship for refugees compared to other third-country nationals. Nevertheless, they follow different, i.e. more or less restrictive policies. In this light, the CJEU clarified that national authorities must conduct individual assessments of the implications of denial of EU citizenship rights when deciding upon national citizenships.

Similar to most EUMS, the US prioritizes the naturalization of refugees in comparison to other immigrants. A 2018 study on naturalization rates assessing the full population of refugees resettled in the US between 2000 and 2010 showed that resettlement refugees in the US were significantly more likely to acquire citizenship than immigrants entering from other programs.[1281] In general, statistics disclosed that resettlement refugees had a relatively high naturalization rate compared to other immigrants to the US, which reflects a less restrictive citizenship policy towards refugees. For instance, resettled refugees benefit from a shorter waiting period: Unlike for other immigrants, already their first year in the US, before adjustment to LPR status, counts.[1282]

5.4.3.5 Re-resettlement

Naturalization impacts the freedom of movement, i.e. the right to leave and enter a country. The freedom of movement not only becomes an issue when an individual wishes to leave the country of (first) refuge in order to be resettled to a receiving country, but also *vice versa*, i.e. in case the naturalized resettled individual wishes to return to his or her initial home

---

1281 See Nadwa Mossaad et al, 'Determinants of refugee naturalization in the United States' in (11 September 2018) 115 PNAS 37, 9178.

1282 See Stephen H Legomsky and David B Thronson, *Immigration Law and Policy*, 1546.

country. The relevant question in terms of the latter is: To what extent can a receiving country justifiably interfere with the right to leave of resettled and naturalized individuals?

Art 12 para 2 ICCPR determines that any country, including the "*own country*", must grant a right to leave. After and arguably before naturalization, a receiving country can be considered as one's "*own country*". This holds particularly true where the respective resettlement beneficiary has established special ties to that country.[1283] If, notwithstanding such special ties to the receiving country, the (naturalized) resettlement beneficiary wants to return to his or her initial home country, he or she is likely to contravene the interests of the former. Especially, the receiving country as the new "*own country*" may have an interest in restricting a resettled naturalized individual's right to leave, because it has invested in his or her long-term integration. Since the right to leave is not absolute, the receiving country may restrict it under certain conditions and in line with the principle of proportionality (see 3.3.2). Under Art 12 para 2 ICCPR, such restrictions can only be based on the grounds of national security, public order, public health or morals, or the rights and freedoms of others. The mere reason that the receiving country "*invested*" in the integration of resettlement beneficiaries and has an interest to keep them as contributors to its economy and society would therefore not be sufficient.

Unjustified derogations from the right to leave may, amongst others, be induced through the expatriation policy of the country of new citizenship. The US constitutes a liberal example in this regard. From an EU law perspective, the above-mentioned CJEU case law makes it clear that the potential loss of national citizenship of an EUMS needs to be assessed in the light of EU citizenship, and with due consideration of risks for the safety and liberty of the individual concerned.

Finally, not all resettlement beneficiaries actually pursue the goal of naturalization. For instance, Palestinians actively denied resettlement offers,

---

1283 See Rutsel Martha and Stephen Bailey, 'The right to enter his or her own country' (*EJIL: Talk!*, 23 June 2020) <https://www.ejiltalk.org/the-right-to-enter-his-or-her-own-country/> accessed 27 March 2021; "*The scope of "his own country" is broader than the concept 'country of his nationality'. It is not limited to nationality in a formal sense, that is, nationality acquired at birth or by conferral; it embraces, at the very least, an individual who, because of his or her special ties to or claims in relation to a given country, cannot be considered to be a mere alien*", OHCHR, 'General Comment No 27: Article 12 (Freedom of Movement)', UN Doc CCPR/C/21/Rev1/Add9 (2 November 1999) para 20.

invoking their collective rights as people because they feared never being able to return to their initial home country.[1284]

5.4.4 Preliminary conclusion

Economic arguments speak in favor of a policy approach that preserves the originally intended long-term integration character of resettlement. A future policy that introduces clear and harmonized requirements for long-term residence status as well as naturalization would help to make resettlement beneficiaries contribute to the local communities. Moreover, harmonization likely decreases discriminatory practice, which is necessary to foster compliance with international law. Notwithstanding, from an EU law perspective, subsidiarity considerations have to be taken into account, especially when it comes to the regulation of specific requirements such as the determination of costs or the content of examinations. Eventually, even naturalized resettlement beneficiaries may want to leave their new home country to return to their prior home country. In such situations, the receiving country as the new home country must not restrict the right to leave of the resettled refugee unless on the basis of legitimate grounds and in line with the principle of proportionality.

1284 See Anne Irfan, 'Rejecting resettlement: the case of Palestinians' in (2017) 54 Forced Migration Review, 68 (70f).

6 Conclusion

The second Chapter of this monography elaborated on the concept of resettlement and revealed that resettlement constitutes a means of responsibility sharing. Yet, a binding international resettlement mechanism has not evolved. Also, at the EU level, a binding obligation to conduct resettlement does not exist and is not provided for in the Proposal for a Union Resettlement Framework Regulation.

There is no binding definition of resettlement under international law. Despite conceptualization efforts of the UNHCR, its resettlement definition has not reached the status of costumery international law. The Commission has defined resettlement at the EU level. Only lately, in the 2021 AMIF regulation, an explicit reference to resettlement as durable solution can be found. The US understanding of resettlement reflects the idea of providing a durable solution to refugees. The firm resettlement bar takes account of the conditions in the country of (first) refuge and makes eligibility for resettlement dependent on whether firm resettlement has already been provided or is accessible in that country.

History confirms that resettlement has been a vital tool in various contexts where countries of (first) refuge were unable to offer firm resettlement to refugees (e.g. Austria in the course of the influx of Hungarian refugees and Thailand with regard to Vietnamese refugees). It also derives from history that global resettlement efforts have depended on the willingness of prospective receiving countries to resettle. Indeed, US and European policy-makers have pursued similar motives when engaging in resettlement. Besides the humanitarian purpose of resettlement, foreign policy, security and economic interests have impacted their decisions. In this light, critics pointed to the discrepancy between a humanitarian measure and a migration control mechanism. When resettlement entails controlling (the entry of) people and discriminating against particular groups, it not only departs from its humanitarian nature, but also entails potential human rights violations. It is up to the states as the main actors in the resettlement process as well as the UNHCR and other non-state actors to uphold the humanitarian nature of resettlement. This predominantly applies to states facing certain responsibilities under international law towards resettlement beneficiaries.

The first major legal question underlying the third Chapter of this monography referred to the international obligations that must be respected in the course of (EU) resettlement. When states engage in resettlement, they must consider obligations under universal and regional human rights treaties as well as the Refugee Convention and its Protocol. With regards to universal human rights treaties and the ECHR, the analysis revealed that the application of these treaties can exceptionally be triggered by the exercises of jurisdiction in the course of targeted extraterritorial actions during selection missions, namely when a receiving country acts through its state officials and implements its resettlement policy on foreign territory. The basis of the jurisdictional link thereby lies in the control over the targeted actions of policy implementation, and is established only with regards to those rights affected by the specific actions in furtherance of the respective policy and/or application of the domestic law of the receiving country.

As opposed to human rights treaties, most rights under the Refugee Convention are territorially limited and even require a certain level of attachment with the receiving country. Nonetheless, Art 3 (non-discrimination) and Art 33 (*non-refoulement*) Refugee Convention apply extraterritorially if the threshold to establish extraterritorial jurisdiction as applied in human rights treaties is met.

If jurisdiction is established, substantive rights under the respective treaties must be granted to resettlement beneficiaries. First, when receiving countries select resettlement beneficiaries on foreign territory, they may face extraterritorial *non-refoulement* obligations arising from implicit and explicit *non-refoulement* provisions under the CAT, ICCPR, CRC, ECHR and the Refugee Convention. Yet, effective control over *non-refoulement* rights in the course of resettlement selection will only be established in exceptional cases and the *non-refoulement* obligations are primarily left to the state on whose territory resettlement beneficiaries are located. Moreover, resettlement beneficiaries must be granted the right to leave, meaning that migration control policies of receiving countries implemented by countries of (first) refuge must not unjustifiably interfere with such right. In addition, potential resettlement beneficiaries have a right to review a negative selection decision when there is an arguable claim of violation of a right under the ICCPR and/or the ECHR. Besides, the Refugee Convention guarantees any refugee access to courts in all Contracting States. However, refugees are limited to rely on judicial remedies in the respective domestic law. Furthermore, international human rights law offers refugees protection in cases where they are discriminated against other refugees, e.g. in the resettlement selection process or with regards to the legal status in the receiving country. However, when it comes to issues of discrimination between refugees and nationals of the receiving country, there is no comprehensive protection under international human rights law. Also, the Refugee Convention does not account for equal treatment between refugees and nationals in a comprehensive manner since only a few rights in this Convention postulate such treatment. Upon arrival on a receiving country's territory, reception conditions must correspond to the rights and freedoms guaranteed under general international and European human rights law as well as the Refugee Convention. Ultimately, receiving countries may not arbitrarily refuse naturalization of a resettled refugee.

When the actors involved in the resettlement process violate the outlined obligations under international law, the ARSIWA and the ARIO provide rules for the attribution of responsibility. The assessment showed that in the context of the resettlement process, certain requirements for attribution, especially the knowledge threshold for receiving countries to establish derivative responsibility due to aid or assistance, are difficult to prove.

The identified pertinent international obligations are also relevant under EU law. In this light, Chapter 4 dealt with the EU legal framework of resettlement. So far, EUMS have engaged in resettlement on the basis of discretionary choices. Still, Art 78 para 1 TFEU requires that EU resettlement legislation must be developed and interpreted in conformity with international refugee law as well as with pertinent international and European human rights. In addition, the principle of solidarity and responsibility sharing (Art 80 TFEU) as well as the principle of consistency (Art 21 para 3 TEU and Art 7 TFEU) apply when regulating and implementing EU resettlement. The relevant rules of EU competence to adopt legislation on resettlement are Art 78 para 2 lit d and lit g TFEU. Art 78 para 2 lit d TFEU allows for the establishment of procedural rules on the resettlement process, including extraterritorial processing. However, this Article does not cover procedures on centralized EU assessment. Art 78 para 2 lit g TFEU can be used in a complementary manner for third-country support to ensure the effective application of international protection obligations.

From an institutional perspective, the EU has financially supported resettlement operations of EUMS through the AMIF. Besides, the EU has provided operational support through the EUAA and its predecessor EASO. The expanded mandate of the EUAA includes binding decision-making power, which can also be relevant for resettlement selection decisions. Conferring such power to the EUAA is covered by the criteria set out in the *Meroni* judgement. While former EASO's advisory opinions lacked means of review, binding decisions of the EUAA can be subject to review by the CJEU under Art 263 TFEU. Moreover, the empowerment of the EUAA has introduced a shift from assisted processing to common processing.

Eventually, the Proposal for a Union Resettlement Framework Regulation reflects the strive for a permanent resettlement framework. However, similar to the EU-Turkey Statement, the Proposal shows inconsistencies regarding the principle of non-discrimination as well as potential violations of Art 31 Refugee Convention (when penalizing those who tried to enter the EU irregularly by excluding them from resettlement).

In the long term, the arguments in favor of a permanent EU resettlement framework prevail to ensure continued resettlement contributions in compliance with international law. Whether such EU framework will set out a mandatory resettlement quota remains a highly political question. The concept of flexible solidarity has been proposed as a way out of the current political deadlock on the issue of mandatory quotas. In the end, flexible solidarity does not relieve EUMS from obligations under international human rights and refugee law.

Lastly, the comparative analysis of European and US resettlement practices identified the following legal issues throughout the resettlement process that demand contemplation *de lege ferenda*. Starting with the pre-selection of potential resettlement beneficiaries, EUMS and the US rely on the UNHCR as major referral entity. In addition to ordinary UNHCR pre-selection, a future increase of cooperation with NGOs as referral entities as well as the involvement of the EUAA and civil society could open up resources for a more comprehensive and diversified case identification system. Furthermore, the harmonization of EUMS national selection practices would enable more comparable and consistent (high) procedural standards.

Concerning the scope of resettlement beneficiaries, individuals who do not qualify as Convention refugees, in particular people fleeing from war, may equally be in need for resettlement. To that effect, relying on the category of 'forced migrants' in the future scope of resettlement beneficiaries would include "*any individual who, owing to the risk of serious harm, is compelled to leave or unable to return to her or his country of origin*".[1285] In addition, IDPs, who have not been able to leave their country of origin, are relevant target groups *de lege ferenda*. So far, the US, as opposed to most

1285 Kiran Banerjee, 'Rethinking the Global Governance of International Protection' in (2018) 56 Columbia Journal of Transnational Law, 319.

EUMS, has considered IDPs for resettlement, but the groups of eligible IDPs have not been determined based on vulnerability and protection needs. If future EU legislation followed the US approach granting resettlement to IDPs, the eligibility of IDPs for resettlement to the EU would have to be based on objective criteria to avoid interference with the principle of non-discrimination under international law. Precisely, the criterion of integration potential as applied by some EUMS is problematic because it lacks objectivity and fails to account for actual humanitarian needs. It constitutes an additional requirement that has no basis in the Refugee Convention and thus could be a source of discrimination between and amongst (groups of) refugees.

For selection decisions, the comparative analysis found that instruments of appeal are scarce. This contradicts international law, where the ICCPR and the ECHR require effective means to appeal decisions when there is an arguable claim of violation of rights under the respective Treaty. Moreover, the right to good administration as stipulated in Art 41 Charter entails that potential resettlement beneficiaries must be granted the right to be heard.

Regarding pre-departure orientation programs, the comparison revealed divergent practices. Future EU regulation could contribute to evening out existing shortfalls and inequalities not only by imposing comparably high standards of pre-departure orientation, but also by ensuring that orientation programs are equally accessible to all refugees. Considerations *de lege ferenda* also need to account for continuity between pre-departure and post-arrival assistance because this kind of practice has already proven successful.

Furthermore, a lesson can be learned from the US public-private partnerships with voluntary agencies, the Volags. With their experience and network, Volags are particularly well suited to match refugee profiles with conditions in the receiving communities. Besides, Volags have supported resettlement beneficiaries arriving in the US in achieving self-sufficiency. The US focus on fast self-sufficiency and labor market entry, combined with meaningful time limits for assistance deserves to be taken into consideration when drafting future EU resettlement legislation. What is more, references in the Refugee Convention and in EU law indicate that the will of resettlement beneficiaries has legal weight in the placement process.

In addition, the analysis of the US' centralized resettlement approach pointed to shortfalls in information sharing and funding. Even if a fully centralized approach is not covered by the current EU Constitutional Framework, similar shortfalls can be avoided *de lege ferenda* in EU resettlement legislation by enhancing information sharing with the local communities as well as ensuring proactive and tailor-made funding to respond to local needs. In particular, direct EU-level funding for those municipalities willing to admit individuals in need for resettlement is necessary to enable efficient use of open capacities.

Moreover, future EU resettlement should be designed in a way to foster EUMS compliance with their obligations (*de lege lata*) concerning reception conditions upon arrival. In addition, sources of unequal treatment among and between (groups of) refugees, particularly in terms of their legal status, need to be addressed *de lege ferenda* in order to avoid violations of non-discrimination obligations under international human rights law.

Facilitated access to long-term residence status corresponds to resettlement's character as a durable solution. The failure of support from their home countries makes refugees so dependent on long-term residence status. Thus, the recommendation *de lege ferenda* consists of reducing disproportionate hurdles to access long-term residence status by harmonizing the requirements for such status in the EU within the limits established by CJEU case law, i.e. keeping examination to a basic level, refraining from excessive examination costs and accounting for the individual situation of the applicant. Still, EUMS must be afforded the opportunity to have their national values reflected in the content of language and civic integration tests.

Concerning the access to citizenship, CJEU case law determines that EUMS authorities must assess the implications of EU citizenship on the individual applicant when deciding on the granting or refusing of national citizenship of resettlement beneficiaries.

Finally, successful integration and naturalization in the receiving country imply that this country becomes the "*own country*" of a resettlement beneficiary. Ideally, the interests of the resettlement beneficiary and the receiving country become blended during the integration process. On the one hand, the resettlement beneficiary should achieve a durable solution and self-sufficiency, and on the other hand, this country gains interest in keeping the resettlement beneficiary, as he or she has become a beneficial contributor to the receiving economy and society.

Ultimately, it seems too idealistic to assume that increased EU regulatory involvement in the field of resettlement will entirely eliminate human rights abuses. Likely, there will be opposing EUMS preferring to build a fortress instead of setting a sign of solidarity with third countries and protection seekers. Nevertheless, within the scope of its competences, the

EU has regulatory power[1286] to foster human rights compliance in EU resettlement, a previously legally grey area. Supposing the claim that the EU "*affects the lives of many people in ways they perceive as profoundly unjust*"[1287] contains a grain of truth, the EU now has the chance to prove the opposite by developing an EU resettlement policy that positively affects the lives of people within and beyond its external borders.

1286 See Anu Bredford, *The Brussels Effect: How the European Union Rules the World* (Oxford University Press 2020) 288.

1287 Dimitry Kochenov, Gráinne de Búrca and Andrew Williams, 'How just is the EU, or: is there a 'new' European deficit?' (*Verfassungsblog*, 10 June 2015) <https://verfassungsblog.de/how-just-is-the-eu-or-is-there-a-new-european-deficit-2/> accessed 27 March 2021.

Bibliography

General

Kenneth W ABBOTT and Duncan SNIDAL, 'Hard and Soft Law in International Governance', in (2000) 54 Legalization and World Politics 3, Special Issue, 'International Organization', 421-456

Tendayi ACHIUME, 'Migration as Decolonialization' in (2020) 71 Stanford Law Review, 1509-1574

Giorgio AGAMBEN, *Homo Sacer Sovereign Power and Bare Life* (Stanford University Press 1998)

AIDA and ECRE, 'Country Report: Introduction to the asylum context in Turkey' (last updated 30 November 2020) <https://asylumineurope.org/reports/country/turkey/introduction-asylum-context-turkey/> accessed 16 June 2021

Jean ALLAIN, 'The Jus Cogens Nature of Non-Refoulement' in (2002) 13 International Journal of Refugee Law, 533-558

AMNESTY INTERNATIONAL, 'Refugee Rights in 2018' (2018) <https://www.amnesty.org/en/latest/research/2018/12/rights-today-2018-refugees/> accessed 20 June 2021

Elena ANDREEVSKA, 'The Legal Protection of Refugee: Western Balkanas' in (2016) 23 Lex ET Scientia International Journal 2, 85-99

Kiran BANERJEE, 'Rethinking the Global Governance of International Protection' in (2018) 56 Columbia Journal of Transnational Law, 313-326

Ilias BANTEKAS and Lutz OETTE, *International Human Rights Law and Practice* (Cambridge University Press 3rd ed 2020)

Carol BATCHELOR and Edwina O'SHEA, 'The internationalization of resettlement: lessons from Syria and Bhutan' in (2017) 54 Forced Migration Review, 9-11 <https://www.refworld.org/docid/58cbcb314.html> accessed 13 February 2021

Alexander BETTS and Jean François DURIEUX, 'Convention Plus as a Norm-Setting Exercise' in (2007) 20 Journal of Refugee Studies 3, 509-530

Albert BLECKMANN, 'Das Souveränitätsprinzip im Völkerrecht' in (1985) 23 Archiv des Völkerrechts 4, 450-477 <https://www.jstor.org/stable/40798156?seq=1> accessed 20 March 2021

Albert BLECKMANN, 'Zur Verbindlichkeit des allgemeinen Völkerrechts für internationale Organisationen' in (1977) 37 Zeitschrift für ausländisches öffentliches Recht und Völkerrecht 107-121

Michael BOTHE, 'Legal and Non-Legal Norms – a meaningful distinction in international relations?' in (1980) 11 Netherlands Yearbook of International Law, 65-95

Başak ÇALI, 'General Comment No 6: Treatment of Unaccompanied and Separated Children Outside Their Country of Origin ' for extra-territorial jurisdiction come of age? Karlsruhe, too, has spoken, now it's Strasbourg's turn' (*EJIL: Talk!*, 21 July 2020) <https://www.ejiltalk.org/has-control-over-rights-doctrine-for-extra-territorial-jurisdiction-come-of-age-karlsruhe-too-has-spoken-now-its-strasbourgs-turn/> accessed 27 March 2021

Brendon J CANNON and Hirotaka FUJIBAYASHI, 'Security, structural factors and sovereignty: Analyzing reactions to Kenya's decision to close the Dadaab refugee camp complex' in (2018) 27 African Security Review 1, 20-41

David CANTOR, Nikolas FEITH TAN, Marianna GKILIATI, Elisabeth MAVROPOULOU et al, 'Externalisation, Access to Territorial Asylum, and International Law' in (2022) International Journal of Refugee Law, 1-37

Randy CAPPS et al, 'Integrating refugees in the United States: The successes and challenges of resettlement in a Global context' in (2015) Statistical Journal of the IAOS, 341-367

Amanda CELLINI, 'The resettlement of Hungarian refugees in 1956' in (2017) 54 Forced Migration Review, 6-8 <https://www.refworld.org/docid/58cbcb314.html> accessed 13 February 2021

Vincent CHETAIL, *International Migration Law* (Oxford University Press 2019)

Vincent CHETAIL and Céline BAULOZ (eds), *Research Handbook on International Law and Migration* (Edward Elgar Publishing 2014)

Bhupinder S CHIMNI, 'The Geopolitics of Refugee Studies: A View from the South' in (1998) 11 Journal of Refugee Studies 4, 350-374

COMMITTEE AGAINST TORTURE, 'General Comment No 4 (2017) on the implementation of Article 3 of the Convention in the context of Article 22', CAT/C/GC/4 (4 September 2018) <https://tbinternet.ohchr.org/_layouts/15/treatybodyexternal/Download.aspx?symbolno=CAT%2fC%2fGC%2f4&Lang=en> accessed 14 February 2021

COMMITTEE ON ECONOMIC SOCIAL AND CULTURAL RIGHTS, 'General Comment No 24 on State obligations under the International Covenant on Economic, Social and Cultural Rights in the context of business activities', UN Doc E/C.12/GC/24 (10 August 2017)

COMMITTEE ON THE ELIMINATION OF DISCRIMINATION AGAINST WOMEN, 'General recommendation No 32 on the gender-related dimensions of refugee status, asylum, nationality and statelessness of women', UN Doc CEDAW/C/GC/32 (14 November 2014) <https://www.refworld.org/docid/54620fb54.html> accessed 21 June 2021

COMMITTEE ON THE RIGHTS OF THE CHILD, 'Decision adopted by the Committee on the Rights of the Child under the Optional Protocol to the Convention on the Rights of the Child on a communications procedure in respect of Communication No 104/2019: Sacchi et al v Argentina', UN Doc CRC/C/88/D/104/2019 (8 October 2021)

COMMITTEE ON THE RIGHTS OF THE CHILD, 'Decision adopted by the Committee under the Optional Protocol to the Convention on the Rights of the Child on a communications procedure, concerning communications No 79/2019 and No 109/2019', UN Doc CRC/C/85/D/79/2019 – CRC/C/85/D/109/2019 (2 November 2020)

COMMITTEE ON THE RIGHTS OF THE CHILD, 'General Comment No 6: Treatment of Unaccompanied and Separated Children Outside Their Country of Origin' (1 September 2006) <https://digitallibrary.un.org/record/566055?ln=en> accessed 14 February 2021

James CRAWFORD, *Brownlie's Principles of Public International Law* (Oxford University Press 9th ed 2019)

James CRAWFORD, *State Responsibility: The General Part* (Cambridge University Press 2013)

James CRAWFORD, 'The ILC's Articles on Responsibility of States for Internationally Wrongful Acts: A Retrospect' in (2002) 96 American Journal of International Law 4, 874-890

James CRAWFORD and Martti KOSKENNIEMI (eds), *The Cambridge Companion to International Law* (Cambridge University Press 2012)

Mary CROCK, Laura SMITH-KAHN, Ron MCCALLUM and Ben SAUL, *The Legal Protection of Refugees with Disabilities, Forgotten and Invisible?* (Elgar Publishing 2017)

Christian DAHLMAN, 'The function of Opinio Juris in Customary International Law' in (2012) Nordic Journal of International Law, 328-339

Milka DIMITROVSKA, 'The Concept of International Responsibility of State in the International Public Law System' in (2015) 1 Journal of Liberty and International Affairs 2, 1-16

Annika DIPPEL, *Extraterritorialer Grundrechtsschutz gemäß Art 16a GG* (Duncker & Humboldt 2020)

Oliver DÖRR and Kirsten SCHMALENBACH (eds), *Vienna Convention on the Law of Treaties: A Commentary* (Springer 2nd ed 2018)

Melonee DOUGLAS, Rachel LEVITAN and Lucy W KIAMA, 'Expanding the role of NGOs in resettlement' in (2017) 54 Forced Migration Review, 34-37

Rebecca DOWD and Jane Mc ADAM, 'International Cooperation and Responsibility-Sharing to Protect Refugees: What, Why, and How?' in (2017) 66 International and Comparative Law Quaterly, 863-892

ECOSOC, 'Guiding Principles on International Displacement', UN Doc E/CN4/1998/53/Add2 (11 February 1998) <https://undocs.org/E/CN.4/1998/53/Add.2> accessed 20 March 2021

Alice EDWARDS, 'Human Rights, Refugees and the Right 'to Enjoy' Asylum' in (2005) 17 International Journal of Refugee Law, 293-330

Molli FEE, 'Pre-resettlement experiences: Iranians in Vienna' in (2017) 54 Forced Migration Review, 23-24

Erika FELLER and Anja KLUG, 'Refugees, United Nations High Commissioner for (UNHCR)' (MPIL, January 2013) <https://opil.ouplaw.com/view/10.1093/law:epil/9780199231690/law-9780199231690-e530> accessed 20 March 2021

Susan FRATZKE and Lena KAINZ, 'Preparing for the unknown: Designing effective predeparture orientation for resettling refugees' (May 2019) 1-38 <https://www.migrationpolicy.org/research/designing-effective-predeparture-orientation-resettling-refugees> accessed 13 February 2021

Bill FRELICK, Ian M KYSEL and Jennifer PODKUL, 'The Impact of Externalization of Migration Controls on the Rights of Asylum Seekers and Other Migrants' in (2016) 4 Journal on Migration and Security 4, 190-220 <https://www.hrw.org/sites/default/files/supporting_resources/jmhs.pdf> accessed 21 June 2021

Michael Lysander FREMUTH, 'Access Denied? – Human Rights Approaches to Compensate forthe Absence of a Right to Be Granted Asylum' in (2020) 4 University of Vienna Law Review 1 Special Issue: Slovenian-Austrian Law Conference, 79-115

Georgio GAJA, 'Articles on the Responsibility of International Organizations' (9 December 2011) <https://legal.un.org/avl/ha/ario/ario.html> accessed 21 June 2021

Thomas GAMMELTOFT-HANSEN, *Access to asylum: international refugee law and the globalisation of migration control* (Cambridge University Press 2011)

Thomas GAMMELTOFT-HANSEN and James C HATHAWAY, 'Non-Refoulement in World of Cooperative Deterrence' in (2015) 53 Columbia Journal of Transnational Law 2, 235-284

Thomas GAMMELTOFT-HANSEN and Jens VEDSTED-HANSEN (eds), *Human rights and the dark side of globalisation: Transnational law enforcement and migration control* (Routledge 2016)

Adèle GARNIER, 'The COVID-19 Resettlement Suspension: Impact, Exemptions and the Road Ahead' (*FluchtforschungsBlog*, 16 June 2020) <https://blog.fluchtforschung.net/the-covid-19-resettlement-suspension/> accessed 13 February 2021

Adèle GARNIER, 'Migration Management and Humanitarian Protection: The UNHCR's 'Resettlement Expansionism' and its Impact on Policy-Making in the EU and Australia' in (2014) 40 Journal of Ethnic and Migration Studies 6, 942-959

Adèle GARNIER, Kristin Bergtora SANDVIK and Amanda CELLINI, 'The COVID-19 Resettlement Freeze: Towards a Permanent Suspension?' (14 April 2020) <https://www.kaldorcentre.unsw.edu.au/publication/covid-19-resettlement-freeze-towards-permanent-suspension> accessed 28 February 2021

Adèle GARNIER, Liliana Lyra JUBILUT and Kristin Bergtora SANDVIK (eds), *Refugee Resettlement: Power, Politics, and Humanitarian Governance* (Berghahn 2018)

N Ela GÖKALP Aras and Zeynep Sahin MENCÜTEK, '*Refugee Protection: Turkey Report*', Paper 2020/30 (January 2020) <https://www.researchgate.net/profile/Zeynep-Mencutek/publication/340236818_Refugee_Protection_Turkey_Report_Working_Papers_Global_Migration_Consequences_and_Responses/links/5e7e4ee192851caef4a56b41/Refugee-Protection-Turkey-Report-Working-Papers-Global-Migration-Consequences-and-Responses.pdf> accessed 16 June 2021

Guy S OODWIN-GILL, 'Article 31 of the 1951 Convention Relating to the Status of Refugees: non-penalization, detention, and protection' (2001) <https://www.unhcr.org/en-us/publications/legal/419c778d4/refugee-protection-international-law-article-31-1951-convention-relating.html> accessed 8 July 2022

Guy S GOODWIN-GILL, *The Refugee in International Law* (Oxford University Press 1983)

Guy S GOODWIN-GILL, Jane Mc ADAM and Emma DUNLOP, *The Refugee in International Law* (Oxford University Press 4th ed 2021)

Guy S GOODWIN-GILL, and Jane Mc ADAM, *The Refugee in International Law* (Oxford University Press 3rd ed 2007)

Guy S GOODWIN-GILL and Philippe WECKEL (eds), *Migration & Refugee Protection in the 21st Century: Legal Aspects – The Hague Academy of International Centre for Research* (Martinus Nijhoff 2015)

Atle GRAHL-MADSEN, *Commentary on the Refugee Convention 1951: Articles 2-11, 13-37* (Division of International Protection of the UNHCR 1997) <https://www.unhcr.org/3d4ab5fb9.pdf> accessed 21 February 2021

Atle GRAHL-MADSEN, *The Status of Refugees in International Law: Volume II* (AW Sijthoff 1972)

Naoko HASHIMOTO, 'Refugee Resettlement as an Alternative to Asylum' in (2018) 37 Refugee Survey Quarterly, 162-186

James C HATHAWAY, *The Rights of Refugees Under International Law* (Cambridge University Press 2nd ed 2021)

James C HATHAWAY, *The Rights of Refugees Under International Law* (Cambridge University Press 2005)

James C HATHAWAY and R Alexander NEVE, 'Making international Refugee Law Relevant again: A proposal of Collectivized and Solution-Orientated Protection' in (1997) 10 Harvard Human Rights Journal, 115-211

Arthur C HELTON, 'What Is Refugee Protection' in (1990) 2 International Journal of Refugee Law, 119-129

Stephan HOBE, 'Non-Governmental Organizations' (MPIL, June 2019) <https://opil.ouplaw.com/view/10.1093/law:epil/9780199231690/law-9780199231690-e968?rskey=LXvy3A&result=1&prd=MPIL> accessed 13 February 2021

Constantin HRUSCHKA (ed), *Genfer Flüchtlingskonvention: Handkommentar* (Nomos 2022)

Chris INGLESE, 'Soft law' in (1993) 20 Polish Yearbook of International Law, 75-90

ILC, 'Draft Articles on the Responsibility of International Organizations, with commentaries' (ARIO Commentary 2011) <https://legal.un.org/ilc/texts/instruments/english/commentaries/9_11_2011.pdf> accessed 27 March 2021

ILC, 'Seventh report on the responsibility of international organizations (prepared by G Gaja, Special Rapporteur)', UN Doc A CN4/610 (2009) <https://legal.un.org/ilc/documentation/english/a_cn4_610.pdf> accessed 21 February 2021

INTERNATIONAL RESCUE COMMITTEE, CARITAS EUROPE, EUROPEAN COUNCIL ON REFUGEES AND EXILES, INTERNATIONAL CATHOLIC MIGRATION COMMISSION, CURCHES' COMMISSION FOR MIGRANTS IN EUROPE, SHARE NETWORK AND RED CROSS EU OFFICE, 'Joint Resettlement: Resettlement Can't Wait' (23 September 2020) <https://www.ecre.org/wp-content/uploads/2020/09/Joint-Statement.-Resettlement-can‘t-wait.pdf> accessed 17 June 2021

IOM, 'Resettlement' <https://eea.iom.int/resettlement> accessed 11 September 2022

IOM, 'UNHCR announce temporary suspension of resettlement travel for refugees' (*Press release*, 17 April 2020) <https://www.iom.int/news/iom-unhcr-announce-temporary-suspension-resettlement-travel-refugees> accessed 27 February 2021

IOM, 'First IOM International Charter Flight from Ethiopia Brings 154 Refugees to New Homes in Germany' (18 October 2019) <https://www.iom.int/news/first-iom-international-charter-flight-ethiopia-brings-154-refugees-new-homes-germany> accessed 14 February 2021

IOM, 'Glossary on Migration No 34' (2019) <https://publications.iom.int/system/files/pdf/iml_34_glossary.pdf> accessed 13 February 2021

Anne IRFAN, 'Rejecting resettlement: the case of Palestinians' in (2017) 54 Forced Migration Review, 68-71

Miles JACKSON, *Complicity in International Law* (Oxford University Press 2015)

Stian Øby JOHANSEN, 'Human Rights Accountability of CSDP Missions on Migration' (*Eumigrationlawblog.eu*, 8 October 2020) <http://eumigrationlawblog.eu/human-rights-accountability-of-csdp-missions-on-migration/#more-2839> accessed 28 February 2021

Stian Øby JOHANSEN, 'Dual Attribution of Conduct to both an International Organization and a Member State' in (2019) 6 Oslo Law Review 3, 178-197

Will JONES and Alexander TEYTELBOYM, ''Matching' refugees' in (2017) 54 Forced Migration Review, 25

Sarah JOSEPH and Melissa CASTAN, *The International Covenant on Civil and Politcal Rights: Cases, Materials and Commentary* (Oxford University Press 3rd ed 2013)

Satvinder Singh JUSS (ed), *Research Handbook on International Refugee Law* (Edward Elgar 2019)

Walter KÄLIN and Jörg KÜNZLI, *The Law of International Human Rights Protection* (Oxford University Press 2nd ed 2019)

Ibrahim KANALAN, 'Extraterritorial State Obligations Beyond the Concept of Jurisdiction' in (2018) 19 German Law Journal 1, 43-63

Susan KNEEBONE (ed), *Refugees, asylum seekers and the rule of law: comparative perspectives* (Cambridge University Press 2009)

Dieter KUGELMANN, 'Refugees' (MPIL, March 2010) <https://opil.ouplaw.com/view/10.1093/law:epil/9780199231690/law-9780199231690-e866> accessed 4 July 2021.

Tally KRITZMAN-AMIR, 'Not In My Backyard: On the Morality of Responsibility Sharing in Refugee Law' in (2009) 34 Brooklyn Journal of International Law 2, 355-393

Mark LICHTBACK and Ellen ZUCKERMAN (eds), *Comparative Politics: Rationality, Culture, and Structure* (Cambridge University Press 1997)

Annelisa LINDSAY, 'Surge and selection: power in the refugee resettlement regime' in (2017) 54 Forced Migration Review, 11-13 <https://www.refworld.org/docid/58cbcb314.html> accessed 28 February 2021

Gil LOESCHER, *The UNHCR and World Politics: A perilious path* (Oxford University Press 2001)

Gil LOESCHER, 'The UNHCR and World Politics: State Interest vs Institutional Autonomy' in (2001) 35 The International Migration Review 1, Special Issue, 'UNHCR at 50: Past, Present and Future of Refugee Assistance', 33-56

Gil LOESCHER and James MILNER, 'Understanding the challenge' in (2009) 33 Forced Migration Review, 9-11 <https://www.fmreview.org/sites/fmr/files/FMRdownloads/ en/FMRpdfs/FMR33/FMR33.pdf> accessed 13 February 2021

Ian MACGIBBON, 'The Scope of Acquiescence in International Law' in (1954) 31 British Yearbook of International Law, 143-186

Jane MCADAM, 'Protecting People Displaced by the Impacts of Climate Change: The UN Human Rights Committee and the Principle of Non-refoulement' (2020) 114 American Journal of International Law 4, 708-725

Rutsel MARTHA and Stephen BAILEY, 'The right to enter his or her own country' (*EJIL: Talk!*, 23 June 2020) <https://www.ejiltalk.org/the-right-to-enter-his-or-her-own-country/> accessed 27 March 2021

Giuseppe de MICHELIS, *Conference international de l'émigration et de l'immigration, Rome 15-31 mai 1924* (Imprimerie de la Chambre des Députés – Raison C Colombo 1925)

David MILLER, *Strangers in our midst* (Harvard University Press 2016)

Harriet MOYNIHAN, 'Aiding or Assisting: Challenges in Armed Conflict' (November 2016) <https://www.chathamhouse.org/sites/default/files/publications/research/2016-11-11-aiding-assisting-challenges-armed-conflict-moynihan.pdf> accessed 27 August 2022

Haruno NAKASHIBA, 'Clarifying UNHCR Resettlement: A few considerations from a legal perspective', UNHCR Research Paper n°264 (November 2013) <https://www.unhcr.org/research/working/528e0a139/clarifying-unhcr-resettlement-few-considerations-legal-perspective-haruno.html> accessed 13 February 2021

Haruno NAKASHIBA, 'Postmillennial UNHCR refugee resettlement: New developments and challenges', UNHCR Research Paper n°265 (November 2013) <https://www.unhcr.org/research/working/528e15259/postmillenial-unhcr-refugee-resettlement-new-developments-old-challenges.html> accessed 13 February 2021

James P NIESSEN, 'The Culture of Welcome and the January, 1957 Austrian Refugee Quota Proposal' (2016) <https://rucore.libraries.rutgers.edu/rutgers-lib/50546/PDF/1/play/> accessed 13 February 2021

Gregor NOLL and Joanne van SELM, 'Rediscovering Resettlement' in (2003) 3 Migration Policy Institute Insight <https://www.migrationpolicy.org/research/rediscovering-resettlement> accessed 13 February 2021

Leomoi OCHAN, Abikar ABDIKAR and Kim HAEUNH, 'Educating for return: Somali refugees in Dadaab' in (2019) Forced Migration Review, 36-37 <https://www.fmreview.org/sites/fmr/files/FMRdownloads/en/return/leomoi-abikar-kim.pdf> accessed 13 February 2021

OHCHR, 'Communication No 3042/2017: AS, DI, OI and GD v Italy', UN Doc CCPR/C/130/D/3042/2017 (27 January 2021)

OHCHR, 'Communication No 2728/2016: Ione Teitiota v New Zealand', UN Doc CCPR/C/127/D/2728/2016 (23 September 2020) <https://demaribus.files.wordpress.com/2020/02/2728-2016.pdf> accessed 19 June 2021

OHCHR, 'Spain's age assessment procedures violate migrant children's rights, UN committee finds' (13 October 2020) <https://ohchr.org/EN/NewsEvents/Pages/DisplayNews.aspx?NewsID=26375&LangID=E> accessed 21 June 2021

OHCHR, 'General Comment No 36: Article 6 (Right to Life)', UN Doc CCPR/C/GC/36 (3 September 2019) <https://tbinternet.ohchr.org/_layouts/15/treatybodyexternal/ Download.aspx?symbolno=CCPR/C/GC/36&Lang=en> accessed 13 February 2021

OHCHR, 'Interim report of the Special Rapporteur on torture and other cruel, inhuman or degrading treatment or punishment', UN Doc CCPR/C/GC/36 (7 August 2015) <https://www.ohchr.org/en/documents/thematic-reports/a77502-interim-report-special-rapporteur-torture-and-other-cruel-inhuman> accessed 5 May 2023

OHCHR, 'Communication No 1539/2006: Mohammad Munaf v Romania', UN Doc CCPR/C/96/D/1539/2006 (21 August 2009) <https://www.refworld.org/cases,HRC,4acf500d2.html> accessed 14 February 2021

OHCHR, 'Communication No 1493/2006: Lecraft v Spain', UN Doc CCPR/C/96/D/1493/2006 (17 August 2009) <https://documents-dds-ny.un.org/doc/UNDOC/GEN/G09/442/84/PDF/G0944284.pdf?OpenElement> accessed 10 July 2022

OHCHR, 'Communication No 1477/2006: Maksudov and Others v Kyrgyzstan', UN Doc CCPR/C/93/D/1461,1462,1476 and 1477/2006 (31 July 2008) <https://www.refworld.org/cases,HRC,4a93a0cd2.html> accessed 18 February 2021

OHCHR, 'General Comment No 32: Article 14: Right to equality before courts and tribunals and to a fair trial', UN Doc CCPR/C/GC/32 (23 August 2007) <https://www.refworld.org/docid/478b2b2f2.html> accessed 18 February 2021

OHCHR, 'Communication No 1136/2002: Bozov v Estonia', UN Doc CCPR/C/81/D/1136/2002 (25 August 2004) <http://hrlibrary.umn.edu/undocs/html/1136-2002.html> accessed 21 February 2021

OHCHR, 'General comment No 31: The nature of the general legal obligation imposed on States Parties to the Covenant', UN Doc CCPR/C/21/Rev1/Add13 (26 May 2004) <https://www.refworld.org/docid/478b26ae2.html> accessed 13 February 2021

OHCHR, 'Communication No 864/1999: Alfonso Ruiz Agudo v Spain', UN Doc CCPR/C/76/D/864/1999 (31 October 2002) <http://www.worldcourts.com/hrc/eng/decisions/2002.10.31_Ruiz_Agudo_v_Spain.htm > accessed 21 July 2022

OHCHR, 'Communication No 919/2000: Mr Michael Andreas Müller and Imke Engelhard v Namibia', UN Doc CCPR/C/74/D/919/2000 (26 March 2002) <http://hrlibrary.umn.edu/undocs/919-2000.html> accessed 20 July 2022

OHCHR, 'General Comment No 27: Article 12 (Freedom of Movement)', UN Doc CCPR/C/21/Rev1/Add9 (2 November 1999) <https://www.refworld.org/docid/45139c394.html> accessed 16 February 2021

OHCHR, 'General Comment No 20: Article 7 (Prohibition of torture, or other cruel, inhuman or degrading treatment or punishment)', UN Doc HRI/GEN/1/Rev9 (Vol I) (10 March 1992) <https://www.refworld.org/docid/453883fb0.html> accessed 14 February 2021

OHCHR, 'General Comment No 19: Article 23 (The Family) Protection of the Family, the Right to Marriage and Equality of the Spouses' (27 July 1990) <https://www.refworld.org/pdfid/45139bd74.pdf> accessed 21 July 2022

OHCHR, 'Communication No 196/1985: Gueye v France' (1989) <http://hrlibrary.umn.edu/undocs/session35/196-1985.html> accessed 10 July 2022

OHCHR, 'General Comment No 18: Non-discrimination', UN Doc HRI/GEN/1/Rev9 (Vol I) (10 November 1989) <https://www.refworld.org/docid/453883fa8.html> accessed 20 February 2021

OHCHR, 'General Comment No 16: Article 17 (Right to Privacy), The Right to Respect of Privacy, Family, Home and Correspondence, and Protection of Honour and Reputation', UN Doc HRI/GEN/1/Rev9 (Vol I) (8 April 1988) <www.refworld.org/docid/453883f922.html> accessed 21 June 2021

OHCHR, 'CCPR General Comment No 15: The position of aliens under the Covenant' UN Doc HRI/GEN/1/Rev1 (11 April 1986) <https://www.refworld.org/docid/45139acfc.html> accessed 20 February 2021

Obiora Chinedu OKAFOR, 'Cascading towards "De-Solidarity"? The Unfolding of Global Refugee Protection' in (30 August 2019) TWAILR Reflections 2 <https://twailr.com/cascading-toward-de-solidarity-the-unfolding-of-global-refugee-protection/> accessed 27 February 2021

Brian OPESKIN, Richard PERRUCHOUD and Jillyann REDPATH-CROSS (eds), *Foundations of International Migration Law* (Cambridge University Press 2012)

Maria O'SULLIVAN, 'Can States cease the protection status of resettled refugees?' (*Asylum Insight*, November 2019) <https://www.asyluminsight.com/maria-osullivan#.Xd0yrndFzt4> accessed 27 March 2021

Annick PIJNENBURG, 'Containment Instead of *Refoulement*: Shifting State Responsibility in the Age of Cooperative Migration Control' in (2020) Human Rights Law Review, 306-322

Margret AM PIPER, Paul POWER and Graham THOM, 'Refugee Resettlement: 2012 and Beyond', UNHCR Research Paper n°253 (February 2013) <https://www.unhcr.org/research/working/510bd3979/refugee-resettlement-2012-beyond-margaret-piper-paul-power-dr-graham-thom.html> accessed 13 February 2021

Janine PRANTL, Mark J WOOD and Michael W DOYLE, 'Principles of Responsibility Sharing: Proximity, Culpability, Moral Accountability and Capability' in (June 2022) California Law Review 3 <https://www.californialawreview.org/print/principles-for-responsibility-sharing-proximity-culpability-moral-accountability-and-capability/> accessed 16 August 2022

REFUGEE COUNCIL OF AUSTRALIA, 'Global resettlement statistics' (as of 2 August 2019) <https://www.refugeecouncil.org.au/global-resettlement-statistics/> accessed 13 February 2021

August REINISCH (ed) *Österreichisches Handbuch des Völkerrechts* I (Manz 5th ed 2013)

Kristin Bergtora SANDVIK and Katja Lindskov JACOBSEN (eds), *UNHCR and the Struggle for Accountability* (Routledge 2016)

William SCHABAS, *The Customary International Law of Human Rights* (Oxford University Press 2021)

Olivier de SCHUTTER, *International Human Rights Law: Cases, Materials, Commentary* (Cambridge University Press 3rd ed 2019)

Joanne van SELM, 'Public-Private Partnerships in Refugee Resettlement: Europe and the US' in (2003) 4 Journal of International Migration and Integration 2, 157-174

William SEWELL, 'Three Temporalities: Toward a Sociology of the Event', CSST Working Paper No 58, CRSO Working Paper No 448 (October 1990) <https://deepblue.lib.umich.edu/bitstream/handle/2027.42/51215/448.pdf?sequence=1&isAllowed=y> accessed 13 February 2021

Yuval SHANY, 'Taking Universality Seriously: A Functional Approach to Extraterritoriality in International Human Rights Law' in (2013) 7 Law and Ethics of Human Rights, 47-71

Malcolm SHAW, *International Law* (Cambridge University Press 6th ed 2008)

Wiebke SIEVERS, Rainer BAUBÖCK, Christoph REINPRECHT (eds), *Flucht und Asyl – Internationale und österreichische Perspektiven* (VÖAW 2021)

James C SIMEON (ed), *The UNHCR and the Supervision of International Refugee Law* (Cambridge University Press 2013)

Nikolaos SITAOPOULOS, 'Why International Migration Law Does not Give a License to Discriminate' (*EJIL: Talk!*, 20 May 2015) <https://www.ejiltalk.org/why-international-migration-law-does-not-give-a-license-to-discriminate/> accessed 20 February 2021

Amy SLAUGHTER, 'How NGOs have helped shape resettlement' in (2017) 54 Forced Migration Review, 32-34

Maja SMRKOLJ, 'International Institutions and Individualized Decision-Making: An Example of UNHCR's Refugee Status Determination' in (2008) 9 German Law Journal 11, 1779-1803

Clara STRAIMER, 'Vulnerable or invisible? asylum seekers with disabilities in Europe', Research Paper No 194 (November 2010) <https://www.unhcr.org/4cd9765b9.pdf> accessed 21 June 2021

Astri SUHRKE, 'Burden-sharing during Refugee Emergencies: The Logic of Collective versus National Action' in (1998) 11 Journal of Refugee Studies 4, 396-415

William Lacy SWING, 'Practical considerations for effective resettlement' in (2017) 54 Forced Migration Review, <https://www.refworld.org/docid/58cbcb314.html> accessed 27 March 2021

TAGUNGSDOKUMENTATION, *Resettlement und komplementäre Zugangswege: Neue Wege – neue Länder* (Frankfurt am Main 13-14 May 2019) <https://resettlement.de/wp-content/uploads/Dokumentation-Fachtagung-Resettlement-Mai-2019.pdf> accessed 14 February 2021

Daniel THÜRER, 'Soft law' (MPIL, March 2019) <https://opil.ouplaw.com/view/10.1093/law:epil/9780199231690/law-9780199231690-e1469> accessed 13 February 2021

Tullio TREVES, 'Customary International Law' (MPIL, November 2006) <https://opil.ouplaw.com/view/10.1093/law:epil/9780199231690/law-9780199231690-e1393> accessed 13 February 2021

Garry G TROELLER, 'UNHCR Resettlement: Evolution and Future Direction' in (2002) 14 International Journal of Refugee Law 1, 85-95

Garry G TROELLER, 'UNHCR Resettlement as an Instrument of International Protection: Constraints and Obstacles in the Arena of Competition for Scarce Humanitarian Resources' in (1991) 3 International Journal of Refugee Law 3, 564-578

Volker TÜRK, 'Prospects for Responsibility Sharing in the Refugee Context' in (2016) 4 Journal on Migration and Human Security 3, 45-58

UN, 'COVID-19: Agencies temporarily suspend refugee resettlement travel' (17 March 2020) <https://news.un.org/en/story/2020/03/1059602> accessed 27 February 2021

UN, 'Interview: "Refugees are the responsibility of the world... Proximity doesn't define responsibility." – Peter Sutherland' (*UN News*, 2 October 2015) <https://news.un.org/en/story/2015/10/511282-interview-refugees-are-responsibility-world-proximity-doesnt-define> accessed 16 June 2021

UN GENERAL ASSEMBLY, 'Final Act of the United Nations Conference of Plenipotentiaries on the Status of Refugees and Stateless Persons', Recommendation D (25 July 1951) <https://www.unhcr.org/protection/travaux/40a8a7394/final-act-united-nations-conference-plenipotentiaries-status-refugees-stateless.html> accessed 13 February 2021

UNHCR, 'Contributions' (as of 29 June 2022) <https://reporting.unhcr.org/contributions> accessed 29 June 2022

UNHCR, 'Procedural Standards for Refugee Status Determination under UNHCR's Mandate' <https://www.refworld.org/pdfid/42d66dd84.pdf> accessed 13 February 2021

UNHCR, 'Projected Global Resettlement Needs 2023' (June 2022) <https://www.unhcr.org/62b18e714> accessed 24 June 2022

UNHCR, 'Resettlement Data' <https://www.unhcr.org/resettlement-data.html> accessed 24 June 2022

UNHCR, 'The Executive Committee's origins and mandate' <https://www.unhcr.org/executive-committee.html> accessed 13 February 2021

UNHCR, 'The 10-Point Plan', Chapter 7 Solutions <https://www.unhcr.org/50a4c17f9.pdf> accessed 24 June 2022

UNHCR, 'Refugee Data Finder' (as of 16 June 2022) <https://www.unhcr.org/refugee-statistics/> accessed 27 June 2022

UNHCR, '2020 Planning Summary' (20 December 2019) <http://reporting.unhcr.org/sites/default/files/pdfsummaries/GA2020-Turkey-eng.pdf> accessed 21 February 2021

UNHCR, 'Global Refugee Forum pledges collective action for better refugee inclusion, education, jobs' (*Press release*, 18 December 2019) <https://www.unhcr.org/news/press/2019/12/5dfa56b54/global-refugee-forum-pledges-collective-action-better-refugee-inclusion.html> accessed 27 March 2021

UNHCR, 'UNHCR troubled by latest US refugee resettlement cut' (*Press release*, 4 November 2019) <https://www.unhcr.org/news/press/2019/11/5dbd87337/unhcr-troubled-latest-refugee-resettlement-cut.html> accessed 13 February 2021

UNHCR, 'Global Trends: Forced Displacement in 2018' (20 June 2019) <https://www.unhcr.org/5d08d7ee7.pdf> accessed 13 February 2021

UNHCR, Report 'Global compact on refugees', UN Doc A/73/12 (Part II) (13 September 2018) <https://www.unhcr.org/gcr/GCR_English.pdf> accessed 13 February 2021

UNHCR, 'Conclusions on International Protection: Adopted by the Executive Committee of the UNHCR Programme 1975-2017 (Conclusion No 1 – 114)', UN Doc HCR/IP/3/Eng/REV 2017 (October 2017) <https://www.refworld.org/pdfid/5a2ead6b4.pdf> accessed 13 February 2021

UNHCR, 'Proposal for a Regulation of the European Parliament and of the Council establishing a Union Resettlement Framework and amending Regulation (EU) No 516/2014 of the European Parliament and the Council, COM(2016) 468 final 2016/0225 (COD): UNHCR's Observations and Recommendations' (November 2016) <https://www.refworld.org/pdfid/5890b1d74.pdf> accessed 21 February 2021

UNHCR, 'Frequently Asked Questions about Resettlement' (September 2013) <https://www.refworld.org/pdfid/4ac0d7e52.pdf> accessed 13 February 2021

UNHCR, *Resettlement Handbook* (revised ed July 2011) <http://www.unhcr.org/protection/resettlement/46f7c0ee2/unhcr-resettlement-handbook-complete-publication.html?query=resettlement> accessed 13 February 2021

UNHCR, 'Comments by the United Nations High Commissioner for Refugees (UNHCR) to the Legislative Proposal amending the Citizenship Law', Nr 52/Lp11 (August 2012) <https://www.refworld.org/pdfid/57ed07954.pdf> accessed 24 July 2021

UNHCR, 'Protection Policy Paper: Maritime interception operations and the processing of international protection claims: legal standards and policy considerations with respect to extraterritorial processing' (November 2010) <https://www.refworld.org/docid/4cd12d3a2.html> accessed 21 February 2021

UNHCR, 'Advisory Opinion on the Extraterritorial Application of Non-Refoulement Obligations under the 1951 Convention relating to the Status of Refugees and its 1967 Protocol' (26 January 2007) <https://www.refworld.org/docid/45f17a1a4.html> accessed 16 February 2021

UNHCR, 'Multilateral Framework of Understandings on Resettlement', FORUM/2004/6 (16 September 2004) <https://www.unhcr.org/protection/convention/414aa7e54/multilateral-framework-understandings-resettlement-emforum20046em.html?query=Multilateral%20Framework%20of% 20Understandings%20on%20Resettlement> accessed 13 February 2021

UNHCR, 'Framework for durable solutions for refugees and persons of concern' (2003) <https://www.unhcr.org/partners/partners/3f1408764/framework-durable-solutions-refugees-persons-concern.html> accessed 24 June 2022

UNHCR, 'The Strategic Use of Resettlement', EC/53/SC/CRP.10/Add.1 (3 June 2003) <https://www.unhcr.org/excom/standcom/3edf57cd4/strategic-use-resettlement.html> accessed 13 February 2021

UNHCR, 'UNHCR receives report on Nairobi' (*Press release*, 25 January 2002) <https://www.unhcr.org/news/press/2002/1/3c513a284/unhcr-receives-report-nairobi-investigation.html> accessed 13 February 2021

UNHCR, *The Haitian Interdiction Case* 1993, Brief *Amicus Curiae* in (1994) 6 International Journal of Refugee Law 85, 94-97

UNHCR, *Handbook on Procedures and Criteria for Determining Refugee Status* (1992) <https://www.unhcr.org/publications/legal/5ddfcdc47/handbook-procedures-criteria-determining-refugee-status-under-1951-convention.html> accessed 14 February 2021

UNHCR, 'Resettlement as an Instrument of Protection: Traditional Problems Achieving This Durable Solution and New Directions in the 1990s', EC/SCP/65 (9 July 1991) <https://www.unhcr.org/excom/scip/3ae68ccc10/resettlement-instrument-protection-traditional-problems-achieving-durable.html> accessed 13 February 2021

UNHCR, 'Report of the United Nations High Commissioner for Refugees', UN Doc A/3585/Rev.1 (1 January 1958) <https://www.refworld.org/docid/3ae68c710.html> accessed 17 June 2021

UNHCR EXCOM Conclusion No 8 (XXVIII) 'Determination of Refugee Status' (1977) <https://www.unhcr.org/excom/exconc/3ae68c6e4/determination-refugee-status.html> accessed 6 July 2022

UNHCR EXCOM Conclusion No 30 (XXXIV) 'The Problem of Manifestly Unfounded or Abusive Applications for Refugee Status or Asylum' (1983) <https://www.unhcr.org/excom/exconc/3ae68c6118/problem-manifestly-unfounded-abusive-applications-refugee-status-asylum.html> accessed 6 July 2022

UNIVERSITY OF MICHIGAN LAW SCHOOL, 'The Michigan Guidelines on Refugee Freedom of Movement' (May 2017) para 10 <https://www.refworld.org/docid/592ee6614.html> accessed 14 February 2021

UN Treaty Collection, Chapter V Refugees and Stateless Persons: Protocol relating to the Status of Refugees (as of 19 September 2020) <https://treaties.un.org/pages/ViewDetails.aspx?src=TREATY&mtdsg_no=V-5&chapter=5#EndDec> accessed 21 February 2021

Sibel URANUES, '"Pushback" – Rechtliches über das "Unwort des Jahres" 2021 (Teil I)' (*Blogasyl*, June 30, 2022) <https://www.blogasyl.at/2022/06/pushback-teil-1/> accessed 6 July 2022.

Markus WAGNER, 'Non-State Actors' (MPIL, July 2013) <https://opil.ouplaw.com/view/10.1093/law:epil/9780199231690/law-9780199231690-e1445?rskey=0oAy0H&result=1&prd=MPIL> accessed 13 February 2021

WH, 'Why climate migrants do not have refugee status' (*The Economist*, 6 March 2018) <https://www.economist.com/the-economist-explains/2018/03/06/why-climate-migrants-do-not-have-refugee-status> accessed 13 February 2021

Michael WOOD, 'Customary international law and human rights' (Working Paper EUI 2016) <https://cadmus.eui.eu/handle/1814/44445> accessed 10 July 2021

Jan WOUTERS et al (eds), *Accountability for Human Rights Violations* (Intersentia 2010)

Marjoleine ZIECK, 'Refugees and the Right to Freedom of Movement: From Flight to Return' in (2018) 39 Michigan Journal of International Law 1, 19-116

Marjoleine ZIECK, 'Doomed to Fail from the Outset? UNHCR's Convention Plus Initiative Revisited' in (2009) 21 International Journal of Refugee Law 3, 387-420

Marjoleine ZIECK, *UNHCR's worldwide presence in the field* (Wolf Legal Publishers 2006)

Andreas ZIMMERMANN (ed), *The 1951 Convention Relating to the Status of Refugees and its 1967 Protocol* (Oxford University Press 2011)

Europe

Guido AMBROSO, 'The Balkans at a crossroads: Progress and challenges in finding durable solutions for refugees and displaced persons from the wars in the former Yugoslavia', UNHCR Research Paper no133 (November 2006) <https://www.unhcr.org/4552f2182.pdf> accessed 13 February 2021

ARBEITSGRUPPE CARITAS, DIAKONIE, IOM, ÖRK, UNHCR, 'Resettlement in Österreich' (revised July 2017) <https://www.caritas.at/fileadmin/storage/global/pdf/Resettlement_Konzept_für_Ö_update_2017.pdf> accessed 13 February 2021

Anthony ARNULL et al (eds), *A Constitutional Order of States? Essays in EU Law in Honour of Alan Dashwood* (Hart 2011)

Fulvio ATTINA, 'Tackling the Migrant Wave: EU as a Source and a Manager of Crisis' in 70 Revista Espanola de Derecho Internacional, 49-70

Katharina BAMBERG, 'The EU Resettlement Framework: From a humanitarian pathway to a migration management tool?', Discussion Paper European Migration and Diversity Programme (26 June 2018) <http://aei.pitt.edu/94238/1/pub_8632_euresettlement.pdf> accessed 13 February 2021

Jacopo BARIAGAZZI, 'Mediterranean countries give green light to deal on EU asylum agency' (*Politico*, 8 June 2021) <https://www.politico.eu/article/mediterranean-countries-green-light-deal-eu-asylum-agency/> accessed 16 June 2021

Hemme BATTJES, *European Asylum Law and International Law* (Martinus Nijhoff 2006)

Moritz BAUMGÄRTEL, *Demanding Rights: Europe's Supranational Courts and the Dilemma of Migrant Vulnerability* (Cambridge University Press 2019)

Petra BENDEL, 'Neustart oder Fehlstart? Zum neuen EU-Pakt für Migration und Asyl' (*Fluchtforschungsblog*, 26 September 2020) <https://blog.fluchtforschung.net/neustart-oder-fehlstart-zum-neuen-eu-pakt-fur-migration-und-asyl/> accessed 27 February 2021

Wolfgang BENEDEK et al (eds) *European Yearbook on Human Rights 2018* (Intersentia 2018)

Samantha BESSON, 'Due Diligence and Extraterritorial Human Rights Obligations – Mind the Gap!' in (2020) 9 ESIL Reflections <https://esil-sedi.eu/wp-content/uploads/2020/04/ESIL-Reflection-Besson-S.-3.pdf> accessed 6 July 2022

Samantha BESSON, 'The Extraterritoriality of the European Convention on Human Rights: Why Human Rights Depend on Jurisdiction and What Jurisdiction Amounts to' in (2012) Leiden Journal of International Law, 857-884

Francesca BIGNAMI (ed), *EU Law in Populist Times: Crises and Prospects* (Cambridge University Press 2020)

Tom de BOER and Marjoleine ZIECK, 'The Legal Abyss of Discretion in the Resettlement of Refugees: Cherry-Picking and the Lack of Due Process in the EU' in (2020) 32 International Journal of Refugee Law 1, 54-85

Daniel BOFFEY, 'African Union seeks to kill EU plan to process migrants in Africa' (*The Guardian*, 24 February 2019) <https://www.theguardian.com/world/2019/feb/24/african-union-seeks-to-kill-eu-plan-to-process-migrants-in-africa> accessed 13 February 2021

Elona BOKSHI, 'Refugee Resettlement in the EU: The capacity to do it better and to do it more', KNOW RESET Research Report 2013/04 (European University Institute 2013) <https://www.ecre.org/wp-content/uploads/2016/03/00013_20140108160733_knowresetrr-2013-04.pdf> accessed 13 February 2021

Christina BOSWELL, 'The 'External Dimension' of EU Immigration and Asylum Policy' in (2003) 79 International Affairs, 619-638

Owen BOWCOTT, 'ICC submission calls for prosecution of EU over migrant deaths' (*The Guardian*, 3 June 2019) <https://www.theguardian.com/law/2019/jun/03/icc-submission-calls-for-prosecution-of-eu-over-migrant-deaths> accessed 13 February 2021

Anu BREDFORD, *The Brussels Effect: How the European Union Rules the World* (Oxford University Press 2020)

Philippe de BRUYCKER, 'Towards a New European Consensus on Migration and Asylum' (*Eumigrationlawblog.eu*, 2 December 2019) <http://eumigrationlawblog.eu/towards-a-new-european-consensus-on-migration-and-asylum/> accessed 13 December 2019

Philippe de BRUYCKER and Evangelia (Lilian) TSOURDI, 'In search of fairness in responsibility sharing' in (2016) 51 Forced Migration Review, 64-65

Christian CALLIESS and Matthias RUFFERT (eds), *EUV/AEUV: Das Verfassungsrecht der Europäischen Union mit Grundrechtecharta* (CH Beck 5th ed 2016)

Christian CALLIESS (ed), *Europäische Solidarität und nationale Identität. Überlegungen im Kontext der Krise im Euroraum* (Mohr Siebeck 2013)

CARITAS EUROPA, CHURCHES' COMMISSION FOR MIGRANTS IN EUROPE, ECRE, INTERNATIONAL REFUGEE COMMITTEE and RED CROSS EU OFFICE, 'Recommendations on a Union Resettlement Framework' (14 November 2016) <https://redcross.eu/positions-publications/recommendations-on-a-union-resettlement-framework> accessed 27 February 2021

Lars CARLSEN, 'An Alternative View on Distribution Keys for the Possible Relocation of Refugees in the European Union' in (2017) 130 Social Indicators Research 3, 1147-1163

Sergio CARRERA, *An Appraisal of the European Commission of Crisis: Has the Juncker Commission delivered a new start for EU Justice and Home Affairs?* (Centre for European Policy Studies 2018) <https://www.ceps.eu/wp-content/uploads/2019/01/Commission%20of%20Crisis.pdf> accessed 13 February 2021

Vincent CHETAIL, Philippe de BRUYCKER and Francesco MAIANI (eds), *Reforming the Common European Asylum System: The New European Refugee Law* (Brill 2016)

Meltem İneli CIĞER, '5 Reasons Why: Understanding the reasons behind the activation of the Temporary Protection Directive in 2022' (*Eumigrationlawblog.eu*, 7 March 2022) <https://eumigrationlawblog.eu/5-reasons-why-understanding-the-reasons-behind-the-activation-of-the-temporary-protection-directive-in-2022/> accessed 18 July 2022

COMMISSION, 'Refugee Fund' <https://ec.europa.eu/home-affairs/financing/fundings/migration-asylum-borders/refugee-fund_en> accessed 21 February 2021

COMMISSION, Communication 'Action plan on Integration and Inclusion 2021-2027', COM(2020) 758 final <https://eur-lex.europa.eu/legal-content/EN/TXT/PDF/?uri=CELEX:52020DC0758&from=EN> accessed 19 July 2022

COMMISSION, 'A fresh start on migration: Building confidence and striking a new balance between responsibility and solidarity' (*Press release*, 23 September 2020) <https://ec.europa.eu/commission/presscorner/detail/en/ip_20_1706> accessed 27 February 2021

COMMISSION, Recommendation on legal pathways to protection in the EU: promoting resettlement, humanitarian admission and other complementary pathways, C(2020) 6467 final

COMMISSION, Proposal for a Regulation on asylum and migration management and amending Council Directive 2003/109 and the proposed Regulation (EU) XXX/XXX [Asylum and Migration Fund], COM(2020) 610 final

COMMISSION, Communication on a New Pact on Migration and Asylum, COM(2020) 609 final

COMMISSION, Communication 'The EU budget powering the recovery plan for Europe', COM(2020) 442 final

COMMISSION, Amended proposal for a Regulation laying down the multiannual financial framework for the years 2021 to 2027, COM(2020) 443 final

COMMISSION DIRECTORATE-GENERAL HOME AFFAIRS, 'Asylum, Migration and Integration Fund (AMIF)' <https://ec.europa.eu/home-affairs/financing/fundings/migration-asylum-borders/asylum-migration-integration-fund_en> accessed 28 February 2021

COMMISSION, Communication 'COVID-19: Guidance on the implementation of relevant EU provisions in the area of asylum and return procedures and on resettlement', OJ [2020] C126/12-27

COMMISSION, 'Resettlement: EU Member States' pledges exceed 30,000 places for 2020' (*Press release*, 18 December 2019) <https://ec.europa.eu/commission/presscorner/ detail/de/ip_19_6794> accessed 13 February 2021

COMMISSION, 'Delivering on resettlement' (16 October 2019) <https://ec.europa.eu/commission/presscorner/detail/en/FS_19_6079> accessed 21 February 2021

COMMISSION, '2018 report on the application of the EU Charter of Fundamental Rights' (2019) <https://ec.europa.eu/info/sites/info/files/2018_annual_report_charter_en_0.pdf> accessed 28 February 2021

COMMISSION, 'EU Trust Fund for Africa: new actions adopted to support vulnerable migrants, foster socio-economic development and improve border management in North of Africa' (14 December 2018) <https://ec.europa.eu/commission/presscorner/detail/ro/IP_18_6793> accessed 8 July 2022

COMMISSION, 'Managing migration: Commission expands on disembarkation and controlled centre concepts' (*Press release*, 24 July 2018) <http://europa.eu/rapid/press-release_IP-18-4629_en.htm> accessed 27 February 2021

COMMISSION, Communication 'A Modern Budget for a Union That Protects, Empowers and Defends: The Multiannual Financial Framework for 2021-2027', COM(2018) 321 final

COMMISSION, Proposal for a Regulation establishing the Asylum and Migration Fund, COM(2018) 471 final 2018/0248 (COD)

COMMISSION, 'The EU-Turkey Statement: Two years on' (April 2018) <https://ec.europa.eu/home-affairs/sites/default/files/what-we-do/policies/european-agenda-migration/20180314_eu-turkey-two-years-on_en.pdf> accessed 17 June 2021

COMMISSION, 'European Agenda on Migration: Continuous efforts needed to sustain progress' (*Press release*, 14 March 2018) <http://europa.eu/rapid/press-release_IP-18-1763_en.htm> accessed 21 February 2021

COMMISSION, Communication 'Progress report on the Implementation of the European Agenda on Migration', COM(2018) 301 final.

COMMISSION, Implementing Decision on the adoption of the work programme for 2017 and the financing of Union actions in the framework for the Asylum, Migration and Integration Fund, C(2017) 2572 final <https://ec.europa.eu/research/participants/data/ref/other_eu_prog/home/wp/amif-awp-2017_en.pdf> accessed 27 March 2021

COMMISSION, 'Relocation: Commission refers the Czech Republic, Hungary and Poland to the Court of Justice' (*Press release*, 7 December 2017) <http://europa.eu/rapid/press-release_IP-17-5002_en.htm> accessed 13 February 2021

COMMISSION, 'Relocation: EU Solidarity between Member States' (14 November 2017) <https://ec.europa.eu/home-affairs/sites/homeaffairs/files/what-we-do/policies/european-agenda-migration/20171114_relocation_eu_solidarity_between_member_states_en.pdf> accessed 13 February 2021

COMMISSION, 'Relocation: Commission launches infringement procedures against Czech Republic, Hungary and Poland' (*Press release*, 14 June 2017) <http://europa.eu/rapid/press-release_IP-17-1607_en.htm> accessed 13 February

COMMISSION, Recommendation (EU) 2017/1803 on enhancing legal pathways for persons in need of international protection [2017] OJ L259/21-24 [notified under the document C(2017)6504]

COMMISSION, Proposal for a Regulation establishing a Union Resettlement Framework and amending Regulation (EU) No 516/2014 of the European Parliament and the Council, COM(2016) 468 final 2016/0225 (COD)

COMMISSION, Communication on establishing a new Partnership Framework with third countries under the European Agenda on Migration, COM(2016) 385 final

COMMISSION, Proposal for a Regulation establishing the criteria and mechanisms for determining the Member State responsible for examining an application for international protection lodged in one of the Member States by a third-country national or a stateless person (recast), COM(2016) 270 final

COMMISSION, 'EMN Ad-Hoc Query on BE AHQ on the waiting period for family reunification for beneficiaries of subsidiary protection' (requested on 10 August 2016) <https://ec.europa.eu/home-affairs/sites/homeaffairs/files/2016.1096_-_be_ahq_on_the_waiting_period_for_family_reunification.pdf> accessed 27 March 2021

COMMISSION, 'Completing the reform of the Common European Asylum System: towards an efficient, fair and humane asylum policy' (*Press release*, 13 July 2016) <http://europa.eu/rapid/press-release_IP-16-2433_en.htm> accessed 21 February 2021

COMMISSION, Communication 'Towards a Reform of the Common European Asylum System and Enhancing Legal Avenues to Europe', COM(2016) 197 final

COMMISSION, Communication 'Action Plan on the Integration of Third Country Nationals', COM(2016) 377 final

COMMISSION, Recommendation on a European resettlement scheme, C(2015) 3560 final

COMMISSION, Communication 'A European Agenda on Migration', COM(2015) 240 final

COMMISSION, 'Relocation & Resettlement' (27 May 2015) <https://ec.europa.eu/home-affairs/sites/homeaffairs/files/what-we-do/policies/european-agenda-migration/background-information/docs/relocation_and_resettlement_factsheet_en.pdf> accessed 13 February 2021

COMMISSION, Communication 'The Global Approach to Migration and Mobility', COM(2011) 743 final

COMMISSION, Green Paper on the right to family reunification of third-country nationals living in the European Union (Directive 2003/86/EC), COM(2011) 735 final

COMMISSION, Amended Proposal for a Regulation on the European Union Agency for Asylum and repealing Regulation (EU) No 439/2010: A contribution from the European Commission to the Leaders' meeting in Salzburg on 19-20 September 2018 COM/2018/633 final

COMMISSION, Directorate-General Home Affairs, 'Study on the Feasibility of Establishing a Mechanism for a Relocation of Beneficiaries of International protection', JLX/2009/ERFX/PR/1005 (Final Report 2010) <https://ec.europa.eu/home-affairs/sites/homeaffairs/files/e-library/docs/pdf/final_report_relocation_of_refugees_en.pdf> accessed 13 February 2021

COMMISSION, Communication 'Establishment of a joint EU resettlement programme', COM(2009) 447 final

COMMISSION, Communication 'Regional Protection Programmes', COM(2005) 388 final

COMMISSION, Communication on the Managed Entry in the EU of Persons in Need of International Protection and the Enhancement of the Protection Capacity of the Regions of Origin 'Improving Access to Durable Solutions', COM(2004) 410 final

COMMISSION, Communication on the common asylum policy and the Agenda for protection (Second Commission Report on the implementation of Communication, COM(2000) 755 final of 22 November 2000), COM(2003) 152 final

COMMISSION, Communication 'Towards a common asylum procedure and a uniform status, valid throughout the Union, for persons granted asylum', COM(2000) 755 final

COMMISSION, White Paper 'Completing the Internal Market', COM(85) 310 final <https://eur-lex.europa.eu/legal-content/EN/TXT/PDF/?uri=CELEX:51985DC0310&from=DE> accessed 21 February 2021

COUNCIL OF EUROPE, 'Chart of signatures and ratifications of Treaty 177' (as of 10 July 2022) <https://www.coe.int/en/web/conventions/full-list/-/conventions/treaty/177/signatures?p_auth=Zn0fdiIA> accessed 10 July 2022

COUNCIL OF EUROPE, 'Realising the right to family reunification of refugees in Europe' (7 February 2017) <https://familie.asyl.net/fileadmin/user_upload/pdf/PREMS_052917_ GBR_1700_Realising_Refugees_160x240_Web.pdf-1.pdf> accessed 27 March 2021

COUNCIL OF THE EU, 'Reform of the Common European Asylum System and Resettlement' (26 February 2019) <https://data.consilium.europa.eu/doc/document/ST-6600-2019-INIT/en/pdf> accessed 23 June 2021

COUNCIL OF THE EU, 'Conclusions of the Representatives of the Governments of the Member States meeting within the Council on resettling through multilateral and national schemes 20000 persons in clear need of international protection', Council Doc 11130/15 (22 July 2015) <https://data.consilium.europa.eu/doc/document/ST-11130-2015-INIT/en/pdf> accessed 21 February 2021

COUNCIL OF THE EU, 'Council Conclusions on a common framework for genuine and practical solidarity towards Member States facing particular pressures due to mixed migration flows', 7115/12 ASIM 20 FRONT 30 (8 March 2012) <https://www.consilium.europa.eu/uedocs/cms_data/docs/pressdata/en/jha/130731.pdf> accessed 27 February 2021

Thomas DAVIES (ed), *Routledge Handbook of NGOs and International Relations* (2019)

Darla DAVITTI, 'Biopolitical Borders and the State of Exception in the European Migration 'Crisis'' in (2018) 29 European Journal of International Law 4, 1173-1196

Katharine M DONATO, Amanda CARRICO and Jonathan M GILLIGAN, 'As more climate migrants cross borders seeking refuge, laws will need to adapt' (*The Conversation*, 8 June 2021) <https://theconversation.com/as-more-climate-migrants-cross-borders-seeking-refuge-laws-will-need-to-adapt-159673> accessed 16 June 2021

Yuval DVIR, Paul MORRIS and Miri YEMINI, 'What kind of citizenship for whom? The 'refugee crisis' and the European Union's conceptions of citizenship' in (2019) 17 Globalization, Societies and Education 2, 208-219

ECRE, 'EU-Turkey Deal 5 Years on: Fundamentals Remain Unchanged' (19 March 2021) <https://mailchi.mp/ecre/ecre-weekly-bulletin-19032021#edito> accessed 17 June 2021

EUAA, 'New EU Agency for Asylum starts work with reinforced mandate' (19 January 2022) <https://euaa.europa.eu/news-events/new-eu-agency-asylum-starts-work-reinforced-mandate> accessed 19 July 2022

EUROPEAN COUNCIL meeting of 28 June 2018 – Conclusions EUCO 9/18 (28 June 2018) <https://www.consilium.europa.eu/media/35936/28-euco-final-conclusions-en.pdf> accessed 21 February 2021

EUROPEAN COUNCIL, 'EU-Turkey statement, 18 March 2016' (*Press Release*, 18 March 2016) <https://www.consilium.europa.eu/en/press/press-releases/2016/03/18/eu-turkey-statement/> accessed 21 February 2021

EUROPEAN COUNCIL, 'Stockholm Programme – An Open and Secure Europe Serving and Protecting Citizens' [2010] OJ C115/1-38

EUROPEAN COUNCIL, 'The Hague Programme – Strengthening Freedom, Security and Justice in the European Union' [2005] OJ C53/1-14

EUROPEAN MIGRATION NETWORK, 'Asylum and Migration Glossary 7.0' (July 2020) <https://ec.europa.eu/home-affairs/what-we-do/networks/european_migration_network/glossary_en> accessed 17 August 2021

EUROPEAN MIGRATION NETWORK, 'Resettlement and Humanitarian Admission Programmes in Europe – what works' (9 November 2016) <https://ec.europa.eu/home-affairs/sites/homeaffairs/files/what-we-do/networks/european_migration_network/reports/docs/emn-studies/emn-studies-00_resettlement_synthesis_report_final_en.pdf> accessed 28 February 2021

EUROPEAN PARLIAMENT, 'Asylum and migration: deal reached on new EU resettlement framework' (*Press release*, 15 December 2022), <https://www.europarl.europa.eu/news/en/press-room/20221214IPR64717/asylum-and-migration-deal-reached-on-new-eu-resettlement-framework>

EUROPEAN PARLIAMENT, 'Legislative Train Schedule: EU Resettlement Framework' (as of 5 May 2022) <https://www.europarl.europa.eu/legislative-train/theme-towards-a-new-policy-on-migration/file-jd-eu-resettlement-framework> accessed 24 June 2022

EUROPEAN PARLIAMENT, 'Community sponsorship schemes under the new pact on migration and asylum' (*Briefing*, June 2021) <https://www.europarl.europa.eu/RegData/etudes/BRIE/2021/690675/EPRS_BRI(2021)690675_EN.pdf> accessed 29 June 2022

EUROPEAN PARLIAMENT, 'Resettlement of refugees: EU framework' (*Briefing*, 2019) <https://www.europarl.europa.eu/RegData/etudes/BRIE/2016/589859/EPRS_BRI%282016%29589859_EN.pdf> accessed 23 June 2021

EUROPEAN PARLIAMENT, 'Resettlement of refugees: EU framework' (*Briefing*, April 2017) <http://www.europarl.europa.eu/RegData/etudes/BRIE/2016/589859/EPRS_BRI%282016%29589859_EN.pdf> accessed 13 February 2021

Marie-Claire FOBLETS and Luc LEBOEUF (eds), *Humanitarian Admission to Europe: The Law between Promises and Constraints* (Hart/Nomos 2020)

FRA, 'Guidance on how to reduce the risk of refoulement in external border management when working in or together with third countries' (5 December 2016) <https://fra.europa.eu/sites/default/files/fra_uploads/fra-2016-guidance-reducing-refoulement-risk-0_en.pdf> accessed 14 February 2021

Nula FREI and Constantin HRUSCHKA, 'Circumventing Non-Refoulement or Fighting "Illegal Migration"?' (*Eumigrationlawblog.eu*, 23 March 2018) <https://eumigrationlawblog.eu/circumventing-non-refoulement-or-fighting-illegal-migration/> accessed 14 February 2021

Rudolf GEIGER, Daniel ERASMUS-KHAN and Markus KOTZUR (eds), *European Union Treaties: Treaty on the European Union, Treaty on the Functioning of the European Union* (CH Beck/Hart 2015)

GERMAN PRESIDENCY, Draft Council Resolution on burden-sharing with regard to the admission and residence of refugees of 1 July 1994, Council Document 7773/94 ASIM 124

Christoph GRABENWARTER, *European Convention on Human Rights: Commentary* (CH Beck/Hart/Nomos 2014)

Christoph GRABENWARTER and Katharina PABEL, *Europäische Menschenrechtskonvention: Ein Studienbuch* (CH Beck/Helbig Lichtenhahn Verlag/Manz 6th ed 2016)

Eberhard GRABITZ, Meinhard HILF and Martin NETTESHEIM (eds), *Das Recht der Europäischen Union* (CH Beck 68th supplement October 2019)

Kay HAILBRONNER and Daniel THYM (eds), *EU Immigration and Asylum Law: A Commentary* (CH Beck/Hart/Nomos 2nd ed 2016)

Ulrich HALTERN, *Europarecht: Dogmatik im Kontext* Vol I (Mohr Siebeck 3rd ed 2017)

Emiliya Bratanova van HARTEN, 'The new EU Resettlement Framework: the Ugly Duckling of the EU asylum acquis?' (*EU Law Analysis*, 3 February 2023) <http://eulawanalysis.blogspot.com/2023/02/the-new-eu-resettlement-framework-ugly.html> accessed 2 May 2023

HEADS OF GOVERNMENT OF THE V4 COUNTRIES, 'Joint Statement of the Heads of Governments of the V4 Countries', 16 September 2016 <https://www.euractiv.com/wp-content/uploads/sites/2/2016/09/Bratislava-V4-Joint-Statement-final.docx.pdf> accessed 20 March 2021

Andrew HENDERSON, '5 Most Expensive Residency Applications in Europe' (last updated 26 December 2019) <https://nomadcapitalist.com/2017/11/06/most-expensive-residency-applications/> accessed 27 March 2021

Satoko HORII, 'Accountability, Dependency, and EU Agencies: The Hotspot Approach in the Refugee Crisis' in (2018) 37 Refugee Survey Quarterly 2, 204-230

Constantin HRUSCHKA, 'Hot Returns Remain Contrary to the ECHR: ND & NT before the ECHR' (*Eumigrationlawblog.eu*, 28 February 2020) <https://eumigrationlawblog.eu/hot-returns-remain-contrary-to-the-echr-nd-nt-before-the-echr/> accessed 6 July 2022

Sandra HUMMELBRUNNER, 'The Unity and Consistency of Union Law: The Core of Review under Article 256(2) and (3) TFEU' in (2018) 73 Zeitschrift für öffentliches Recht, 295-315

Timothy J HUTTON, 'Asylum Policy in the EU: The Case for Deeper Integration' in (2015) 61 CESifo Economic Studies 3, 605-637

Thomas JAEGER and Karl STÖGER (eds), *Kommentar zu EUV und AEUV* (238th supplement June 2020)

Lyra JAKULEVIČIENÉ and Mantas BILEIŠIS, 'EU refugee resettlement: Key challenges of expanding the practice into new Member States' in (2016) 9 Baltic Journal of Law & Politics 1, 93-123

Tobias KLARMANN, *Illegalisierte Migration: Die (De-)Konstruktion migrationsspezifischer Illegalitäten im Unionsrecht* (Nomos 2021)

Dimitry KOCHENOV, Gráinne de BÚRCA and Andrew WILLIAMS, 'How just is the EU, or: is there a 'new' European deficit?' (*Verfassungsblog*, 10 June 2015) <https://verfassungsblog.de/how-just-is-the-eu-or-is-there-a-new-european-deficit-2/> accessed 27 March 2021

Markus KOTZUR, 'Flexible Solidarity – Effective Solidarity?' (*Völkerrechtsblog*, 16 November 2016) <https://voelkerrechtsblog.org/flexible-solidarity-effective-solidarity/> accessed 27 February 2021

Andreas KUMIN, Julia SCHIMPFHUBER, Kirsten SCHMALENBACH and Lorin-Johannes WAGNER (eds), *Außen- & sicherheitspolitische Integration im Europäischen Rechtsraum – Festschrift Hubert Isak* (Jan Sramek 2020)

Iris G LANGE and Boldizsár NAGY, 'External Border Control Techniques in the EU as a Challenge to the Prnciple of Non-Refoulement' in (2021) European Constitutional Law Review, 1-29

Koen LENAERTS and Piet van NUFFEL, *European Union Law* (Sweet & Maxwell 3rd ed 2011)

Marcel LEUBECHER, 'Warum die meisten Flüchtlinge Merkels Appell nicht folgen werden' (*Die Welt*, 1 February 2016) <https://www.welt.de/politik/deutschland/article151744427/Warum-die-meisten-Fluechtlinge-Merkels-Appell-nicht-folgen-werden.html> accessed 27 March 2021

Ursula von der LEYEN, 'A Union that strives for more: My agenda for Europe' (Political guidelines for the next European Commission 2019-2024) <https://ec.europa.eu/info/sites/info/files/political-guidelines-next-commission_en_0.pdf> accessed 20 March 2021

Eva LUTTER, Vanessa ZEHNDER and ELENA KNEŽEVIĆ, 'Resettlement und humanitäre Aufnahmeprogramme' in (2018) Asylmagazin, 29-36

Francesco MAIANI, 'A "Fresh Start" or One More Clunker? Dublin and Solidarity in the New Pact' (*Eumigrationlawblog.eu*, 20 October 2020) <http://eumigrationlawblog.eu/a-fresh-start-or-one-more-clunker-dublin-and-solidarity-in-the-new-pact/> accessed 27 March 2021

Francesco MAIANI, '"Regional Disembarkation Platforms" and "Controlled Centres": Lifting Drawbridge, Reaching out Across The Mediterranean, or Going Nowhere?' (*Eumigrationlawblog.eu*, 18 September 2018) <http://eumigrationlawblog.eu/regional-disembarkation-platforms-and-controlled-centres-lifting-the-drawbridge-reaching-out-across-the-mediterranean-or-going-nowhere> accessed 21 February 2021

Zaini MAJEED, 'European Nations To Resettle 40,000 Afghan Refugees To Prevent 'irregular Arrivals'' (11 December 2021) <https://www.republicworld.com/world-news/europe/european-nations-to-resettle-40000-afghan-refugees-to-prevent-irregular-arrivals.html> accessed 24 June 2022

Alfredo MÄRKER and Stephan SCHLOTHFELDT (eds), *Was schulden wir Flüchtlingen und Migranten?: Grundlagen einer gerechten Zuwanderungspolitik* (Springer 2002)

Heinz MAYER and Karl STÖGER (eds), *Kommentar zu EUV und AEUV* (141st supplement 2012)

Valsamis MITSILEGAS, Violeta MORENO-LAX and Niovi VAVOULA (eds), *Securitising Asylum Flows: Deflection, Criminalisation and Challenges for Human Rights* (Brill 2020)

Jesus Férnandez-Huertas MORAGA and Hillel RAPOPORT, 'Tradable Refugee-admission Quotas and EU Asylum Policy' in (2015) 61 CESifo Economic Studies 3, 638-672

Violeta MORENO-LAX, 'The Architecture of Functional Jurisdiction: Unpacking Contactless Control – On Public Powers, *SS and Others v Italy*, and the "Operational Model"' in (2020) German Law Journal, 385-416

Andreas Th MÜLLER, 'Solidarität in der gemeinsamen europäischen Asylpolitik' in (2015) Zeitschrift für öffentliches Recht, 463-489

Martin NETTESHEIM, 'Migration im Spannungsfeld von Freizügigkeit und Demokratie' in (2019) Archiv des öffentlichen Rechts, 358-424

Milan NIČ, 'The Visegrád Group in the EU: 2016 as a turning-point?' in (2016) European View, 281-290

Arne NIEMANN and Natascha ZAUN, 'EU Refugee Policies and Politics in Times of Crisis: Theoretical and Empirical Perspectives' in (2018) 56 Journal of Common Market Studies 1, 3-22

Andreas ORATOR, *Möglichkeiten und Grenzen der Einrichtung von Unionsagenturen* (Mohr Siebeck 2017)

David OWEN, 'Refugees, EU Citizenship and the Common European Asylum System A Normative Dilemma for EU Integration' in (2019) Ethical Theory and Moral Practice, 347-368

Daphne PANAYOTATOS, 'Undermining Protection in the EU: What Nine Trends Tell Us About The Proposed Pact on Migration and Asylum' (June 2021) <https://www.refugeesinternational.org/reports/2021/6/1/undermining-protection-in-the-eu-what-nine-trends-tells-us-about-the-proposed-pact-on-migration-and-asylum> accessed 17 June 2021

Steve PEERS, 'Residents of everywhere?' (*EU Law Analysis*, 26 January 2022) <http://eulawanalysis.blogspot.com/2022/01/residents-of-everywhere-cjeu-rules-on.html?m=1> accessed 24 July 2022

Steve PEERS, Violeta MORENO-LAX, Madeline GARLICK and Elspeth GUILD, *EU Immigration and Asylum Law (Text and Commentary)* (Brill 2nd ed 2015)

Delphine PERRIN and Frank MCNAMARA, 'Refugee Resettlement in the EU: Between Shared Standards and Diversity in Legal and Policy Frames', KNOW RESET Research Report 2013/03 (European University Institute 2013) <https://cadmus.eui.eu/bitstream/handle/1814/29400/KnowReset_RR-2013_03.pdf> accessed 13 February 2021

Natalia PESTOVA, 'Differential treatment of refugees in Ireland' in (2017) 54 Forced Migration Review, 45-47

Ségolène Barbou des PLACES, 'Burden Sharing in the Field of Asylum: Legal Motivations and Implications of a Regional Approach' (2012) <https://hal.archives-ouvertes.fr/hal-01614068/document> accessed 21 February 2021

Janine PRANTL, 'The UNHCR in 2021: Refugee Resettlement as a Challenge of Underfunding, Power Imbalance and Impartiality' (*Völkerrechtsblog*, 20 July 2021) <https://voelkerrechtsblog.org/the-unhcr-in-2021-refugee-resettlement-as-a-challenge-of-underfunding-power-imbalance-and-impartiality/> accessed 7 August 2021

Janine PRANTL, ''Lessons to be learned' für ein zukünftiges, gemeinsames EU Resettlement' in (2020) Europarecht Supplement 3, 117-132

Janine PRANTL, 'A strong EU resettlement program is more important than ever' (*FluchtforschungsBlog*, 13 May 2020) <https://blog.fluchtforschung.net/a-strong-eu-resettlement-program-is-more-important-than-ever/> accessed 21 February 2021

Janine PRANTL and Ian KYSEL, 'Generous, but Equal Treatment? Anti-Discrimination Duties of States Hosting Refugees Fleeing Ukraine' (*EJIL: Talk!*, 2 May 2022) <https://www.ejiltalk.org/generous-but-equal-treatment-anti-discrimination-duties-of-states-hosting-refugees-fleeing-ukraine/> accessed 10 July 2022

Sarah PROGIN-THEUERKAUF, 'Grenzen des Verbots von Kollektivausweisungen: Das Urteil des EGMR im Fall ND und NT gegen Spanien' in (2020) sui generis, 309-315

Tihomir SABCHEV and Moritz BAUMGÄRTEL, 'The path of least resistance? EU cities and locally organised resettlement' in (February 2020) 63 Forced Migration Review <https://citiesofrefuge.eu/sites/default/files/2020-02/sabchev-baumgartel-fmr.pdf> accessed 27 March 2021

Mattia di SALVO et al, 'Flexible Solidarity: A comprehensive strategy for asylum in the EU', MEDAM Assessment Report (15 June 2018) <https://www.medam-migration.eu/fileadmin/Dateiverwaltung/MEDAM-Webseite/Publications/Assessment_Reports/2018_MEDAM_Assessment_Report/MEDAM_Assessment_Report_2018_Full_report.pdf> accessed 20 March 2021

Sertan SANDERSON, 'EU relocation scheme ends to mixed reviews' (*InfoMigrants*, 26 September 2017) <https://www.infomigrants.net/en/post/5270/eu-relocation-scheme-ends-to-mixed-reviews> accessed 27 June 2022

William A SCHABAS, *The European Convention on Human Rights: A Commentary* (Oxford University Press 2015)

Konrad SCHIEMANN, 'Europe and the Loss of Sovereignty' in (2007) 56 The International and Comparative Law Quarterly 3, 475-489

Jan SCHNEIDER and Anna-Lucia GRAFF, 'EASO Reloaded: Can The New EU Asylum Agency Guarantee A Standardised System of Protection?' (June 2018) <https://www.svr-migration.de/en/publications/eu_asylum_agency/> accessed 17 July 2022

Dana SCHMALZ, 'Rights that are not Illusory' (*Verfassungsblog*, 9 July 2021) <https://verfassungsblog.de/rights-that-are-not-illusory/> accessed 9 July 2021

Dana SCHMALZ, *Refugees, Democracy and the Law: Political Rights at the Margins of the State* (Routledge 2020)

Dana SCHMALZ, 'Am Ende der Kraft' (*Verfassungsblog*, 14 September 2020) <https://verfassungsblog.de/am-ende-der-kraft/> accessed 27 February 2021

Hanna SCHNEIDER, 'Implementing the Refugee Resettlement Process: Diverging Objectives, Interdependencies and Power Relations' in (2021) Frontiers in Political Science <https://www.frontiersin.org/articles/10.3389/fpos.2021.629675/full> accessed 21 June 2021

Miroslava SCHOLTEN and Marloes van RIJSBERGEN, 'The ESMA-Short Selling Case: Erecting a New Delegation Doctrine in the EU upon the *Meroni-Romano* Remnants' in (2014) 41 Legal Issues of Economic Integration 4, 389-406

Robert SCHÜTZE, *Foreign Affairs and the EU Constitution: Selected Essays* (Cambridge University Press 2014)

Joanne van SELM, 'Are asylum and immigration really a European Union issue?' in (2016) 51 Forced Migration Review, 60-62

Joanne van SELM, 'European Refugee Policy: is there such a thing?', UNHCR Research Paper n°115 (May 2005) <https://www.refworld.org/pdfid/4ff166f31e.pdf> accessed 13 February 2021

Joanne van SELM et al, Study on 'The Feasibility of setting up resettlement schemes in EU Member States or at EU Level, against the background of the Common European Asylum system and the goal of a Common Asylum Procedure' (European Communities 2004)

Priyanka SHANKAR, 'EU, fearful of refugee crisis, delays response on Afghan asylum' (*Al Jazeera*, 15 October 2021) <https://www.aljazeera.com/news/2021/10/15/eu-fearful-of-refugee-crisis-delays-response-on-afghan-asylum-2> accessed 24 June 2022

Omer SHATZ and Juan BRANCO et al, 'EU Migration Policies in the Central Mediterranean and Libya (2014-2019)' (PSIA – Sciences Po 2017/2018, 2018/2019) <https://www.statewatch.org/news/2019/jun/eu-icc-case-EU-Migration-Policies.pdf> accessed 13 February 2021

Thomas SPIJKERBOER, 'Bifurcation of people, bifurcation of law: externalization of migration policy before the EU Court of Justice' in (2017) 31 Journal of Refugee Studies 2, 216-239.

Vladislava STOYANOVA, 'M.N. and Others v Belgium: no ECHR protection from refoulement by issuing visas' (*EJIL: Talk!*, 12 May 2020) <https://www.ejiltalk.org/m-n-and-others-v-belgium-no-echr-protection-from-refoulement-by-issuing-visas/> accessed 6 July 2022

Rudolf STREINZ (ed), *EUV/AEUV Kommentar* (CH Beck 3rd ed 2018)

Tineke STRIK, 'The Global Approach to Migration and Mobility' in (2017) 5 Groningen Journal of International Law 2, 310-328

Eiko R THIELEMANN, 'Why Refugee Burden-Sharing Initiatives Fail: Public Goods, Free-Riding and Symbolic Solidarity in the EU' in (2018) 56 Journal of Common Market Studies 1, 63-82

Eiko R THIELEMANN, 'Between Interests and Norms: Explaining Burden-Sharing in the European Union' in (2003) 16 Journal of Refugee Studies 3, 253-273

Daniel THYM, 'Temporary Protection for Ukrainians: the Unexpected Renaissance of 'Free Choice'' (*Eumigrationlawblog.eu*, 7 March 2022) <https://eumigrationlawblog.eu/temporary-protection-for-ukrainians-the-unexpected-renaissance-of-free-choice/> accessed 18 July 2022

Daniel THYM, 'Secondary Movements: Overcoming the Lack of Trust among the Member States?' (*Eumigrationlawblog.eu*, 29 October 2020) <http://eumigrationlawblog.eu/secondary-movements-overcoming-the-lack-of-trust-among-the-member-states/> accessed 21 February 2021

Daniel THYM, 'Mehr Schein als Sein?: Legislative Unklarheiten und operative Fallstricke des EU-Asylpakets' (*Verfassungsblog*, 24 September 2020) <https://verfassungsblog.de/mehr-schein-als-sein/> accessed 27 February 2021

Daniel THYM, 'A Restrictionist Revolution?: A Counter-Intuitive Reading of the ECtHR's ND & NT-Judgment on 'Hot Expulsions' at the Spanish-Moroccan Border' (*Verfassungsblog*, 17 February 2020) <https://verfassungsblog.de/a-restrictionist-revolution/> accessed 15 February 2021

Evangelia (Lilian) TSOURDI, 'The New Pact and EU Agencies: an ambivalent approach towards administrative integration' (*Eumigrationlawblog.eu*, 6 November 2020) <http://eumigrationlawblog.eu/the-new-pact-and-eu-agencies-an-ambivalent-approach-towards-administrative-integration/> accessed 28 February 2021

Evangelia (Lilian) TSOURDI, 'Holding the European Asylum Support Office Accountable for its role in Asylum Decision-Making: Mission Impossible?' in (2020) 21 German Law Journal, 506-531

Sara de VIDO, 'The ratification of the Council of Europe Istanbul Convention by the EU: A step forward in the protection of women from violence in the European legal system' in (2017) 9 European Journal of Legal Studies 2, 69-104

Natalie WELFENS and Yasemin BEKYOL, 'The Politics of Vulnerability in Refugee Admissions Under the EU-Turkey Statement' in (2021) Frontiers in Political Science, 5 <https://www.frontiersin.org/articles/10.3389/fpos.2021.622921/full> accessed 13 July 2022

Vera WRIEDT, 'Expanding Exceptions? AA and Others v North Macedonia, Systematic Pushbacks and the Fiction of Legal Pathways' (*Eumigrationlawblog.eu*, 7 June 2022) <https://eumigrationlawblog.eu/expanding-exceptions-aa-and-others-v-north-macedonia-systematic-pushbacks-and-the-fiction-of-legal-pathways/> accessed 18 July 2022

US

Thomas Alexander ALEINIKOFF, David A MARTIIN, Hiroshi MOTOMURA, Maryellen FULLERTON and Juliet P STUMPF, *Immigration and Citizenship: Process and Policy* (West Academic Publishing 8th ed 2016)

AMERICAN IMMIGRATION COUNCIL, 'An Overview of US Refugee Law and Policy' (8 January 2020) <https://www.americanimmigrationcouncil.org/research/overview-us-refugee-law-and-policy> accessed 27 March 2021

Kathryn M BOCKLEY, 'A Historical Overview of Refugee Legislation: The Deception of Foreign Policy in the Land of Promise' in (1995) 21 North Carolina Journal of International Law and Commercial Regulation 1, 253-292

Anastasia BROWN and Todd SCRIBNER, 'Unfulfilled Promises, Future Possibilities: The Refugee Resettlement System in the United States' in (2014) 2 Journal on Migration and Human Security 2, 101-120

CENTER FOR APPLIED LINGUISTICS, 'Immigrant & Refugee Integration' <http://www.cal.org/areas-of-impact/immigrant-refugee-integration> accessed 27 March 2021

Muzaffar CHISHTI and Sarah PIERCE, 'Despite Trump Invitation to Stop Taking Refugees, Red and Blue States Alike Endorse Resettlement' (29 January 2020) <https://www.migrationpolicy.org/article/despite-trump-invitation-stop-taking-refugees-red-and-blue-states-alike-endorse-resettlement> accessed 13 February 2021

CITIZEN PATH, 'Adjustment of Status Package Fees' <https://citizenpath.com/adjustment-of-status-fee/> accessed 27 July 2022

Sarah CLEVELAND, 'The United States and the Torture Convention, Part I: Extraterritoriality' (*Just Security*, 14 November 2014) <https://www.justsecurity.org/17435/united-states-torture-convention-part-i-extraterritoriality/> accessed 7 July 2022

Dree K COLLOPY, *AILA's Asylum Primer* (American Immigration Lawyers Association 7th ed 2015)

COMMITTEE ON THE JUDICIARY, Letter of 13 September 2019 <https://judiciary.house.gov/sites/democrats.judiciary.house.gov/files/documents/2019-09-13%20Letter%20to%20Admin%20re%20Refugee%20Admissions.pdf> accessed 13 February 2021

COMMITTEE ON THE JUDICIARY, 'Grassley, Feinstein: Congress Requires More Thorough Engagement with State Dept. on Refugee Numbers' (27 September 2017) <https://www.judiciary.senate.gov/press/rep/releases/grassley-feinstein-congress-requires-more-thorough-engagement-with-state-dept-on-refugee-numbers> accessed 13 February 2021

CULTURAL ORIENTATION RESOURCE CENTER, 'Overseas CO' <http://50.116.32.248/index.php/providing-orientation/overseas> accessed 21 March 2021

Kevin J FANDL, 'States' Rights and Refugee Resettlement' in (2017) 52 Texas International Law Journal 1, 71-101

Ashley FANTZ and Ben BRUMFIELD, 'More than half the nation's governors say Syrian refugees not welcome' (19 November 2014) <https://edition.cnn.com/2015/11/16/world/paris-attacks-syrian-refugees-backlash/index.html> accessed 13 February 2021

Michael FIX, Kate HOOPER and Jie ZONG, 'How Are Refugees Faring: Integration at US and State Levels' (June 2017) <https://www.migrationpolicy.org/research/how-are-refugees-faring-integration-us-and-state-levels> accessed 27 March 2021

Mark FRANKEN, 'Admitting Refugees for Resettlement: A Mission of Rescue' in (2003) 26 In Defense of the Alien, 188-200

Adam GAFFNEY and Danny MCCORMICK, 'The Affordable Care Act: implications for health-care equity' in (2017) 389 The Lancet 10077, 1442-1452

Robert Kogod GOLDMAN and Scott M MARTIN, 'International Legal Standards Relating to the Rights of Aliens and Refugees and United States Immigration Law' in (1983) 5 Human Rights Quarterly 3, 302-326

Ted HESSON, 'Trump officials pressing to slash refugee admissions to zero next year' (*Politico*, 18 July 2019) <https://www.politico.com/story/2019/07/18/trump-officials-refugee-zero-1603503> accessed 13 February 2021

Ted HESSON and Kristina COOKE, 'Explainer: Why did the United States resettle only 12 Ukrainian refugees in March?' (*Reuters*, 11 April 2022) <https://www.reuters.com/world/why-isnt-us-accepting-more-ukrainian-refugees-2022-03-16/> accessed 28 June 2022

INITIATIVE OF THE HARVARD IMMIGRATION AND REFUGEE CLINICAL PROGRAM, 'Fulfilling US Commitment to Refugee Resettlement: Protecting Refugees, Preserving National Security, & Building the US Economy through Refugee Admissions' in (2017) 5 Texas A&M Law Review, 155-236

INTERNATIONAL CRISIS GROUP, 'How to Save the US Refugee Admissions Program', Crisis Group United States Report N°2 (12 September 2018) <https://www.crisisgroup.org/united-states/002-how-save-us-refugee-admissions-program> accessed 13 February 2021

INTERNATIONAL REFUGEE ASSISTANCE PROJECT, 'Refugee Reset: Mid-Year Increase to the US Refugee Admission Target' (28 January 2021) <https://refugeerights.org/wp-content/uploads/2021/01/Refugee-Reset-Mid-Year-Increases-to-the-U.S.-Refugee-Admissions-Target.pdf> accessed 13 February 2021

INTERNATIONAL RESCUE COMMITTEE, 'What does a Joe Biden presidency mean for refugees and asylum seekers?' (8 November 2020) <https://www.rescue.org/article/what-does-joe-biden-presidency-mean-refugees-and-asylum-seekers> accessed 13 February 2021

INTERNATIONAL RESCUE COMMITTEE, 'How immigrants and refugees become US citizens' (3 July 2018) <https://www.rescue.org/article/how-immigrants-and-refugees-become-us-citizens> accessed 27 March 2021

Zolan KANNO-YOUNGS, 'After backlash, Biden will increase the limit on refugee admissions' (*The New York Times*, 16 April 2021) <https://www.nytimes.com/2021/04/16/us/biden-refugees-cap.html> accessed 16 April 2021

Donald KERWIN, 'The US Refugee Resettlement Program – A Return to First Principles: How Refugees Help to Define, Strengthen, and Revitalize the United States' in (2018) 6 Journal on Migration and Human Security 3, 205-225 <https://journals.sagepub.com/doi/full/10.1177/2331502418787787> accessed 13 February 2021

Donald KERWIN, 'The Faltering US Refugee Protection System: Legal and Policy Responses to Refugees, Asylum-Seekers, and Others in Need of Protection' in (2012) 31 Refugee Survey Quarterly 1, 1-33

KEMAL KIRIŞCI and Fulya MEMISOGLU, 'Biden's decision to pull troops from Afghanistan risks a major refugee crisis' (26 April 2021) <https://www.brookings.edu/articles/bidens-decision-to-pull-troops-from-afghanistan-risks-a-major-refugee-crisis/> accessed 15 May 2022

Harold Hongju KOH, 'Memorandum Opinion on the Geographic Scope of the Convention Against Torture and Its Application in Situations of Armed Conflict' (21 January 2013) <https://www.documentcloud.org/documents/20986585-20130121-dos-torture-convention> accessed 7 July 2022

Stephen H LEGOMSKY, *Immigration Law and Policy* (The Foundation Press 1992)

Stephen H LEGOMSKY and David B THRONSON, *Immigration and Refugee Law and Policy* (The Foundation Press 7th ed 2019)

Nadwa MOSSAAD et al, 'Determinants of refugee naturalization in the United States' in (11 September 2018) 115 PNAS 37, 9175-9180

NATIONAL IMMIGRATION FORUM, 'Explainer: Private Sponsorship Programs for Refugees' (25 April 2022) <https://immigrationforum.org/article/a-guide-to-private-sponsorship-for-refugees/> accessed 29 June 2022

Kathleen NEWLAND, 'Legislative Developments and Refugee Resettlement in the Post-Cold War Era' in (1996) 19 In Defense of the Alien, 134-139

Michael J PARRISH, 'Redefining the Refugee: The Universal Declaration of Human Rights as a Basis for Refugee Protection' in (2000) 22 Cardozo Law Review, 223-267

Kristie de PEÑA, 'Congress is letting the administration violate consultation requirements for refugee admissions' (*The Hill*, 26 August 2019) <https://thehill.com/opinion/immigration/458860-congress-is-letting-the-trump-administration-violate-consultation> accessed 13 February 2021

Michael POSNER, 'How To Address The Legal Status of Afghan Refugees' (*Forbes*, 8 September 2021) <https://www.forbes.com/sites/michaelposner/2021/09/08/how-to-address-the-legal-status-of-afghan-refugees/?sh=7d25a18d572f> accessed 27 June 2022

Janine PRANTL, 'Afghan Mass Displacement: The American Response in Light of International Human Rights and Refugee Law, and the Need for International Cooperation to achieve a Satisfactory Solution' in (2022) ALJ, 17-46

Janine PRANTL and Stephen YALE-LOEHR, 'Let Private Citizens Sponsor Refugees' (*NY Daily News*, 15 October 2022) <https://www.nydailynews.com/opinion/ny-oped-let-private-citizens-sponsor-refugees-20221015-dtepnanthfegnpf6anjirwt3by-story.html> accessed 23 November 2022

REFUGEE COUNCIL USA, 'Resettlement Process' <https://rcusa.org/resettlement/resettlement-process/> accessed 27 March 2021

REFUGEE COUNCIL USA, 'Where are the Refugees?: Drastic Cuts to Refugee Resettlement Harming Refugees, Communities, and American Leadership' (12 June 2019) <http://www.rcusa.org/report> accessed 13 February 2021

Nayla RUSH, 'The FY 2020 Refugee Ceiling? 15,000 could cover all UNHCR urgent and emergency submissions worldwide next year' (*Center for Immigration Studies*, 27 August 2019) <https://cis.org/Rush/FY-2020-Refugee-Ceiling> accessed 21 February 2021

Maanvi SINGH, 'Biden raises US refugee admissions cap to 62,500 after delay sparks anger' (*The Guardian*, 3 May 2021) <https://www.theguardian.com/world/2021/may/03/biden-refugee-cap-us-immigration?utm_term=Autofeed&CMP=twt_gu&utm_medium&utm_source=Twitter#Echobox=1620096721> accessed 5 May 2021

Daniel J STEINBOCK, 'The Qualities of Mercy: Maximizing the Impact of US Refugee Resettlement' in (2003) 36 University of Michigan Journal of Law Reform, 951-1006

Jim P STIMPSON and Fernando A WILSON, 'Medicaid Expansion Improved Health Insurance Coverage For Immigrants, But Disparities Persist' in (2018) 37 Health Affairs 10, 1656-1662

Vasudha TALLA (with the assistance of IRAP and Human Rights First), 'Private Sponsorship of Refugee Resettlement in the United States: Guiding Principles and Recommendations' (October 2016) <https://www.humanrightsfirst.org/sites/default/files/Private_Sponsorship_of_Refugees_in_the_United_States_White_Paper.pdf#page=3> accessed 29 June 2022

Amanda TAUB and Max FISHER, 'Trump's Refugee Cuts Threaten Deep Consequences at Home and Abroad' (*The New York Times*, 11 September 2019) <https://www.nytimes.com/2019/09/11/world/middleeast/bahamas-refugees.html> accessed 13 February 2021

Michael S TEITELBAUM and Miron WEINER (eds), *Threatened Peoples, Threatened Borders* (WW Norton Company 1995)

THE WORLD STAFF, 'Refugees to be assessed on ability to 'assimilate'' (The World, 18 October 2017) <https://theworld.org/stories/2017-10-18/refugees-be-assessed-ability-assimilate> accessed 22 July 2022

UNITED STATES COMMITTEE FOR REFUGEES AND IMMIGRANTS, 'World Refugee Survey 2009 – United States' (17 June 2009) <http://www.refworld.org/docid/4a40d2b580.html> accessed 21 October 2018

USCIS, 'Check Case Processing Times' <https://egov.uscis.gov/processing-times/> accessed 27 July 2022

USCIS, 'Green Card for Refugees' <https://www.uscis.gov/greencard/refugees> accessed 27 March 2021

USCIS, 'I-485, Application to Register Permanent Residence or Adjust Status' <https://www.uscis.gov/i-485> accessed 27 March 2021

USCIS, 'N-600K, Application for Citizenship and Issuance of Certificate Under Section 322' <https://www.uscis.gov/n-600k > accessed 27 July 2022.

USCIS, 'Our Fees' <https://www.uscis.gov/forms/our-fees> accessed 27 March 2021

USCIS, 'Refugee Processing and Security Screening' <https://www.uscis.gov/refugeescreening#Enhanced%20Review> accessed 27 March 2021

USCIS, 'Request for Review Tip Sheet' <https://www.uscis.gov/humanitarian/refugees-asylum/refugees/request-review-tip-sheet> accessed 27 March 2021

USCIS, 'Process for Venezuelans' (as of 19 October 2022) <https://www.uscis.gov/venezuela> accessed 15 November 2022

USCIS, 'Uniting for Ukraine' (April 2022) <https://www.uscis.gov/ukraine> accessed 12 August 2022

USCIS, 'RAIO Combined Training Program: Firm Resettlement' (20 December 2019) <https://www.uscis.gov/sites/default/files/document/foia/Firm_Resettlement_LP_RAIO.pdf> accessed 24 August 2022

USCIS, 'Inadmissibility on Public Charge Grounds' (14 August 2019) <https://www.govinfo.gov/content/pkg/FR-2019-08-14/pdf/2019-17142.pdf> accessed 27 March 2021

USCIS, 'I am a refugee or asylee... How do I become a US permanent resident?' (October 2013) <https://www.uscis.gov/sites/default/files/USCIS/Resources/D3en.pdf> accessed 27 March 2021

US DEPARTMENT OF HOMELAND AND SECURITY, 'Privacy Impact Assessment for the United Nations High Commissioner for Refugees (UNHCR) Information Data Share', DHS/USCIS/PIA-081 (13 August 2019) <https://www.dhs.gov/sites/default/files/publications/privacy-pia-uscis081-unhcr-august2019.pdf> accessed 11 July 2021

US DEPARTMENT OF STATE, 'Reception and Placement', <https://www.state.gov/refugee-admissions/reception-and-placement/> accessed 17 September 2022

US DEPARTMENT OF STATE, 'US Refugee Admissions Program Access Categories' <https://2017-2021.state.gov/refugee-admissions/u-s-refugee-admissions-program-access-categories/index.html> accessed 20 July 2022

US DEPARTMENT OF STATE, 'US Refugee Admissions Program' (Fact Sheet, 10 June 2022), <https://www.state.gov/u-s-refugee-admissions-program/> accessed 24 June 2022

US DEPARTMENT OF STATE, 'Launch of the Sponsor Circle Program for Afghans' (25 October 2021) <https://www.state.gov/launch-of-the-sponsor-circle-program-for-afghans/> accessed 29 June 2022

US DEPARTMENT OF STATE, 'US Refugee Admissions Program Priority 2 Designation for Afghan Nationals' (2 August 2021) <https://www.state.gov/u-s-refugee-admissions-program-priority-2-designation-for-afghan-nationals/> accessed 20 July 2021

US DEPARTMENT OF STATE, DEPARTMENT OF HOMELAND AND SECURITY, DEPARTMENT OF HEALTH AND HUMAN SERVICES, 'Report to Congress on Proposed Refugee Admissions for Fiscal Year 2023' (8 September 2022) <https://www.state.gov/report-to-congress-on-proposed-refugee-admissions-for-fiscal-year-2023/>

US DEPARTMENT OF STATE, DEPARTMENT OF HOMELAND AND SECURITY, DEPARTMENT OF HEALTH AND HUMAN SERVICES, 'Report to Congress on Proposed Refugee Admissions for Fiscal Year 2022' (20 September 2021) <https://www.state.gov/report-to-congress-on-proposed-refugee-admissions-for-fiscal-year-2022/> accessed 15 May 2022

US DEPARTMENT OF STATE, DEPARTMENT OF HOMELAND AND SECURITY, DEPARTMENT OF HEALTH AND HUMAN SERVICES, 'Report to Congress on Proposed Refugee Admissions for Fiscal Year 2021' <https://www.state.gov/wp-content/uploads/2020/10/FY21-USRAP-Report-to-Congress-FINAL-for-WEBSITE-102220-508.pdf> accessed 13 February 2021

US DEPARTMENT OF STATE, DEPARTMENT OF HOMELAND AND SECURITY, DEPARTMENT OF HEALTH AND HUMAN SERVICES, 'Report to Congress on Proposed Refugee Admissions for Fiscal Year 2020' <https://www.politico.com/f/?id=0000016d-bb51-d0d8-af6d-ff79261f0002> accessed 13 February 2021

US DEPARTMENT OF STATE, DEPARTMENT OF HOMELAND AND SECURITY, DEPARTMENT OF HEALTH AND HUMAN SERVICES, 'Report to Congress on Proposed Refugee Admissions for Fiscal Year 2019' <https://www.state.gov/wp-content/uploads/2018/12/Proposed-Refugee-Admissions-for-Fiscal-Year-2019.pdf> accessed 13 February 2021

US DEPARTMENT OF STATE, DEPARTMENT OF HOMELAND AND SECURITY, DEPARTMENT OF HEALTH AND HUMAN SERVICES, 'Report to Congress on Proposed Refugee Admissions for Fiscal Year 2018' <https://s3.documentcloud.org/documents/4063604/Report-to-Congress-Proposed-Refugee-Admissions.pdf> accessed 22 July 2022

US TOGETHER, COMMUNITY REFUGEE & IMMIGRATION SERVICES, WORLD RELIEF COLUMBUS and CITY OF COLUMBUS, 'Impact of Refugees in Central Ohio' (2015) <https://www.crisohio.org/wp-content/uploads/2016/04/IMPACT-OF-REFUGEES-ON-CENTRAL-OHIO_2015-SP_I.pdf> accessed 27 March 2021

Lauren WOLFE, 'The Trump Administration Wants Refugees to Fit In or Stay Out' (*Foreign Policy*, 12 October 2017) <https://foreignpolicy.com/2017/10/12/the-trump-administration-wants-refugees-to-fit-in-or-stay-out/> accessed 22 July 2022

James Y XI, 'Refugee Resettlement Federalism' in (2017) Stanford Law Review 69, 1197-1236

Danilo ZAK, 'Bill Summary: The Afghan Afjustment Act' (*National Immigration Forum*, 11 August 2022) <https://immigrationforum.org/article/bill-summary-the-afghan-adjustment-act/> accessed 3 September 2022

Cases

ICJ

Ahmado Sadio Diallo (Republic of Guinea v Democratic Republic of the Kongo) [2010] ICJ Rep 639

Application of the Convention on the Prevention and Punishment of the Crime of Genocide (Bosnia and Herzegovina v Serbia and Montenegro) [2007] ICJ Rep 43

Armed Activities on the Territory of Congo Case (Democratic Republic of the Congo v Uganda) [2005] ICJ Rep 168

Legal Consequences of the Construction of a Wall in the Occupied Palestinian Territory (Advisory Opinion) [2004] ICJ Rep 136

Military and Paramilitary Activities in and against Nicaragua Case (Nicaragua v United States of America) (Merits) [1986] ICJ Rep 14

North Sea Continental Shelf [1969] ICJ Rep 3

South West Africa, Second Phase (Dissenting Opinion of Judge Tanaka) [1966] ICJ Rep 250

Reparation for injuries suffered in the service of the United Nations (Advisory Opinion) [1949] ICJ Rep 174

ECtHR and European Commission on Human Rights

AA and others v North Macedonia App Nos 55798/16 and 4 others (ECtHR 2nd Section 5 April 2022)

MH and others v Croatia App Nos 15670/18 and 43115/18 (ECtHR 4 April 2022)

Shahzad v Hungary App No 12625/17 (ECtHR 8 July 2021)

MN and Others v Belgium App No 3599/18 (ECtHR 5 May 2020)

ND and NT v Spain App No 8675/15 and 8697/15 (ECtHR 13 February 2020)

Güzelyurtlu and Others v Cyprus and Turkey App No 36925/07 (ECtHR 29 January 2019)

Big Brother Watch and Others v UK Apps Nos 58170/13 (ECtHR 13 September 2018)

Romeo Castaño v Belgium App No 8351/17 (ECtHR 9 July 2018)

Fábián v Hungary App No 78117/13 (ECtHR 5 September 2017)

Petropavlovskis v Latvia App No 44230/06 (ECtHR 13 January 2015)

Tarakhel v Switzerland App No 29217/12 (ECtHR 4 November 2014)

The Church of Jesus Christ of Latter-Day Saints v Great Britain App No 7552/09 (ECtHR 28 March 2014)

Hirsi Jamaa & Others v Italy App No 27765/09 (ECtHR 23 February 2012)

Al-Skeini and Others v United Kingdom App No 55721/07 (ECtHR 7 July 2011)

Al-Jedda v the United Kingdom App No 27021/08 (ECtHR 7 July 2011)

MSS v Belgium and Greece App No 30696/09 (ECtHR 21 January 2011)

Clift v the United Kingdom App No 7205/07 (ECtHR 22 November 2010)

Al-Sadoon and Mufdhi v United Kingdom App No 61498/08, Merits and Just Satisfaction (ECtHR 2 March 2010)

Andrejeva v Latvia App No 55707/00 (ECtHR 18 February 2009)

KRS v UK App No 32733/08 (ECtHR 2 December 2008)

Saadi v Italy App No 37201/06 (ECtHR 28 February 2008)

DH and Others v Czech Republic App No 57325/00 (ECtHR 13 November 2007)

Behrami and Behrami v France, and Saramati v France, Germany and Norway App No 71412/01 and 78166/01 (ECtHR 2 May 2007)

Timishev v Russia App No 55762/00 and 55974/00 (ECtHR 13 December 2005)

Bader and Others v Sweden App No 13284/04 (ECtHR 8 November 2005)

Bosphorus Hava Yollari Turizm ve Tizaret Anonim Şirketi v Ireland App No 45036/98 (ECtHR 30 June 2005)

Öcalan v Turkey App No 46221/99 (ECtHR 12 May 2005)

Ilaşcu and Others v Moldowa and Russia App No 48787/99 (ECtHR 8 July 2004)

Koua Poirrez v France App No 40892/98 (ECtHR 30 December 2003)

Banković and Others v Belgium and 16 Other Contracting States App No 52207/99 (ECtHR 19 December 2001)

Cyprus v Turkey App No 25781/94 (ECtHR 10 May 2001)

GHH and Others v Turkey App No 43258/98 (ECtHR 11 October 2000)

Maaouia v France App No 39652/98 (ECtHR 5 October 2000)

TI v UK App No 43844/98 (ECtHR 7 March 2000)

Beer and Regan v Germany App No 28934/95 (ECtHR 18 February 1999)

Matthews v the United Kingdom App No 24833/94 (ECtHR 18 February 1999)

Chahal v United Kingdom App No 22414/93 (ECtHR 15 November 1996)

Gayusuz v Austria App No 17371/90 (ECtHR 16 September 1996)

Amuur v France App No 19776/92 (ECtHR 20 May 1996)

M v Denmark App No 17392/90 (Commission Decision 14 October 1992)

Soering v United Kingdom App No 14038/88 (ECtHR 7 July 1989)

"Relating to certain aspects of the laws on the use of languages in education in Belgium" v Belgium App No 1474/62; 1677/62; 1691/62; 1769/63; 1994/63; 2126/64 (ECtHR 23 July 1968)

W v Ireland App No 9360/81 (Commission Decision 28 February 1983)

CJEU

Case C-432/20, *Landeshauptmann von Wien* [2022] EU:C:2022:39

Joined Cases C-133/19, C-136/19 and C-137/19 *BMM, BS, BM and BMO v État belge* [2020] EU:C:2020:577

Joined Cases C-715/17, C-718/17 and C-719/17 *Commission v Republic of Poland, Hungary and Czech Republic* [2020] EU:C:2020:257

Joined Cases C-715/17, C-718/18 and 719/17 *European Commission v Republic of Poland, Hungary and Czech Republic* [2019] EU:C:2019:917, Opinion of AG Sharpston

Joined Cases C-391/16, C-77/17 and C-78/17 *M v Ministerstvo vnitra, X and X v Commissaire général aux réfugiés et aux apatrides* [2019] EU:C:2019:403

Case C-257/17 *C, A v Staatssecretaris van Veiligheid en Justitie* [2018] EU:C:2018:876

Joined Cases C-208/17 P to C-210/17 P *NF and Others v European Council* [2018] EU:C:2018:705, Order of the Court (First Chamber)

Joined Cases C-177/17 and C-178/17 *Demarchi Gino Sas and Graziano Garavaldi v Ministero della Giustizia* [2017] EU:C:2017:656

Joined Cases C-643/15 and C-647/15 *Slovak Republic and Hungary v Council* [2017] EU:C:2017:631

Case C-258/14 *Eugenia Florescu and others v Casa Județeană de Pensii Sibiu and others* [2017] EU:C:2017:448

Joined cases C-490/16 and 646/16 *AS v Republic of Slovenia* and *Jafari* [2017] EU:C:2017:443, Opinion of AG Sharpston

Case C-638/16 PPU *X and X v État belge* [2017] EU:C:2017:173

Cases T-192/16, T-193/16 and T-257/16 *NF, NG and NM v European Council* [2017] EU:T:2017:128, Orders of the General Court

Case C-578/16 PPU *CK, HF and AS v Republic of Slovenia Reform* [2017] EU:C:2017:127

Opinion 2/13 *Accession of the European Union to the European Convention for the Protection of Human Rights and Fundamental Freedoms* [2014] EU:C:2014:2454

Case C-270/12 *The United Kingdom of Great Britain and Northern Ireland v European Parliament and the Council of the European Union* [2014] EU:C:2014:18

Case C-277/11 *MM v Minister for Justice Equality and Law Reform* [2012] EU:C: 2012:744

Joined Cases C-411/10 and C-493/10 *NS v Secretary of State for the Home Department and ME and Others v Refugee Applications Commissioner and Minister for Justice, Equality and Law Reform* [2011] EU:C:2011:865

Case C-175/08 *Aydin Salahadin Abdulla v Bundesrepublik Deutschland* [2010] EU:C:2010:105

Case C-322/88 *Salvatore Grimaldi v Fonds des Maladies Professionnelles* [1989] EU:C:1989:646

Case 98/80 *Giuseppe Romano v Institut national d'assurance maladie-invalidité* [1981] EU:C:1981:104

Case 128/78 *Commission of the European Communities v United Kingdom of Great Britain and Northern Ireland* [1979] EU:C:1979:32

Case C-39/72 *Commission of the European Communities v Italian Republic* [1973] EU:C:1973:13

Case C-22/70 *Commission v Council* [1971] EU:C:1971:32

Case C-26/62 *Van Gend en Loos v Administratie der Belastingen* [1963] ECLI:EU:C:1963:1

Cases C-9/56 and C-10/56 *Meroni & Co, Industrie Metallurgiche, SpA v High Authority of the European Coal and Steel Community* [1958] EU:C:1958:7

US Supreme Court

California et al v Texas et al 593 US __ (2021)

Acting Commissioner, Immigration and Naturalization Service, et al v Haitian Centers Council, Inc 509 US 155 (1993)

Other courts

African Court on Human and Peoples' Rights, *Robert John Penessis v United Republic of Tanzania* (Judgement) App No 013/2015 (28 November 2019)

BVerfG, Judgment of the First Senate of 19 May 2020 – 1 BvR 2835/17 <https://www.bundesverfassungsgericht.de/SharedDocs/Entscheidungen/EN/2020/05/rs20200519_1bvr283517en.html;jsessionid=616AA65B0D67A6BAEA9FCF97F6FFA0AB.1_cid37> accessed 28 March 2021

BVerfG, Order of the First Senate of 14 July 1999 – 1 BvR 2226/94 [BVerfGE 100, 313 (363f) Telekommunikationsüberwachung I] <https://www.bundesverfassungsgericht.de/SharedDocs/Entscheidungen/DE/1999/07/rs19990714_1bvr222694.html> accessed 28 March 2021

IACtHR, Advisory Opinion OC-23/17 *The Environment and Human Rights* (15 November 2017)

IACtHR, Advisory Opinion OC-4/84 *Proposed Amendments to the Naturalization Provision of the Constitution of Costa Rica* (January 1984)

M70 v Minister for Immigration and Citizenship, 244 CLR 144 (2011)

R (European Roma Rights Centre and Others) v Immigration Officer at Prague Airport [2003] EWCA Civ 666 (Eng CA, 20 May 2003)

Affaire d'Indemnite Russe (Russia v Turkey), 11 RIAA 431 (Perm Ct Arb 1912) <https://pcacases.com/web/sendAttach/643> accessed 17 July 2020

Legal texts and International Treaties

Agreement between the United States and Kosovo (25 August 2021) <https://www.state.gov/wp-content/uploads/2021/11/21-825-Kosovo-Transit-Afghanistan.pdf>

Council of Europe Convention on preventing and combating violence against women and domestic violence (entered into force 1 August 2014) CETS No 210

Consolidated version of the Treaty on the Functioning of the European Union [2012] OJ C326/47-390

Consolidated version of the Treaty on European Union [2012] OJ C326/13-390

ILC, Draft Articles on Responsibility of International Organizations (adopted 2011) <http://legal.un.org/ilc/texts/instruments/english/draft_articles/9_11_2011.pdf> accessed 21 February 2021

United Nations Convention on the Rights of Persons with Disabilities (adopted 13 December 2006, entered into force 3 May 2008) 2515 UNTS 3

Protocol No 12 to the Convention for the Protection of Human Rights and Fundamental Freedoms (entered into force 1 April 2005) ETS No 177

ILC, 'Draft Articles on Responsibility of States for Internationally Wrongful Acts, with commentaries' (adopted November 2001, ARSIWA Commentary 2001) <http://legal.un.org/ilc/texts/instruments/english/commentaries/9_6_2001.pdf> accessed 21 February 2021

Charter of Fundamental Rights of the European Union [2000] OJ C364/1-22

The Schengen *acquis* – Convention implementing the Schengen Agreement of 14 June 1985 between the Governments of the States of the Benelux economic Union, the Federal Republic of Germany and the French Republic on the gradual abolition of checks at their common borders [2000] OJ L239/19-62

European Convention on Nationality (signed 6 November 1997, entered into force 1 March 2000) ETS No 166

Treaty of Amsterdam amending the Treaty on European Union, the Treaties establishing the European Communities and certain related acts [1997] OJ C340/1-144

Convention determining the State responsible for examining applications for asylum lodged in one of the Member States of the European Community – Dublin Convention [1997] OJ C254/1-12

United Nations Convention on the Rights of the Child (adopted 20 November 1989, entered into force 2 September 1990) 1577 UNTS 3

International Convention against Torture and Other Cruel, Inhuman or Degrading Treatment or Punishment (adopted 10 December 1984) 1465 UNTS 85

Convention on the Elimination of All Forms of Discrimination Against Women (adopted 18 December 1981, entered in to force 3 September 1981) 1249 UNTS 13

African Charter on Human and Peoples' Rights (adopted 27 June 1981, entered into force 21 October 1986) 1520 UNTS 217

American Convention on Human Rights, OAS Treaty Series No 36 (adopted 22 November 1969, entered into force 18 July 1978) <https://www.oas.org/dil/treaties_b-32_american_convention_on_human_rights.pdf> accessed 13 May 2021

Vienna Convention on the Law of Treaties (adopted 23 May 1969, entered into force 27 January 1980) 1155 UNTS 331

Convention on the Reduction of Statelessness (adopted 30 August 1961, entered into force 13 December 1975) 989 UNTS 175

Protocol No 4 to the Convention for the Protection of Human Rights and Fundamental Freedoms, securing certain rights and freedoms other than those already included in the Convention and in the first Protocol thereto (entered into force 2 May 1968) ETS No 46

Protocol to the Convention Relating to the Status of Refugees (adopted 31 January 1967, entered into force 4 October 1967) 606 UNTS 267

International Covenant on Civil and Political Rights (adopted 16 December 1966, entered into force 23 March 1976) 999 UNTS 171

International Covenant on Economic, Social and Cultural Rights (adopted 16 December 1966, entered into force 3 January 1976) 993 UNTS 3

International Convention on the Elimination of All Forms of Racial Discrimination (adopted 21 December 1965, entered into force 4 January 1969) 660 UNTS 195

Convention Relating to the Status of Refugees (adopted 28 July 1951, entered into force 22 April 1954) 189 UNTS 137-220

Convention for the Protection of Human Rights and Fundamental Freedoms (adopted 4 November 1950, entered into force 3 September 1953) ETS No 5

Statute of the Office of the United Nations High Commissioner for Refugees (14 December 1950) <https://www.unhcr.org/4d944e589.pdf> accessed 13 February 2021

Universal Declaration of Human Rights (adopted 10 December 1948) UNGA Res 217 A(III)

Charter of the United Nations (adopted 26 June 1945, entered into force 24 October 1945) 1 UNTS XVI

EU secondary legislation

Council Implementing Decision 2022/382 (EU) establishing the existence of a mass influx of displaced persons from Ukraine within the meaning of Article 5 of Directive 2001/55/EC, and having the effect of introducing temporary protection [2022] OJ L71/1-6

Regulation 2021/1147 (EU) establishing the Asylum, Migration and Integration Fund [2021] OJ L251/1-47 (consolidated version of 12 April 2022)

Regulation 2021/2303 (EU) on the European Union Agency for Asylum and repealing Regulation (EU) No 439/2010 [2021] OJ L468/1-54

Council Regulation 2020/2093 (EU, Euratom) laying down the multiannual financial framework for the years 2021 to 2027 [2020] OJ L433/11-22

Regulation 2016/1624 (EU) on the European Border and Coast Guard and amending Regulation (EU) 2016/399 and repealing Regulation (EC) No 863/2007, Regulation (EC) No 2007/2004 and Decision 2005/267/EC [2016] OJ L251/1-76

Council Decision 2015/1601 (EU) establishing provisional measures in the area of international protection for the benefit of Italy and Greece [2015] OJ L248/80-94

Council Decision 2015/1523 (EU) establishing provisional measures in the area of international protection for the benefit of Italy and of Greece [2015] OJ L239/146-156

Regulation 2014/516 (EU) establishing the Asylum, Migration and Integration Fund [2014] OJ L150/168-195

Directive 2013/33 (EU) laying down standards for the reception of applicants for international protection [2013] OJ L180/96-116

Directive 2013/32 (EU) on common procedures for granting and withdrawing international protection [2013] OJ L180/60-95

Regulation 2013/604 (EU) establishing the criteria and mechanisms for determining the Member State responsible for examining and application for international protection lodged in one of the Member States by a third-country national or a stateless person [2013] OJ L180/31-59

Directive 2011/95 (EU) on standards for the qualification of third-country nationals or stateless persons as beneficiaries of international protection, for a uniform status for refugees or for persons eligible for subsidiary protection, and for the content of the protection granted [2011] OJ L337/9-26

Regulation 2010/439 (EU) establishing a European Asylum Support Office [2010] OJ L132/11-28

Council Decision 2010/48 (EC) concerning the conclusion, by the European Community, of the United Nations Convention on the Rights of Persons with Disabilities [2010] OJ L23/35-61

Decision of the European Parliament and of the Council (EC) 573/2007 of 23 May 2007 establishing the European Refugee Fund for the period 2008 to 2013 as part of the General programme 'Solidarity and Management of Migration Flows' [2007] OJ L144/1-21

Directive 2004/38 (EC) on the right of citizens of the Union and their family members to move and reside freely within the territory of the Member States [2004] OJ L158/77-123

Directive 2003/109 (EC) concerning the status of third-country nationals who are long-term residents [2004] OJ L16/44 amended by Directive 2011/51/EU [2011] OJ L132/1

Council Regulation No 343/2003 (EC) establishing the criteria and mechanisms for determining the Member State responsible for examining an asylum application lodged in one of the Member States by a third-country national [2003] OJ L50/1–10

Directive 2003/86 (EC) on the right to family reunification [2003] OJ L251/12-18

Directive 2001/55 (EC) on minimum standards for giving temporary protection in the event of a mass influx of displaced persons and on measures promoting a balance of efforts between Member States in receiving such persons and bearing the consequences thereof [2001] OJ L212/12-23

Decision 2000/596 (EC) establishing a European Refugee Fund [2000] OJ L252/12-18

Council Resolution on burden-sharing with regard to the admission and residence of displaced persons on a temporary basis [1995] OJ C262/1

US legislation

Extending Government Funding and Delivering Emergency Assistance Act 2021 <https://www.congress.gov/117/plaws/publ43/PLAW-117publ43.pdf>

Emergency Security Supplemental Appropriations Act 2021 <https://www.congress.gov/bill/117th-congress/house-bill/3237> accessed 27 June 2022

Executive Order 13888 'Enhancing State and Local Involvement in Refugee Resettlement' (26 September 2019) <https://www.hsdl.org/?view&did=829794> accessed 13 February 2021

Executive Order 13780 'Protecting The Nation from Foreign Terrorist Entry Into The United States' (6 March 2017) <https://trumpwhitehouse.archives.gov/presidential-actions/executive-order-protecting-nation-foreign-terrorist-entry-united-states-2/> accessed 20 March 2021

Executive Order 13769 'Protecting The Nation from Foreign Terrorist Entry Into The United States' (27 January 2017) <https://trumpwhitehouse.archives.gov/presidential-actions/executive-order-protecting-nation-foreign-terrorist-entry-united-states/> accessed 20 March 2021

Code of Federal Regulations 2012 <https://www.govinfo.gov/content/pkg/CFR-2012-title8-vol1/pdf/CFR-2012-title8-vol1-part208.pdf> accessed 13 February 2021

Immigrant Responsibility Act 1996 <https://www.govinfo.gov/content/pkg/PLAW-104publ208/pdf/PLAW-104publ208.pdf> accessed 27 March 2021

Refugee Act 1980 <https://www.govinfo.gov/content/pkg/STATUTE-94/pdf/STATUTE-94-Pg102.pdf> accessed 13 February 2021

Indochina Migration and Refugee Assistance Act 1975, Public Law 94-23, 89 Stat 87

The Immigration and Nationality Act Amendments 1965, Public Law 89-236, 79 Stat 911

Fair Share Refugee Act 1960, Public Law 86-648, 74 Stat 504

Refugee Escape Act 1957, Public Law 85-316, 71 Stat 639

Refugee Relief Act 1953, Public Law 203, 67 Stat 400, Chapter 336

Immigration and Nationality Act 1952 <https://www.uscis.gov/laws-and-policy/legislation/immigration-and-nationality-act> accessed 13 February 2021

Displaced Persons Act 1948, Public Law 80-774, 62 Stat 1009, Chapter 647